The
ILLUSTRATOR

Book

The ILLUSTRATOR 5 Book

Deke McClelland

Peachpit Press
Berkeley, California

The Illustrator 5 Book

Deke McClelland

Peachpit Press
2414 Sixth Street
Berkeley, California 94710
(800) 283-9444, (510) 548-4393
fax: (510) 548-5991

Trademarks

Adobe Illustrator is a registered trademark of Adobe Systems Inc.

Many of the designations used by manufacturers and resellers to distinguish their products are claimed as trademarks. Where those designations appear in this book, and Peachpit was aware of a trademark claim, the designations have been printed in initial caps or all caps.

Notice of Liability

The information in this book is distributed on an "As Is" basis, without warranty. While every precaution has been taken in the preparation of this book, neither the author nor Peachpit Press, Inc. shall have any liability to any person or entity with respect to liability, loss, or damage caused or allowed to be caused directly or indirectly by the instructions contained in this book or by the computer software and hardware products described herein.

ISBN 1-56609-090-3

Printed and bound in the United States of America

0 9 8 7 6 5 4 3 2

PRINTED ON RECYCLED PAPER

To Daniel
for making it
possible

and Toni
for putting up
with it

Acknowledgments

Thank you to everyone who helped
in making this book:

The awesome folks at Peachpit
for getting it out there.

Marjorie Baer and Paul King
for copy editing and
psychological damage control.

Carol Person and Wendy Sharp
for giving a guy who can't schedule a break.

All the folks at Adobe who
provided products and assistance.

Dane Spangler
for the most-excellent
part illustrations.

Tom Midgley
of Blue Fire Design.

Scott Harmon of
Johnson Publishing for imagesetting.

Craig Danuloff,
RD, JG, SR, AE, and JM
for all those things PRI does.

And EP for being w/ me.

CONTENTS AT A GLANCE

TABLE OF CONTENTS

Chapter 6:
Reshaping Paths That Frankly Need Help 207

Chapter 7:
Creating and Editing Type 261

Chapter 8:
Filling Graphic Objects and Type 333

Appendix:
Installing Adobe Illustrator 5.0 621

Index 629

THE ILLUSTRATOR 5 BOOK

1

When it was first released in 1987, Adobe Illustrator was a graphic arts tool without equal. Unlike anything that had come before it, Illustrator applied the power of the personal computer to the full range of visual expression. Suddenly, artists and non-artists alike could create technical drawings, logotypes, business graphics, fine art, product illustrations, and countless other art forms on affordable computer systems with uncompromisingly professional results.

Illustrator was unique and powerful because it removed the artificial constraints that had previously plagued affordable computer-graphics tools—the trade-offs between power, precision, and performance. With its Bézier curve drawing model, its fantastic range of manipulative tools, and its ability to produce truly professional-quality output, Adobe Illustrator provided an incredible tool to anyone with the need or desire to produce high-quality artwork.

That was then; this is five versions later. With Illustrator 5.0, Adobe is again turning heads. New automatic gradations, the ability to work directly in the preview mode, improved ease of use functions, and a slew of filters that add capabilities to the basic program bring Illustrator into the new world order. Illustrator 5.0 allows users who have been taking advantage of previous versions of the software to expand their capabilities; it also allows new users to benefit from the success and experience of a powerful industry leader.

About this book

With the power of Adobe Illustrator 5.0 comes responsibility. Although the package adheres strictly to all the friendly interface guidelines required of a Macintosh application and is basically straightforward and easy to use, you will get the full benefit of this software only if you *master* it. This means becoming familiar with the drawing model on which Illustrator is based; understanding the tools, commands, and dialog box options that Illustrator provides; and gaining hands-on experience by completing a wide variety of quick but informative exercises. *The Illustrator 5 Book* is dedicated to the relentless, exhaustive delivery of this knowledge. And then some.

In the chapters that follow, you will find each of the concepts, features, and functions of Illustrator described completely, including functional descriptions required by novices, advice aimed at intermediate users, and advanced discussions demanded by power-users. Throughout, *The Illustrator 5 Book* adopts the viewpoint of the user. In addition to objective, technical details, Illustrator's strengths and weaknesses are considered, what to avoid and what to rely on. In every manner possible, this book captures the insights born from years of artistic and computing experience, with the hope that *The Illustrator 5 Book* will become your personal Illustrator 5.0 trainer, providing both bookwise details *and* street-smart tips and tricks.

Conventions

This book employs the following conventions to make it easier for you to understand Adobe Illustrator 5.0 and to glean useful information without slogging through a lot of words:

 The *keyboard equivalent icon* calls out commands, options, and other features that can be accessed from the keyboard, allowing you to increase your speed and devote your mouse hand to the more important task of drawing.

The *power tips icon* calls out tips. Not press-this-key-to-get-this tips, but real, honest-to-goodness thoughtful tips that will improve your drawing capability by leaps and bounds. If you didn't think it was possible to do something with Illustrator, here's where I'll show you how.

Chapter summaries

The Illustrator 5 Book is composed of 15 chapters, an appendix, and an index. The following is a summarization of their contents:

- **Chapter 1** looks at the concepts behind creating graphics in programs like Adobe Illustrator. In this discussion I provide a brief history of how computer graphics developed on the Apple Macintosh, featuring applications like MacPaint, MacDraw, and Adobe Illustrator 1.1.

- **Chapter 2** opens with a glossary of basic Macintosh terminology, followed by a comprehensive tour of the Illustrator toolbox and menu commands. This chapter is designed to familiarize you with the software in case you want to begin using Illustrator 5.0 immediately. If you are an experienced Macintosh user, you will probably be able to begin creating graphics after a brief survey of this chapter. If you are new to Macintosh or to this type of graphics application, this chapter will provide a thorough introduction to your new tools.

- **Chapter 3** discusses how to create a new illustration or open an existing illustration in Illustrator, including how to introduce, use, and change tracing templates. I take you on a brief tour through Illustrator's on-screen environment, including view sizes and page setup. I also introduce the DOCUMENT SETUP and GENERAL PREFERENCES dialog boxes, Illustrator's central control stations. The chapter finishes by addressing the topics of saving your illustration and quitting the application.

- **Chapter 4** uses a conceptual tutorial to focus on the strategy used to draw complex graphics in Illustrator. Here, the creation of a sample illustration is approached from an entirely theoretical vantage; no specific commands or tools are discussed. Instead, this chapter addresses the thought process required to solve electronic drawing problems. This chapter will be beneficial to both the novice and the experienced graphic creator.

- **Chapter 5** examines how to draw geometric and free-form images from scratch using the rectangle and oval tools, the freehand tool, the brush tool, and the all-powerful pen tool. Here's everything you ever wanted to know about point and path theory, but were afraid to ask your local philosopher. The chapter ends with a look at tracing bitmapped and scanned images. If you can't draw, you can trace using the auto trace tool.

- **Chapter 6** focuses on the manipulation of existing lines and shapes. Everything in Illustrator can be molded and reshaped to your heart's desire. I look first at moving points and segments and measuring distances. I next turn my attention to three new tools for adding, subtracting, and converting points. Finally, you will learn all there is to know about Bézier control handles.

- **Chapter 7** explains how to create type on a point, in a path, and on a path. Want to import type? No problem. Want to wrap it around a graphic? That's easy, too. Want to convert it to a path and manipulate it until it doesn't even look like text any more? Check out Chapter 7.

- **Chapter 8** is about fills. The chapter starts out easy, but then I turn on the steam with exhaustive discussions of tile patterns, gradations, clipping paths, and compound paths. The automated gradient feature, completely super new to Illustrator 5.0, allows you to design custom gradations, utilizing multiple colors, and then use them as fills.

- **Chapter 9** is about the other side of the painting coin—strokes. Everything's here: line weights, line caps, dash patterns, dash patterns with line caps, dash patterns and line caps with line weights layered on each other . . . well, you get the idea. It's a really boring chapter.

- **Chapter 10** colorizes your artwork. This chapter includes information on using the color libraries included in the Color Systems folder, as well as a theoretical introduction to the issues of color as they relate to working with computer-generated art and four-color process printing. I also discuss the new paint bucket and eyedropper tools, which are so exciting, you'll fall over dead. Discretion is advised.

- **Chapter 11** dwells on transformations and duplications. You will learn how to create a precision drawing environment using rulers and guides. Next I discuss the four transformation tools, with which you can scale, flip, rotate, and slant any graphic object or text block. The last half of the chapter covers duplication and layering, with and without the LAYERS palette.

- **Chapter 12** explores the new world of Illustrator 5.0's filters. This misnomer describes a bizarre assortment of plug-in modules that affords you a number of extra capabilities, from creating specialized objects to adding special effects to the graphic objects and text blocks in your illustration. Here Adobe takes care of many of the gripes that I had with Illustrator 3.0. This break-neck tour exposes the nuances of each filter, with the intent of saving you the trouble of cursing the nearly worthless coverage that the manual provides.

- **Chapter 13** discovers the six graphing tools. These are charts as only a true drawing program can make them. I demonstrate how to create bar graphs, percentage charts, pie graphs, line graphs, area charts, and scatter graphs, all by entering a few values into Illustrator's GRAPH DATA window, complete with spreadsheet and import options. You can also create *pictographs*, which feature images stretched to various heights.

- **Chapter 14** looks at the importing and exporting of graphic images. Illustrator supports the popular Encapsulated Post-Script format used by most scanning software, drawing programs, and desktop publishing software available for the Macintosh computer.

- **Chapter 15** focuses on printing your illustrations. This chapter also examines all issues related to the creation and use of color separations generated by the Adobe Separator utility.

- **Appendix A** describes how to install Adobe Illustrator on your hard drive, just in case you need some help getting started. Even if you're already up and running, you may want to check out my detailed description of the Adobe Type Manager.

Each chapter contains practical tips and advice designed to increase your user potential. In addition, I provide essential warnings to minimize unforeseen problems and aggravation. From cover to cover, *The Illustrator 5 Book* is designed to provide you with all the information that you will need to get the most out of this powerful application.

PART 1
NAVIGATION

CHAPTER

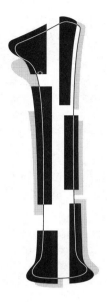

THE EMERGENCE OF DRAWING ON THE MACINTOSH

For a few thousand lucky users in 1984, the first image of the Macintosh computer was a seemingly handwritten "Hello" scrawled across a tiny black-and-white screen. From this image alone, it was immediately apparent that the Mac was unlike everything computing had been before. Sure, the computer was a new shape, sort of like a miniature arcade game, but that wasn't the giveaway. The scribbled "Hello" signaled something much more important.

Gone was the monotonous computer lettering that was a constant reminder of a computer's robotic nature. In its place was a free-form word, written at an angle in letters three inches high and looking distinctly friendly. The image on the screen, we'd later learn, was from a new piece of software called MacPaint.

MacPaint was as much of a revolution in applications software as the Macintosh itself was in hardware and the System/Finder was in operating systems, and it was probably as responsible for Mac's early success as were these other items. Looking back, it is easy to recognize MacPaint's arrival as a real turning point for personal-computer graphics. All the promise held in that handwritten "Hello" unfolded as MacPaint became a familiar tool. Gone were the boxlike constrictions and programming tedium that had previously epitomized personal-computer graphics. Instead, a diverse set of familiar drawing tools, such as the pencil, paintbrush, and spraypaint can were now *on-screen* drawing tools, adapted for computer use with an amazing similarity to their real-world counterparts.

The advent of MacPaint was important for two reasons. First, skilled artists were quickly able to produce terrific artwork using MacPaint. The diversity of MacPaint's tools proved up to the task of creating thousands of images that soon turned up in publications, art exhibits, and on clip-art disks and computer screens everywhere. The second important result of MacPaint was the effect the program had on "the rest of us," the nonartist masses who had never dreamed of lifting brush to canvas or stroking pen to paper in anything more elaborate than a telephone doodle. To this group, MacPaint provided freedom to try, forgiveness to correct, and tools to empower. Just as word processors had encouraged the writing process, MacPaint encouraged graphic creation and placed it within the grasp of everyone.

While the inevitable wish list for additional MacPaint features grew, the more important limitation had already become apparent: MacPaint's low-resolution bitmapped nature—largely responsible for its power—was a limiting factor on the printed page. Many images require fluid curves, and MacPaint's stair-stepped approximations inhibited this new brand of computer art from establishing itself in the many areas where quality was the paramount concern.

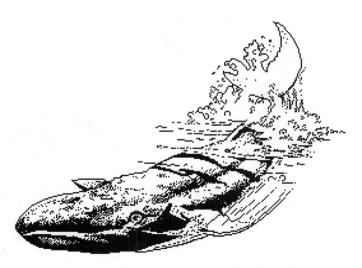

Figure 1-1: Soon after its introduction, MacPaint became synonymous with low-resolution graphics.

This limitation became more pronounced with the introduction of the LaserWriter. With the PostScript language built in, this toner-based laser printer was actually capable of printing words and pictures created on the Mac at 300 dots per inch—four times the resolution of the computer's screen. On paper, the stair steps that appeared on the screen were replaced with nearly perfect curves. The catch was that only PostScript-compatible typefaces and mathematically defined graphics could utilize the full resolution of PostScript printers. Alas, MacPaint was still MacPaint, cemented at the 72-dot-per-inch resolution of the software.

MacDraw, on the other hand, which took advantage of the full resolution of the LaserWriter, suddenly moved from its role as a technically oriented specialty application to the center stage of Macintosh graphics. MacDraw's shortcoming—a limited set of tools useful for creating rather boxy images—was overlooked in favor of its sharp, smooth output. The result was a compromise: Computer graphics could now match the clarity of traditional graphics, but they were limited in their expressive range.

Figure 1-2: MacDraw took advantage of the LaserWriter's high resolution, but its output was typically stylized and simplistic.

As the abilities of the PostScript interpreter inside the LaserWriter became better understood, users began to search for an application powerful enough to drive the LaserWriter's precise laser-printing engine. Measured against this potential, MacPaint was seen as the toy its critics had always proclaimed it to be. Even MacDraw, which took advantage of only the most basic of PostScript's capabilities, was inadequate. It wasn't until Adobe Systems released Illustrator and, later, Aldus Corporation released FreeHand, that artists could tap into the full power of PostScript.

Figure 1-3: The new breed of PostScript drawing applications offered artistic freedom and high-resolution output.

These new programs offered the resolution capabilities of Mac-
Draw combined with drawing freedom similar to that of MacPaint.
Precise lines and shapes could be drawn in any weight, turning and
curving limitlessly. Enclosed areas could be filled with any screen
density or pattern that could be defined in the PostScript language.
Not only were the vast quantity of PostScript typefaces useful for traditional writing tasks, but type itself became an object that could be
manipulated to produce any graphic effect.

By providing users with the ability to harness the full power of the
PostScript language, programs like Adobe Illustrator have shattered
the distinction between computer art and traditional art.
Graphic illustration, technical drawing, and many
other art forms finally enjoy the power of the
personal computer.

*Figure 1-4: Graphic art now
enjoys the full power of the
personal computer.*

CHAPTER

TERMS, TOOLS, MENUS, AND SHORTCUTS

Adobe Illustrator very closely follows the Macintosh interface. Your proficiency with Illustrator thus depends on how well you use your mouse and keyboard to interact with a collection of menus, tools, and dialog boxes. This chapter is an introduction to these fundamental aspects of Illustrator.

Each Illustrator tool and menu command, as well as many associated dialog boxes, will be discussed. After reading this chapter, you will have a good understanding of the range of capabilities Adobe Illustrator provides. More experienced users—especially those familiar with previous versions of Illustrator—may find this information sufficient to allow them to begin their own experimentations with Illustrator 5.0. Less experienced users may find these summaries a bit overwhelming. In either case, remember that this is only a brief tour; the remainder of this book provides all the details you need to master the range of possibilities suggested in this chapter.

Basic terminology

Before touring the menus and tools, I'll take a moment to define the terms used throughout this book to describe the basic Macintosh interface—terms like *select*, *choose*, *options*, and so on—to remove ambiguity and to facilitate your learning experience. Because most of these terms are used differently by different computer authors—heck, they're even used differently by a single computer author within a single book—I recommend that even experienced Macintosh users review this section before going on to the other chapters of the book. (If you're one of those wonderful people who has kept me alive by purchasing past versions of this book, back when it was called *Mastering Adobe Illustrator*, you already know all this terminology stuff. In fact, I don't know what you're doing even reading this section. Go on, get out of here. Skip ahead to *The toolbox* section on page 19.)

You probably already know how to perform at least a few functions required for the fundamental operation of your Macintosh, including turning on your computer, inserting a disk, and copying files. You should also be familiar with the meaning of the terms *mouse*, *monitor*, *window*, *icon*, *cursor*, and *desktop*. If you are not, please consult your Macintosh operation manual.

Terminology specific to using Adobe Illustrator will be introduced in later chapters. Whether defined in this chapter or later on down the line, these vocabulary words appear in *italic type*.

Mouse operations

First let's review mouse operations. To *click* the mouse is to press the mouse button and immediately *release*. To *drag* is to press and hold down the mouse button, move your mouse to a new location, and release. To *double-click* is to press and release the mouse button twice in rapid succession. Each of these operations is illustrated in Figure 2-1.

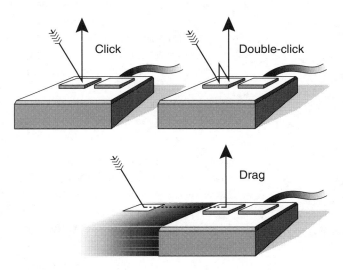

Figure 2-1: The three fundamental mouse operations.

Menus

Commands are organized into related groups called *menus*. Each menu has a name, which appears along the top of your screen in the *menu bar*. To *choose* a command is to pick it from a menu by clicking and holding your mouse button down on the menu name, then dragging down the list of commands. When the command you want to choose is *highlighted*—displayed with white letters against a black background—release the mouse button.

Like other Macintosh applications, Illustrator offers four kinds of menu commands:

- **Commands followed by ellipses**. Choosing a command whose name is followed by an ellipsis (...) causes a *dialog box* to appear. The dialog box is Illustrator's way of requesting information before executing the command.

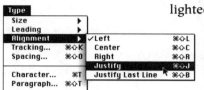

- **Submenu commands**. As soon as these commands are highlighted, a second menu pops up either to the right or to the left of the command (depending upon the space available on your screen). This second menu, called a *hierarchical submenu*, contains a list of *options* that you choose in the same way you choose menu commands. Drag onto the submenu, then drag up or down the menu until the desired option is highlighted, and release the mouse button. If the entire submenu is not visible, it will scroll as you drag toward its top or bottom.

- **Toggling command options**. These are commands that turn on and off a particular Illustrator function. In some cases, these commands display a check mark in front of the command name when the feature is turned on. In other cases, the name of the command itself changes to reflect its new purpose.

- **Executing commands**. Commands that do not fall into one of the above categories simply execute immediately after you choose them.

Many menu commands may be chosen by simultaneously pressing two or more keys on your keyboard. Such a key sequence is called a *keyboard equivalent*. In most cases, the keyboard equivalent for a command is listed to the right of the command in its menu. Throughout this book, I will list any applicable keyboard equivalents in parentheses each time I introduce a menu command. The cloverleaf symbol (⌘) represents the COMMAND key, just as it does on your keyboard. The up arrow (⇧) represents the SHIFT key, the switch symbol (⌥) represents the OPTION key, and the hollow caret (⌃) represents the CONTROL key.

Dialog boxes

A *dialog box* can present information, request information, or both. In most cases, dialog boxes appear in response either to a command you have chosen or to some action you have taken. When a dialog box requests information, it presents you with a series of options.

Four kinds of options are found in dialog boxes:

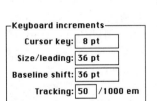

- **Radio buttons.** When you can select only one option within a group of options, small round *radio buttons* appear before each option name. To *select* a radio button option, click on either the button itself or on the name of the option following the button. Several sets of radio buttons may appear in a single dialog box, but only one from each set can be selected at any one time. Selecting any one radio button therefore *deselects* any other in the group. A radio button filled with a black dot indicates that the option is selected; a hollow radio button is deselected.

- **Check boxes.** When you can select several options in a group of options, small square *check boxes* appear before each option name. To select or deselect a check box option, click on either the box itself or on the option name. If that option was previously deselected, it becomes selected; if it was selected, the option becomes deselected. A check box is selected when an × is displayed and is deselected when the box is empty. Multiple check boxes within a set can be selected or deselected.

- **Option boxes.** Options that require you to enter data are called *option boxes.* Most option boxes contain default data when the dialog box first appears. When this default data is selected (highlighted with a colored background), you can enter new values from the keyboard and the default data will be replaced. To *select* a value in an option box, double-click on the value or drag over it.

 When a dialog box contains several option boxes, you can move from one option box to the next by pressing the TAB key. To move to the previous option box, press SHIFT-TAB.

• **Pop-up menus**. Options that are presented as *pop-up menus* display only the current option setting when the dialog box first appears. To view the list of alternatives, you must select the current option—or an icon in some cases—by moving the cursor over the option and pressing and holding down the mouse button. This will "pop up" a menu displaying the available options. You select an option from the pop-up menu by dragging up or down the listing and releasing the mouse button when the name of the desired alternative is highlighted. If an option in a pop-up menu is followed by an ellipsis (...), choosing it will bring up yet another dialog box with additional options.

When you have finished entering, selecting, and choosing options in a dialog box, you can exit by clicking on buttons. The most common buttons are the OK and CANCEL buttons. Buttons may also function as commands when they are placed within dialog boxes, where they are used to initiate an action or bring up another dialog box. To activate the button with a heavy outline (usually OK), press the RETURN or ENTER key.

Dialog boxes that do not request information are known as *alert boxes*, since their purpose is to alert you to some fact. Some alert boxes warn you of the consequences of the action you are about to take and allow you to abort that action. Others inform you of some event that has already happened, allowing you only to acknowledge that you are aware of the event.

Dialog boxes that can remain open and available while you perform other operations are called *palettes*. To see a palette, choose any of the commands from the middle portion of the WINDOWS menu. Altogether, Illustrator 5.0 provides seven palettes, including the toolbox. You can move a palette by dragging on its title bar. To close a palette, click inside the close box on the left side of the title bar. Otherwise, the options found in a palette are nearly identical to those found in a dialog box.

Sometimes you will discover that an option, command, or menu is *dimmed*, which indicates that it has no effect on a certain situation. You cannot choose or select dimmed items.

Typographic conventions

Occasionally, this book will instruct you to press a key while performing a mouse operation. When not represented by symbols (⌘, ⇧, ⌥, ⌃)—as in the case of keyboard equivalents—keys are indicated in small caps (COMMAND, SHIFT, OPTION, CONTROL). Menus (FILE, EDIT), commands (SAVE, OPEN...), buttons (APPLY, CANCEL), and dialog box names (PREFERENCES, TYPE STYLE) are also displayed in small caps to set them apart from standard text. Option names are set apart with quotation marks, whether they appear in pop-up menus ("Helvetica," "Justified") or in dialog boxes ("Snap to point," "Magenta").

The toolbox

The following are brief descriptions of the *tools* Adobe Illustrator 5.0 offers for creating and manipulating the lines, shapes, and text that will make up your Illustrator documents. These provide just a taste of the possibilities that exist. More thorough descriptions follow in the succeeding chapters.

You select a tool from the *toolbox*, or *tool palette*, by clicking on it. The selected tool will become highlighted. The Illustrator toolbox is entirely independent of all other elements of the Illustrator desktop, so if you reduce the size of a drawing window, the toolbox remains unchanged with all tools visible and easily accessible. You can move the toolbox by dragging at its title bar, or hide the toolbox by clicking in its close box. To redisplay the toolbox, choose the SHOW TOOLBOX command from the WINDOW menu. One toolbox serves, and is positioned in front of, any and all open Illustrator documents.

Illustrator 5.0's toolbox contains 22 tool *slots*. The tools that appear in these slots when you first launch Illustrator are called the *default tools*, but Illustrator offers also 8 *alternate tools* that are initially hidden. For example, of the three selection, or arrow, tools available, only two appear in the top two slots at any one time. To display the third alternate selection tool, click and hold the mouse button down on the topmost right tool icon. Tool slots that hide alternate tools have a small right-facing arrowhead in the upper right corner of the tool slot. All alternates for that tool will display to the right of the slot, as shown in Figure 2-2. Select the desired alternate tool as you would a command—that is, by dragging, highlighting the tool, and releasing the mouse button.

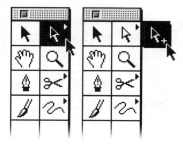

Figure 2-2: Drag at a slot that features a small arrowhead to select an alternate tool.

The default tool and all alternates for each slot in the toolbox appear in Figure 2-3. The following sections explain how they work.

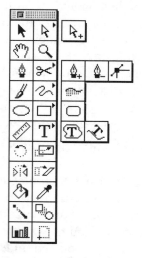

Figure 2-3: The toolbox with all default and alternate tools displayed.

The **Illustrator 5** Book

The selection tool slot

The *selection tool* (also called the *arrow tool*) is the tool most commonly used in Adobe Illustrator. You use it to select, move, and duplicate existing objects in your illustration. You can use the selection tool as follows:

- Click on a point, segment, group, or text block to select it and deselect the previous selection.

- Press SHIFT and click an object to add it to the selection.

- Drag on an empty portion of the screen to create a *marquee* (a rectangle defined by a dotted line boundary). All objects that fall, even partially, within the marquee boundaries will become selected.

- Drag a selected object to move all selected objects.

- Drag a selected object and press OPTION before completing the drag to clone all selected objects.

 To temporarily access the most recently used selection tool when you have any other tool selected, press and hold the COMMAND key. Releasing the COMMAND key returns you to the original tool. Press COMMAND with the TAB key to *toggle* between the selection tool and the direct-selection tool or the group-selection tool, whichever of the two appears in the topmost right slot. For example, if the selection tool is active, and the direct-selection tool appears in the topmost right slot, pressing COMMAND-TAB selects the direct-selection tool. Pressing COMMAND-TAB again selects the regular selection tool.

Pressing OPTION and clicking on the selection tool slot in the toolbox brings up the MOVE dialog box (just as if you had chosen the MOVE... command from the ARRANGE menu).

The direct-selection tool slot

The *direct-selection tool*, which appears as a hollow arrow, allows you to select individual points and segments inside an object, a compound path, or a path that is joined with type. You can also use this tool to edit the shape of a text block and flow large amounts of text into multiple columns. The following items explain how the direct-selection tool works:

- Click on a point, segment, group, or compound path to deselect the previous selection and select the nearest point or segment. Click inside a filled path to select the entire object.

- Press SHIFT and click a point, segment, or object to add it to the current selection.

- Press OPTION and click on a point or segment to select an entire path.

- Press OPTION and click a second time on an object that is part of a group to select the entire group.

The other tool that may appear in this slot is the *group-selection tool*, which looks like a hollow arrow with a plus sign. This tool allows you to select an entire path, whether inside a group or independent. If you click a second time on a selected path, you select the group to which the path belongs. It works just like OPTION-clicking with the direct-selection tool.

The hand tool slot

You use the hand tool to *scroll* the illustration; that is, move the drawing area with respect to the Illustrator window boundaries. Dragging with the hand tool allows you to scroll simultaneously along both the vertical and horizontal just as the vertical and horizontal scroll bars allow you to scroll separately.

To temporarily access the hand tool at any time, press and hold the SPACEBAR. Releasing the SPACEBAR will return you to the previously selected tool.

Double-clicking on the hand tool icon changes the current view size—defined below—to the *fit-in-window* view, which permits you to see the entire drawing area in the window (the same as choosing the FIT IN WINDOW command from the VIEW menu).

The zoom tool slot

Use the *zoom tool*, which appears as a magnifying glass, to expand or contract the *view size* of the current illustration. The image itself is not affected. Rather, the tool allows you to zoom in on a detail or zoom out to take in the big picture. Illustrator 5.0 provides 17 pre-defined view sizes ranging from as small as $\frac{1}{16}$ of the actual (or 100%) size to as large as 16 times the actual size.

When the zoom tool is selected, the cursor appears as a magnifying glass with a plus sign, indicating that it is in magnification mode. Press OPTION while the zoom tool is selected and the magnifying glass appears instead with an inset minus sign, indicating that it is in view reduction mode. The zoom tool works as follows:

- Click anywhere in the drawing area to magnify your illustration to the next larger view size.

- Press OPTION and click anywhere in the drawing area to reduce the view size of your illustration to the next lower level of magnification.

- Drag on your illustration to draw a marquee around the portion of your illustration that you want to magnify. When you release the mouse button, Illustrator magnifies the view size so that only the marqueed area fills the window.

- Press CONTROL and drag to form, instead, a *center-to-corner* marquee (in which the center of the marquee appears at the appears at the beginning of the drag and the lower right corner appears at the end of the drag).

- Illustrator expresses the view size as a percentage value in the title bar. A value of 100% indicates actual view size. Any value over 100% indicates a magnified view size; any lower percentage indicates a reduced view size.

To temporarily access the zoom tool with inset plus sign at any time, press and hold both the COMMAND key and the SPACEBAR. Then click to magnify the view size. Release both keys to return to the previously selected tool. Press COMMAND-OPTION-SPACEBAR to access the zoom tool with inset minus sign. Click while pressing these keys to reduce the view size.

Double-clicking on the zoom tool icon changes the current view size to the 100% view size, just as if you had chosen the ACTUAL SIZE command from the VIEW menu.

The pen tool slot

The *pen tool* is used to draw a path as a series of individual points. Typically, you click or drag to establish the first point in a path. As you click or drag to create a second point, Illustrator draws a *segment* joining the two points. Another segment joins the second point to the third, the third to the fourth, and so on. (For complete information about points and segments, read Chapter 5.)

Drawing with the pen tool is more laborious than drawing with the brush, freehand, or auto trace tool (see pages 26 and 27), but it tends to be more accurate. You can use the pen tool as follows:

- Click on an empty portion of the screen to create a *corner point*.

- Press SHIFT and click to constrain the segment to an angle that is a multiple of 45°.

- Drag on an empty portion of the screen to create a *smooth point* with two symmetrical *Bézier control handles*.

- Click on an existing smooth endpoint to change it to a corner point with only one Bézier control handle.

- Press OPTION and drag from an existing smooth endpoint to change it to a *cusp*, a corner point with two independent control handles.

- Press CONTROL and click on an existing segment to add a smooth point and divide the segment into two segments. Press CONTROL and click on an existing point to remove the point and join the two segments divided by the point into a single segment.

Press the CONTROL key to temporarily access the pen tool when the freehand tool is selected. Release the CONTROL key to return to the freehand tool.

The scissors tool slot

The *scissors tool* is used to split segments and to add points to a path. Illustrator automatically determines the identity of the points based on the form of the path. The scissors tool may be used as follows:

- Click on a segment to insert two endpoints, splitting the segment. This technique can be used to open a closed path or to divide an open path into two open paths.

- Click on a point to convert the point into two endpoints, thus opening a closed path or dividing an open path into two open paths.

- Press OPTION and click on a segment to add a single point to the path without splitting it.

The three alternate tools for this slot are the *add-anchor-point tool*, which appears as a pen icon with a plus sign; the *delete-anchor-point tool*, which appears as a pen icon with a minus sign; and the *convert-direction-point tool*, which looks like a corner point flanked by Bézier control handles. The add-anchor-point tool inserts a point into a path segment, just as if you had OPTION-clicked with the scissors tool or CONTROL-clicked with the pen tool on a segment. Conversely, clicking with the delete-anchor-point tool deletes a point. However, it does not break the path, as happens when you delete a selected point by pressing the DELETE key. Instead, a new segment connects the two points neighboring the deleted point.

The convert-direction-point tool is used to convert corner points to smooth points, and smooth points to cusps or corner points. The convert-direction-point tool may be used as follows:

- Click on a smooth point to convert it to a corner point with no Bézier control handle.

- Drag one of the Bézier control handles of a smooth point to move it independently of the other Bézier control handle, thus converting the smooth point to a cusp.

- Drag from a corner point to convert it to a smooth point with two symmetrical Bézier control handles.

Press the CONTROL key to temporarily access the convert-point tool when any tool from the selection tool slot is selected. When any other tool (except the pen, freehand, or auto trace tool) is selected, press COMMAND-CONTROL to access the convert-point tool. When the pen, freehand, or auto trace tool is selected, press COMMAND-OPTION-CONTROL to bring up the convert-direction-point tool.

The brush tool slot

The *brush tool* is new to Illustrator 5.0. It allows you to create a closed path of any size that, with the addition of a color fill, gives the appearance of a traditional paint stroke. Now, in one fell swoop, you can make a filled shape that, in previous versions of Illustrator, you had to draw meticulously with the pen tool or the freehand tool. A shape created with the brush tool consists of segments, points, and handles—just like a shape created with any other drawing tool—and can be adjusted accordingly. With the brush tool, it is possible to achieve a calligraphic style, particularly if you use the tool with a pressure-sensitive drawing tablet. Double-clicking on the brush tool icon displays the Brush dialog box.

The freehand tool slot

The *freehand tool*, which appears as a squiggly line, is used to draw free-form paths. Illustrator automatically determines the placement and identity of the points required to define a free-form path. You can use the freehand tool as follows:

- Drag on an empty portion of the screen to create a free-form path.
- Press COMMAND while dragging with the tool to erase portions of the path you have just drawn.
- Drag from either end of an existing open path to extend the length of the path.
- Drag from one end of an existing open path to the other end of the same path to close the path.
- Drag from the end of one existing open path to the end of another open path to join the two paths into one.
- Press OPTION and drag from the end of an existing open path to ensure that the point from which you drag is a corner point.

The only alternate tool for this slot is the *auto trace tool*, which appears as a line above a small hill of dots. This tool is used to convert imported *bitmaps* (from a painting application such MacPaint or Photoshop) into smooth object-oriented graphics by tracing the outline of an image with a closed path. The auto trace tool may be used as follows:

- Click within six pixels of an imported bitmap to create a single closed path that traces the outline of the image.

- Drag from one point within six pixels of a bitmap to another point similarly close to the same bitmap to trace only that portion of the image that lies between the click and release points.

- Drag from either end of an existing open path within six points of a bitmap to extend the length of the path.

- Press OPTION and drag from the end of an existing open path situated near a bitmap to ensure that the point from which you drag is a corner point.

You can also extend an existing open path with the auto trace tool in the same way described for the freehand tool, provided that the existing path follows the outline of an imported bitmap.

The oval tool slot

The *oval tool* is used to create an ellipse with a center point. You can use the oval tool as follows:

- Drag to draw an ellipse from the middle of one arc to the middle of the opposite arc.

- Press OPTION and drag to draw an ellipse from center to arc.

- Press SHIFT and drag to draw a circle from arc to opposite arc or SHIFT-OPTION-drag to draw a circle outward from its center.

- Click to display a dialog box requesting you to enter the dimensions of the prospective ellipse. The click point becomes the middle of the upper left arc.

- Press OPTION and click to display a dialog box requesting you to enter the dimensions of the prospective ellipse. The click point becomes the center of the shape.

The rectangle tool slot

The *rectangle tool* creates a simple rectangle with a center point. Here's how it works:

- Drag to draw a rectangle from corner to opposite corner.

- Press OPTION and drag to draw a rectangle from center point to corner.

- Press SHIFT and drag to draw a square from corner to corner or SHIFT-OPTION-drag to draw a square outward from its center.

- Click to display a dialog box requesting you to enter the dimensions and corner radius of the prospective rectangle. A "Corner radius" value greater than zero makes the rectangle a rounded-rectangle. The click point becomes the upper left corner of the shape.

- Press OPTION and click to display a dialog box requesting you to enter the dimensions and corner radius of the prospective rectangle. This time, the point where you OPTION-clicked becomes the center of the shape.

The alternate tool for this slot is the *rounded-rectangle tool*. The rounded-rectangle tool draws a rectangle with rounded corners. You can use the rounded rectangle tool as follows:

- Drag to draw a rounded-rectangle from corner to opposite corner.

- Press OPTION and drag to draw a rounded-rectangle from center point to corner.

- Press SHIFT and drag or SHIFT-OPTION-drag to draw a rounded-square from the corner or center, respectively.

- Click to display a dialog box requesting you to enter the dimensions and corner radius of the prospective rectangle. Be sure to enter a "Corner radius" value greater than zero. The click point becomes the upper left corner of the shape.

- When you OPTION-click with the rounded-rectangle tool, the click point becomes the center of the shape.

The measure tool slot

The *measure tool* measures the distance and direction from one point to another. To use the measure tool, click twice, once at each of two different screen locations; or drag from the first location to the second. The INFO palette will display, listing the distance and angle between the two points, as well as the horizontal and vertical components of the measure.

To precisely move objects, first measure the distance that you want to move an object with the measure tool. OPTION-click on the selection tool icon or choose the MOVE... command from the ARRANGE menu. The information from the INFO palette now displays in the MOVE dialog box. Press RETURN to complete the move.

The type tool slot

The *type tool* lets you add and edit existing text directly on the page. You can also create type inside a path or along a path. Use the type tool as follows:

- Click outside an existing text block to position an *alignment point*. Text entered from the keyboard will align to this point.

- Drag outside an existing text block to draw a *column*. Text entered from the keyboard will appear inside this column.

- Click on an existing closed path or OPTION-click on an open path to create *area type*. Text entered from the keyboard will appear inside the path.

- Click on an existing open path or OPTION-click on a closed path to create *path type*. Text entered from the keyboard will follow along the path.

- Click inside an existing text block to position the blinking *insertion marker*. Text entered from the keyboard will begin at the marker.

- Drag inside an existing text block to select multiple characters of type. Selected text appears highlighted and can be formatted or replaced with new text entered from the keyboard.

- Double-click inside a text block to select a word of type.

- Triple-click inside a text block to select a paragraph.

The two other tools in this slot are the *area-type tool*, which appears as a letter inside a shape, and the *path-type tool*, which appears as a letter on a curve. The area-type tool allows you to set type inside an existing free-form path. The path-type tool joins the *baseline* of a block of type to an existing free-form path to create text on a curve. Each tool is operated by clicking on the desired path and entering text from the keyboard.

Press the CONTROL key to temporarily access the type tool when the area-type tool or path-type tool is selected. Release the CONTROL key to return to the selected type tool.

Regardless of the tool used to create it, a text block can be edited with any of the three type tools.

The rotate tool slot

The *rotate tool* is used to rotate one or more selected objects in your illustration around a single point, called a *rotation origin*. The rotate tool may be used as follows:

- Click to establish the rotation origin. Then drag the selected object around the origin to rotate it.

- Click to establish the rotation origin, then SHIFT-drag to rotate the selected object by any angle that is a multiple of 45°.

- Click to establish the rotation origin, then OPTION-drag to simultaneously rotate and clone the selected object.

- Press OPTION and click to display a dialog box requesting you to enter the angle by which you want to rotate the selected object.

The scale tool slot

The *scale tool* is used to reduce or enlarge one or more selected objects in your illustration. An object is resized with respect to a single point, called a *scale origin*. The scale tool may be used as follows:

- Click to establish the rotation origin. Then drag toward the scale origin to reduce the selected object.

- Click to establish the scale origin. Then drag away from the scale origin to enlarge the selected object.

- Click to establish the scale origin, then SHIFT-drag to resize the selected object proportionally.

- Click to establish the scale origin, then OPTION-drag to simultaneously resize and clone the selected object.

- Press OPTION and click to display a dialog box requesting you to enter the percentage by which you want to reduce or enlarge the selected object.

The reflect tool slot

The *reflect tool* is used to flip one or more selected objects around a *reflection axis*, which may be oriented horizontally, vertically, or at some angle. The reflect tool may be used as follows:

- Click to secure one end of the reflection axis. Then click or drag to determine the location of the other end of the axis, around which Illustrator flips the selected object.

- Click to secure one end of the reflection axis. Then SHIFT-click or SHIFT-drag to constrain the angle of the axis to any angle that is a multiple of 45°.

- Click to secure one end of the reflection axis, then OPTION-click or OPTION-drag to simultaneously flip and clone the selection.

- Press OPTION and click to display a dialog box requesting you to enter the orientation of the reflection axis around which you want to flip the selected object.

The shear tool slot

The *shear tool* is used to slant (or *skew*) one or more selected objects. An object is skewed with respect to a single point, called a *shearing origin*. The shear tool may be used as follows:

- Click to establish the shearing origin. Then drag with respect to the origin to skew the selected object.

- Click to establish the shearing origin. Then SHIFT-drag to constrain the angle of the skew to any angle that is a multiple of 45°.

- Click to establish the shearing origin. Then OPTION-drag to simultaneously skew and clone the selected object.

- Press OPTION and click to display a dialog box requesting you to enter the angle by which you want to skew the selected object and the angle of the *shearing axis*.

The paint bucket tool slot

The *paint bucket tool*, new to Illustrator 5.0, allows you to fill and stroke a graphic object or text block according to the specifications in the PAINT STYLE palette. Here's how to use the paint bucket tool:

- Double-click on the paint bucket tool icon in the toolbox to display the PAINTBUCKET/EYEDROPPER dialog box, which allows you to specify which attributes are affected by the paint bucket tool. You can select from several varieties of fill and stroke attributes by clicking on check boxes.

- Click on a graphic object or text block to select it and change its fill and stroke to those displayed in the PAINT STYLE palette (in accordance with your specifications in the PAINTBUCKET/EYEDROPPER dialog box).

- Press COMMAND and click on an object, then release the COMMAND key and click on a second object to copy the fill and stroke attributes from the first object to the second.

- Press the SHIFT key and click on a graphic object or text block to add it to the current selection. The fill and stroke attributes of this object will also change to those displayed in the PAINT STYLE palette.

Press the OPTION key to temporarily access the eyedropper tool while the paint bucket tool is selected. Release the OPTION key to return to the paint bucket tool.

The eyedropper tool slot

The *eyedropper tool*, also new to Illustrator 5.0, records the color of the fill and stroke of an existing graphic object or text block. To use the eyedropper tool, click on an object in your illustration. The settings in the PAINT STYLE palette change to match the fill and stroke of that object (according to your specifications in the PAINTBUCKET/EYEDROPPER dialog box).

Press the OPTION key to temporarily access the paint bucket tool while the eyedropper tool is selected. Release the OPTION key to return to the eyedropper tool.

Select an object, then select the eyedropper tool and double-click on a second object to copy the fill and stroke attributes from the second object to the first.

Double-click on the eyedropper tool icon to display the PAINTBUCKET/EYEDROPPER dialog box.

The gradient vector tool slot

The *gradient vector tool* allows you to change the position, direction and size of a gradient fill in a shape. Illustrator 5.0 incorporates an automatic gradation feature as a one of seven possible fills. You can use the gradient vector tool as follows:

- Drag across a selected object filled with a linear gradation to change the direction of the gradation. When you release the mouse, the gradation will start at the point at which you began dragging and extend to where you stopped dragging.

- Drag across a selected object filled with a radial gradation to change the center and edges of the gradation. When you release the mouse, the center of the gradation will appear at the point at which you began dragging; the last ring of color will appear at the point where you stopped dragging.

- SHIFT-drag with the gradient vector tool to constrain the angle of the drag to a multiple of 45°.

- Double-click on the gradient vector tool icon in the toolbox to display the GRADIENT palette, which lets you create and edit the colors in a gradient fill.

The blend tool slot

The *blend tool* creates intermediate form, fill, and stroke manipulations between two selected open paths or between two selected closed paths. To use the blend tool, select one or more points in each of the two paths. The two paths need not have a similar number of points. Click twice, once on a selected point in each path, to bring up the BLEND dialog box. Enter the number of steps desired and press the RETURN key. Illustrator then creates the requested number of intermediary steps as instructed.

The graph tool slot

The *graph tool* automatically generates a standard bar chart (also known as a *cluster bar chart* or a *grouped column chart*) from a spreadsheet of numbers. The graph tool may be used as follows:

- Drag to draw the rectangular boundary for the chart from corner to corner.
- Press OPTION and drag to draw the rectangular boundary for the chart from center to corner.
- Press the SHIFT key and drag or SHIFT-OPTION-drag to draw a square boundary from the corner or center, respectively.
- Click to display a dialog box requesting you to enter the dimensions of the prospective chart boundary. The click point becomes the upper left corner of the chart.
- Press OPTION and click to display a dialog box requesting you to enter the dimensions of the prospective chart boundary. The click point becomes the center of the chart.

After you determine the size of the chart, Illustrator displays the GRAPH DATA window. Here you may enter or import data into a typical spreadsheet matrix made up of rows and columns. Press the ENTER key to instruct Illustrator to process the data and generate the chart.

Five alternate charting tools are available for the graph tool slot. To access a different tool, double-click on the graph tool icon in the toolbox to display the GRAPH STYLE dialog box. Then select a radio button from the "Graph type" list and press RETURN. In addition to the default grouped-column graph tool, you can select from the *stacked-column-graph tool*, the *line-graph tool*, the *pie-graph tool*, the *area-graph tool*, and the *scatter-graph tool*. Each tool organizes the data in the GRAPH DATA window into a different kind of chart.

The stacked-column-graph tool stacks related values for different *series* (columns of data in the spreadsheet) one upon another, rather than positioning them side by side, as in a standard bar chart. When each row of values adds up to 100%, a stacked bar chart is called a *percentage chart*.

The line-graph tool maps your data as points on an XY-coordinate grid. Ordinarily, the X axis represents time and the Y axis displays the values. Straight segments connect points in a single series, clearly displaying rising and falling values.

The pie-graph tool creates a pie for each series of data (organized in rows in the spreadsheet), so that values in a series can be compared to the series as a whole. Pie graphs illustrate percentages rather than specific values.

The area-graph tool generates what amounts to a filled-in line graph. Each series is stacked upon the previous one to avoid overlapping, emphasizing the total performance of all series over time.

The scatter-graph tool maps *paired data* on an XY-coordinate grid. The first series of data produces Y-axis values, the second series produces X-axis values. Each point is therefore the intersection of the two values in a single row of data.

The page tool slot

Use the *page tool* to relocate the central *page tile* (represented by the dotted outline) within the drawing area. To use the page tool, first choose the FIT IN WINDOW command from the VIEW menu. Then click or drag with the page tool to position the lower left corner of the tile boundary. If the page tile is not visible, choose SHOW PAGE TILING from the VIEW menu.

Resetting the toolbox

The default tools that appear in the toolbox when you first run Illustrator represent the most commonly used tools. However, as you work on an illustration, you will no doubt select various alternate tools, changing the composition of the toolbox.

You can reset a single slot to display its default tool by pressing SHIFT and double-clicking the desired slot. To quickly reset the entire toolbox, press both SHIFT and COMMAND and double-click any slot.

Menus and commands

Following are brief descriptions of the menus and commands offered by Adobe Illustrator 5.0. Again, these descriptions are intended simply as introductions to the commands. You'll find more thorough descriptions throughout later chapters. Keyboard equivalents are listed in parentheses when applicable.

The Apple (🍎) menu

The APPLE menu behaves exactly as it does within all other Macintosh applications and at the Finder. You have access to all desk accessories currently available to your System file and to any items that you have added to your Apple Menu Items folder.

ABOUT ADOBE ILLUSTRATOR... displays the same startup screen that displays when you launch the program. Normally, the only people who use this command are those whose names appear in the credits and their relatives.

ABOUT PLUG-IN displays the credits for the individual plug-in modules. For use of the command, see above.

The File menu

As in most Macintosh applications, the Adobe Illustrator FILE menu controls broad, document-level activities, including opening, closing, printing, and saving illustrations. Additionally, the FILE menu controls the importation of text and graphic images and the exportation of EPS (*Encapsulated PostScript*) files.

NEW... (⌘-N) creates a new file without a template.

OPEN... (⌘-O) brings up the PLEASE OPEN ILLUSTRATION OR TEMPLATE dialog box, which allows you to open any available Illustrator 1.1, 88, 3.0, 4.0, or 5.0 file; open a bitmap tracing template saved in the MacPaint or PICT format; or cancel the open operation. By pressing the OPTION key when choosing OPEN... (⌘-⌥-O) you may add, change, or discard the template for an existing illustration.

File	
New	⌘N
Open...	⌘O
Close	⌘W
Save	⌘S
Save As...	
Place Art...	
Import Styles...	
Doc. Setup...	⌘⇧D
Page Setup...	
Print...	⌘P
Preferences	▶
Quit	⌘Q

CLOSE (⌘-W) closes the current illustration, but does not quit the Illustrator application. If any changes have been made to a document before it is closed, a warning box will display giving you the opportunity to save the changes, close without saving the changes, or cancel the close command. If you choose to save, a SAVE CHANGES dialog box appears, allowing you to save your changes or, again, cancel the close operation.

SAVE (⌘-S) updates the disk file of your current document to include all changes made since it was last saved. If the current document already has a name, you are given no opportunity to confirm the save or to change the location or name of the file. If the current document is "Untitled art" followed by a number, the SAVE ILLUSTRATION dialog box will appear, allowing you the opportunity to enter a name for the document and to determine on which drive and in which folder you would like to save your file. You may also indicate that a new Illustrator file should include a Macintosh or IBM Encapsulated PostScript screen representation for importation into a page-layout program such as Aldus PageMaker or QuarkXPress, and with what versions of Illustrator the file will be compatible. The SAVE command will be dimmed if no changes have been made to the current document since it was last saved.

SAVE AS... brings up the SAVE ILLUSTRATION dialog box, which allows you to change the name or location of the file you are saving. You may also add a Macintosh or IBM EPS screen representation to an existing Illustrator file, and change the compatibility.

PLACE ART... brings up the PLEASE OPEN EPS FILE dialog box, which allows you to place an Encapsulated PostScript document into an illustration or cancel the place operation. You can also place Illustrator files that were not saved with EPS previews, although they will not preview correctly.

IMPORT TEXT... appears in place of the PLACE ART... command when you activate or create a text block using one of the type tools. Choosing this command brings up the SELECT FILE TO IMPORT dialog box, which allows you to import a text document. Illustrator 5.0 supports Microsoft Word 3.0, 4.0, and 5.0; RTF (Rich Text Format); MacWrite 4.0, 5.0, and II; WriteNow 3.0; DOS and Windows versions of WordPerfect 5.1; WordPerfect 2.0 for the Mac; and text-only file formats.

File

New	⌘N
Open...	⌘O
Close	⌘W
Save	⌘S
Save As...	
Place Art...	
Import Styles...	
Doc. Setup...	⌘⇧D
Page Setup...	
Print...	⌘P
Preferences	▶
Quit	⌘Q

IMPORT STYLES... brings up the PLEASE OPEN ILLUSTRATION OR TEMPLATE dialog box, which allows you to import the styles attributes that were saved with any Illustrator file, whether the file is an illustration or a template. The imported style attributes include custom colors, tile patterns, gradations. Imported attributes augment but do not replace existing attributes in the destination file. In the scrolling list, locate the file that contains the style attributes you want to import and click the IMPORT button to add the styles.

DOCUMENT SETUP... (⌘-⇧-D) brings up DOCUMENT SETUP dialog box, in which you control the elements that define your *artboard*, which is Illustrator's on-screen analogy for a real-world sketchbook. Here you can choose from seven pre-defined page sizes or create your own size up to 120 inches square. (That should pretty well accommodate anyone's mural-making inclinations.) Select an "Orientation" icon to select whether the page is upright or on its side. If you check the "Use Page Setup" check box, the size and orientation specifications will match the those defined in the PAGE SETUP dialog box, as explained in the next entry. You can also specify whether tile patterns and placed images preview and whether tile patterns print; you can control how large documents divide when printing; you can change the resolution of paths (in dots per inch) and select whether very long paths are broken into smaller ones when printed or saved; and you can specify the unit of measure employed by the rulers and various option-box values inside dialog boxes.

PAGE SETUP... brings up Apple's standard LASERWRITER PAGE SETUP dialog box, provided that you have selected a PostScript-compatible printer using the Chooser desk accessory. The dialog box allows you to specify the size and orientation of the printed page and the percentage enlargement or reduction of the illustration when printed. Other options have little effect in Illustrator.

PRINT... (⌘-P) brings up Apple's standard LASERWRITER PRINT dialog box, provided that you have selected a PostScript-compatible printer in the Chooser. The dialog box allows you to specify which pages you wish to print, the number of copies, and the paper source.

File	
New	⌘N
Open...	⌘O
Close	⌘W
Save	⌘S
Save As...	
Place Art...	
Import Styles...	
Doc. Setup...	⌘⇧D
Page Setup...	
Print...	⌘P
Preferences	▶
Quit	⌘Q

PREFERENCES... displays four commands that allow you to adjust a number of Illustrator's settings.

GENERAL... (⌘-K) command brings up the GENERAL PREFERENCES dialog box, from which you can specify several basic attributes affecting the on-screen drawing environment. You can change the values for the angle for the constraint axis; the corner radius for rectangles; the freehand tolerance; the auto trace gap; the movement equivalent of cursor keystrokes; the degree to which keystrokes affect the type size, leading, vertical shift, and tracking; the number of undo levels; and the stage at which Illustrator displays text as gray bars. You can also control how points snap together, whether patterns transform, the scaling of line weights, whether clicking an area's fill selects the surrounding path, and whether precise Illustrator displays the ostensibly more precise crosshair cursors. Finally, you can select the unit of measure used throughout the program. (This last item affects all future illustrations, whereas the similar option in the DOCUMENT SETUP dialog box affects the foreground illustration only.)

COLOR MATCHING... brings up the COLOR MATCHING dialog box. Here you can change the way Illustrator displays color— for example, just how blue your cyan or how bright your magenta appears on screen. Changes in the COLOR MATCHING dialog box directly affect the colors in the Paint Style palette.

HYPHENATION... command allows you to define exceptions to the auto-hyphenation function that appears in the PARAGRAPH dialog box. None of the words that appear in the scrolling field will be hyphenated, which means the entire word will drop down to the next line in a text block intact, instead of breaking between lines.

PLUG-INS... lets you switch between different folders of filters.

QUIT (⌘-Q) exits the Illustrator application, closing all open illustrations and returning control to the Macintosh Finder or to another application. A SAVE CHANGES alert box will appear for every illustration that has unsaved changes. If you opt to save an untitled illustration, the SAVE ILLUSTRATION dialog box will appear.

```
┌─ Edit ──────────┐
│ Undo         ⌘Z │
│ Redo        ⌘⇧Z │
├─────────────────┤
│ Cut          ⌘H │
│ Copy         ⌘C │
│ Paste        ⌘U │
│ Clear           │
│ Select All   ⌘A │
│ Select None ⌘⇧A │
├─────────────────┤
│ Paste In Front ⌘F │
│ Paste In Back  ⌘B │
├─────────────────┤
│ Publishing    ▶ │
├─────────────────┤
│ Show Clipboard  │
└─────────────────┘
```

The Edit menu

Most of the commands in the EDIT menu will be familiar to you if you have worked in other Macintosh applications. These commands control the duplication of objects via the Macintosh Clipboard, common layering manipulations, and so on. Two EDIT commands— PASTE IN FRONT and PASTE IN BACK—are unique to Illustrator, although they conform to the EDIT menu tradition of working directly with the Clipboard.

UNDO (⌘-Z) steps backward through the last operation performed in Illustrator. Undoing an operation reverses all effects created by the operation; the file returns to its exact state prior to the operation. To help you keep track of previous operations, the UNDO command lists the command it will undo if chosen, such as UNDO MOVE. Under Illustrator 5.0, you can now undo multiple operations in a row.

REDO (⌘-⇧-Z) steps forward through the most recently undone operation in Illustrator, effectively undoing the last UNDO command. Redoing an operation reapplies all effects undone with the last UNDO; the file returns to its exact state prior to UNDO. To help you keep track of the last undone operation, the REDO command lists the command it will undo if chosen, such as REDO MOVE. The REDO command is dimmed any time UNDO was not the last operation.

CUT (⌘-X) deletes one or more selected objects from your illustration and stores them in the Macintosh Clipboard, replacing the Clipboard's previous contents. If no object is selected, the CUT command is dimmed.

COPY (⌘-C) makes a copy of one or more selected objects in your illustration and stores them in the Macintosh Clipboard, replacing the Clipboard's previous contents. If no object is selected, the COPY command is dimmed.

PASTE (⌘-V) makes a copy of the items in the Macintosh Clipboard and places them inside the current illustration. If the Clipboard is empty, the PASTE command is dimmed.

CLEAR (DELETE, BACKSPACE, or CLEAR) deletes one or more selected objects from your illustration but does not place them in the Clipboard or alter the Clipboard's contents. You can bring back the objects by choosing UNDO CLEAR. If no object is selected, the CLEAR command is dimmed.

```
Edit
Undo          ⌘Z
Redo          ⌘⇧Z

Cut           ⌘X
Copy          ⌘C
Paste         ⌘U
Clear
Select All    ⌘A
Select None   ⌘⇧A

Paste In Front ⌘F
Paste In Back  ⌘B

Publishing      ▶

Show Clipboard
```

SELECT ALL (⌘-A) selects every element—including all points—within the drawing area of the current document. The only exception to this is that if a text block has been activated with one of the type tools, choosing SELECT ALL highlights all text in the current *story* (one or more linked text blocks).

SELECT NONE (⌘-⇧-A) deselects every element—including all points—within the drawing area of the current document. The only exception to this occurs if a text in a text block has been selected with one of the type tools, in which case the Select None command is dimmed.

PASTE IN FRONT (⌘-F) pastes the contents of the Clipboard in front of any and all selected objects at the exact location from which the Clipboard contents were cut or copied. If nothing is selected, the newly pasted objects become the foremost objects in the Illustrator drawing area. This command is dimmed if the Clipboard is empty.

PASTE IN BACK (⌘-B) pastes the contents of the Clipboard in back of any and all selected objects at the exact location from which the Clipboard contents were cut or copied. If nothing is selected, the newly pasted objects become the rearmost objects in the Illustrator drawing area. This command is dimmed if the Clipboard is empty.

PUBLISH displays a submenu of four commands that allow you to take advantage of System 7's edition manager, which allows you to link elements inside a drawing to one or more files created in other applications and saved to disk.

CREATE PUBLISHER... displays the edition-destination dialog box, requesting that you enter a name and specify a drive and a folder in which to store an *edition file* which will contain all selected objects. The edition file can be imported into any other application. After choosing the command, the selected objects in the drawing area are surrounded by a gray border, indicating the portions of the document included in the edition. The edition file updates automatically every time you choose the SAVE command from the FILE menu.

SUBSCRIBE TO... displays the edition-selection dialog box, which allows you to *subscribe* to an edition file saved to disk. After choosing the command, the contents of the edition file appear in the current drawing, surrounded by a gray border. The *edition object* updates automatically every time the publisher application saves the file.

Edit

Undo	⌘Z
Redo	⌘⇧Z
Cut	⌘H
Copy	⌘C
Paste	⌘U
Clear	
Select All	⌘A
Select None	⌘⇧A
Paste In Front	⌘F
Paste In Back	⌘B
Publishing	▶
Show Clipboard	

PUBLISHER OPTIONS... displays the edition-management dialog box, which allows you to view the location of the selected edition object on disk and to determine how often the corresponding edition file should update. You may also cancel the link between the selected edition object and the editions file on disk.

SHOW/HIDE BORDERS toggles the display of the gray borders that surround edition objects that have been saved to disk using the CREATE PUBLISHER... command.

SHOW/HIDE CLIPBOARD toggles the display of the content of the clipboard, just as the SHOW CLIPBOARD command does at the Finder level. The contents supposedly reflect the last cut or copy operation. Unfortunately, the CLIPBOARD window frequently doesn't accurately display objects cut or copied from Illustrator, instead displaying the phrase "1 objects." In such a case, you must execute the PASTE command to view the Clipboard contents.

The Arrange menu

Arrange

Repeat Transform	⌘D
Move...	⌘⇧M
Bring To Front	⌘=
Send To Back	⌘-
Group	⌘G
Ungroup	⌘U
Lock	⌘1
Unlock All	⌘2
Hide	⌘3
Show All	⌘4

As the menu title suggests, commands in the ARRANGE menu allow you to arrange selected elements within the drawing window and with respect to other elements. Many of these commands are standards that have been included in Adobe Illustrator since its initial release.

REPEAT TRANSFORM (⌘-D) repeats the transformation just performed on the current selection, including any cloning. REPEAT TRANSFORM is particularly useful for experimenting with slight transformations; you can nudge the effect along until the object meets your exact requirement. This command is dimmed if a transformation was not the most recently performed operation.

MOVE... (⌘-⇧-M) displays the MOVE dialog box, which allows you to move any and all selected objects a specified distance in a specified direction. You can access this dialog box by OPTION-clicking the selection tool slot in the toolbox. If no object is selected, the MOVE... command is dimmed.

BRING TO FRONT (⌘-=, COMMAND-EQUAL) moves any and all selected objects in front of all other objects in the illustration. Although this command acts somewhat like a combined CUT-and-PASTE IN FRONT command, the Clipboard is not affected. If no object is selected, the BRING TO FRONT command is dimmed.

The **Illustrator 5** Book

Arrange	
Repeat Transform	⌘D
Move...	⌘⇧M
Bring To Front	⌘=
Send To Back	⌘-
Group	⌘G
Ungroup	⌘U
Lock	⌘1
Unlock All	⌘2
Hide	⌘3
Show All	⌘4

SEND TO BACK (⌘- –, COMMAND-HYPHEN) moves any and all selected objects in back of all other objects in the Illustrator drawing area. Again, the contents of the Clipboard are not affected. If no object is selected, the SEND TO BACK command is dimmed.

GROUP (⌘-G) combines all currently selected elements into a single object. You can even group multiple groups. The GROUP command changes the layering order of selected objects, bringing them forward to just behind the foremost object in the group. You can select and adjust a single element in a group without first ungrouping it by using the direct-selection tool. If no object is selected, the GROUP command is dimmed.

UNGROUP (⌘-U) separates a selected group into its original elements. Some objects are created as groups, including blends and graphs. (In Illustrator 5.0, rectangles and ellipses are no longer grouped.) Ungrouping these objects allows you to edit them with the selection tool; however, it may also prevent you from editing the object in different ways. For example, if you ungroup a graph, you can no longer edit it using commands from the GRAPH menu. If no object is selected, the UNGROUP command is dimmed.

LOCK (⌘-1) locks any and all selected objects so that they cannot be selected or manipulated in any manner. Locking one or more points or segments in a single path locks the entire path. Pressing the OPTION key when choosing the LOCK command locks all objects that are *not* currently selected.

UNLOCK ALL (⌘-2) unlocks *all* locked objects in the foreground illustration. You cannot unlock a single locked object independently of other locked objects in the same illustration.

HIDE (⌘-3) hides any and all selected objects so that they are not visible on screen, nor can they be selected or manipulated in any manner. Hiding one or more points or segments in a single path hides the entire path. An object will neither print nor preview when it is hidden. Pressing the OPTION key when choosing the HIDE command hides all objects that are *not* currently selected. Hiding is not saved: hidden objects therefore reappear the next time the illustration is opened.

SHOW ALL (⌘-4) displays *all* hidden objects in the foreground illustration. You cannot display a single hidden object independently of other hidden objects in the same illustration.

```
View
✓Preview        ⌘Y
 Artwork        ⌘E
 Preview Selection ⌘⌥Y

 Hide Template
 Show Rulers    ⌘R
 Hide Page Tiling
 Hide Edges     ⌘⇧H
 Hide Guides

 Zoom In        ⌘]
 Zoom Out       ⌘[
 Actual Size    ⌘H
 Fit In Window  ⌘M

 New View...    ⌘⌃V
 Edit Views...
```

The View menu

The VIEW menu contains commands that affect how you see elements in the drawing area. The first three commands control the display mode. The next five toggle on and off commands that display drawing aids. The next four alter the view size. The last two commands allow you to record and use your own personalized drawing window "look" through view size and artwork orientation.

PREVIEW (⌘-Y) previews an illustration, displaying all objects as they will appear when printed, complete with strokes, fills, patterns, colors, and so on. Illustrator 5.0 also displays guides and tracing templates in the preview mode, though these do not print. Furthermore, you can now create and edit objects in the preview mode.

ARTWORK (⌘-E) displays graphic objects with transparent fills and black, hairline strokes. Type is displayed with black fills and no stroke. Guides appear as dotted lines. A grayed version of the bitmapped tracing template is also visible, provided that a template exists in the current document. The advantage of artwork mode over preview mode is that the screen refreshes considerably faster, which is especially helpful when an illustration consists of a large number of objects with complex fills, such as gradations and tile patterns. You can also get to objects that may be partially or completely hidden and therefore inaccessible in the preview mode.

PREVIEW SELECTION (⌘-⌥-Y) previews any and all selected objects, including all strokes and fills. Objects that are not selected are hidden. As in the preview mode, you can move and reshape objects when previewing a selection. Generally, this display mode is most useful for previewing a detail of a drawing, a less time-consuming operation than previewing an entire illustration.

SHOW/HIDE TEMPLATE toggles the display of a grayed version of the bitmapped tracing template that was scanned or created in a similar program, provided that a template exists in the current document. The appearance of the rest of the illustration is dependent on which of the three display modes (described above) is selected.

SHOW/HIDE RULERS (⌘-R) toggles the display of horizontal and vertical rulers on the bottom and right sides of the current Illustrator window. Rulers display in the unit of measure specified in the GENERAL PREFERENCES or DOCUMENT SETUP dialog box.

Uiew

✓Preview   ⌘Y
 Artwork   ⌘E
 Preview Selection ⌘⌥Y

 Hide Template
 Show Rulers   ⌘R
 Hide Page Tiling
 Hide Edges   ⌘⇧H
 Hide Guides

 Zoom In   ⌘]
 Zoom Out   ⌘[
 Actual Size   ⌘H
 Fit In Window   ⌘M

 New Uiew...   ⌘⌃U
 Edit Uiews...

SHOW/HIDE PAGE TILING toggles the display of the dotted out-line that defines the printable portion of your artwork board. You can change the tiling method using options in the DOCUMENT SETUP dialog box. The page tool allows you to move the tiles.

SHOW/HIDE EDGES (⌘-⇧-H) toggles the display of the colored outlines and points that normally appear when objects are selected. By hiding edges, you can better see how a move or transformation affects selected objects. You can manipulate selected objects as usual even when edges are hidden.

SHOW/HIDE GUIDES toggles the display of *guides*—non-printing dotted lines that enable you to exactly align objects in the drawing area—within your illustration. See the discussion of the MAKE (GUIDES) command on page 48.

ZOOM IN (⌘-], COMMAND-RIGHT BRACKET) magnifies your view of the illustration to twice the previous view size. This is the same as clicking with the zoom tool in the middle of the screen.

ZOOM OUT (⌘-[, COMMAND-LEFT BRACKET) reduces your view of the illustration to half the previous view size. This is the same as OPTION-clicking with the zoom tool in the middle of the screen.

ACTUAL SIZE (⌘-H) changes the view of the current document to a full-size representation. This view size displays all objects in an il-lustration at the size at which they will print. The size of your screen determines how much of the document can be seen at a time. You can also access the actual view size by double-clicking on the zoom tool icon in the toolbox.

FIT IN WINDOW (⌘-M) changes the view size of the current document so that the entire drawing area is visible on your screen. The exact size at which your illustration is displayed depends on the size of your monitor. You can also access the fit-in-window view size by double-clicking on the hand tool icon in the toolbox.

NEW VIEW... (⌘-⌃-V) displays the NEW VIEW dialog box, which allows you to name and record the current view size and position of the artwork board within the drawing window. Once named, the view will display at the bottom of the ARRANGE menu. When you choose the named view, Illustrator returns you to the recorded view size and board position. You can record up to 25 views, the first ten of which receive the keyboard equivalent ⌘-⌃ followed by 0 through 9.

EDIT VIEW... displays the EDIT VIEW dialog box, which allows you to rename or delete any of the views that you have previously recorded. Click on one of the view names in the scrolling field to select the view. Press the TAB key to highlight the NAME option box and type in the new name or click on the DELETE button to remove the view from the VIEW menu.

The Object menu

Commands in the OBJECT menu are used to specify the strokes and fills of objects in your illustration. You can create special tile patterns and colors using the commands in this menu. You can also combine objects into *compound paths*, so that one path cuts a hole through another.

PAINT STYLE... (⌘-I) brings up the PAINT STYLE palette, which allows you to specify the fill and stroke of one or more selected objects. Fill attributes include tint, color, pattern, and gradation. Stroke attributes include all those applicable to fill except for gradation, as well as line weight, line cap, line join, miter limit, and dash pattern. You may also turn on the "Overprint" option, which produces transparent colors when printing. If you turn off the "Auto" check box, selected elements will not adopt changes made in the PAINT STYLE palette until you click on the APPLY button.

CUSTOM COLOR... brings up the CUSTOM COLOR dialog box, which is used to define and edit *custom colors*. The selected color appears in the top right corner, either in color or as a black-and-white composite, depending upon the color capabilities of your monitor. This dialog box is used to define colors as a combination of cyan, magenta, yellow, and black tints. You can then use colors defined in the CUSTOM COLOR dialog box in the stroke or fill of an object via the PAINT STYLE palette.

PATTERN... brings up the PATTERN dialog box, which is used to define and edit *tile patterns*. The selected pattern appears in the top right corner. To define a new pattern, select a rectangle with a collection of pattern elements in front of it, choose the PATTERN... command, and click on the NEW button. You can then apply the tile pattern to the stroke or fill of an object via the PAINT STYLE palette.

The **Illustrator** 5 Book

Object	
Paint Style...	⌘I
Custom Color...	
Pattern...	
Gradient...	
Attributes...	⌘⌃A
Join...	⌘J
Average...	⌘L
Guides	▶
Masks	▶
Compound Paths	▶
Cropmarks	▶
Graphs	▶

GRADIENT... brings up the GRADIENT palette, which allows you to define and edit *gradient fills* (also called *gradations*). The selected gradation appears along the top of the dialog box, as a combination of two or more process or custom colors. To define a new gradient fill, click on the NEW button and a white-to-black gradation will appear at the top of the GRADIENT palette. Click on the tab on the left side of the gradient strip and select a new color to define the color at the beginning of the gradation. Do the same for the right tab to define the color at the end of the gradation. Click along the bottom of the strip to add more tabs and more colors. Select either the "Linear" or "Radial" radio button to specify the style of gradation. Gradations are not applicable to strokes or text blocks.

ATTRIBUTES... (⌘-⇧-A) lets you toggle the display of the center point of a shape, reverse the direction of a path, and specify the resolution of a path. You can also attach a note that will appear in the PostScript definition of a path. If no element is selected, the ATTRIBUTES command is dimmed.

JOIN... (⌘-J) is used to join two selected endpoints, thereby fusing two open paths into one or closing a single open path. If one selected endpoint is directly in front of the other, the JOIN... command brings up the JOIN dialog box, which allows you to select the identity (corner or smooth) of the resulting single point. If the two selected endpoints exist at separate locations, a straight segment is drawn between them. If no object is selected, the JOIN... command is dimmed.

AVERAGE... (⌘-L) repositions several selected elements according to the vertical and horizontal averages of their current locations. Choosing this command brings up the AVERAGE dialog box, which allows you to specify repositioning along a horizontal axis, a vertical axis, or at a single average location along both axes. This command is most frequently applied in preparation for using the JOIN... command. If no object is selected, the AVERAGE... command is dimmed.

 To simultaneously average and join two endpoints, select the two points and then press COMMAND-OPTION-J. No dialog box will appear. If you want to undo the operation, you'll have to press COMMAND-Z twice, first to split the points and second to move them back to their original locations.

Object
Paint Style...   ⌘I
Custom Color...
Pattern...
Gradient...
Attributes...   ⌘^A
Join...   ⌘J
Average...   ⌘L
Guides   ▶
Masks   ▶
Compound Paths   ▶
Cropmarks   ▶
Graphs   ▶

GUIDES displays a submenu of commands that control the conversion and locking of guides in your illustration. Guides appear as dotted outlines in both the artwork and preview modes. Since they do not print, you cannot fill or stroke them.

MAKE (⌘-5) converts any and all selected objects into guides. Converting one or more selected points in a path converts the entire path to a guide. If no object is selected, this command is dimmed.

RELEASE (⌘-6) converts selected guides back into printable objects. (You can select a guide by SHIFT-CONTROL-clicking on it with a selection tool.) If no guide is selected, this command is dimmed.

LOCK (⌘-7) allows you to lock and unlock guides. When a guide is locked, you cannot move or manipulate it in any way. All guides lock and unlock when you choose this command; a guide cannot be locked or unlocked individually. Guides are locked when a check mark appears next to the LOCK command and are unlocked when no check mark appears.

The RELEASE and LOCK commands effect *ruler guides* the same as guides created with the MAKE command. Ruler guides are guides created by dragging from a ruler into the drawing area.

 You can move guides by SHIFT-CONTROL-dragging them with any selection tool. To delete a guide, SHIFT-CONTROL-click on it and press the DELETE key.

MASK displays a submenu of commands that allow you to create and break up *clipping paths*, which are paths that appear to be filled with other objects, called *masked elements*. Those portions of the masked elements that fall inside the clipping path preview and print; portions that fall outside the clipping path are invisible except when selected or when viewed in the artwork mode.

MAKE converts two or more selected objects into a mask. The frontmost object becomes the clipping path; all other objects get clipped. If no object is selected, this command is dimmed.

RELEASE converts selected masks back into everyday average objects. If no mask is selected, this command is dimmed.

The **Illustrator 5** Book

Object	
Paint Style...	⌘I
Custom Color...	
Pattern...	
Gradient...	
Attributes...	⌘⌃A
Join...	⌘J
Average...	⌘L
Guides	▶
Masks	▶
Compound Paths	▶
Cropmarks	▶
Graphs	▶

COMPOUND PATHS displays a submenu of commands that allow you to create and break up *compound paths*, which are objects in which one path cuts a hole in another. You can determine which objects cut holes and which do not by selecting individual objects with the direct-selection tool and using the "Reverse" option in the ATTRIBUTES dialog box.

MAKE (⌘-8) converts two or more selected objects into a compound path. After you apply this command, all overlapping areas of the selected objects become transparent and all non-overlapping areas adopt the fill of the rearmost object. You cannot combine objects from different groups with the MAKE command. If no object is selected, this command is dimmed.

RELEASE (⌘-9) converts selected compound paths back into everyday average objects. If no compound path is selected, this command is dimmed.

CROPMARKS displays a submenu of commands that allow you to create and release *cropmarks*, which are printable guides that indicate the boundaries of the trimmed page. They cannot be selected or manipulated.

MAKE converts any selected rectangle into eight cropmarks. Cropmarks always have a 0.5-point line weight, regardless of the fill and stroke of the original rectangle. Only one set of cropmarks can appear in an illustration, so choosing MAKE always deletes any previous crop marks. If no rectangle is selected and the "Single full page" option is selected in the DOCUMENT SETUP dialog box, the MAKE command creates crop marks around the page size.

RELEASE converts cropmarks back into an editable rectangle. The RELEASE command is useful primarily when you want to alter the crop marks. To do so, choose RELEASE, resize and move the rectangle, and choose MAKE to convert the rectangle back into cropmarks. If no cropmarks exist in your illustration, this command is dimmed.

```
┌─ Object ─────────┐
│ Paint Style...   ⌘I │
│ Custom Color...     │
│ Pattern...          │
│ Gradient...         │
│ Attributes...   ⌘⌃A │
├─────────────────────┤
│ Join...         ⌘J │
│ Average...      ⌘L │
├─────────────────────┤
│ Guides            ▶ │
│ Masks             ▶ │
│ Compound Paths    ▶ │
│ Cropmarks         ▶ │
│ Graphs            ▶ │
└─────────────────────┘
```

GRAPH displays a submenu of commands that allow you to manipulate charts created with the graph tool.

STYLE... brings up the same GRAPH STYLE dialog box that appears when you double-click on the graph tool icon in the toolbox. Here you can change the graph style used to represent a selected graph or series. For example, if you change a grouped column chart to a line chart, the data will remain the same, only the way in which it is represented will change. You can also select various graph attributes, such as the "Axis" options, which determine the position of the Y axis, the size of tick marks, and the location of labels.

DATA... displays the same GRAPH DATA dialog box that appears after you click or drag with one of the graph tools in the drawing area. Here you can enter, import, and edit data associated with the selected chart; transpose rows and columns in the spreadsheet; switch the X and Y axes; adjust the number of significant digits in decimals; and change the width of columns in the spreadsheet matrix. If no object is selected, the DATA... command is dimmed.

DESIGN... brings up the DESIGN dialog box, used to define, name, and organize graph designs. The selected design appears in the bottom right corner of the dialog box. To define a new design, select both a rectangle and the collection of design elements in front of it, choose the DEFINE GRAPH DESIGN... command, and click the NEW button. You can then apply your new design to the bars in a grouped or stacked column chart using the COLUMN... command, or to markers in a line or scatter chart using the MARKER... command. If no object is selected, the DESIGN... command is dimmed.

COLUMN... allows you to select from a library of *graph designs*, created using the DESIGN... command; these will appear as columns in a grouped or stacked chart. You may also specify whether the design is scaled to represent different values, repeated, or stretched in a predetermined area. For example, if the design were a drawing of a hammer, you might create it so that the handle stretched to represent large values, but that the base and head of the hammer remain constant in size. If no design has yet been defined, the COLUMN... command is dimmed.

MARKER... allows you to select from a library of graph designs, created using the DESIGN... command; these will appear as markers in a line or scatter chart. If no design has yet been defined, the MARKER... command is dimmed.

The Font menu

The Font menu displays the names of all typefaces available to your system software. A check mark next to a font name indicates the typeface assigned to the selected characters or, if no type is selected, the default typeface. If the selected text is set in more than one typeface, no check mark will display.

To add more typefaces to the FONT menu, you merely switch to the Finder, add the desired fonts to the Fonts folder (System 7.1) or the Extensions folder (System 7.0), and switch back to Illustrator. Mind you, this convenience is a function of System 7 and later. If you are not running System 7, you must restart Illustrator after you add any fonts.

Illustrator 5.0 automatically organizes type styles into submenus by family. In this respect, the program incorporates the functionailty of another Adobe product called Type Reunion, quite the change of events considering that previous versions of Illustrator were not even compatible with Type Reunion, which meant that a single large family like Helvetica could fill an entire screen.

The Type menu

Ever since version 3.0, Illustrator has been the premier type-handling program on the planet. Illustrator 5.0 continues this relatively new tradition with the introduction of the PARAGRAPH and the FIT HEADLINE commands.

SIZE displays a pop-up menu of type-size options (measured in points). These options represent the most common sizes, but any size between 0.1 and 1296 points is permitted. To access an uncommon size, choose the "Other..." option (⌘-⇧-S) to bring up the CHARACTER palette. Enter a size and leading value. A check mark next to an option indicates the type size of the selected characters. If the selected text is set in more than one type size, no check mark will display.

Type	
Size	▶
Leading	▶
Alignment	▶
Tracking...	⌘⇧K
Spacing...	⌘⇧O
Character...	⌘T
Paragraph...	⌘⇧T
Link Blocks	⌘⇧G
Unlink Blocks	⌘⇧U
Make Wrap	
Release Wrap	
Fit Headline	
Create Outlines	

KE You can adjust type size from the keyboard by the amount specified in the GENERAL PREFERENCES dialog box. Press COMMAND-SHIFT-< to make the selected characters smaller; press COMMAND-SHIFT-> to increase the type size.

LEADING displays a pop-up menu of *leading* options (the amount of space between lines of type, measured in points). These options represent the most common leadings, but any size between 0.1 and 1296 points is permitted. To access an uncommon leading, choose the "Other..." option (⌘-⇧-S) to bring up the CHARACTER palette. Enter a size and leading value. A check mark next to an option indicates the leading value of the selected characters. If the selected text is not uniformly leaded, no check mark will display.

KE You can adjust leading from the keyboard by the amount specified in the GENERAL PREFERENCES dialog box. Press OPTION-↑ to decrease the amount of space between selected lines of type; press OPTION-↓ to increase the leading.

ALIGNMENT displays a submenu menu of alignment commands for one or more selected paragraphs. Your choices are LEFT (⌘-⇧-L), CENTERED (⌘-⇧-C), RIGHT (⌘-⇧-R), JUSTIFY (⌘-⇧-J), and JUSTIFY LAST LINE (⌘-⇧-B). A check mark next to an option indicates the alignment of the selected characters. If the selected paragraphs are aligned differently, no check mark will display.

KERN/ TRACKING... (⌘-⇧-K) brings up the CHARACTER palette, which allows you to tighten or loosen the spacing between selected characters of type. *Kerning* is measured in increments of $\frac{1}{1000}$ of an *em space* (a space as wide as the current type size—for example, a 12-point em space is 12 points wide). Negative values squeeze the letters closer together; positive values spread them apart. The KERN... command appears when you click between two characters with the type tool; the TRACKING... command appears when one or more characters are selected.

KE Both tracking and kerning can be adjusted from the keyboard by the distance specified in the GENERAL PREFERENCES dialog box. Press OPTION-← to squeeze characters together, press OPTION-→ to spread them apart. To squeeze or spread selected characters by five times the distance, press COMMAND-OPTION-← or COMMAND-OPTION-→.

```
┌─────────────────────┐
│ Type                │
├─────────────────────┤
│ Size            ▶   │
│ Leading         ▶   │
│ Alignment       ▶   │
│ Tracking...    ⌘⇧K  │
│ Spacing...     ⌘⇧O  │
├─────────────────────┤
│ Character...    ⌘T  │
│ Paragraph...   ⌘⇧T  │
├─────────────────────┤
│ Link Blocks    ⌘⇧G  │
│ Unlink Blocks  ⌘⇧U  │
│ Make Wrap           │
│ Release Wrap        │
├─────────────────────┤
│ Fit Headline        │
│ Create Outlines     │
└─────────────────────┘
```

SPACING... (⌘-⇧-O) brings up the PARAGRAPH palette, which provides "Word spacing" and "Letter spacing" options that control the amount of horizontal space between words and characters in a selected paragraph. Both word spacing and letter spacing are measured in percentages of the width of a standard space character in the current type size and font.

CHARACTER... (⌘-T) brings up the CHARACTER palette, in which you can alter the font, type size, leading, baseline shift, tracking, and horizontal scaling of the currently selected type or, if no text is selected, the next text entry. If a text block is selected with the selection tool, the new formatting specifications affect the entire block. If you select type with one of the type tools, the formatting affects only the highlighted text.

PARAGRAPH... (⌘-⇧-T) brings up the PARAGRAPH palette, in which you can control paragraph formatting, including alignment, indentation, the amount of vertical space before a paragraph, hanging punctuation, hyphenation spacing, and word and letter spacing.

LINK Block (⌘-⇧-G) is used to link columns of text. If you enter or import more text than will fit into a single column drawn with the type tool, a small plus sign will display in the bottom right corner of the column rectangle. To *flow* the type into additional columns, select both the overfull column and one or more paths (which can be any shape or size, open or closed) and choose the LINK command. Paths from different groups may not be combined with the LINK command. If no object is selected, this command is dimmed.

UNLINK Block (⌘-⇧-U) separates linked text blocks and the type they contain. All paths contain the same type as they did before, but now each text block is separate; changing the shape of a path with the direct-selection tool will not cause text to flow from one text block to another. If no object is selected, the UNLINK command is dimmed.

MAKE WRAP forces type to flow around the boundary of a graphic image. To wrap text, position the paths that make up the graphic image in front of the text you want to wrap. Select text and graphics and choose the MAKE WRAP command. All selected objects are combined into a single *wrapped image*. If no object is selected, the MAKE WRAP command is dimmed.

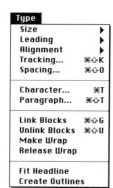

Type	
Size	▶
Leading	▶
Alignment	▶
Tracking...	⌘⇧K
Spacing...	⌘⇧O
Character...	⌘T
Paragraph...	⌘⇧T
Link Blocks	⌘⇧G
Unlink Blocks	⌘⇧U
Make Wrap	
Release Wrap	
Fit Headline	
Create Outlines	

To change the amount of gutter (called *standoff*) between text and graphics, rewrap the text around an unpainted path that matches the basic outline of the graphic image. Then use the direct-selection tool to reshape the path to conform to the graphic image.

RELEASE WRAP separates a selected wrapped image into its original text and graphic objects. Type will pass behind the paths that make up the graphic just as it did prior to choosing the MAKE WRAP command. If no object is selected, the RELEASE WRAP command is dimmed.

FIT HEADLINE is specifically designed to work with *multiple masters* fonts, in which a variety of custom typefaces can be generated from a single font file. Whereas a regular PostScript printer font consists of 256 characters all created from a single design, a multiple masters font comprises characters that cover a spectrum of weights and widths. The FIT HEADLINE command can make text formatted with a multiple masters font fit perfectly inside a text block by increasing or decreasing the weight and width. Using the command on type formatted in a standard font simply increases or decreases the tracking.

CREATE OUTLINES converts a block of text selected with a selection tool into a collection of editable paths. For example, the letter *A* would be converted into a path that looks exactly like a letter *A*. In addition to filling and stroking the converted text as you would regular type, you can apply a gradient fill, use the path as a clipping path, and apply special effects from the FILTERS menu, all impossible with standard type. This command is most useful for converting large type that you intend to use to create logos and other textual effects. Note that this command will only function with PostScript fonts if Adobe Type Manager 3.6 (included with Illustrator 5.0) has been copied to your System folder and is currently running.

As a side note, while the CREATE OUTLINE command now works with TrueType fonts under System 7, it does not work with PostScript Type 3 fonts, a format that fell out of popular use several years ago. The selected type must be set in a Type 1 font, which most PostScript fonts are, including those marketed by Adobe, Linotype, Bitstream, and many other major distributors. As a rule of thumb, unless you know you are using a Type 3 font, you probably aren't.

Filter
Last Filter ⌘⇧E

Colors   ▶
Create   ▶
Distort   ▶
Objects   ▶
Pathfinder   ▶
Select   ▶
Stylize   ▶
Text   ▶

The Filters menu

Each command in the FILTERS menu brings up a submenu that provides access to a number of plug-in filters, meaning that they are separate modules that reside in the Plug-Ins folder. This setup allows you to boost Illustrator's functionality as more filters become available by simply dragging the modules into the Plug-Ins folder and restarting Illustrator. Most filters allow you to apply special effects to a graphic object. In one easy step, these effects can produce startling transformations that would be difficult if not downright impossible to produce by hand.

LAST FILTER (⌘-⇧-E) applies the most recently chosen filter to the selected portion of your illustration. When you choose the first command in the FILTER menu, the effect is carried out immediately without displaying a dialog box. You will not be allowed to change any of the filter's settings, so the effect will repeat with the same settings as when you last chose the filter. To apply the filter differently, press the OPTION key while choosing the command to display the dialog box.

COLORS displays a submenu of commands that allow you to manipulate the colors of the selected objects. In this way, you can quickly tweak the colors of an object without having to change the colors individually in the PAINT STYLE palette.

CREATE displays a submenu of six filters, four of which enable you to make special objects that would otherwise be very difficult or very tedious to draw by hand. The remaining two filters, MOSAIC... and TRIM MARKS, require you to select previously created artwork.

DISTORT displays a submenu of five filters that change the outlines of selected objects. The first, FREE DISTORT, is a common graphics function that lets you stretch and bend paths dynamically. The other four automatically alter the shape by a specified amount.

OBJECT displays a submenu of seven or nine filters, depending on your computer. The first three filters allow you to align and distribute selected objects, the next one doubles the number of points in a selected path, and three others apply individualized transformations. If your computer is equipped with a math coprocessor, two additional filters allow you to trace objects with new paths.

PATHFINDER displays a submenu of several filters that allow you to combine simple objects into complex ones. You can clip chunks out

Filter

Last Filter ⌘⇧E

Colors ▶
Create ▶
Distort ▶
Objects ▶
Pathfinder ▶
Select ▶
Stylize ▶
Text ▶

of paths and mix paths together in ways that neither masks nor compound paths can emulate. Unfortunately, all of these filters require that your Mac be equipped with a math coprocessor. Otherwise, the PATHFINDER submenu will not appear in the FILTER menu at all.

SELECT displays a submenu of seven filters that gives you a few different ways to select objects. The first three filters select objects based on common colors. The fourth selects objects that share a common line weight. The last two select all masks or independent points.

STYLIZE displays a submenu of six filters that add specific style features to a selected object. With these filters, you can create arrowheads, drop shadows, and calligraphic lines. You can also bloat objects, scrunch them up, and round off the corners.

TEXT displays a submenu that contains two filters to export text and locate specific phrases. These are the only filters applicable to text blocks.

The Window menu

Window

New Window

Hide Toolbox ⌘⌃T
Show Layers ⌘⌃L
Show Info ⌘⌃I
Show Paint Style
Show Gradient
Show Character
Show Paragraph

✓Untitled art 1 <50%>

The commands in the WINDOW menu control the display of the palettes that can stay open while you work in the drawing window. They also allow you to juggle illustrations and create multiple views of a single illustration.

NEW WINDOW displays a new view of the current window. Each new window that you create can take advantage of a different display mode and view size. Furthermore, it will continuously update as you create and manipulate objects.

SHOW/HIDE TOOLBOX (⌘-⌃-T) toggles the display of the Illustrator toolbox. Like any other palette, the toolbox is independent of the document window.

SHOW/HIDE LAYERS (⌘-⌃-L) toggles the display of the LAYERS palette, which lets you create, delete, and rename *layers*. Much like different transparencies, one on top of another, layers allow you to organize and isolate objects in a complex illustration. To help you keep track of what's going on, selected objects on different layers are automatically colored differently. Using options in the LAYERS palette, you can hide and show, lock and unlock, and change the view mode of each layer independently.

The **Illustrator** 5 Book

SHOW/HIDE INFO (⌘-⌃-I) toggles the display of the INFO palette, which displays up to three categories of information depending on which tool is selected. First, it displays the horizontal and vertical location of the cursor with respect to the ruler origin. Second, it displays the height and width of the selected object. Third, it displays information pertinent to the transformation in progress. Not all operations register information in all three categories in the palette.

SHOW/HIDE PAINT STYLE toggles the display of the PAINT STYLE palette, discussed back on page 46.

SHOW/HIDE GRADIENT toggles the display of the GRADIENT palette, discussed on page 47.

SHOW/HIDE CHARACTER toggles the display of the CHARACTER palette, discussed on page 53. Don't you just love how many of these commands repeat functions provided by commands I've already discussed? You can choose any one of five commands to display the CHARACTER palette, for example, four of which offer entirely different keyboard equivalents.

SHOW/HIDE PARAGRAPH toggles the display of the PARAGRAPH palette, also discussed on page 53.

Below these are the names of all open illustrations. The name of the current or foremost illustration is preceded by a check mark. Selecting any file name command will bring that window to the front of your screen.

The Help menu

The HELP menu is a function of System 7 that provides access to the Apple's balloon help feature. Adobe didn't create any balloon help specifically for Illustrator and thus the information provided by the balloons is helpful only for discovering extremely basic stuff about the Macintosh interface.

ABOUT BALLOON HELP... displays the ABOUT BALLOON HELP... dialog box, which includes instructions on how to activate and use the balloons. Help for using help, in other words.

SHOW/HIDE BALLOONS toggles the display of the dialog balloons filled with general facts about the Macintosh interface. You may find that the balloons outlive their usefulness almost instantaneously.

Hide Illustrator 5.0
Hide Others
Show All

✓ Illustrator 5.0
Photoshop 2.5
Finder
PageMaker 4.2

The Applications menu

Like the HELP menu, the APPLICATIONS menu is unique to System 7.0 and later. Here you can access all running applications and control which applications are hidden or displayed.

HIDE ADOBE ILLUSTRATOR 5.0 hides Illustrator and switches you to the next open program. To redisplay Illustrator, select it from the lower part of the APPLICATIONS menu.

HIDE OTHERS hides all other open applications while leaving Illustrator untouched. If Illustrator is the only application currently displayed, then this command is dimmed.

SHOW ALL revives all applications that were hidden as a result of the last two commands. If no applications are hidden, this command is dimmed.

Directly below the SHOW ALL command are the names and icon of all running applications. The foreground application is preceded by a check mark. A dimmed icon denotes a hidden application. Choose a name to bring the application to the foreground.

Press the OPTION key while choosing an application to simultaneously hide the foreground application and bring the chosen application to the foreground.

Shortcuts

As with any drawing program, most interaction with Adobe Illustrator must be performed using your mouse or some other input device. However, a number of commands, options, and other operations can also be executed by way of the keyboard or via keyboard and mouse combinations. The charts in this section contain all keyboard equivalents applicable to Illustrator, categorized by function.

In each keyboard equivalent, keyboard symbols are separated by hyphens. This indicates that you should simultaneously press all keys displayed. For example, the keyboard equivalent for the SELECT ALL command under the EDIT menu is ⌘-A. This means that you should press both the COMMAND key and the A key *at the same time* to perform the SELECT ALL command.

Mouse actions are a little more complicated. If one or more key symbols precede a mouse symbol, you should press the key(s), perform the mouse operation, and then release the key(s). For example,

The **Illustrator** 5 Book

the shorthand for selecting multiple objects is ⇧-➤. This means to press and hold SHIFT, click on the object, and release the SHIFT key; the SHIFT key is held down throughout the completion of the mouse operation. On the other hand, if the key symbol appears *after* the mouse symbol, you should begin performing the mouse operation, *then* press the key, release the mouse button, and finally release the key. To constrain the movement of one or more selected objects in a perpendicular direction, for example, you should perform the operation ⋯➤-⇧, which means to begin dragging the selected object before pressing the SHIFT key. When you are pleased with the new positioning, release the mouse button and then release the SHIFT key.

The following is a list of commonly accepted Apple keyboard symbols used throughout our charts:

⌘	COMMAND (cloverleaf) or APPLE (🍎) key
⇧	SHIFT key
⌥	OPTION key
⌃	CONTROL key
⇥	TAB key
↵	RETURN key
⌤	ENTER key
⌫	DELETE or BACKSPACE key
▦	precedes keys to be access from the numeric keypad
▦ ⌧	CLEAR key
␣	SPACEBAR
↑	UP CURSOR ARROW key
←	LEFT CURSOR ARROW key
↓	DOWN CURSOR ARROW key
→	RIGHT CURSOR ARROW key

This book also makes use of the following mouse symbols:

➤	mouse click
➤➤	double-click
➤➤➤	triple-click
⋯➤	mouse drag

Menu commands

The following list shows how to access most of the menu commands included in Adobe Illustrator 5.0 using keystrokes and simple mouse operations. All commands that are not listed cannot be accessed from the keyboard and must be chosen from a menu.

Command or option	Keystroke and/or mouse action
Actual Size	⌘-H or ✒✒ zoom tool icon in toolbox
Average…	⌘-L
Artwork	⌘-E
Attributes…	⌘-⌥-A
Bring To Front	⌘-= (COMMAND-EQUAL)
Centered (Alignment)	⌘-⇧-C
Character…	⌘-P
Clear	⌫ or ⌨⌦
Close	⌘-W or ▲ close box in title bar
Copy	⌘-C
Cut	⌘-X
Document Setup	⌘-⇧-D
Fit In Window	⌘-M or ✒✒ hand tool icon in toolbox
General Preferences…	⌘-K
Group	⌘-G
Hide (selected objects)	⌘-3
Hide Rulers (if shown)	⌘-R
Hide Edges (if shown)	⌘-⇧-H
Hide Info (if shown)	⌘-⌥-I or ▲ close box in palette title bar
Hide Layers (if shown)	⌘-⌥-L or ▲ close box in palette title bar
Hide Toolbox (if shown)	⌘-⌥-T or ▲ close box in toolbox title bar
Join…	⌘-J
Justify (Alignment)	⌘-⇧-J
Justify Last Line (Alignment)	⌘-⇧-B
Kern…	⌘-⇧-K
Last Filter… (repeat)	⌘-⇧-E
Left (Alignment)	⌘-⇧-L
Link Blocks	⌘-⇧-G
Lock	⌘-1

The **Illustrator** 5 Book

Command or option	Keystroke and/or mouse action
Lock Guide	⌘-7
Make Compound Paths	⌘-8
Make Guide	⌘-5
Move...	⌘-⇧-M or ⬿-⬈ selection tool icon
New...	⌘-N
New View... (define)	⌘-⌃-N
Open...	⌘-O
Other... (Size or Leading)	⌘-⇧-S
Paint Style...	⌘-I
Paragraph...	⌘-⇧-T
Paste	⌘-V
Paste In Back	⌘-B
Paste In Front	⌘-F
Preview Illustration	⌘-Y
Preview Selection	⌘-⬿-Y
Print...	⌘-P
Quit	⌘-Q
Redo	⌘-⇧-Z
Release Compound Paths	⌘-⬿-9
Release Guides	⌘-6
Reset Toolbox (all slots)	⌘-⇧-⬈⬈ any slot in toolbox
Reset Toolbox (single slot)	⇧-⬈⬈ specific slot in toolbox
Right (Alignment)	⌘-⇧-R
Save	⌘-S
Select All	⌘-A
Select None	⌘-⇧-A
Send To Back	⌘-– (COMMAND-HYPHEN)
Show All	⌘-4
Show Rulers (if hidden)	⌘-R
Show Edges (if hidden)	⌘-⇧-H
Show Info (if hidden)	⌘-⌃-I
Show Layers (if hidden)	⌘-⌃-L
Show Paint Style (if hidden)	⌘-I
Show Toolbox (if hidden)	⌘-⌃-T
Spacing...	⌘-⇧-O

Command or option	Keystroke and/or mouse action
Transform Again	⌘-D
Tracking…	⌘-⇧-K
Undo	⌘-Z
Ungroup	⌘-U
Unlink	⌘-⇧-U
Unlock All	⌘-2
Zoom In	⌘-]
Zoom Out	⌘-[

Tools

This list shows how to access many of the Adobe Illustrator tools. In most cases, a tool can be accessed temporarily while a key is pressed. Releasing the key returns you to the previously selected tool. Such equivalents are distinguished by the symbol ⭦, to indicate that the key must be held down. All tools that are not listed cannot be accessed from the keyboard and must be selected normally.

Tool	Keystroke
Last selection tool used	⭦⌘ when any tool is selected
Selection	⌘-➔ when direct-selection or group-selection tool is selected
Tool in direct-selection slot	⌘-➔ when selection tool is selected
Group-selection	⭦⌘-⬦ when direct-selection tool was last tool used; otherwise, ⌘-➔, ⭦⌘-⬦
Zoom	⭦⌘-⎵ when any tool is selected
Zoom-out	⭦⌘-⬦-⎵ or ⭦⬦ when zoom tool is selected
Hand	⭦⎵ when any tool is selected
Type	⭦⩘ when area-type tool or path-type tool is selected
Area-type	⭦ on closed path or ⬦-⭦ on open path with type tool
Path-type	⭦ on open path or ⬦-⭦ on closed path with type tool
Paint bucket	⭦⬦ when eyedropper tool is selected

Tool	Keystroke
Eyedropper	⬉⌥ when paint bucket tool is selected
Pen	⬉⌃ when freehand tool is selected
Add-anchor-point	⬉⌃ when pen tool is selected; ⬉⌥ when scissors tool or delete-anchor-point tool is selected; ⬉⌘-⌃ when freehand tool is selected
Delete-anchor-point	⬉⌥ when add-anchor-point tool is selected
Convert-point	⬉⌘ when selection tool is selected; ⬉⌘-⌥ when pen tool is selected; ⬉⌘-⌥-⌃ when freehand tool is selected; ⬉⌘-⌃ when any other tool is selected

Creating and manipulating type

This list explains how to create, select, flow, and reposition type using tools available from the selection tool and type tool slots.

Type manipulation	Keystroke and/or mouse action
Create type at origin point	⬉ with type tool, enter text
Create type in column	⸱⸱⸱⬉ with type tool, enter text
Create type inside path	⬉ on path with type tool or area-type tool, enter text
Create type on path	⬉ on path with type tool or path-type tool, enter text
Insert type in text block	⬉ in block with any type tool, enter text
Select type in text block	⸱⸱⸱⬉ in block with any type tool
Select word	⬉⬉ in block with any type tool
Select paragraph	⬉⬉⬉ in block with any type tool
Delete type in text block	⸱⸱⸱⬉ in block with any type tool, ⌫ or ⌦
Delete word	⬉⬉ in block with any type tool, ⌫ or ⌦
Delete paragraph	⬉⬉⬉ in block with any type tool, ⌫ or ⌦
Replace type in text block	⸱⸱⸱⬉ in block with any type tool, enter text
Replace word	⬉⬉ in block with any type tool, enter text
Replace paragraph	⬉⬉⬉ in block with any type tool, enter text
Flow text into new column	⌥-⸱⸱⸱⬉ column with direct-selection tool

Type manipulation	Keystroke and/or mouse action
Flow text into new path	⌥-⋯➤ path with direct-selection tool
Move text along path	⋯➤ I-beam with selection tool
Flip direction of text on path	➤➤ I-beam with selection tool

Formatting type

Although all text created in Illustrator must be entered from the keyboard, much of the formatting must be accomplished by choosing a command and applying various options. The list below includes the handful of formatting functions that can be accessed from the keyboard. All keyboard formatting controls except alignment rely on increments set in the GENERAL PREFERENCES dialog box. Text must first be selected with one of the selection or type tools before formatting can be applied.

Formatting function	Keystroke
Increase type size	⌘-⇧->
Decrease type size	⌘-⇧-<
Increase leading	⌥-↓
Decrease leading	⌥-↑
Kern together by increment	⌥-←
Kern apart by increment	⌥-
Kern together by 5× increment	⌘-⌥-←
Kern apart by 5× increment	⌘-⌥-
Increase tracking	⌥-
Decrease tracking	⌥-←
Increase track by 5× increment	⌘-⌥-
Decrease track by 5× increment	⌘-⌥-←
Increase vertical shift	⇧-⌥-↓
Decrease vertical shift	⇧-⌥-↑
Force hyphenate word	⌘-⇧- – (COMMAND-SHIFT-HYPHEN)
Center-align paragraph	⌘-⇧-C
Justify paragraph	⌘-⇧-J
Justify (including last line) para.	⌘-⇧-B
Left-align paragraph	⌘-⇧-L
Right-align paragraph	⌘-⇧-R

Using dialog boxes

Keyboard equivalents can also be used to select options and activate buttons inside dialog boxes. Most of the keystrokes listed below work inside all dialog boxes. The only exception is the NONE button, which is available only in the PLEASE OPEN TEMPLATE dialog box.

Dialog box function	Keystroke
Advance to next option box	➜⏐
Cancel button	⌘-. (COMMAND-PERIOD)
None button	⌘-N
OK button	↵ or ⤫
Select contents of option box	⌘-A
Delete contents of option box	⌘-A, ⌫

Entering graph data

The GRAPH DATA dialog box operates differently from all other dialog boxes in Adobe Illustrator. It provides additional and alternate keyboard equivalents, as listed below.

Dialog box function	Keystroke
Select cell data	⭢ in cell
Select multiple cells	⋯⭢ over cells
Clear multiple cells	⋯⭢ over cells, ⌨⊘
Return character in cell data	| (vertical line character, ⇧-\)
Use numerical value as label	" (straight quote marks) around number
Move one cell right	→ or ↵
Move one cell left	←
Move one cell up	↑
Move one cell down	↵ or ↓
Change width of cell	⋯⭢ column handle
OK button	⤫
Cancel change to cell data	⌘-Z
Cancel all changes	⭢ close box, ⭢ DON'T SAVE button

Creating and reshaping objects

The items below describe ways to create and edit various common elements in Adobe Illustrator. All of these items require the use of a mouse in one way or another. Many require the keyboard as well.

Drawing operation	Keystroke and/or mouse operation
Circle, draw from arc	⇧-⌖ with oval tool
Circle, draw from center	⇧-⌥-⌖ with oval tool
Circle, adjust curvature	⌖ Bézier control handle with direct-selection tool
Close open path	⌖ around endpoints with selection tool, ⌘-J
Corner point, create	⌖ with pen tool
Corner point, add handle	⌖, ⌥-⌖ same point with pen tool
Corner point, make smooth	⌖ point with convert-point tool
Curved line, draw	⌖, ⌖ separate locations with pen tool
Curved segment, adjust	⌖ Bézier control handle or segment with selection tool
Cusp point, create	⌖, ⌥-⌖ same point with pen tool
Delete point, break path	⌖ point with direct-selection tool, ⌫
Delete point, do not break	⌖ point with delete-point tool
Ellipse, draw from arc	⌖ with oval tool
Ellipse, draw from center	⌥-⌖ with oval tool
Ellipse, adjust curvature	⌖ Bézier control handle with direct-selection tool
Extend open path	⌖ endpoint with pen, freehand, or auto trace tool
Insert point in path	⌥-⌖ segment with scissors tool
Insert two endpoints in path	⌖ segment with scissors tool
Join two endpoints into one	⌖ around points with direct-selection tool, ⌘-⇧-J
Join two endpoints straight segment	⌖ around points with direct-selection tool, ⌘-J
Move	→, ↑, ←, or ↓ with any selected object
Move and clone	⌘-⌥-⇧-→, -↑, -←, or -↓ with any selected object
Open closed path	⌖ segment with selection tool, ⌫; or ⌖ point or segment with scissors tool

Drawing operation	Keystroke and/or mouse operation
Perpendicular line, draw	▶, ⇧-▶ separate locations with pen tool
Rectangle, draw from corner	⌖ with rectangle tool
Rectangle, draw from center	⬚-⌖ with rectangle tool
Rounded rect., from corner	⌖ with rounded-rectangle tool
Rounded rect., from center	⬚-⌖ with rounded-rectangle tool
Rounded rect., adjust corner	⌖ Bézier control handle with direct-selection tool
Rounded square, from corner	⇧-⌖ with rounded-rectangle tool
Rounded square, from center	⇧-⬚-⌖ with rounded-rectangle tool
Rounded sqr., adjust corner	⌖ Bézier control handle with direct-selection tool
Select grouped path	▶ point or segment with selection tool
Select ungrouped paths	▶ point or segment with selection tool
Select single path in group	▶ point or segment with direct-selection tool
Select point	▶ point with selection tool
Select point in group	▶ point with direct-selection tool
Select multiple points	⌖ around points or ▶ one, ⇧-▶ another with selection or direct-selection tool
Select segment	▶ segment with selection tool
Select segment in group	▶ segment with direct-selection tool
Smooth point, create	⌖ with pen tool
Smooth point, delete handle	⌖, ⬚-▶ same point with pen tool
Smooth pt., make corner	▶ point with convert-point tool
Smooth pt., make cusp	⌖ Bézier control handle with convert-point tool
Split point into endpoints	▶ point with scissors tool
Square, draw from corner	⇧-⌖ with rectangle tool
Square, draw from center	⇧-⬚-⌖ with rectangle tool
Straight line, draw	▶, ▶ separate locations with pen tool

Manipulating objects

Manipulating elements in Adobe Illustrator also requires some use of a mouse as well as occasional keystrokes. The following are the most common transformations and duplications.

Manipulation	Keystroke and/or mouse operation
Clone entire object	⌥-···▶ object with selection tool
Clone partial object	···▶-⌥ object with selection tool
Move object	···▶ object with selection tool
Move object perpendicularly	···▶-⇧ object with selection tool
Move by specified increment	↑, ←, ↓, or →
Reflect selected object	▶, ▶ separate locations with reflect tool
Reflect object horizontally	▶, ⇧-▶ to left or right with reflect tool
Reflect object vertically	▶, ⇧-▶ above or below with reflect tool
Reflect and clone object	▶, ⌥-▶ with reflect tool
Reflect and duplicate object	▶, ⌥-▶ with reflect tool, ⌘-D
Rotate selected object	▶, ···▶ separate locations with rotate tool
Rotate object multiple of 45°	▶, ⇧-···▶ with rotate tool
Rotate and clone object	▶, ⌥-···▶ with rotate tool
Rotate and duplicate object	▶, ⌥-···▶ with rotate tool, ⌘-D
Scale selected object	▶, ···▶ separate locations with scale tool
Scale object horizontally	▶, ⇧-···▶ to left or right with scale tool
Scale object proportionally	▶, ⇧-···▶ diagonally with scale tool
Scale object vertically	▶, ⇧-···▶ above or below with scale tool
Scale and clone object	▶, ⌥-···▶ with scale tool
Scale and duplicate object	▶, ⌥-···▶ with scale tool, ⌘-D
Slant selected object	▶, ···▶ separate locations with shear tool
Slant object horizontally	▶, ⇧-···▶ to left or right with shear tool
Slant object vertically	▶, ⇧-···▶ above or below with shear tool
Slant and clone object	▶, ⌥-···▶ with shear tool
Slant and duplicate object	▶, ⌥-···▶ with shear tool, ⌘-D

The **Illustrator 5** Book

CHAPTER

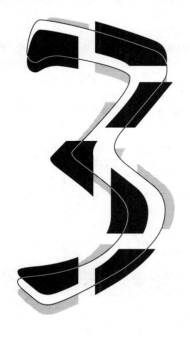

A BRIEF TOUR OF ADOBE ILLUSTRATOR 5.0

Now that I've defined some of the terms I'll use to discuss Adobe Illustrator 5.0 and now that you've had a look at the tools and menus in the application, it is time to start using the darn thing. This chapter will introduce the most basic activities you will perform when using Illustrator: starting the application, creating new files, opening existing files, altering the view size of your drawing area, previewing your drawing, saving files, closing files, and quitting Illustrator.

Starting Illustrator

After you have installed Adobe Illustrator and its related utilities and documents as described in Appendix A, *Installing Illustrator*, you must *launch* the application before you can begin drawing. Illustrator may be launched in any of the following ways:

- **Double-click the Illustrator application icon**. The Illustrator application icon is shown with an Illustrator document in Figure 3-1 as it appears inside a folder at the Finder level. You can double-click the icon to launch the program, or select the icon by clicking on it and choose the OPEN command from the Finder FILE menu.

Figure 3-1: The Illustrator application (left) with an illustration file (right) as they appear at the Finder level.

- **Double-click an Illustrator 5.0 document**. Figure 3-1 displays a typical Illustrator 5.0 file, also called an *illustration*. Double-clicking on this file will launch Illustrator and immediately open the file. Alternatively, you can select the file and choose OPEN from the Finder FILE menu.

   To open several illustrations at once, press SHIFT and click on each of the files you want to open. Then double-click on any one of the selected files.

- **Use a System 7 alias**. You can create an alias of the Illustrator application icon by choosing MAKE ALIAS from the FILE menu. Then throw the alias in the Apple Menu Items folder inside the System folder to be able to launch Illustrator from the Apple menu.

- **Use a launching utility**. If you own a launching utility such as OnCue, Disktop, or MasterJuggler, you can launch Illustrator by choosing it as a command from a menu of application names. Using a macro program like QuicKeys or Tempo, you may launch Illustrator by pressing a sequence of keys, such as CONTROL-I.

When you launch Illustrator for the first time (assuming no one has launched this copy of the application previously), you will be presented with the PLEASE PERSONALIZE dialog box shown in Figure 3-2. Here, you must personalize your copy of Illustrator by entering the appropriate information into the "Name," "Organization," and "Serial Number" option boxes. (It is not necessary to enter an organization in order to run the application.)

Figure 3-2: The Please personalize dialog box appears the first time you launch Adobe Illustrator.

Each time you launch Illustrator, the startup screen shown in Figure 3-3 will appear, displaying the name, organization, and serial number that you entered into the PLEASE PERSONALIZE dialog box. The startup screen is provided simply as an introduction, to let you know that you are in fact running the Illustrator application. It will disappear after a few seconds. Incidentally, if you ever wish to see the startup screen again, choose ABOUT ADOBE ILLUSTRATOR... from the APPLE menu. This screen features an extra line of text listing the amount of free space that currently remains available in the portion of your computer's RAM allocated to Adobe Illustrator (known as *application RAM*). To prevent system errors that may crash your machine and result in the loss of time and data, at least 300K of application RAM should remain unused at all times while using Adobe Illustrator.

Figure 3-3: The Adobe Illustrator 5.0 startup screen, which lists copyright, memory, and personalized user information.

After Illustrator finishes launching and the startup screen disappears, you will find yourself at the *Illustrator desktop*. An empty artboard appears with the toolbox shown along the left side and you may now commence a'drawing. In previous versions of Illustrator, when the program first started, no artwork window would display. Instead, you would have to choose NEW from the FILE menu to create a new document or choose OPEN from the FILE menu to open a previously created document. Though this is no longer the case, it does present a good place to start the discussion of Illustrator. At sometime or another you will encounter the case where no document is open (i.e. you have closed all open artwork windows via the CLOSE command from the FILE menu or by clicking the close button in the left corner of the title bar).

Creating a new illustration

You create a new illustration by choosing the NEW command under the FILE menu (⌘-N). Choosing NEW creates a new drawing window just like the one that is created when you first launch Illustrator.

Another way to create a new illustration is to press the OPTION key while you choose the NEW command from the FILE menu. Doing so allows you to create a new document with a *tracing template*, a grayed rendering of a bitmapped image to aid in the creation of your new illustration. Creating a document in this way displays the PLEASE OPEN TEMPLATE dialog box, shown in Figure 3-4.

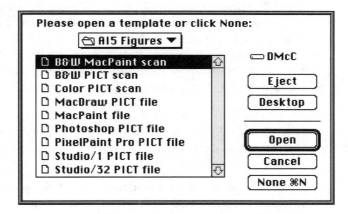

Figure 3-4: The Please Open Template dialog box allows you to select a bitmapped tracing template.

This dialog box allows you to select a tracing template, create a new illustration without a template just as if you had chosen NEW without pressing the OPTION key, or cancel the document creation process entirely. If you intend to use a tracing template for your illustration (as discussed on the next page), select a template document from the *scrolling file list* and click the OPEN button or press RETURN, or double-click on the template file name.

As in most Macintosh dialog boxes of this type, you can quickly locate a specific file by entering the first few letters in its name. The first file in alphabetical order whose name begins with these letters will be selected. (Typing performed in the PLEASE OPEN TEMPLATE dialog does not appear on screen.) You may also press ↑ or ↓ to move up and down the scrolling file list.

If the file that you want to open is on a disk or hard drive volume other than the one containing your Illustrator application, use the DESKTOP (⌘-D) and EJECT (⌘-E) buttons to move between available drives and remove disks so that other disks can be inserted. Double-clicking a folder name in the scrolling file list opens that folder and displays the files it contains. Drag down on the *folder bar* above the scrolling file list to close a folder and display the contents of the drive or folder in which the previous folder resides.

 Press TAB to activate the DRIVE button under System 6. There is no DRIVE button under System 7, but you can advance from one drive to the next by pressing COMMAND-→ or COMMAND-←. Press COMMAND-SHIFT-1 to eject a disk from the floppy drive. If your computer offers more than one drive, press COMMAND-SHIFT-2 to eject a disk from the lower drive. Press COMMAND-↓ to open the selected folder; press COMMAND-↑ to close the current folder. Press COMMAND-PERIOD to cancel.

Clicking on the NONE button (⌘-N) instructs Illustrator to create a new illustration without a template. (You can always add a template later if you so desire.) Clicking on the CANCEL button directs the application to cancel the creation of the new document.

After opening a tracing template or clicking the NONE button, Illustrator creates a new document. An untitled *illustration window* and the Illustrator toolbox will appear.

Using tracing templates

To aid in the creation of high-resolution artwork, you can open a MacPaint or PICT file to use as a *tracing template*. The template appears in the background of your illustration so that you can trace it using one of Illustrator's drawing tools. In many cases, it is easier to begin an illustration by tracing an existing image than by drawing the illustration from scratch. This is true even when the template is inexact or is only a partial representation of the graphic you wish to create, because Illustrator's powerful tools allow you to easily edit the image after you have traced it.

Any document saved in either the *MacPaint format* or the *PICT format* can be a tracing template. MacPaint-format documents can originate not only from MacPaint itself but also from other popular painting programs such as SuperPaint, PixelPaint Pro, Color It, and Photoshop, as well as from scanning applications like Thunderware. The MacPaint format is one of the most widely supported graphics formats for the Macintosh computer. Unfortunately, it is also the most limited. MacPaint files are exclusively *monochrome* (black and white—no colors or gray values), no larger than 8 inches by 10 inches, vertically oriented, and always bitmapped at a resolution of 72 dots per inch. (See Chapter 1, *The Emergence of Drawing on the Macintosh*).

The PICT (QuickDraw picture) format, on the other hand, provides much more flexibility. The PICT format is most commonly associated with moderately powerful drawing applications such as MacDraw and Canvas. In fact, PICT goes much farther. It is the original file-swapping format Apple developed for the purpose of transferring both bitmapped and object-oriented pictures from one graphics application to another. PICT can accommodate any size graphic, resolutions exceeding 300 dots per inch, and over 16 million colors. For this reason, nearly all scanning and image-editing applications support this format. Sadly, Illustrator only marginally supports the PICT format. Object-oriented graphics are converted to bitmaps. Regardless of the resolution of the PICT image, Illustrator displays the file at 72 dot per inch. And although you can open color PICT files, Illustrator converts them to black and white; light colors are changed to white, dark colors are changed to black. Typically, the result is a highly polarized graphic in which details become hard to trace or are completely obscured.

 When working from a color tracing template, convert the scan to black and white in your scanning or image-editing software before opening it in Illustrator.

Figure 3-5 on the next page demonstrates how a typical color scan appears when opened directly in Illustrator and when converted to black and white prior to being opened in Illustrator.

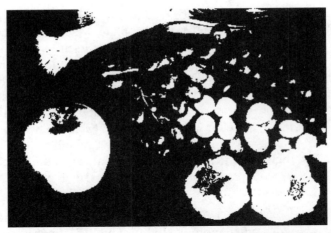

Figure 3-5: A color template converted to black and white by Illustrator (top) provides less detail than one that is converted to black and white in an image-editing software and then opened in Illustrator (bottom).

Whether the tracing template is a MacPaint or PICT file, Illustrator places it in the background of an illustration. A template image generally displays on screen in a uniform gray tone, as shown in Figure 3-6, so you can easily distinguish it from the illustration itself. No more than one template can exist within an illustration at any one time. Also, you cannot move, transform, or duplicate a tracing template; in fact, you can't manipulate it in any manner. The placement

The **Illustrator 5** Book

of a template within the Illustrator window corresponds directly to the image's placement within the software from which it originated. To manipulate a template, you must perform the manipulation in the original application prior to introducing the template into an Illustrator file. Once in Illustrator, a template is not considered to be an integral part of an illustration. Templates do not print. In Illustrator, a template is useful for tracing, and nothing more.

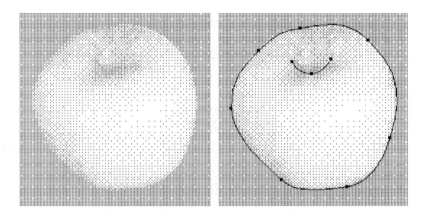

Figure 3-6: A tracing template appears grayed in the background of an Illustrator window to distinguish it from the lines and shapes used to trace it (right).

Kinds of tracing templates

The best way to think of a tracing template is in terms of its purpose, which may fall into one of three broad categories:

- **Scans** are electronic images of photographs, prints, or drawings. Black-and-white scans are commonly saved as MacPaint documents. Oversized or color scans may use the PICT format. Scans, especially when taken from photographs, offer exceptionally accurate tracing backgrounds. They are useful for detail work, such as schematic drawings, medical illustrations, and other situations where accuracy is paramount. They are also useful for people who want to draw, but do not consider themselves very skilled in drawing. Scans can be the perfect bridge between an amateur effort and a professional product.

- **Sketches** are deeply embedded in the artistic tradition. If you were creating an oil painting, for example, you might make several sketches before deciding how the finished piece should look. After arriving at a satisfactory design, you would pencil it onto the canvas. Only after finalizing the sketch would you begin laying down the oils. Like oil paint, Illustrator is ill-suited to sketching. Sketches are best created in a painting application like MacPaint, Expert Color Paint, or Color It. Painting programs provide an environment conducive to spontaneity, allowing you to scribble, erase, and draw quickly and freely, much as you would with a pencil. When the final sketch is complete, you can use it as a template in Illustrator, where the high-resolution, final artwork is created.

- **Drafts** are CAD (*computer-aided design*), schematic, or structured drawings created in MacDraw, MacDraft, Claris CAD, and similar applications. Perhaps the original drawing program did not provide the array of free-form illustration tools and capabilities available in Illustrator 5.0, or you want to add details that can be coupled with the graphic in a page-layout program like PageMaker or QuarkXPress. Draft templates are typically transported via the PICT format.

The Illustrator desktop

Figure 3-7 on the next page shows the result of pressing the OPTION key while choosing NEW... and selecting a bitmapped sketch as the tracing template. This is the same Illustrator desktop that appears immediately after launching the Illustrator application, only now it contains a bitmapped template in the *illustration* or *artwork window*. The desktop in Figure 3-7 clearly displays the following items (labeled items appear in bold type):

- **The menu bar** provides access to the twelve menus discussed in the *Menus and commands* section of Chapter 2. Drag at a menu name to display a menu; release on a command name to choose a command.

- **The toolbox** includes the 22 default tools and the 8 alternate tools discussed in *The toolbox* section of Chapter 2. Also known as the *palette*, the toolbox includes its own title bar and close box.

Drag the **toolbox title bar** to move the toolbox; click the **toolbox close box** to hide the toolbox.

- The **illustration window** is the large window in the middle of the desktop. A window appears for every open illustration. Like the toolbox, the illustration includes a **window title bar** and a **window close box** for moving and closing the current illustration window. The title bar lists the names of the current illustration and the current tracing template file, separated by a colon. If the illustration has not been saved, the name appears as "Untitled art" followed by a number. The title bar also includes a **window zoom box**, which when clicked enlarges the window to fill the entire screen (although it has no effect on the illustration itself). Click the zoom box again to reduce the window to normal size. Drag the **window size box** in the bottom right corner of the window to manually enlarge or reduce the size of the window.

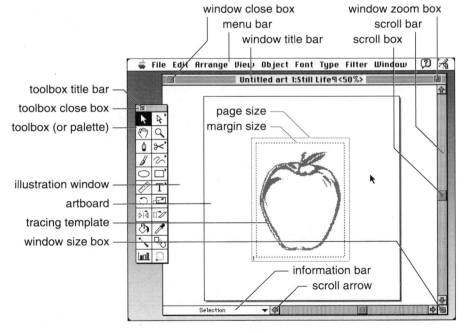

Figure 3-7: The Adobe Illustrator 5.0 desktop, with all parts labeled.

- The **artboard** is the page with the drop shadow where you'll create the graphic objects and type in your illustration. You specify the size of the artboard using the DOCUMENT SETUP... command. Though you can view, create, and manipulate an object if it is moved outside the artboard, the artboard serves as the primary *drawing area*; the area around it is designed for storing objects that may be in the way.

- The dotted lines inside the drawing area indicate the **page size**, specified using the PAGE SETUP... command, and the **margin size**, which defines the area of the page that can be printed (known as the *imageable area*). Objects in the *margin*—the space between the page size and the margin size borders—usually won't print. The grayed **tracing template** also appears in the artboard. Page boundaries and templates cannot go outside the artboard boundaries.

- The **scroll bars** appear along the right and bottom edges of the illustration window, as they do in most Mac applications. They allow you to *scroll* the window; that is, move the window with respect to the drawing area. Click a **scroll arrow** to scroll the window a small distance and click in the gray area of a scroll bar to scroll the window a large distance. Drag a **scroll box** to manually determine the distance scrolled.

- The **information bar** in the bottom left portion of the illustration window lists information about the program. Click the arrowhead to the right to access a pop-up menu that allows you to select from four categories of information: the name of the current tool or operation, the time and date, the amount of free memory, and the number of undos and redos. Press the OPTION key while you click to access a few additional categories.

The cursor

The final item in Figure 3-7 is the arrow-shaped *cursor*, the most important item in any graphics software. The cursor tracks the movement of your mouse as it relates to the Macintosh screen area. When positioned in any other part of the desktop but the illustration window, the cursor appears as a black arrow. In the illustration window, the cursor changes to reflect the current tool or operation. Table 3-1 shows every cursor that may appear in Illustrator 5.0 and describes the action that it implies.

Table 3-1: Cursors that may appear in the illustration window and their meanings

▶	selecting objects with selection tool
▷	selecting objects with direct-selection tool
▷₊	selecting objects with group-selection tool
▶	dragging with any selection, pen, transformation, graph, or page tool
▶▷	cloning (option-dragging) with any selection or transformation tool
▷	snapping to point or guide when dragging with any selection, oval, rectangle, rounded-rectangle, transformation, or graph tool
▷▷	cloning and snapping with any selection or transformation tool
✋	ready to scroll with hand tool
✋	scrolling window with hand tool
⊕	magnifying view size to next larger size
⊖	reducing view size to next smaller size
🔍	view size has reached maximum level of magnification or reduction
✒ₓ	pen tool when no point or path is active
✒	ready to add point to active path with pen tool
✒	ready to convert direction of point just created with pen tool
✒ₒ	ready to close active open path with pen tool
✒/	pen tool positioned over endpoint of previously created open path when no point or path is active
✒□	ready to connect active open path to previously created open path with pen tool

-¦-	scissors, auto trace, measure, gradient vector, blend, graph, or page tool active; oval, rectangle, rounded-rectangle, or any transformation tool prior to operation
	adding point with add-anchor-point tool
	removing point with delete-anchor-point tool
	changing point type with convert-anchor-point tool
	drawing with brush tool
	drawing with freehand tool
	connecting an open path (active or not) with freehand tool
	erasing with freehand tool (command key pressed)
	ready to draw center-to-arc oval with oval tool
	ready to draw a center-to-corner rectangle, rounded-rectangle, or graph
	creating text inside a column or aligned to a point with type tool
	creating text inside a free-form path with area-type tool
	fixing text to a free-form path with path-type tool
	entering or editing existing type with any type tool
	ready to perform an exact transformation (via the respective dialog box) with any transformation tool (option key pressed)
	using paint bucket tool
	using eyedropper tool
	selecting a color with eyedropper tool

entering date into the Graph Date dialog box

adjusting column width in the Graph Data dialog box

pen tool when no point or path is active and CAPS LOCK key is pressed

ready to add point to active path with pen tool when
    CAPS LOCK key is pressed

ready to convert direction of point just created with
    pen tool when CAPS LOCK key is pressed

ready to close active open path with pen tool when CAPS LOCK key
    is pressed

pen tool positioned over endpoint of previously created open path
    when no point or path is active and CAPS LOCK key is pressed

ready to connect active open path to previously created open path
    with pen tool when CAPS LOCK key is pressed

adding point with add-anchor-point tool when CAPS LOCK key
    is pressed

removing point with delete-anchor-point tool when
    CAPS LOCK key is pressed

drawing with brush or freehand tool or using paint bucket tool when
    the CAPS LOCK key is pressed

connecting an open path (active or not) with freehand tool when
    the CAPS LOCK key is pressed

erasing with freehand tool (COMMAND key pressed) when the CAPS
    LOCK key is pressed

using eyedropper tool when the CAPS LOCK key is pressed

selecting a color with eyedropper tool when the CAPS LOCK
    key is pressed

waiting patiently for an operation to conclude

Opening an existing file

You can open existing illustrations while in Illustrator or directly from the Finder level. Illustrator 5.0 can also open files created in older versions of Illustrator. Both alternatives are discussed in the following sections.

Opening illustrations at the Finder

If Illustrator is not already running, you can simultaneously open the Illustrator 5.0 application and a specific illustration file by double-clicking an illustration file icon at the Finder level. Figure 3-8 shows the various kinds of icons that may be associated with Illustrator documents. Double-clicking any of the files shown in the first column of the figure will launch the Illustrator 5.0 application. The next three columns of files belong to Illustrator 3.0, Illustrator 88, and Illustrator 1.1, respectively. Double-clicking any of these files will launch an older version of Adobe Illustrator or display the message "Application not found" if the older version of the Adobe Illustrator application does not reside on an available disk or hard drive. Such illustrations must be opened from inside Illustrator 5.0, as described in the next section.

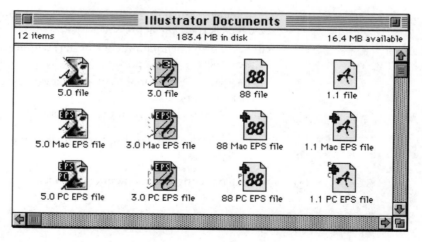

Figure 3-8: The twelve types of Illustrator documents viewed by icon at the Finder level.

The **Illustrator 5** Book

Figure 3-9 shows the files from Figure 3-8 when viewed by name. Be sure to double-click the small page icon rather than the file name when launching an illustration displayed in this manner.

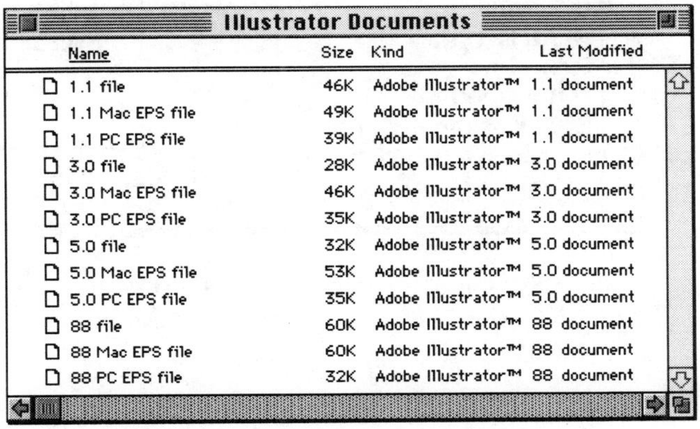
Illustrator Documents
Name
Size
Kind
Last Modified
1.1 file 46K Adobe Illustrator™ 1.1 document
1.1 Mac EPS file 49K Adobe Illustrator™ 1.1 document
1.1 PC EPS file 39K Adobe Illustrator™ 1.1 document
3.0 file 28K Adobe Illustrator™ 3.0 document
3.0 Mac EPS file 46K Adobe Illustrator™ 3.0 document
3.0 PC EPS file 35K Adobe Illustrator™ 3.0 document
5.0 file 32K Adobe Illustrator™ 5.0 document
5.0 Mac EPS file 53K Adobe Illustrator™ 5.0 document
5.0 PC EPS file 35K Adobe Illustrator™ 5.0 document
88 file 60K Adobe Illustrator™ 88 document
88 Mac EPS file 60K Adobe Illustrator™ 88 document
88 PC EPS file 32K Adobe Illustrator™ 88 document

Figure 3-9: The same illustration files viewed by name at the Finder level.

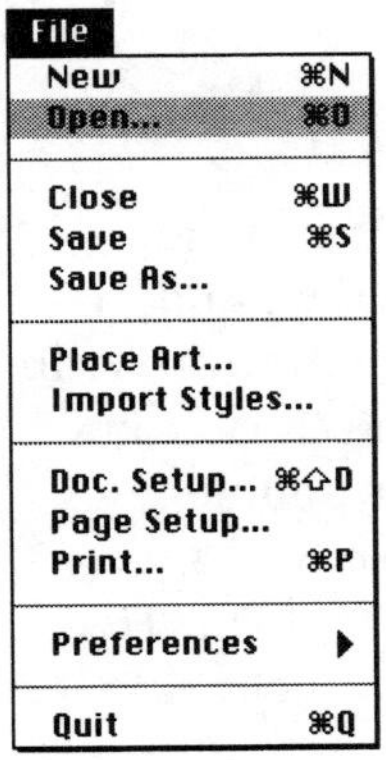
File
New ⌘N
Open... ⌘O
Close ⌘W
Save ⌘S
Save As...
Place Art...
Import Styles...
Doc. Setup... ⌘⇧D
Page Setup...
Print... ⌘P
Preferences
Quit ⌘Q

Opening files inside Illustrator 5.0

To open an existing illustration while inside Illustrator 5.0, choose the OPEN... command from the FILE menu (⌘-O). Figure 3-10 displays the PLEASE OPEN ILLUSTRATION OR TEMPLATE dialog box that appears after you choose this command. To open an Illustrator document, double-click its name in the scrolling file list, or select the file and click the OPEN button or press RETURN. You can open an illustration created in any version of Illustrator. You can also open a template document, creating a new document with a tracing template just as if you had pressed the OPTION key while choosing the NEW... command and selected a template.

The PLEASE OPEN ILLUSTRATION OR TEMPLATE dialog box makes no distinction between illustration and tracing template documents in its scrolling file list. To avoid confusion, I recommend that you employ a consistent naming scheme. For example, I typically append a ¶ symbol (OPTION-7) to the end of PICT file names.

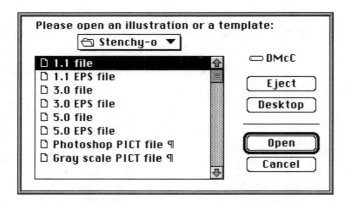

Figure 3-10: The Please Open Illustration or Template dialog box allows you to open either an illustration or template file.

The DESKTOP and EJECT buttons, folder bar, and keyboard equivalents operate the same way as described for the PLEASE OPEN TEMPLATE dialog box in the *Creating a new illustration* section earlier in this chapter. Click the CANCEL button or press COMMAND-PERIOD to cancel the OPEN... operation.

Swapping tracing templates

Normally, when you open an existing illustration, the tracing template that was used to create the illustration is also opened and displayed in the drawing area. If you prefer to open an illustration with a different template or with no template at all, press the OPTION key while you choose the OPEN... command (⌘-⬥-O). After double-clicking an illustration name in the PLEASE OPEN ILLUSTRATION OR TEMPLATE dialog box, the PLEASE OPEN TEMPLATE dialog will appear. Here you may select a new template, eliminate the template by clicking NONE (⌘-N), or cancel the OPEN... command. In this way, you can add a template to an illustration that originally had none, subtract a template from an existing illustration, or replace one template with another.

You can open multiple files in Adobe Illustrator, provided that sufficient application RAM is available. All open illustrations will display in windows similar to the one shown in Figure 3-7.

Working in the illustration window

Once you have opened an illustration or created a new one, it is important to know how to use tools, commands, and scroll bars to move around inside the illustration window. This section discusses how to change the view size, scroll the drawing area inside the window, preview your illustration, and adjust the page size and placement.

Changing the view size

Illustrator provides 17 *view sizes*, which are levels of magnification at which the drawing area can be displayed in the illustration window. Magnified view sizes provide great detail but allow only small portions of a page to be displayed at a time. Reduced view sizes show you a larger portion of the drawing area, but may provide insufficient detail for creating and manipulating objects. Because Illustrator makes it easy to quickly change between various view sizes, you can accurately edit your artwork and still maintain an overall design consistency.

When you first enter a new document, the drawing area is at *fit-in-window* size, which reduces the artwork area so that it can be displayed in the illustration window in its entirety. The actual magnification level required to produce the fit-in-window view size depends on the size and resolution of your monitor as well as the artboard size as specified in the DOCUMENT SETUP dialog box, a calculation that Illustrator makes automatically. Whenever you want to get the scoop on the big picture, choose FIT IN WINDOW from the VIEW menu (⌘-M) or just double-click on the hand tool icon in the toolbox.

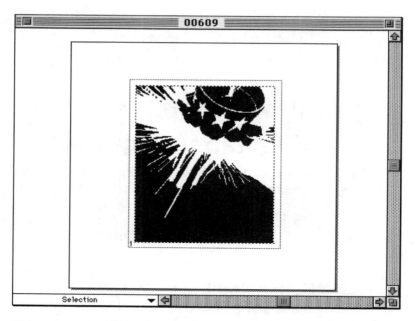

Figure 3-11: An illustration viewed at the fit-in-window view size.

View
✓Preview   ⌘Y
Artwork   ⌘E
Preview Selection   ⌘⌃Y

Hide Template
Show Rulers   ⌘R
Hide Page Tiling
Hide Edges   ⌘⇧H
Hide Guides

Zoom In   ⌘]
Zoom Out   ⌘[
Actual Size   ⌘H
Fit In Window   ⌘M

New View...   ⌘⌃V
Edit Views...

Another useful view size is *actual size*. At actual size, the details of your illustration are displayed on screen at the size they will appear when printed. For this reason, actual size generally provides the most natural visual feedback concerning the progress of your artwork. You can change the view size to actual size at any time by choosing the ACTUAL SIZE command from the VIEW menu (⌘-H).

You can access each of Illustrator 5.0's 17 levels of magnification by using the *zoom tool*. When the zoom tool is selected, your cursor becomes a magnifying glass that displays a plus sign, a minus sign, or nothing in its center. The magnifying glass with inset plus sign functions as a *zoom-in tool*. Clicking in the drawing area with the zoom-in tool magnifies the view size by roughly 150 percent, depending on the relationship between the current view size and the next view size. This affords you greater detail, but it shows less of your artwork.

Drag with the zoom tool to surround the portion of the illustration that you want to magnify with a rectangular marquee. Illustrator zooms in until the surrounded area fills the entire screen. Press the CONTROL key while dragging to marqee the area from the center outward.

The **Illustrator 5** Book

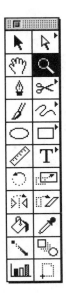

When you press the OPTION key, the magnifying glass displays an inset minus sign, showing that it will function as a *zoom-out tool*. Pressing OPTION while clicking with the zoom tool reduces the view size to somewhere in the neighborhood of 70 percent of the previous level of magnification. You can see more of your artwork, but less detail. The magnifying glass cursor is empty when your current view size is at either the maximum (1600%) or minimum (6.25%) level of magnification possible; at that point, you can zoom in or out no further.

Figure 3-12: The same illustration viewed at actual size.

KE To temporarily access the zoom tool when some other tool is selected, press and hold the COMMAND key and SPACEBAR. Releasing both keys will return the cursor to its previous appearance. Press COMMAND-OPTION-SPACEBAR to temporarily access the zoom-out tool.

Scrolling the drawing area inside the illustration window

Since most Macintosh screens are not as large as a full page, you probably won't be able to see your entire illustration at actual size or a higher level of magnification. Therefore, Illustrator provides you with the ability to move the artboard inside the illustration window, a technique known as *scrolling*. It's like looking through a pair of binoculars, in a way. You can see the action more clearly, but you can see only part of the action at any one time. To look at something different, you have to move the binoculars (and your head) to adjust your view. This is the same thing that happens when you scroll in Adobe Illustrator.

The first method for scrolling the artboard is to use the two *scroll bars*, which are located at the bottom and right sides of the window. (Refer to Figure 3-7 for their location in respect to the Illustrator desktop.) At both ends of each scroll bar are the *scroll arrows*. Clicking directly on a scroll arrow scrolls the illustration window just barely in that direction. But because the window remains stationary in the Illustrator desktop, the artboard appears to move in the opposite direction. For example, if you click the *up* scroll arrow, the artboard and its objects appear to move *down*. This is because your window into the artboard has been raised.

To scroll the window more quickly, drag one of the two *scroll boxes* that move back and forth inside the scroll bars. Be sure to drag in small increments; if you drag a scroll bar all the way to one side or the other of a scroll bar, you will scroll completely outside the artboard.

You can also click within the gray area of a scroll bar. This causes the artboard to move roughly 12 times further in one direction or another than when you click on a scroll arrow. When you click to the right of a scroll box in a horizontal scroll bar, the window scrolls to the right (and your drawing area appears to move to the left). When you click to the left of the scroll box, the window scrolls to the left. This same principle applies when clicking in the vertical scroll bar.

A more convenient way to move about your drawing area is to use the *hand tool*. You can select the hand tool by clicking on the

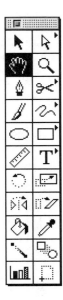

icon in the toolbox. The hand tool allows you to drag the drawing area in increments, the same increments that apply to the scroll arrows. In most situations, dragging with the hand tool is more predictable and more accurate than clicking on arrows and dragging on boxes in the scroll bars.

KE To temporarily access the hand tool when some other tool is selected, press and hold the SPACEBAR. Releasing the SPACE-BAR returns the cursor to its previous appearance. The hand tool cannot be accessed from the keyboard when you are editing text.

Using display modes

Display modes provide another way to control the way you see images in the drawing area. When you first create a new illustration or open an existing one, you view it in one of three display modes. Objects either appear as they will print (preview mode), as fine black outlines with transparent interiors (artwork mode), or as a combination of both (preview-selection mode).

In the *artwork mode*, text appears as solid black, graphic objects have thin, black outlines with transparent interiors, and no colors are shown. Any tracing template appears in the background as grayed. You enter this mode by choosing the ARTWORK command from the VIEW menu (⌘-E). Only the objects that make up your artwork and the template are visible. To its credit, the artwork mode is very fast, because Illustrator doesn't have to spend time displaying complicated visual effects. However, drawing in the artwork mode takes some getting used to. Figure 3-13 shows a drawing of some flowers. The grayed image is the template, the black outlines represent lines and shapes that make up the illustration. With some imagination and experience, you can become accustomed to drawing in this mode.

Sometimes, the template obscures the objects that make up your artwork. This is particularly true if you are making changes to an image as you trace it. To hide the template (provided you have one open), choose the HIDE TEMPLATE command from the VIEW menu. Whether a template is shown or hidden has no effect on any manipulation you make to the illustration. You can redisplay the tracing template by choosing SHOW TEMPLATE from the VIEW menu.

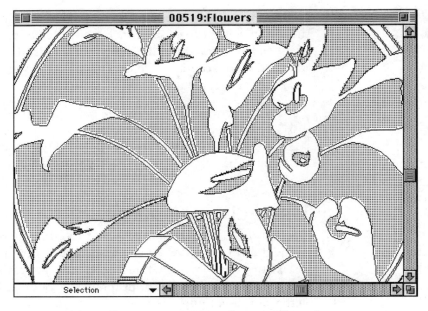

Figure 3-13: An illustration viewed in the artwork mode.

In previous versions of Illustrator, if you wanted to display the tracing template independently of your artwork, you could choose the *template mode* and all artwork and text objects would disappear. In Illustrator 5.0, if you wish to display the template alone, you must choose SELECT ALL from the EDIT menu (⌘-A) and then choose HIDE from the ARRANGE menu (⌘-3). The gray template will now appear alone. To restore all artwork and text objects, choose SHOW ALL from the ARRANGE menu (⌘-4) and then choose SELECT NONE from the EDIT menu (⌘-⇧-A).

Previewing an illustration

Illustrator also allows you to *preview* the printed appearance of your illustration by choosing PREVIEW from the VIEW menu (⌘-Y). Figure 3-14 shows how the flowers appear in the preview mode. Figure 3-15 shows the flowers when printed. The two are very similar, making the preview mode a useful method for assessing the appearance of your artwork. Though you can now create and manipulate type and graphic objects in the preview mode, keep in mind that doing so may be considerably slower than working in the artwork mode.

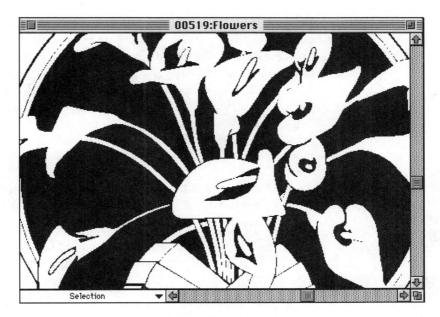

Figure 3-14: An illustration viewed in the preview mode.

Figure 3-15: The same illustration as it appears when printed.

As I mentioned earlier, previous versions of Illustrator did not permit you to create or manipulate type or graphic objects in the preview mode. You could get around this problem by taking the following steps. Though the problem no longer exists, this method may still appeal to you if you want to work with more than one view. For example, if you prefer to draw in the artwork mode because of the way it permits you to easily access overlapping objects, but you find yourself frequently switching to the preview mode to see how things will print, try this:

1. Drag the window size box—found in the bottom right corner of the illustration window—to the left to shrink the window to about half its current width.

2. Choose the NEW WINDOW command from the WINDOW menu. A new copy of the current illustration appears on your screen.

3. Drag the title bar of the new window to the right side of the screen so that it sits side by side with the original window.

4. Choose the view mode not in effect in the first window. For example, if you were working in the artwork mode, switch to the preview mode. Also change the view size and scroll the drawing area as desired. Notice that the window on the left side of the screen remains unaffected.

5. Click the title bar of the window showing the artwork mode to activate it. Any object you draw will preview in the other window just as if you were drawing in the preview mode.

In Figure 3-16, I've used the NEW WINDOW command to create two windows for the flower drawing. In the left window, I've dragged an object to a new location. The right window previews the result. The NEW WINDOW command allows you to create as many alternate views of the current illustration as you desire, each of which you can scroll independently and set its own view size and display mode.

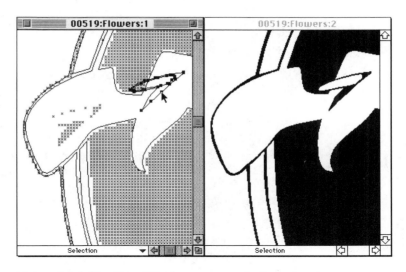

Figure 3-16: The New Window command allows you to simultaneously manipulate and preview an illustration.

By and large, I recommend that you simply execute an illustration in either the preview or artwork mode without bothering with multiple windows, which tend to slow things down and limit your work area. However, if you have a big monitor—or better yet, multiple monitors—and a powerful computer, you may find multiple views very helpful.

To save additional time when previewing a complex illustration, Illustrator allows you to preview only the selected objects by choosing the PREVIEW SELECTION command from the VIEW menu (⌘-⌥-Y). Objects that are not selected appear in the artwork mode. For complete information about selecting objects, see the *Selecting elements* section of Chapter 7.

KE Whether instigated using the PREVIEW or PREVIEW SELECTION command, you can cancel a screen preview in progress by pressing COMMAND-PERIOD. Illustrator immediately returns your illustration to the artwork mode.

Adjusting the page
and artboard size

Another issue related to your perception of an illustration is *page size* versus *artboard size*; that is, the size and orientation of the printable area as opposed to that of the drawing area on the screen. The fact that Illustrator 5.0 is being promoted in some marketing niches as the only single-page document-creation program you'll ever need makes this issue even more important. Page size governs how text and graphic objects sit on a sheet of paper. Just as Frank Lloyd Wright designed private homes to both compliment and exploit their natural surroundings, you must design your artwork to compliment and exploit the dimensions of a printed page.

Since it's possible to create documents on screen that are much larger than the maximum size your printer can handle, it's important to keep an eye on the page size or face the possibility of printing an illustration that runs off the paper. The size and orientation of the printable area is reflected on screen in the dotted line display of the page tile, discussed later in this chapter. Adjusting the page size is a two step process. First, choose the CHOOSER command from the APPLE menu. The Chooser desk accessory will appear, as shown in Figure 3-17. One or more *printer drivers* display on the left side of the window. Click on the icon labeled "LaserWriter," which is the driver for all PostScript-compatible printers. This allows you to prepare your illustration to be printed to a PostScript printer even if no such printer is currently hooked up to your Mac. Then click the close box to return to the Illustrator desktop.

The second step is to choose the PAGE SETUP... command from the FILE menu. The LASERWRITER PAGE SETUP dialog box will appear, as shown in Figure 3-18. You can select from five "Paper" options to select the page size you want to use: "US Letter" (8½ by 11 inches, the default and the most common selection), "US Legal" (8½ by 14 inches), "A4 Letter" (a European size measuring 210 by 297 millimeters), "B5 Letter" (also European, 182 by 250 millimeters), and "Tabloid" (11 by 17 inches). If you are using version 6 or 7 of the LaserWriter driver (included with System 6.0.4 and later), you can drag on the "Tabloid" option to display a pop-up menu of other page sizes, including "A3 Tabloid" (European, 296 by 420 millimeters, a little wider and shorter than the American tabloid), and "No. 10 Envelope" (which in Illustrator merely decreases the margin size to about 3⅞ inches by 9⅛ inches inside a standard letter-sized page).

File	
New	⌘N
Open...	⌘O
Close	⌘W
Save	⌘S
Save As...	
Place Art...	
Import Styles...	
Doc. Setup...	⌘⇧D
Page Setup...	
Print...	⌘P
Preferences	▶
Quit	⌘Q

If you are using LaserWriter driver 8—also called PSPrinter and included on the Illustrator Deluxe CD-ROM—you select from a "Paper" pop-up menu that contains only those paper sizes that your printer can print. To see the dimensions of a page size, click on the large page icon on the left side of the dialog box. It will then display information about the selected paper size, as shown in Figure 3-18.

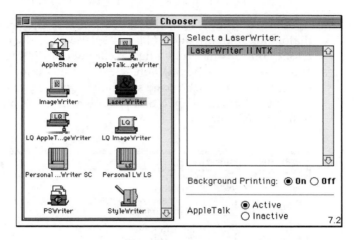

Figure 3-17: Use the Chooser desk accessory to select the LaserWriter printer driver.

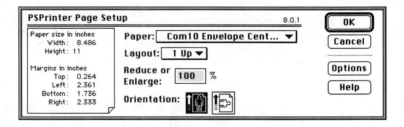

Figure 3-18: Click on the left-hand page icon to display information about the selected page size.

You specify whether your printed page is set vertically (the portrait setting) or horizontally (the landscape setting) by selecting from the two "Orientation" page icons. Finally, the LASERWRITER PAGE SETUP dialog allows you to specify a scaling percentage by entering a number into the "Reduce or Enlarge" option box. This value alters the size of your printed illustration. Any value under 100% will reduce your illustration; any value over 100% will enlarge your illustration.

The four "Printer Effects" options have no influence over Adobe Illustrator files and are not included in version 8 of the LASERWRITER PAGE SETUP dialog box. What is included with the new dialog box is a "Layout" pop-up menu that lets you divide large documents into multiple page tiles, each of which will print on a separate piece of paper.

Click on the OPTIONS button to bring up the LASERWRITER OPTIONS dialog box, like the one in Figure 3-19. While the dialog box contains a lot of options, the only one we care about right now is the "Larger Print Area" check box. When selected, this option enlarges the dotted *margin size* within the page size boundary. The margin size determines the *imageable area* of a page, which is the portion of the page that can be printed.

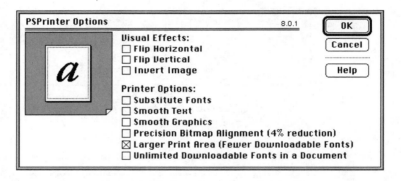

Figure 3-19: Use the LaserWriter Option dialog box to increase the margin size in the drawing area.

To specify the size and orientation of the artboard, choose DOCU-MENT SETUP from the FILE menu (⌘-⇧-D). Here you can select one of seven predefined artboard sizes or create your own custom size by entering values into the "Dimensions" option boxes. The maximum artboard size is 120 by 120 inches. To avoid the problem of creating an artboard larger than what your printer can accommodate in a single printing, click on the "Use Page Setup" checkbox. When checked, the dimensions of the artboard change to exactly match the dotted outline of the page-size boundary. For further information, see the *Document setup* section later in this chapter.

Moving the page size in the drawing area

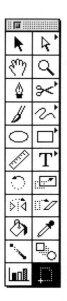

After specifying the page and margin sizes, you may want to alter their placement in the drawing area. Before starting, make sure that the dotted page boundary, also called the *page tile*, is visible. If necessary, choose the SHOW PAGE TILING command from the VIEW menu. You can move the page boundary using the *page tool*, the last tool on the right side of the palette. By clicking or dragging inside the drawing area with this tool, you mark the bottom left corner of the page boundary. After releasing the mouse button, Illustrator displays the page boundary in its new location.

When adjusting the placement of an illustration on a page, it is usually easier and always faster to move the page size with respect to the artwork than to move the artwork inside the page, for the simple reason that you are moving only one element (the page boundary) instead of many graphic objects and text blocks. Moving the page boundary, however, does not affect the location of the artboard, which is forever fixed in place.

Creating a two-page layout

Illustrator is a wonderful program for creating single-page design, but it can also accommodate larger documents. The following steps describe how to create a two-page design with facing pages, the kind required for center pages in a newsletter or fold-up flyer:

1. Choose the DOCUMENT SETUP... command from the FILE menu (⌘-⇧-D). The DOCUMENT SETUP dialog box will appear.

2. Enter values in the "Dimensions" boxes to create an artboard that can accommodate at least two page boundaries. For letter-sized pages, you might try 18 by 18 inches, or 1296 points square. It's okay if your artboard is too big; you just don't want it to be too small.

3. Select the "Tile full pages" radio button from the "View" options to display as many whole pages as will fit in the drawing area. Press RETURN.

4. Choose FIT IN WINDOW from the VIEW menu (⌘-M).

Illustrator will display two or more pages, side-by-side in the drawing area, as shown in Figure 3-20. If it displays only one page, you need to use the page tool to drag the page boundary to the lower left corner of the artboard. You can now create text and graphic objects that extend across both pages.

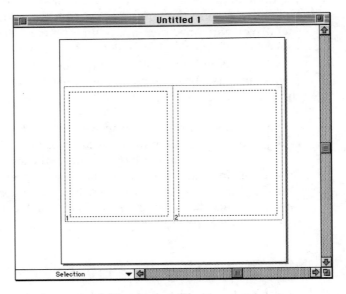

Figure 3-20: The page size moves to accommodate as many whole pages as will fit in the artboard area.

You can also change the appearance of the page-size boundary to display multiple partial pages by choosing the DOCUMENT SETUP... command and selecting the "Tile imageable areas" radio button from the "View" options. Under the current settings, selecting this option would cause the drawing area to appear as shown in Figure 3-21. The dotted lines represent the bordering margin-size boundaries, rather than page sizes. In this way, you can subdivide large artwork onto multiple pages for proofing to a laser printer. See Chapter 15, *Printing Your Illustrations*, for more information.

John Pedley

⚛ The **Illustrator 5** Book

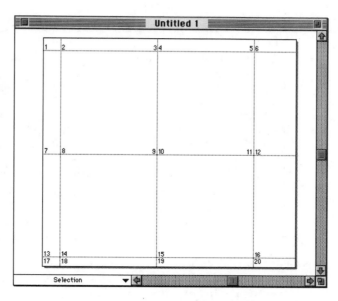

Figure 3-21: Dotted tile lines represent imageable page boundaries without margins, allowing you to divide a large drawing onto multiple printed pages.

Document setup

In addition to letting you change the size of the artboard and the appearance of the page-size boundary within the artboard, the DOCUMENT SETUP... command allows you to adjust a few other settings affecting your illustration. Choosing DOCUMENT SETUP... from the FILE menu (⌘-⇧-D) displays the DOCUMENT SETUP dialog box, shown in Figure 3-22 on the next page. I've already described some of this stuff; but just so you can see it all in one location, the following pages contain a quick summary of the options in the DOCUMENT SETUP dialog box.

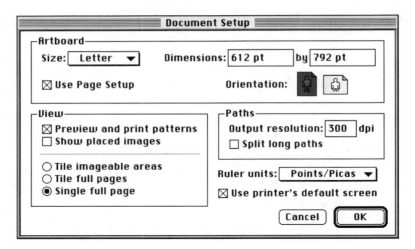

Figure 3-22: The Document Setup dialog box.

- **Size**. This pop-up menu allows you to choose from seven pre-defined artboard sizes.

- **Dimensions**. The values here reflect the height and width dimensions of the artboard size. The smaller of the two values is displayed first, despite the selected orientation. To create a custom page size, enter new values.

- **Orientation**. Here you specify whether your artboard is set vertically or horizontally. Be sure to specify an option. Regardless of how you enter values in the "Dimensions" option boxes, Illustrator conforms to the selected orientation.

- **Use page setup** If checked, the artboard will adopt the size and orientation specified in the PAGE SETUP dialog box.

- **Preview and print patterns**. This option determines whether tile patterns in the fills and strokes of objects in the drawing area preview and print accurately or whether they simply preview and print as gray. Deselect this option to speed up previewing and printing operations.

- **Show placed images**. When this option is turned off, any imported EPS image in your illustration does not display properly in the artwork mode. Instead, the image appears as a rectangular boundary line with intersecting diagonal lines.

When selected, a monochrome version of the image appears. Placed EPS images always preview and print regardless of this option.

- **Page tile views**. These three radio buttons determine how the page size and margin size appear in the drawing area. By selecting the "Single full page" radio button, you instruct Illustrator to display one page whose size and orientation correspond to the settings in the LASERWRITER PAGE SETUP dialog box. "Tile full pages" displays as many whole pages as will fit in the drawing area. "Tile imageable areas" subdivides large artwork into printable regions.

- **Output resolution**. The value in this option should reflect the *resolution* of the final output device. This option affects Illustrator's automatic path-splitting function (described next) and the accuracy at which curves print. (For complete information, see the *Splitting long paths* section of Chapter 15.)

- **Split long paths**. This option automatically breaks up complex paths with gobs of points into smaller paths in an attempt to eliminate printing errors. Illustrator determines which paths are split and to what degree based on the value entered into the "Output resolution" option box. The program automatically splits paths whenever you save or print a file. Do not select this check box unless you are experiencing printing problems. There is no way to automatically reassemble paths that have been split apart; paths must be joined back together manually.

- **Ruler units**. This pop-up menu allows you to select from three units of measurement: "Centimeters," "Inches," and "Points/Picas." (A *pica* is almost exactly equal to $1/6$ inch; a *point* is $1/12$ pica, or about $1/72$ inch.) The selected unit determines the measurement system used throughout all dialog boxes and the horizontal and vertical rulers.

- **Use printer's default screen** When you print a color or grayscale drawing to a black-and-white printer, the printer has to employ some *halftone* scheme to compensate for the colors and gray values. Illustrator automatically optimizes the halftone choice for printing, if you wish. If you would rather use your printer's built-in halftone scheme, which generally works faster, select this option to override the optimization.

Setting preferences

Everyone does not draw alike. For people who draw to a different drummer (in other words, all of us), Illustrator provides the PREFER-ENCES submenu, which provides four commands that allow you to edit a variety of attributes that control the performance of Adobe Illustrator. Choosing GENERAL PREFERENCES... from the FILE menu (⌘-K) displays the GENERAL PREFERENCES dialog box, shown in Figure 3-23. Here you may control the manner in which certain objects in an illustration preview, how elements react to transformations, the distance a selected object is moved when you press an arrow key, the sensitivity of the freehand and auto trace tools, whether dialog boxes display information in points or inches, plus much, much more.

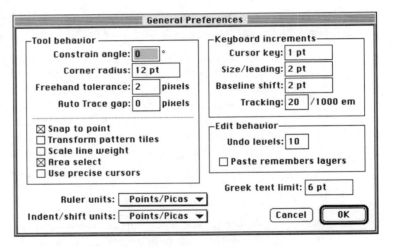

Figure 3-23: The General Preferences dialog box allows you to change a variety of settings that affect the performance of Adobe Illustrator 5.0.

The list that starts on the next page describes each option available in this dialog box. Very little of the background required to fully understand these options has been discussed so far. But have no fear, each option is covered in greater detail in one or more later chapters.

The **Illustrator** 5 Book

The options available in the PREFERENCES dialog box are:

- **Constrain angle**. If you press the SHIFT key while dragging an object, you constrain the direction of its movement to a multiple of 45°; that is, straight up, straight down, left, right, or one of the four diagonal directions. These eight angles make up the *constraint axes*. You can rotate the entire constraint axes by entering a value—measured in degrees—in the "Constrain angle" option box. This value affects the creation of geometric paths (rectangles and ellipses) and text blocks as well as the performance of transformation tools.

- **Corner radius**. This option allows you to round off the corners on shapes drawn with the rounded-rectangle tool. A value of 0 indicates perpendicular corners; larger values make for progressively more rounded rectangles. Radius values are measured in centimeters, inches, or *points* ($1/72$ inch), depending on the unit currently selected in the "Ruler units" pop-up menu.

- **Freehand tolerance**. This option controls the sensitivity of the freehand and auto trace tools. Any value between 0 and 10 is permitted, measured in screen pixels. Lower values make the tools very sensitive, so that—in the case of the freehand tool—the finished path closely matches your cursor movements, or—in the case of the auto trace tool—the finished path closely matches the form of the tracing template. Higher values give Illustrator license to ignore small jags and other imperfections in creating the path. Incidentally, this value has no effect on the performance of the brush tool.

- **Auto Trace gap**. Tracing templates frequently contain loose *pixels* (screen dots) and rough edges, areas where black pixels do not butt up against each other in a consistent manner. Using this option, you can instruct Illustrator to trace over these gaps. A value of 0 turns the option off, so that the auto trace tool traces rough edges as they appear in the template. A value of 1 allows paths to jump over single-pixel gaps; a value of 2 (the highest value allowed) allows paths to hurdle two-pixel gaps.

- **Snap to point**. This option controls whether a dragged object moves sharply toward a stationary point or guide object when the arrowhead cursor comes within two pixels of the point or guide in the drawing area. When a snap occurs, the arrowhead cursor becomes hollow.

- **Transform pattern tiles**. When an object is filled or stroked with a *tile pattern* (as discussed in Chapter 8, *Filling Graphic Objects and Type*), you can specify whether the pattern is *transformed* (moved, scaled, flipped, rotated, or slanted) when the object is transformed, or whether the pattern remains stationary within the object.

- **Scale line weight**. This option determines whether, when an object is scaled, its *line weight* (the thickness of a stroke) is also scaled or the line weight remains constant. This option only affects objects that are scaled proportionally.

- **Area select**. This option controls how you go about selecting filled objects in the preview mode. When checked, you can click anywhere inside an object to select the object, so long as that object is filled and displayed in the preview mode. When the option is off, you can select an object only by clicking on the points and segments that make up the outline of the object.

- **Use precise cursors**. When this option is checked, Illustrator displays the more exacting crosshair cursors in place of the standard cursors for most of the drawing and editing tools. These so-called *precise cursors* allow you to better see what you're doing, but they're not so fun to look at. To see which specific cursors are affected, take a look at the final portion of Table 3-1 on page 83.

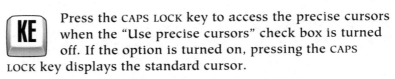 Press the CAPS LOCK key to access the precise cursors when the "Use precise cursors" check box is turned off. If the option is turned on, pressing the CAPS LOCK key displays the standard cursor.

- **Cursor key distance**. Illustrator allows you to move any selected object by pressing one of the four arrow keys (↑, ←, ↓, →). Each keystroke moves the selection the distance entered into this option box, measured in centimeters, inches, or points, depending on the unit selected in the "Ruler units" pop-up menu.

- **Size/Leading**. This option specifies the increment by which type size and leading of selected text can be adjusted from the keyboard (using the COMMAND-SHIFT->, COMMAND-SHIFT-<, OPTION-↑, and OPTION-↓ keyboard equivalents). This value is measured in centimeters, inches, or points, depending on the unit selected in the "Indent/Shift units" pop-up menu.

- **Baseline Shift**. This option specifies the increment by which selected type can be raised and lowered with respect to the *baseline* using the SHIFT-OPTION-↑ and SHIFT-OPTION-↓ keyboard equivalents. The baseline is the vertical line that appears under a block of text. The "Baseline Shift" option is measured in centimeters, inches, or points, depending on which unit is currently selected from the Indent/Shift units pop-up menu.

- **Tracking**. This option specifies the increment by which the horizontal spacing between characters of selected text may be squeezed together or spread apart from the keyboard (using the OPTION-← and OPTION-→ or the COMMAND-OPTION-← and COMMAND-OPTION-→ keyboard equivalents). The "Tracking" option is always measured in 1/1000 of an *em space* (a space as wide as the current type size is tall).

- **Undo levels**. Here you enter the total number of undos and redos that Illustrator can perform in a row. In other words, if you set the "Undo levels" value to 5, you can undo the last five consecutive operations. Changing the value to a higher number will not allow you to undo operations that you couldn't undo prior to changing the value.

- **Paste remembers layers**. Select this check box if you want to paste objects back onto the layers from which they were originally copied. When this option is deselected, Illustrator pastes all objects onto the current layer, regardless of where they were copied from.

- **Ruler units**. This pop-up menu allows you to select from three units of measurement: "Centimeters," "Inches," and "Points/Picas." The selected unit determines the measurement system used throughout all dialog boxes and the horizontal and vertical rulers. Unlike the similar option in the DOCUMENT SETUP dialog box, this option will apply to all future illustrations; it does not affect existing ones.

- **Indent/Shift units**. Select an option from this pop-up menu to specify the measurement system used throughout all options that affect text formatting attributes, including type size, leading, baseline shift, and paragraph indents.

- **Greek text limit**. Here you enter a size value below which Illustrator will show text blocks as gray bars, an operation called *greeking*. Both type size and view size figure into the equation. For example, if you have a block of 6-point type in your illustration and you set the "Greek text limit" value to 6, Illustrator will greek the text at the 100% view size, but it display normally at larger view sizes. Greeking speeds up the screen display because gray bars are easier to draw than individual characters of type.

Next in the PREFERENCES submenu is the COLOR MATCHING... command, which displays the COLOR MATCHING dialog box shown in Figure 3-24.

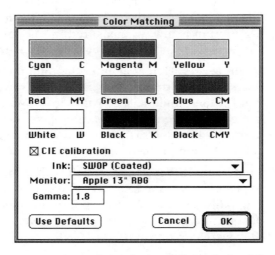

Figure 3-24: The Color Matching dialog box includes options for altering the increments by which selected type can be formatted from the keyboard.

The top portion of the dialog box shows nine colors, each of which you can compare to the corresponding color on the color card included in the Adobe Illustrator 5.0 package. If the color does not quite match, click the color to display the APPLE COLOR WHEEL dialog box and select a more accurate progressive color. For more information, refer to Chapter 10, *Filling and Stroking in Color*.

The other options in this dialog box work as follows:

- **CIE calibration**. When selected, this option enables you to *calibrate* your monitor to more accurately display colors. You have to select this check box to use the following options.

- **Ink**. Select the kind of paper on which you will be reproducing your artwork from this pop-up menu.

- **Monitor**. This option displays a pop-up menu of output devices that Illustrator 5.0 knows how to calibrate. When you select a model, the nine color boxes at the top of the dialog box and the value in the "Gamma" option box update automatically to the required settings.

- **Gamma**. The *gamma* controls the brightness of the medium-range colors (or midtones) displayed on your monitor. A value of 1.8 will accommodate most brands of monitors.

- **Use Default**. Click on this button to return the nine color boxes and the three CIE options to their original settings. For more information on all these options, read the *CIE calibration* section of Chapter 10.

Moving onward, choose the HYPHENATION OPTIONS.... command from the PREFERENCES submenu to display the HYPHENATION OPTIONS dialog box shown in Figure 3-25.

Figure 3-25: The Hyphenation Option dialog box lets you specify words that should not hyphenate.

You can activate Illustrator 5.0's automatic hyphenation feature by selecting the "Auto hyphenate" check box in the PARAGRAPH palette. However, there may be particular words, such as proper nouns, that you do not want to hyphenate under any condition. You can exclude such a word in the HYPHENATION OPTIONS dialog box. To do so, select the language that you're working in from the "Language" pop-up menu, enter the word into the "Entry" option box, and click on the ADD button when you are finished. To remove a word from the list of exceptions, select it from the scrolling list and click on the DELETE button. Click on the DONE button to exit the dialog box.

The final item in the PREFERENCES submenu is the PLUG-INS... command, which allows you to tell Illustrator the location of the folder that contains the *plug-in modules* that you want to use. Plug-ins are separate programs that augment Illustrator's built-in capabilities. Most show up as commands under the FILTERS menu. Since plug-ins consume a large amount of RAM, you may want to locate the ones that you almost never use in a separate folder from those that you use on a regular basis. Then choose the PLUG-INS command to display the dialog box shown in Figure 3-26, locate the folder than contains the useful plug-ins, select the folder so its name appears in the SELECT button, and click on the SELECT button. Then restart Illustrator to make your changes take effect.

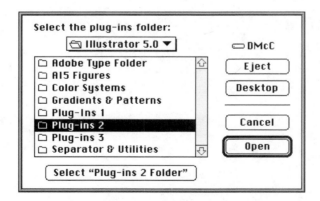

Figure 3-26: The Select Plug-ins folder dialog box lets you select the folder of plug-ins that Illustrator will load the next time you start the program.

The **Illustrator 5** Book

All settings specified in the GENERAL PREFERENCES, COLOR MATCHING, HYPHENATION OPTIONS, and PLUG-INS dialog boxes are saved to a file called Adobe Illustrator Prefs, located in the Preferences folder inside the System folder. Your settings will affect every file that you create or modify from this moment on.

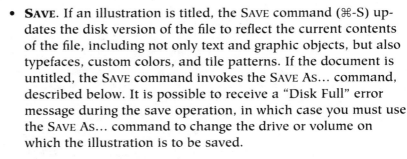 To reset all the PREFERENCES and related dialog boxes to their original settings, quit Illustrator and drag the Adobe Illustrator Prefs file into the Trash at the Finder level. Then choose the EMPTY TRASH command from the SPECIAL menu and restart Illustrator 5.0. This can be a particularly good thing to do when Illustrator starts flaking out on you.

Saving an illustration

Your computer is not immune to external forces. In the event that your computer crashes due to a system error or a power failure or fluctuation, it is possible to lose much of the work that you have performed on the current illustration. To prevent as much wasted time and effort as possible, you should frequently save your illustration to disk (hard disk or floppy disk) by choosing the SAVE or SAVE AS... command from the FILE menu.

These two file-saving commands work as follows:

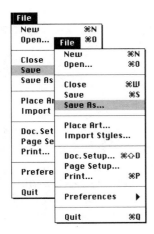

- **SAVE**. If an illustration is titled, the SAVE command (⌘-S) updates the disk version of the file to reflect the current contents of the file, including not only text and graphic objects, but also typefaces, custom colors, and tile patterns. If the document is untitled, the SAVE command invokes the SAVE AS... command, described below. It is possible to receive a "Disk Full" error message during the save operation, in which case you must use the SAVE AS... command to change the drive or volume on which the illustration is to be saved.

- **SAVE AS...**. Use this command to determine the name and location of an illustration before it is saved. Choosing the SAVE AS... command from the FILE menu brings up the SAVE ILLUSTRATION dialog box, shown in Figure 3-27.

The SAVE AS... command provides security. By saving multiple versions of an illustration in various locations, you dramatically reduce your chance of losing substantial amounts of work due to file corruption or a system crash.

If your illustration is titled, the current file name appears in the "Save illustration as" option box directly below the scrolling file list. If your illustration is untitled, no name appears. Enter or edit the file name you want, using up to 31 characters.

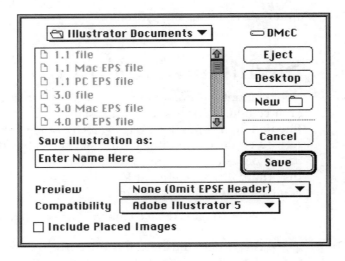

Figure 3-27: The Save illustration dialog box, which appears when you choose the Save As... command and when you choose the Save command for an untitled illustration.

Use the DESKTOP and EJECT buttons and the folder bar to determine a location for the file in the same way as described for the PLEASE OPEN TEMPLATE dialog box in the *Creating a new illustration* section earlier in this chapter.

File-saving options

Click on "Preview" to display a pop-up menu of options used to determine whether your illustration is saved as a standard Illustrator
PostScript file or with an EPS (Encapsulated PostScript) screen representation, which allows it to be imported into other applications running on a Macintosh or an IBM PC-compatible computer. If you
intend to use the file only in Adobe Illustrator, select the default
"None (Omit EPS Header)" option. For more information on saving
an illustration as an EPS file using one of the other options, see
Chapter 14, *Importing and Exporting Artwork*.

You may also save your illustration so that it can be opened by
earlier versions of Adobe Illustrator. Click on "Compatibility" to display a pop-up menu of five options, each of which conform to a previous version of the program. Use this option if you want to send an
Illustrator 5.0 file to a colleague who doesn't own the most recent release of the software. Also, a few other drawing applications, such as
Aldus FreeHand on the Mac and Corel Draw on the PC, will open Illustrator 1.1 files, making this a useful format for swapping images
between different programs.

Select the "Include Placed Images" option to include any and all
placed EPS files in the description of the current illustration. Use this
option only when saving an EPS file. Regardless of whether this option is selected, Illustrator requires that the placed image be available
on disk to open an illustration containing a placed file. For complete
information on importing EPS files into Illustrator and saving illustrations as EPS files, see Chapter 14. This option is dimmed if the illustration you are saving contains no placed EPS files.

When you have selected a name, location, and any other option
for your current illustration, click on the OK button or press RETURN
to complete the SAVE AS... command. You can also click the CANCEL
button or press COMMAND-PERIOD to return to the illustration window
without completing the save operation.

Replacing an existing file

If you try to save an illustration with the same name as an existing illustration in the current drive and folder, Illustrator will present the REPLACE EXISTING alert box, shown in Figure 3-28, asking you to confirm that you want to replace the existing file. Click REPLACE to save over the existing file; click CANCEL or press RETURN to return to the SAVE ILLUSTRATION dialog box, where you can change the name or location of the current illustration.

Figure 3-28: The Replace existing alert box.

If the disk you have selected does not have enough room for the file being saved, a "Disk Full" error message will appear. Click the CONTINUE button to return to the SAVE ILLUSTRATION dialog box so that you can select another drive or volume and reinitiate the save operation.

Finishing an illustration

When you finish working on an illustration, you can close the illustration window. Then you may begin a new illustration, open a different illustration, work on a different illustration that is already open, or quit the Adobe Illustrator application altogether.

Closing an illustration

To close the current illustration, choose the CLOSE command from the FILE menu (⌘-W), or click the close box in the upper left corner of the illustration window. If you have made any changes to the illustration

since it was last changed, a SAVE CHANGES? alert box will appear, as shown in Figure 3-29, asking if you would like to save the illustration before closing it. Clicking the SAVE button or pressing RETURN will perform a SAVE operation (or display the SAVE ILLUSTRATION dialog box if the illustration is untitled) and then close the file; clicking the DON'T SAVE button will close the illustration without saving the changes; and clicking CANCEL or pressing COMMAND-PERIOD will return you to the illustration window without either saving the file or closing it. Cancelling is useful if you want to choose the SAVE AS... command in order to change the name or location of the file, or if you would like to continue working on the publication.

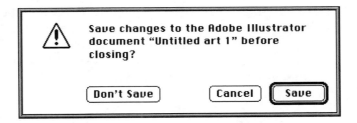

Figure 3-29: The Save changes? dialog box.

Press COMMAND-D to activate the DON'T SAVE button in the SAVE CHANGES? alert box. Illustrator will close the illustration without saving the changes.

If more than one illustration is currently open, closing an illustration will bring one of the remaining illustration windows to the front of the desktop. If only one illustration is open, the illustration window will disappear when you choose the CLOSE command. You will be able to create a new illustration, open an existing illustration, alter the Preferences dialog box settings, or quit Illustrator and return to the Macintosh Finder.

This final operation is discussed on the next page.

Quitting Illustrator

File	
New	⌘N
Open...	⌘O
Close	⌘W
Save	⌘S
Save As...	
Place Art...	
Import Styles...	
Doc. Setup...	⌘⇧D
Page Setup...	
Print...	⌘P
Preferences	▶
Quit	⌘Q

When you have finished your work in the Illustrator application, choose the QUIT command from the FILE menu (⌘-Q) to close any and all open illustrations and return control of your Macintosh to the Finder or the next open application. Like the CLOSE command, the QUIT command prompts the appearance of a SAVE CHANGES? alert box for every illustration to which changes have been made since it was last saved. Clicking on the SAVE button or pressing RETURN will perform a SAVE operation (or display the SAVE ILLUSTRATION dialog box if the illustration is untitled) and then close the file; clicking on the DON'T SAVE button or pressing COMMAND-D will close the illustration without saving the changes; and clicking on CANCEL or pressing COMMAND-PERIOD will return you to the illustration window without saving the file or quitting the application. If no illustration window is open or if no changes have been made to any open window since the last time it was saved, Illustrator will quit without presenting a verification dialog box.

PART 2
DRAWING

CHAPTER

THE GRAPHIC-CREATION PROCESS

In Chapter 1, I examined some of the differences between bitmapped painting software and object-oriented drawing software. In this chapter, I'll introduce you to the process of creating graphics using a drawing application like Adobe Illustrator 5.0. This chapter will prove most helpful to beginning users, because Illustrator relies on drawing concepts different from those required when using painting software or when drawing by conventional means.

As in Chapter 2, I will begin this chapter by defining the terms and concepts on which my ensuing discussions rely. Terms such as *point*, *segment*, *path*, and *element* are the focus of the introductory pages.

Once these are explained, I will step you through the creation of a moderately complex illustration so that you can share in the thought process of creating such a graphic. It's not my intent that you follow along and actually create the illustration; few of the specific Illustrator tools and commands required to produce this graphic have as yet been properly introduced. Perhaps later, after reading future chapters, you will want to return to this chapter and follow the steps to complete this graphic. For now, however, just read along, paying particular attention to the approach I take to each aspect of the graphic-creation process.

Drawing with objects

No matter what type of drawing you want to create, its production in Illustrator must be approached as a combination of *objects* belonging to two simple categories: *lines* and *shapes*.

Suppose that you are about to create a collage. Illustrator provides an inexhaustible stack of lines and another stack of shapes. Each line and shape can be stretched, bent, and otherwise *reshaped* to any extent that you choose, as if it were made of putty. Colors can be changed. You can then lay these manipulated lines and shapes down on your collage in the locations and order that you decide is best. Because it exists on a computer, this collage is impermanent; you can pick up any line or shape and put it down in a new position, slip it between two other objects, or discard it altogether. An element can be exactly duplicated, manipulated in a new way, or left as is.

Every drawing, however complicated or simple, can be expressed as an interacting collection of lines and shapes. The trick is to start simple and work toward complexity. In this manner, you can successfully evaluate an illustration and break it down into its most basic parts. The first step in learning to identify the parts of a prospective illustration is to learn about lines and shapes themselves.

The line

Conceptually, lines in Illustrator are the same as lines drawn with a pencil on a piece of paper. Any line starts at one location and ends at another. Lines may be any length. They may be mere scratch marks or they may stretch from the top of a page to the bottom and loop around like a roller coaster.

Lines in Illustrator are made up of the most basic building blocks—*points*. The simplest line is created as a connection between only two points, one at each end. Anyone familiar with a little geometry will recognize this principle: two points make a line.

But in Illustrator, the concept of a line has been broadened to incorporate many points. *Segments* are drawn between points to connect them. A segment can be straight, as if it were drawn against the edge of a ruler. A straight segment flows directly from one point to another in any direction. A segment may also curve, like the outline of an oval. Curved segments connect two points in an indirect manner, bending inward or outward along the way.

Segments can be linked together so that neighboring segments share a common point. In this way, you can think of a line in Illustrator as a dot-to-dot puzzle. Each point is a dot. You draw one segment from dot A to dot B, a second segment from dot B to dot C, a third segment from dot C to dot D, and so on. The completed dot-to-dot image is called a *path*. A path may consist of only one segment or one hundred.

Figure 4-1 on the next page shows two separate dot-to-dot images. Each dot is a point. A segment is drawn from one point to the next point. The points of one image are numbered; the points of the other are labeled with letters. No segment connects a numbered point to a lettered point, or vice versa. The numbered and lettered images are therefore separate paths.

Obviously, the form of each straight and curved segment in a path determines an image's overall appearance. The appearance of a path is equally affected by the manner in which one segment meets another segment at a point. Segments can meet at a point in two ways. First, the two segments can curve symmetrically on either side of a point. For example, each of the four segments in the numbered path in Figure 4-1 meets with its neighbor to form a seamless *arc* around their shared point. Second, two segments may meet to form a *corner*.

Two segments can meet to form a corner, such as at point D in the figure. Or a straight segment and a curved segment can meet at a corner like the one at point E. Two curved segments can also meet to form a corner like the one at point H.

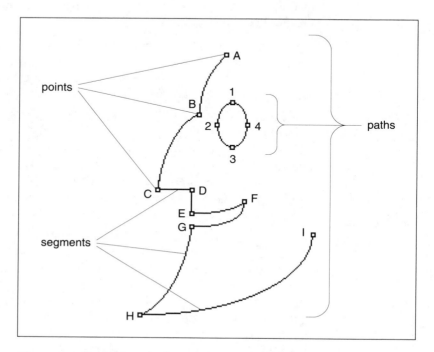

Figure 4-1: Examples of a line (lettered) and a shape (numbered). Elements within both paths are labeled.

The shape

The lettered path in Figure 4-1 is an example of an *open path*, because no segment connects its last point, I, to its first point, A. The numbered path is called a *closed path*, because a segment does connect its last point, 4, to its first point, 1. An open path in Illustrator is what is ordinarily called a line; a closed path is a *shape*. Lines and shapes have various characteristics, as described in the following section.

The **Illustrator 5** Book

Properties of lines and shapes

Unlike a line drawn with a pencil on paper, any path in Illustrator must be consistent in thickness, or *weight*. Certainly, a line drawn with a very dull pencil will be heavier than a line drawn with a newly sharpened pencil, but because a graphite pencil is an imprecise tool, the weight of a pencil line will fluctuate, depending on how hard you press the tip to the page. This is not the case in Illustrator. Different lines can have different weights, but the weight of each line must be constant throughout its length.

Also, drawing a path in Illustrator is like having countless differently colored pencils at your disposal. A line can be black, as if drawn with pen and ink, or it can be light gray or dark gray. It can also be red, or green, or blue, or any one of 16 million other colors. A line can even be white, transparent, or multicolored.

Line weight and color combine to determine the *stroke* of a line or the outline of a shape. In addition, you can manipulate the area inside a path separately from the outline itself. This area is called the *fill*. Just like a line, the fill of a shape may be black or white, transparent or colored. It can even combine many colors interacting or fading into one another.

Determining a path

Before creating a path in Illustrator, you must evaluate the segments that it will follow. This is done one point at a time. Each point indicates 1) where a corner occurs, 2) where a path begins to curve or stops curving, or 3) where a path changes its curve. One segment ends at a point and another segment begins.

To fully understand the point/segment/path relationship, imagine that you are driving on a winding mountain road. You will see many yellow, diamond-shaped signs indicating what kind of path lies ahead of you. In Figure 4-2 on the next page, the center sign indicates that the path of the road curves gradually to the right. The sign on the left indicates that the road turns dramatically to the left, forming a corner. The sign on the right indicates that the road curves all the way around so that your car will eventually face the opposite direction.

Figure 4-2: Points guide segments in a path just as street signs interpret a road.

There is one sign for every change in the path of the road. For example, you will never see a sign like the one shown in Figure 4-3. If a road were actually to curve about following the path described on this sign, you as a driver would not be told about all of these turns at the same time. You would be warned at every change in direction.

Figure 4-3: Too much information for a single point.

The course of a path must be defined at the beginning of every new segment—the point. Think of each point as a road sign. The road sign of a point defines how one segment enters the point and how the next segment exits.

Conclusion: Points define segments. A path follows a number of segments, which determine the form of a line or shape. Strokes and fills are added to a line or shape to imitate real-life images. Finally, these images are brought together like a collage to represent the finished illustration.

A sample illustration

As the preceding discussion suggests, the first step in approaching any prospective drawing in Illustrator is to break the illustration down into its fundamental parts. As an example, suppose I want to create the cartoon image of Groucho Marx shown in Figure 4-4. For the remainder of this chapter I will explain the steps you would undertake to create this drawing in Adobe Illustrator. Remember, this discussion is intended to introduce the overall methods I use to approach such a project. It is not intended as a "how-to" lesson in Illustrator. This task is left to the remaining chapters of the book.

Figure 4-4: A bitmapped sketch of Groucho Marx created in MacPaint.

I have created this sketch in MacPaint, and although I am pleased with its general appearance and form, it is riddled with jagged edges. Since MacPaint images are limited to a 72-dpi resolution, they rarely meet professional standards. My cartoon of Groucho is presently defined as a collection of pixels. I will now describe Groucho as a series of object-oriented shapes and lines. My final Illustrator-created Groucho will be identical in form and superior in resolution.

If you are not an artist, the idea of creating a cartoon of Groucho Marx may seem beyond your ability. However, as with most creative endeavors, creating an drawing in Illustrator has more to do with how you think than with your dexterity or experience. That is why this tutorial has been constructed from an entirely theoretical vantage. No menu commands are used; no tools are mentioned. By avoiding the details of the application, I am able to more fully concentrate on the intellectual process. An illustration must be created in your head before it can be created on paper or on a computer screen.

Also, if it makes you more comfortable, imagine that you are tracing the cartoon of Groucho rather than creating it from scratch. In Illustrator, it is often more efficient to trace from a sketch or photographic scan. For the purposes of this example, it is not important that you feel confident that you can create the sketch of Groucho shown in Figure 4-4. It is only important that you understand how to trace it.

1: The eyes

I will begin by creating Groucho's eyes. Groucho's left eye is shown in Figure 4-5. The eye is *grayed* to show that it is part of the *tracing template*. In Illustrator, the template is the background element containing the MacPaint image that I am sketching. Graying the template is Illustrator's way of showing that it is not a part of the actual drawing.

In Figure 4-6, I have traced a perfect oval around the left eyeball. The oval and template are shown together to give you a perspective for the rest of the illustration. However, these are the only figures in this chapter where the underlying template will be shown. Hiding the template will help to avoid confusion and to present each portion of the drawing in sharp focus. Keep in mind, however, that the tracing template does exist, and that every line and shape I create is traced over some part of it.

The **Illustrator** 5 Book

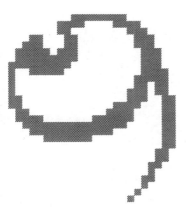

Figure 4-5: The left eye of the Groucho tracing template.

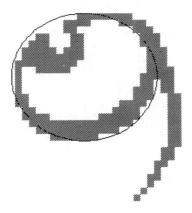

Figure 4-6: Create an oval that traces around the left eye.

The oval that I have created as Groucho's left eyeball is a shape composed of four points. Each of the four points helps to define the path that the outline of the oval follows. I mentioned before that making a line follow a path is like driving a car on a mountain road. Each point is like a small street sign indicating where the line should go. In the case of my oval, all four points are identical. Suppose the outline of the oval follows its path in a counterclockwise direction. Each point would then act like the street sign shown in Figure 4-7 on the following page. As the outline progresses, the points tell the curve to continue to the left in a consistent manner.

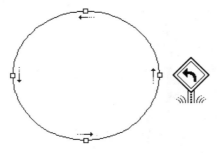

Figure 4-7: The points in the oval tell the path to continue in a counterclockwise direction.

The next few parts of Groucho's eye can be created from my present oval. I will do this by *cloning* and *scaling*. Cloning creates a copy of an object without using the Clipboard. This is useful any time that you are tracing several lines or shapes that are very similar in form. You need only create one original and then clone all objects from that. Cloned objects can then be manipulated separately, so that the finished object only vaguely resembles the original from which it was cloned.

After cloning the oval, I scale the resulting shape to 85% of original. Scaling makes an object larger or smaller. In this case I have two distinct ovals, the newer one 85% the size of the original. I situate the cloned shape so that the tops of both ovals meet as shown in Figure 4-8.

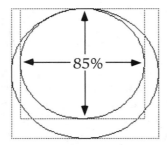

Figure 4-8: Clone the oval and scale it to 85% of its original size.

Next I clone my newest oval and scale its clone to 55% of original. Then I clone that oval and scale this clone to 75%. I move each of the clones to the positions shown in Figure 4-9. I have all shapes required for the left eyeball. Now for the wrinkle under the eye.

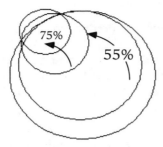

Figure 4-9: Scaling two additional clones.

The wrinkle is only slightly more difficult than the ovals I have created thus far. Figure 4-10 shows how to create this shape. The wrinkle is simply a long, thin crescent defined by four points. Each point is labeled according to one of three analogous street signs. Each sign is shown as if you were approaching the point in the direction indicated by the small arrows. Therefore, if you were driving counterclockwise along the outline of this shape, you would meet with four signs, two notifying you of sharp corners in the path.

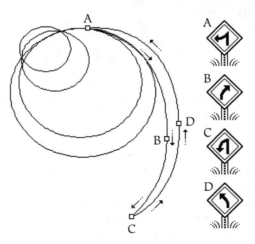

Figure 4-10: Each of the street signs on the right corresponds to a point in the crescent.

Every one of the five objects I have created so far is a shape. This means they all have the properties of both line and fill. So far, all have very thin, black strokes and transparent fills. They will need to change in order to match my template.

For the present purpose, I don't need to make use of any strokes. Groucho's eye can be easily created from fills alone. Therefore, I make all of the strokes transparent. I will fill three shapes, the first and third ovals and the crescent wrinkle, with solid black. The second and fourth ovals are filled with white. The result is shown in the left portion of Figure 4-11.

Note that the image on the left side of Figure 4-11 is displayed in the *preview mode*, as are most of the following figures in this chapter. The preview mode allows you to see how an image will appear when printed. With Illustrator 5.0, you may now actually draw or manipulate images in this mode.

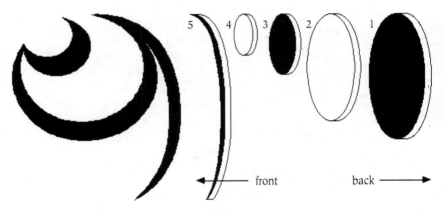

Figure 4-11: The most recently created shapes cover up their predecessors when viewed in the preview mode.

New shapes cover up shapes that were created before them. In the right side of Figure 4-11, the five shapes are numbered 1 through 5, 1 being the first shape created and 5 being the last. Each shape is shown as if seen from the side and as if it had depth. This imaginary view demonstrates how Illustrator places the most recently created object in front, while its predecessors remain in back. In this way, the five shapes are stacked upon each other so that they appear as one continuous black form. If I had painted this version of Groucho's eye

✺ The **Illustrator 5** Book

on a canvas, it might have been a combination of three brush strokes. In Illustrator, it is five shapes. A computer can yield painterly results, but the approach must often be technical and carefully considered.

Having created one of Groucho's eyes, it is now very easy to create the other. First, I gather my five shapes and *group* them, so that they all become one object. Grouping protects the relative placement and size of line and shapes within the group.

Next, I clone the group and *reflect* the clone around a –70° *axis* as shown in Figure 4-12. To more fully understand this process, think of the axis as a double-sided mirror. Suppose that the mirror is mounted like an old cheval glass, so that it is free to tilt within a support. The mirror is normally situated horizontally, like a table top. But if I angle the mirror 70° downward (–70°, or 290°), it would produce the exact reflection shown in Figure 4-12. That is what is meant by reflecting about an axis. The axis is simply a mirror tilted at a prescribed angle.

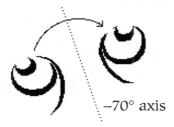

–70° axis

Figure 4-12: Clone the five shapes that make up the left eye and reflect them about a –70° axis.

Since the cartoon of Groucho faces slightly away from the viewer, it is not appropriate for both eyes to be the same size. The right eye, which is farther away from us, should be smaller to give the illusion of depth. Therefore, I must scale the eye. However, to follow the template, I must reduce the eye so that it is proportionally narrower than it is tall. This is no problem, since Illustrator allows for separate vertical and horizontal percentages when scaling. Figure 4-13 on the next page shows how I scale the eye to 80% of its original width and 90% of its original height. The original size is shown as the larger, dotted box. Now both of Groucho's eyes match my template almost perfectly.

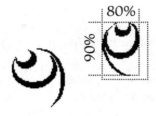

Figure 4-13: Scale the right eye by 80% horizontally and 90% vertically.

2: The eyebrows

Now it is time to create the eyebrows. I will begin with the left brow. This is a slightly more difficult shape than any I have created so far. It involves eight points, labeled A through H in Figure 4-14. Each point is analogous to the street sign that bears the same letter. Keep in mind that, for the purpose of this example, you are seeing these street signs as if you were traveling counterclockwise on the path.

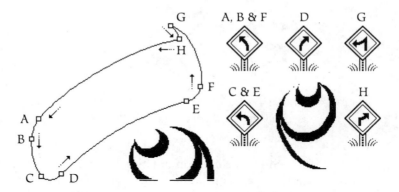

Figure 4-14: The left eyebrow is made up of eight points, each corresponding to one of the street signs shown above.

Once again, I make the stroke of this shape transparent and fill the shape with solid black. Then I clone the eyebrow and reflect the clone about a −75° axis. Figure 4-15 shows the result.

✦ The **Illustrator 5** Book

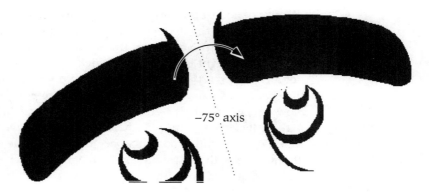

Figure 4-15: Clone the eyebrow shape and reflect it across a −75° axis.

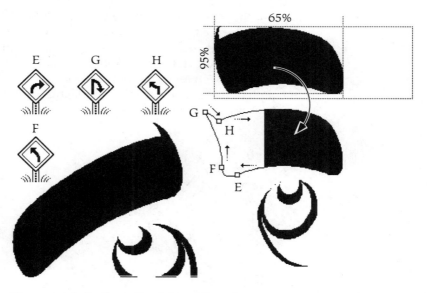

Figure 4-16: Reshape the right eyebrow by converting points F, G, and H.

The newly reflected right eyebrow is not the correct size, nor does its path entirely correspond to the form of the right eyebrow in my template. To remedy the first problem, I must scale the brow to 65% of its original width and 95% of its original height, as shown in the top part of Figure 4-16. To change the path of the shape, I must convert the identity of a few appropriate points. Converting the *identity* is like changing the street sign. Figure 4-16 demonstrates which points I change, and how. Notice that the street sign analogous to point E now curves to the right instead of to the left as it did in Figure 4-14. This is not a change but the result of the reflection about the –75° axis. When the shape was reflected, the identity of every point was also reflected. Now notice point F. Its street sign is identical to that shown in Figure 4-14. It has been changed; otherwise it would have been reflected as well. Points G and H have also been changed. The result is an alteration in the path of the shape. The identity of each and every point directly influences the path.

3: The cigar

Next I will work on Groucho's prominent cigar. First I trace an oval around the lighted ashes at the tip of the cigar. Then I clone this oval and reduce the clone so that I have two concentric ovals. I again clone the larger oval, and move its clone about one-quarter inch to the left. In Figure 4-17, each of the four points of the oval is shown along with the street sign that is analogous to all four. I will change the path of this shape not by changing the identity of its points, but by deleting and adding points.

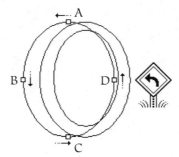

Figure 4-17: Drawing the tip of Groucho's cigar.

From the labeled shape in Figure 4-17, I delete point D and join points A and C with a single, straight segment. The result is shown in Figure 4-18. Notice that both of the street signs analogous to points A and C have been changed so that a corner occurs at each point. Points are thus directly influenced by the points that surround them.

The **Illustrator 5** Book

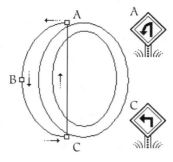

Figure 4-18: Deleting point D and adding a straight
segment in its place changes the identities of neighboring
points A and C.

Before I go any further, I need to *copy* my most recent shape.
Copying an object places a copy of the selected object into the Macintosh Clipboard. I'll need to recall this image in a few moments.

In Figure 4-19, I add two points D and E to the shape. The identities of points A and C update to fit in with their new neighbors. Since
point B is nestled between points A and C, its identity remains constant.

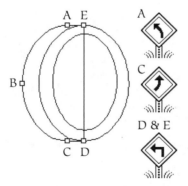

Figure 4-19: Adding points D and E further alters the
identities of points A and C.

I have now created the very tip of Groucho's cigar, though one
would hardly recognize it. I still need to define the line and fill of each
of the three shapes. I will make all lines transparent. I fill the first oval
with a dark gray and the second, smaller oval with a light gray. I fill my

most recent shape with black. The result is shown in Figure 4-20. You may notice that I have a problem. Since the black shape is the most recent, it covers up both of the gray ovals. The black shape is in front of both ovals. The solution is to send the black shape to the back. No matter when an object was created, it can be sent to back or brought to front. By sending an object to back, you tell Illustrator to assume that the object was the first created, and by bringing it to front, you tell Illustrator to assume it was the most recently created. Now, Illustrator first draws the black shape, then the dark gray oval, then the light gray oval. The result is the cigar's end of glowing ashes.

Figure 4-20: The most recent black shape covers up the shapes behind it.

A moment ago, I copied an object to the Macintosh Clipboard. Now I need to retrieve that image. I do this by *pasting*, which takes a copy from the image in the Clipboard and places it on the drawing area. Once I have pasted the shape, I move it into position, as shown in Figure 4-21, and open the path so that no path segment links points A and C.

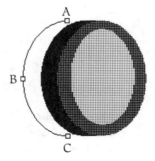

Figure 4-21: Paste the shape copied earlier and open it.

The **Illustrator** 5 Book

By opening my path, I convert the shape into a line. Now I add the necessary points to this line to cause its path to trace the form of the cigar as it goes into Groucho's mouth. As I create the last point in the line, I reclose the line to form a shape.

This time, I stroke the outline of the shape with a heavy, black line weight and fill the shape with white. By filling my shape with white rather than leaving it transparent, the shape will cover up any objects that I create and send to back later in the drawing process. The finished cigar is shown in Figure 4-22.

Figure 4-22: A heavy, black stroke finishes the cigar.

4: The nose and mustache

Groucho's nose is created as a series of eight points, as shown in Figure 4-23. In this figure, I am no longer zoomed in as closely as in some of the other figures, which allows me to see all of Groucho created so far in one glance.

Figure 4-23: Because the outline of the nose tapers at both ends, it must be expressed as a filled shape.

I assign to the shape of Groucho's nose a transparent stroke and a black fill. Looking at the nose, you might wonder why I created it as a shape rather than as a line. It is, after all, very much a line in the traditional sense. The problem is that the weight of this line in not uniform. In fact, it is downright calligraphic, beginning thin and becoming fatter as it sweeps around, then becoming thin again at its end. Lines in Illustrator cannot have this property. I said earlier that while the thickness of a stroke is determined by its line weight, the thickness of a fill is determined by the path that surrounds it. Therefore, to express a calligraphic line, I must create a path that surrounds both sides of the "line," then fill the resulting shape. This is what I have done in the case of the nose and will do throughout the remainder of this illustration.

In setting out to create Groucho's mustache, the first thing to notice is how similar it is to his eyebrows. Therefore, I clone the left eyebrow and move it into the position shown in Figure 4-24, between the nose and the cigar. Incidentally, you may notice that although I have cloned a shape that has no stroke and a black fill, the clone has a thin outline and no fill. I have purposely changed the stroke and fill of this shape to make it stand out from the shapes around it.

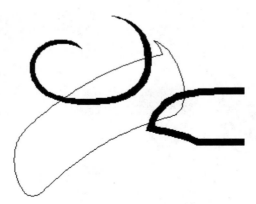

Figure 4-24: Clone the left eyebrow to serve as a starting point for the mustache.

I reflect the mustache shape about a 25° axis. This reflection is interesting because the axis runs directly through the shape, so that the shape actually reflects upon itself, as shown in Figure 4-25. A reflection axis can be angled in any way you desire.

✪ The **Illustrator 5** Book

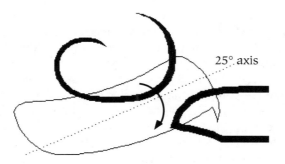

Figure 4-25: Reflect the eyebrow clone about a 25° axis.

The mustache is considerably larger than either of the eyebrows, therefore I enlarge it to 130% of its original size.

The next step is to *skew*, or slant, the shape. In this case, I want to skew it –25° horizontally. Figure 4-26 shows how the skew is measured from the mean horizontal axis. Dotted lines show roughly the angle at which the shape sat before the skew and the resulting new angle of the shape.

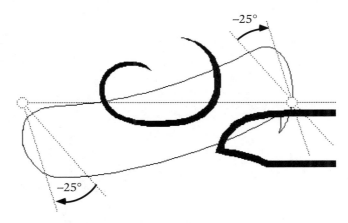

Figure 4-26: Skew the eyebrow clone –25° horizontally.

The basic form of the mustache is still not what it should be, so I must alter the path to match my template. I accomplish this as a combination of changing the identities of present points and adding new points. Figure 4-27 shows the number and location of the points that existed before the alteration. There are eight points, just as in the eyebrow from which it was cloned. Figure 4-28 shows the points after alteration. Notice that there are now nine points, and all the points have been moved at least slightly. I have moved some dramatically and have changed the identities of several as well. Yet my alteration has been subtle in its effect on the appearance of the path. Though every point has been changed in some way, the outline of the shape in Figure 4-28 follows a path very similar to that of its predecessor in Figure 4-27. The subtleties of a path can make or destroy a successful illustration.

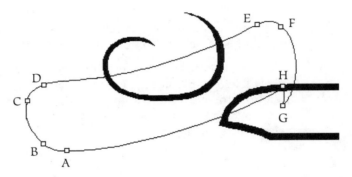

Figure 4-27: The eight points in the eyebrow clone before reshaping the path.

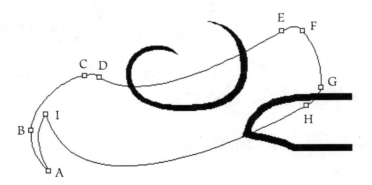

Figure 4-28: After reshaping, the path has nine points, many of which differ from their predecessors.

The **Illustrator** 5 Book

Like the eyebrows, the mustache is assigned a transparent stroke and a black fill. I then send it to back. The result is shown in Figure 4-29. Because of its white fill, the cigar effectively covers a portion of the mustache to appear as if it is jutting from Groucho's hidden mouth. Unfortunately, the same cannot be said for the nose. The nose appears to be behind the mustache, because the fill of the nose shape is acting like the outline of the nose. A second fill is needed to create the flesh of the nose.

Figure 4-29: Despite having been sent to back, the black mustache obscures the shape of the nose.

The fill of the shape that will act as the flesh of the nose must exactly fit into the shape that acts as the outline of the nose. So, I must clone the existing shape. The fill of the cloned shape should cover the area enclosed by the original shape. A segment of the path must connect the points that represent the top of the nose and the tip of the nostril. This is easily accomplished by deleting all of the points that form the inner rim of the nose and then closing the remaining path. The result is shown in Figure 4-30 on the following page.

Notice that this figure shows shapes with no fills and thin strokes. As I mentioned earlier, most of the figures in this chapter display images as they appear in the preview mode. However, for Figure 4-30, I show the paths in the *artwork mode*, which displays all lines and outlines are shown with very thin, black strokes and all fills as transparent. By viewing the paths in this figure in the artwork mode, I can more clearly view the most recent developments.

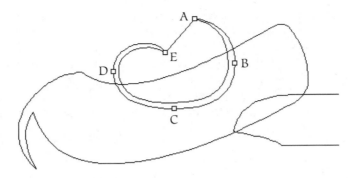

Figure 4-30: The nose and mustache shapes displayed in the artwork mode.

I fill the most recent shape with white and send it to the back so that it does not cover the shape that is the outline of the nose. Then I again send the mustache to the back. Zooming out from the illustration in Figure 4-31 lets me see the result of everything that I have done so far. It looks to be about half finished, but looks can be deceiving. I am actually much closer than that.

Figure 4-31: My progress so far as viewed in the preview mode. Note that the nose now appears in front of the mustache.

5: Finishing the face

Many of Groucho's features are still missing. I have yet to draw his glasses, the bridge of his nose, his ear, his hair, the outline of his face, and a few wrinkles. But, if you will recall my template (refer to Figure 4-4), all of these features are more suggestive than those I have created so far. The subtle features in a template are often harder to approach than their more obvious or outstanding counterparts. The best advice I can offer is to dive right in. Create object after object in a rhythmic sequence, forging on with alacrity and grace. These are the incidental parts of an illustration that round it out, giving it a lucid flappearance.

Figure 4-32: The wrinkles in the flesh and portions of the glasses are expressed as many small shapes, most comprising three points or fewer.

In Figure 4-32, I have created a series of small shapes that act as calligraphic swashes. The majority of the shapes are made up of only two or three points each. The identity of each point causes one path segment to curve more than another, so that the fill creates a free-flowing stroke, simple but highly effective. The most complicated shape is constructed of only five points. Each of these shapes convey flourish and playfulness, yet they must be approached intentionally and with care.

Figure 4-33: Most of the outline of the face as well as several incidental features can be expressed as a single complex shape.

The next shape is very extensive, comprising 48 points, as shown in Figure 4-33. With one shape, I have created the hair, most of Groucho's ear, lip, chin, neck, and part of his glasses. But the process itself is no more difficult than creating any of the other shapes I have created. The most difficult part may be recognizing that such a large portion of the template can be expressed as a single shape. Such recognition comes with practice. Once you have seen the shape, you need only trace its outline point by point, carefully and patiently. Never be intimidated by a large shape. The only difference between a simple line with two points and a complex shape with one hundred is that the latter takes longer to produce.

After filling the complex shape with solid black, only two shapes remain to finish Groucho's face. These are the remainder of the ear and the bridge of the nose. The ear requires eleven points and the nose

🔬 The **Illustrator 5** Book

requires six, as shown in Figure 4-34. Always use points sparingly. If you find that you don't have enough points, you can always add more. But just one point too many means that someplace there are two path segments where there should be only one. The result is a needlessly complicated object, whose path is slightly clumsy and malformed.

Figure 4-34: Finish the face with two shapes, one representing the details of the ear and the other the bridge of the nose.

6: The collar

By now, you can probably easily imagine how to draw Groucho's collar. But there are a couple of stumbling blocks along the way. Figure 4-35 on the next page shows the points required to create the jacket lapel and the shirt collar—four shapes altogether. Both of the lapel shapes get no line and a black fill. The collars get a medium-weight black line and a white fill. Figure 4-36 shows the results. Notice how

I have matched up the line of the collars exactly with the fill of the shape that wraps around to form the throat. Here is a case where the fill of a shape and the weight of a line are designed to be identical.

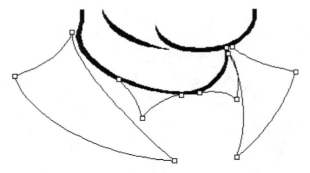

Figure 4-35: The four shapes required to create the collar and lapel.

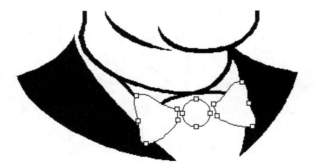

Figure 4-36: The three shapes that make up the bow tie.

Figure 4-36 also shows that the tie is made of three separate shapes. One is a simple oval and the other two have five points apiece. The tie must cover the lapels in an unusual manner, requiring that I consider the stroke as well as the fill of each shape. In the template, there is a white line between the black color of the tie and the black color of the jacket. Therefore, all three shapes of the tie get a medium-weight white stroke with a black fill. The white stroke provides the necessary definition between the tie and the jacket to distinguish the two as independent objects. Last, I bring both of the collar shapes to the front of the other objects so that the tie nestles where it belongs, as shown in Figure 4-37.

🔬 The **Illustrator** 5 Book

Figure 4-37: The white stroke of the tie shapes distinguishes them from the lapels.

7: Smoke from the cigar

Often a last detail adds spirit to a drawing. Here, the last detail will be smoke rising from Groucho's cigar. Granted, it's an unnecessary addition, but it will give the cartoon a touch of realism that it needs.

Figure 4-38: The points required to express the cigar smoke and the same path when stroked with a gray outline.

I trace the smoke with one shape containing 21 points. Figure 4-38 shows the path. Then I assign the shape a thin, light gray stroke with no fill. The shape is simple, yet also elegant and functional.

The completed Groucho

The illustration is finished. Figure 4-39 shows the completed Groucho as he appears when printed from Adobe Illustrator. Despite the large size, the resolution is far better than in the MacPaint template. Every detail is crisp and accurate. His appearance is clean and smooth. All things said and done, I have created a highly professional product.

I have now laid a groundwork for creating almost any electronic illustration. The following chapters discuss the tools, commands, and dialog box options required to create such a drawing in Illustrator 5.0. However, the secret to achieving a professional illustration does not rely in the specific environment provided by the application. Rather, it depends on your approach.

Figure 4-39: The completed Groucho cartoon printed from Adobe Illustrator 5.0.

CHAPTER

DRAWING
PATHS
FROM
SCRATCH

In the previous chapter, you learned that an image drawn in Adobe Illustrator must be constructed as a network of lines and shapes called *paths*. This chapter demonstrates how to draw the paths themselves from scratch using each of the drawing tools or trace a path with the auto trace tool.

I'll start with the most basic paths that you can create in Illustrator—rectangles, squares, ovals, and circles—objects known collectively as *geometric paths*. If you are an experienced Macintosh user, you will probably recognize the tools used to create these paths. Each tool works similarly to tools in Mac-Paint, MacDraw, PageMaker, and other common Macintosh applications. Even if you have never used any of these programs, there is little doubt that you can master the creation of any geometric path.

Geometric paths

Illustrator 5.0 offers six tools for creating geometric shapes. Each tool is operated by clicking or by dragging from one location to another. The points at which you begin and end the drag establish the boundary limits of the simple rectangle or oval. Although limited in utility, these geometric shapes are very easy to draw, because they involve no planning and little guesswork.

Drawing a rectangle

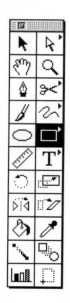

Consider the *rectangle tool*, displayed by default in the fifth tool slot on the right side of the toolbox. After selecting this tool, you drag inside the drawing area to create a rectangle. This is the same process used to create a rectangle in all graphics applications that run on the Macintosh. One corner of the rectangle is determined by the point at which you begin the drag; the opposite corner is determined by the point at which you release (see Figure 5-1). The two remaining corners line up vertically or horizontally with their neighbors. A fifth point, the *center point*, is also created.

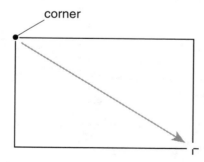

Figure 5-1: Operate the rectangle tool by dragging from one corner to the opposite corner of the desired shape.

The **Illustrator 5** Book

If you press the OPTION key while drawing with the rectangle tool, the beginning of your drag becomes the center point of the rectangle, as shown in Figure 5-2. As before, the release point becomes a corner point and also determines the distance and direction from the center that each of the three other corner points are located.

center

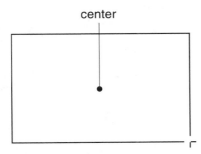

Figure 5-2: Option-drag with the rectangle tool to draw a rectangle from center point to corner point.

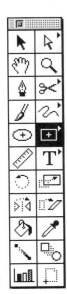

Alternatively, you can select the *centered-rectangle tool* by double-clicking on the rectangle (or the oval) tool slot. The rectangle and oval tools are then displayed with a plus sign in the middle. The centered-rectangle tool allows you to create rectangles from center point to corner point without pressing the OPTION key. Pressing the OPTION key while dragging with the centered-rectangle tool draws a rectangle from corner to corner.

Pressing the SHIFT key while drawing with the rectangle tool *constrains* the resulting shape. To constrain the creation or manipulation of an element is to attach certain guidelines to the effects of your mouse movements. In this case, pressing SHIFT ensures that each corner of the rectangle is equidistant from both of its neighbors; in other words, it creates a square.

Pressing both SHIFT and OPTION while drawing with the rectangle tool or pressing shift while drawing with the centered-rectangle tool creates a square from center to corner.

To get a feel for the rectangle tool, try the following exercise:

1. Select the rectangle tool from the toolbox.

2. Drag with the tool to create a rectangle that is about four times as wide as it is tall, but do not release your mouse button. (You will be keeping it pressed throughout the rest of this exercise.)

3. Press the OPTION key. The rectangle grows to twice its original size. Notice that the point at which you began your drag has become the center of the shape.

4. Now release the OPTION key. The center point reverts to the corner point and the rectangle shrinks to its previous size.

5. Press the SHIFT key. The rectangle expands to a square. Since the rectangle was taller than wide, the square adopts the height as the length of its sides.

6. While still holding down the SHIFT key, drag downward. The square remains the same size until you drag beyond the bottom border.

7. Release the SHIFT key. No longer constrained to a square, the corner of the rectangle will abruptly return to the location occupied by your cursor.

8. Release the mouse button. The rectangle becomes fixed to the drawing area. A corner point appears at each of the shape's four corners.

You can also use the rectangle tool to access a dialog box that allows you to create a rectangle, not by drawing the shape, but by specifying its boundaries numerically. Click—yep, that's it, just click—in the drawing area with the rectangle tool to display the RECTANGLE dialog box shown in Figure 5-3. Here, you may enter values for the "Width," "Height," and "Corner radius" options (the last of which is explained in the section *Drawing a rectangle with rounded corners*, later in this chapter). After pressing RETURN, Illustrator creates a rectangle to your exact specifications.

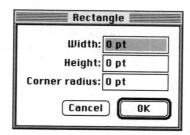

Figure 5-3: Click with any rectangle tool to display the Rectangle dialog box.

The **Illustrator 5** Book

Since no placement options are given in the RECTANGLE dialog box, the point at which you clicked with the rectangle tool acts as the upper left corner point of your new rectangle. Clicking with the centered-rectangle tool (or OPTION-clicking with the rectangle tool), makes the click point the center point in the shape.

Notice that each option box in Figure 5-3 includes "pt," an abbreviation for "points." This refers to the current *unit of measure*, which is set using the "Ruler units" option in the PREFERENCES dialog box (first introduced in the *Setting preferences* section of Chapter 3). The unit of measure in Illustrator can be centimeters ("cm"), inches ("in"), or picas and points. When picas and points are the current unit of measure, all dialog box option values that pertain to length or distance are measured in points.

Values entered into option boxes that pertain to length or distance in Illustrator 5.0 are accurate to within $\frac{1}{100}$ the current unit of measure.

Drawing a rectangle with rounded corners

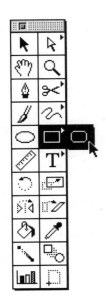

In Illustrator, you can create rectangles with rounded corners using the *rounded-rectangle tool*. You can choose the rounded-rectangle tool by dragging from the rectangle tool slot. Unlike those of a standard rectangle, the horizontal and vertical segments of a rounded rectangle do not meet to form right-angle corners. Instead, perpendicular segments curve to meet one another. Figure 5-4 shows a standard rectangle with perpendicular corners and the same rectangle drawn with the rounded-rectangle tool.

The extent to which the corners of a rectangle are rounded is controlled by specifying a *corner radius*. The corner radius of a standard rectangle is 0, indicating that there is no corner radius and that neighboring sides meet perpendicularly. As the corner radius increases, the rounded corner consumes a larger and larger portion of the rectangle.

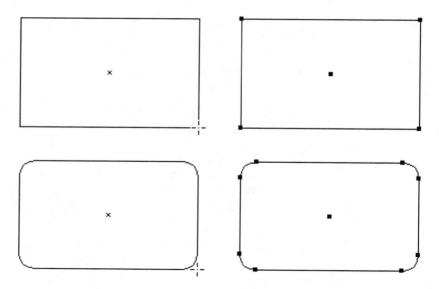

Figure 5-4: Drawing similar shapes with the rectangle and rounded-rectangle tools (left) and the same shapes shown when completed (right).

It may be useful here to review a little geometry. The *radius* is the distance from the center of a circle to any point on its outline. Think of a rounded corner as one quarter of a circle, as shown in Figure 5-5 on the following page spread. The four rounded corners of a rectangle therefore make up an entire circle. Specifying a corner radius determines the radius of this circle. Since the size of the circle will increase as the radius increases, a rounded corner with a large radius consumes proportionally more of a rectangle than a rounded corner with a small radius. Notice how the rounded corner displayed in Figure 5-6 (also on the following page) occupies more space than the corner in Figure 5-5. This is because its corner radius is larger. The radius arrows from Figure 5-5 are superimposed on those of Figure 5-6 to demonstrate this difference.

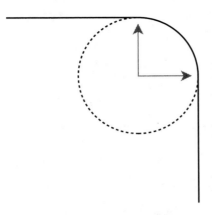

Figure 5-5: The corner of a rounded rectangle is actually a quarter circle. Arrows represent its radius.

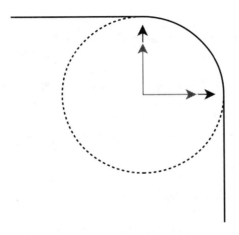

Figure 5-6: An enlarged corner radius with the smaller corner radius superimposed.

The radius of a circle is half the circle's total width, which is called the *diameter*. If the diameter of a rounded corner is at least equal to the longest side of a rectangle—that is, if the radius is at least *half* the longest side—then the rounded corner will consume the entire rectangle. Figure 5-7, for example, shows a series of inset squares, each with a larger corner radius than that of its predecessor. Eventually, the corner radius becomes so large that it takes over the square, resulting in a circle.

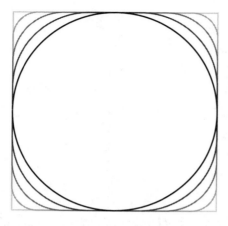

Figure 5-7: The largest of rounded corners will completely consume a rectangle and will result in a circle.

You can specify rounded corners in three ways. First, there is a "Corner radius" option in the RECTANGLE dialog box (see Figure 5-3). Second, you can use the "Corner radius" option in the GENERAL PREFERENCES dialog box, introduced in Chapter 3. Both of these methods require you to specify the corner radius before drawing the rounded rectangle. To round off the corners in an existing rectangle, use the third method, which is to choose the ROUND CORNERS command from the STYLIZE submenu under the FILTERS menu, then enter a value into the "Radius" option box, as discussed in Chapter 12.

If you click with the rectangle tool and enter a value greater than 0 for the "Corner radius" option, Illustrator will automatically move the rounded-rectangle tool into the rectangle tool slot. Conversely, if you click with the rounded-rectangle tool and enter a "Corner radius" value of 0, the rectangle tool will reappear in the slot.

Whether entered into the RECTANGLE or GENERAL PREFERENCES dialog box, the "Corner radius" value is saved with the Adobe Illustrator 5.0 Prefs file in the Preferences folder in the System folder. (The "Radius" value in the ROUND CORNERS dialog box is not saved.) From then on, the value will affect not only the current rounded rectangle, but also future shapes drawn with the rounded-rectangle tool and the centered-rounded-rectangle tool.

🔬 The **Illustrator 5** Book

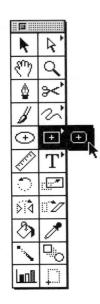

If you press OPTION while drawing with the rounded-rectangle tool, the beginning of your drag becomes the center point of the rectangle. Alternatively, you can double-click on the rectangle (or oval) tool and choose the *centered-rounded-rectangle tool* from the centered-rectangle tool slot. This tool allows you to draw rounded rectangles from the center point without pressing the OPTION key. Pressing OPTION and dragging with the centered-rounded-rectangle tool draws the shape normally, from corner to corner.

Pressing SHIFT and dragging with the rounded-rectangle tool creates a rounded square. Pressing both SHIFT and OPTION while drawing with the rounded-rectangle tool or pressing the SHIFT key while drawing with the centered-rounded-rectangle tool creates a rounded square from the center point.

Drawing an ellipse

The *oval tool*—displayed by default in the fifth tool slot on the left of the toolbox—is used in the same manner as the rectangle tool. The difference, of course, is that the oval tool is used to create *ellipses* (ovals) and circles rather than rectangles and squares.

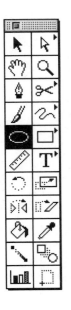

As is the case with the rectangle tool, the click and release points created with the oval tool reside on the path of the ellipse. In this sense, you might think of an ellipse as a rectangle with so large a percentage of its path devoted to rounded corners that the vertical and horizontal segments altogether disappear (see Figure 5-7). However, unlike the rectangle tool, the click and release points of an oval tool drag do not represent opposite corners, since an ellipse has no corners; they represent the middles of opposite *arcs*. While you drag with the oval tool, imagine that a dotted rectangle is formed, displaying the area of drag, as shown in Figure 5-8 on the next page. This rectangle exists entirely within the path of the ellipse. This is different from drawing with an oval tool in most other Macintosh applications, because the simple ellipse in Illustrator is always slightly larger than the area of your drag. An ellipse will always be taller and wider by a factor of $\sqrt{2}$ (roughly 140%) than the height and width of your drag. For example, if you drag four inches horizontally, the resulting ellipse will be $4\sqrt{2}$ (approximately 5½) inches wide.

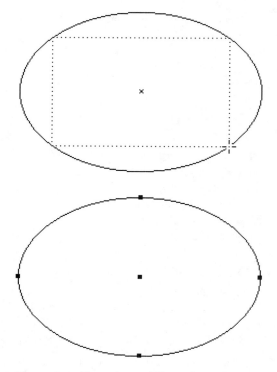

*Figure 5-8: Drawing an ellipse from arc to opposite arc
(with inset rectangle, top) and the same ellipse shown
when completed (bottom).*

This arc-to-arc model may make the oval tool seem overly complicated—at least that's what I thought the first time I ran into it—
but in fact, it makes a more efficient tracing tool. As demonstrated in
Figure 5-9, you trace an elliptical or circular template shape simply by
dragging from the middle of one arc to the middle of the opposite arc.
A dotted rectangle displays the course of your drag. There is no guesswork, since you begin and end your drag on portions of the template
shape. This is preferable to the model adopted by more conventional
drawing programs, such as MacDraw or Aldus FreeHand, in which you
must begin and end your drag well outside the template shape, guess-
ing at imaginary points where the vertical and horizontal extremes of
the circle intersect.

For more information about tracing template images, see *Automated tracing* later in this chapter.

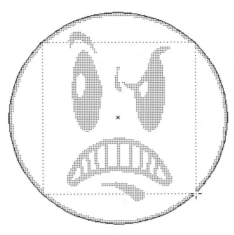

*Figure 5-9: Tracing a bitmapped circle with the
oval tool by dragging from arc to arc.*

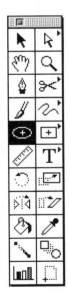

If you press OPTION while drawing with the oval tool, the beginning of your drag becomes the center point of the ellipse. As before, the release point becomes the middle of an arc, determining the size and shape of the ellipse. Alternatively, you can double-click on the oval (or rectangle) tool slot and choose the *centered-oval tool* from the oval tool slot. This tool allows you to draw ellipses from center point to arc without pressing the OPTION key. Pressing OPTION and dragging with the centered-oval tool draws the shape from arc to opposite arc.

Pressing SHIFT and dragging with the oval tool creates a circle. Pressing both SHIFT and OPTION while drawing with the oval tool or pressing the SHIFT key while drawing with the centered-oval tool creates a circle from center point to arc.

Click with the oval tool to bring up the OVAL dialog box shown in Figure 5-10 on the next page. This dialog contains both "Width" and "Height" options, like the RECTANGLE dialog. The values in both option boxes are measured in centimeters, inches, or points, depending on the currently selected "Ruler units" option in the GENERAL PREFERENCES dialog box, as described earlier in this chapter. After entering values for these options and pressing RETURN, Illustrator creates an ellipse to your specifications.

Since no placement options are given in the OVAL dialog box, the point at which you click with the oval tool defines the middle of the upper left arc in your new ellipse. If you click with the centered-oval

---

Chapter 5: **Drawing Paths from Scratch**   157 tool or OPTION-click with the oval tool, the click point becomes the center point in the shape.

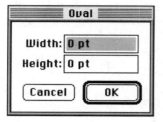

Figure 5-10: Click with the oval or centered-oval tool to display the Oval dialog box.

Geometric paths at an angle

In the course of drawing a shape with one of the six geometric path tools, you may find that your path rotates at some odd angle, as demonstrated by the rectangle in Figure 5-11. This is not happening because you are misusing the tool; rather, you or someone else using this same copy of Illustrator 5.0 has altered the "Constrain angle" option in the GENERAL PREFERENCES dialog box. The *constraint axes* control the angles at which objects can be moved and transformed when you press the SHIFT key. But they also control the creation of geometric paths and text blocks. If any value besides 0 is entered in the "Constrain angle" option box, geometric paths will be rotated to that degree as you draw.

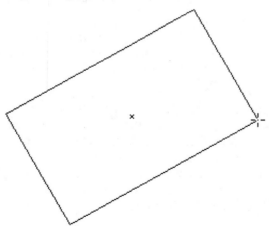

Figure 5-11: Drawing a rectangle when the constraint axes have been rotated by 30°.

To draw rectangle and ellipses that are not rotated, you must reset the constraint axes to their normal orientation. This may be accomplished using one of two methods:

- Choose the GENERAL... command from the PREFERENCES submenu in the EDIT menu (⌘-K). Enter 0 for the "Constrain angle" option and press RETURN.

- Quit the Illustrator application (⌘-Q). At the Finder level, open the System folder and then open the Preferences folder. Select the file named Adobe Illustrator 5.0 Prefs and drag it into the Trash. Choose EMPTY TRASH from the SPECIAL menu and restart the Illustrator application. Obviously, this is a drastic way to solve the problem, but this way you can reset all preference settings at once and make a clean start of things.

Any geometric paths that you draw will now be oriented normally.

Free-form paths

The geometric path tools allow you to create simple shapes quickly and easily. However, Illustrator's true drawing power is based in its ability to define free-form lines and shapes. Such paths may be simple anomalies, like triangles or crescents. Or they may be intricate polygons and naturalistic forms that meet the most complex specifications.

The freehand tool

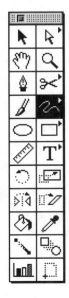

Displayed by default in the fourth tool slot on the right of the Illustrator palette, the *freehand tool* is used for real-time drawing. After choosing this tool, you can click and drag as if you were drawing with a pencil on a sheet of paper. Illustrator tracks the exact movement of your mouse on screen, creating a sketchy line between the locations at which you begin and end your drag. After you release the mouse button, Illustrator automatically determines the number and location of points and segments, and creates the freehand path.

Consider the example of the valentine in Figure 5-12 on the next page. I started drawing with the tool at the upper cusp of the valentine, then swept around in a great rightward arc and down to the lower tip, back upward and around to the left, and finally met up with my first point in one continuous movement, as shown by the position of the cursor in the figure.

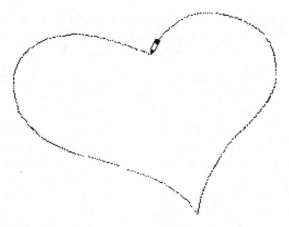

Figure 5-12: Drawing a valentine with the freehand tool.

Notice that the outline of the valentine has a few tiny jagged edges. These jagged edges exist for two reasons. First, I drew this figure with a mouse, which is not a precise drawing instrument. When you move a mouse, a ball within its chamber rolls about against the surface of the table or mouse pad. This ball in turn causes two internal tracking wheels to move, one vertically and one horizontally. Based on the activity of these two wheels, the mouse conveys movement information to the computer. No matter how thoroughly you clean a mouse, there will be some sort of interference between the ball and the wheels, even if it is only some small particles of dust. For example, if you draw a 45° diagonal line, both the vertical and horizontal tracking wheels should move at exactly the same pace. If some interference comes between the ball and the horizontal wheel, causing the wheel to remain motionless for only a moment, the mouse will send purely vertical movement information to the computer until the interference has passed. The result is a momentary jag in an otherwise smooth line.

Second, most people—even skilled artists—are not very practiced in drawing with a mouse. It takes time to master this skill. You may find that your first drawing efforts look much different from what you had planned—possibly far worse than Figure 5-12, for example. Luckily, the freehand tool is capable of smoothing out many imperfections.

The **Illustrator 5** Book

If you're comfortable with drawing with a mouse but you want to avoid some of the tracking problems associated with the standard Apple mouse, consider purchasing an *optical mouse*. My favorite is the A+ Mouse ADB from Mouse Systems, (415) 656-1117. For about $100, this pointing device projects two lights that bounce off a reflective pad. Because it lacks moving parts, an optical mouse tends to last longer and perform more consistently than any trackball device.

Once you release your mouse button, having completed the path, Illustrator begins its calculations to determine how many points your path should have, as well as their locations. Thus, drawing with the freehand tool is entirely automatic.

Freehand tolerance

In Chapter 4, I recommended that you use points sparingly, even when drawing complex images. Too many points needlessly complicate a path, making it clumsy and malformed. You may find, however, that Illustrator does not always follow this advice. When Illustrator finishes its calculations, freehand paths are frequently riddled with far too many points. As often as not, the path that you expected to be a smooth free-form line turns out to be a jagged mess.

To fully understand the freehand tool, you must understand how points get assigned to a freehand path. Illustrator makes its determinations based on three factors:

- **Consistency**. Illustrator assigns a point to every location at which your freehand drag changes direction. Thus, smooth, consistent mouse actions produce smooth, elegant paths; jerky or unsteady mouse actions produce overly complex lines.

- **Speed**. The speed at which you draw can also affect the appearance of a freehand path. If your mouse lingers, Illustrator is more likely to assign a point at this location. However, if you draw too quickly, Illustrator will ignore many of the subtleties in your drag. A slow but steady technique is the most reliable.

- **Tolerance**. Illustrator allows you to control the sensitivity of the freehand tool using the "Freehand tolerance" option in the GENERAL PREFERENCES dialog box. A low *tolerance* setting results in extremely complex paths, a high tolerance setting results in overly smooth paths.

File	
New	⌘N
Open...	⌘O
Close	⌘W
Save	⌘S
Save As...	
Place Art...	
Import Styles...	
Doc. Setup...	⌘⌥D
Page Setup...	
Print...	⌘P
Preferences	▶
Quit	⌘Q

To access the "Freehand tolerance" option, choose the GENERAL... command from the PREFERENCES submenu in the EDIT menu (⌘-K). You can enter any value between 0 and 10 into the option box. Values are measured by Illustrator in screen pixels; by entering the number 2, for example, you instruct Illustrator to ignore any jags that do not exceed 2 pixels in length or width when determining point information of future freehand paths. Setting the "Freehand tolerance" value to 0 makes the freehand tool extremely sensitive; setting the value to 10 smooths out your freehand paths.

Figure 5-13 shows the number and location of the points that Illustrator has automatically set into my valentine shape when the tolerance level is set to 0 pixel. Illustrator has captured every imperfection in the path from the previous figure, including imperfections you may not even have noticed. The result is an overly complicated path. Such a low tolerance value is rarely useful.

Figure 5-13: The points assigned to the valentine shape when the "Freehand tolerance" option is set to 0 pixels. The white squares are points. The small lines with circles at the end of them are Bézier control handles, which will be introduced later in this chapter.

The five paths in Figure 5-14 are Illustrator's interpretations of my valentine when the tolerance value is set to 1, 2, 3, 5, and 10 pixels, respectively. If you compare this figure to Figure 5-14, you'll notice dramatic differences in the way that Illustrator interprets paths at tolerances of 0, 1, and 2 pixels. Paths with tolerances of 3, 5, and 10, however, are strikingly similar.

Figure 5-14: Five examples demonstrating the points assigned to the valentine shape when the freehand tolerance is set to 1, 2 (top), 3 (center), 5, and 10 (bottom), respectively.

A "Freehand tolerance" of 2 or 3 is generally adequate for most users, but you should experiment with this option to determine your preferred setting. If your drawing technique is steadier or more precise than mine, lower your tolerance. If you have problems drawing a straight line, raise your tolerance. Keep in mind, Illustrator saves the "Freehand tolerance" value in the Adobe Illustrator 5.0 Prefs file and will apply it to all future illustrations until you enter a new value.

You cannot alter the tolerance value for a path after the path is created, because Illustrator calculates the points for a path only once, after your release when dragging with the freehand tool. For each of the paths in Figures 5-13 and 5-14, I had to change the tolerance value and draw a new valentine from scratch.

Pressing ⌘ while drawing

Normally, a continuous path tracks every movement as you draw with the freehand tool. If you press the COMMAND key while drawing, however, the cursor changes from a pencil cursor to an eraser cursor, indicating that the freehand tool is prepared to track your movements differently. This COMMAND-dragging can be used to produce either of two results:

- **Erasing**. You can press COMMAND to erase a mistake while in the process of dragging with the freehand tool. In the middle of drawing, press COMMAND and trace back over a portion of a path that you have just drawn. You will see it disappear. In other words, you can draw a path with the freehand tool, immediately "undraw" part of it while pressing the COMMAND key, and then release COMMAND and continue drawing.

- **Adding a single segment**. Rather than COMMAND-dragging back over your path, COMMAND-drag away from it and then release the COMMAND key and continue to draw. Notice that Illustrator does not display your path between the point where the COMMAND key was pressed and the point where it was released. At the end of your drag, Illustrator calculates the number and position of the points necessary to represent your freehand path virtually the same as it has in past examples. The only difference is that any portion of your path that was created while the COMMAND key was pressed is represented by a single segment. This segment may be very nearly straight but it will always curve slightly.

To experiment with adding a single segment with the freehand tool, try the following exercise:

1. Drawing a squiggle with the freehand tool, as shown below.

Figure 5-15: Draw a squiggle with the freehand tool, press the command key and drag away from the line.

2. Press the COMMAND key and drag to the location represented by the hollow eraser cursor in Figure 5-15. For as long as the COMMAND key remains pressed, no line will appear. Your drag will be interpreted by Illustrator to represent a single, slightly curved segment.

3. Release the COMMAND key and draw another squiggle. Your movements are interpreted exactly as they were before. As shown in Figure 5-16, the freehand cursor again becomes a pencil, indicating that the COMMAND key has indeed been released.

4. Release your mouse button. Figure 5-17 shows the completed path, displaying a single, selected segment between the COMMAND key press and release points.

Note that the COMMAND key cannot be pressed before dragging with the freehand tool or released after the drag is finished. The single segment produced by pressing COMMAND must be preceded and followed by normal freehand path segments. Pressing the command key while not drawing with the freehand tool temporarily changes it to the selection tool last used.

Figure 5-16: Continue to draw after releasing the command key.

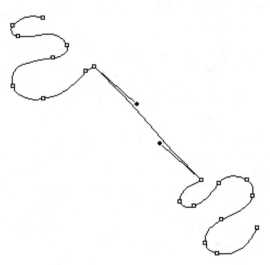

Figure 5-17: The completed path contains a single, slightly curved segment between the points where the command key was pressed and released.

The **Illustrator 5** Book

Extending a line

You can also use the freehand tool to *extend* an open path. For example, suppose you have drawn a line with the freehand tool some time ago, but now want to make the line longer or to close the path. Drag from an *endpoint*—that is, the point at either end of the line—with the freehand tool, as shown in Figure 5-18. Illustrator treats the line created by dragging with the tool as an extension of the existing open path. To extend a path, drag from an endpoint and end your drag when the line has become the desired length. To close the path, drag from one endpoint to the other.

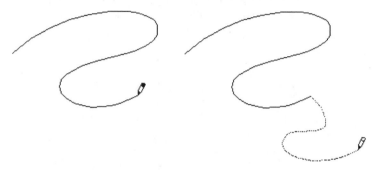

Figure 5-18: To extend an open path (left) with the freehand tool, drag from either of its endpoints (right).

Normally, an endpoint will be converted to a *smooth point* regardless of its original identity when you drag from it with the freehand tool, as shown in Figure 5-19 on the next page. A smooth point ensures a continuous *arc* between two segments, as discussed in *The line* section of Chapter 4. This is even true when the point appears to be a corner, a fact that can affect future manipulations as discussed in Chapter 6, *Reshaping Paths that Frankly Need Help*.

To make an endpoint into a *corner point*—where two segments meet to form a sharp corner—press and hold the OPTION key before you begin your drag. This technique is demonstrated in Figure 5-20. If you are closing a path, the endpoint at which you release will also be a smooth point unless you press OPTION before ending your drag and hold the key down until after the mouse button has been released.

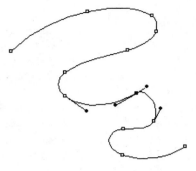

Figure 5-19: Dragging from an endpoint with the freehand tool converts the point to a smooth point (displayed as selected).

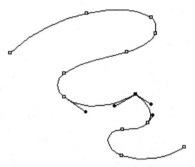

Figure 5-20: Press the option key to convert an endpoint to a corner point (displayed as selected).

Sketching complicated paths

The freehand tool can be used to sketch complicated objects, especially line drawings. If you are skilled in drawing with the mouse, you may find that the immediacy of producing high-resolution images in real time is very appealing. Drawing with the freehand tool can soften the computer-produced appearance of an illustration, and may convey a sense of immediacy to those who view the piece. Regardless of your drawing ability or preferences, however, the freehand tool rarely renders images that can be considered professional in quality.

Suppose that I draw a fish as a single line with the freehand tool. The first example in Figure 5-21 shows the path as I originally draw it, before Illustrator calculates the number and location of points and segments. The second example shows the points that Illustrator has assigned to our fish. The third example shows the fish as a deselected path.

Figure 5-21: Three steps in the process of sketching a fish with the freehand tool.

The finished product represents the original movement of the free-hand tool with amazing accuracy. This is primarily due to the "Free-hand tolerance" option, discussed earlier in this chapter. (The tolerance was set to 3 for the examples in Figure 5-21.) The final path is by no means perfect, mainly because the original drawing isn't perfect, but it is a very good place to start.

Most illustrations created with the freehand tool need to be extensively manipulated in order to print acceptably. Like a Polaroid camera, there's a tradeoff between the immediate satisfaction offered by the freehand tool and the resulting accuracy and elegance. For this reason, I suggest that you use the tool primarily for sketching images and you prepare yourself for the time required to properly reshape them (as described in Chapter 6).

The brush tool

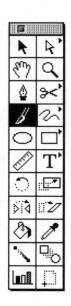

Displayed in the fourth tool slot on the left, the *brush tool* is the other free-form path creation tool. New to Illustrator 5.0, the brush tool is comparable to the paintbrush tool in a paint program. It allows you to create shapes that closely mimic the stroke of a paintbrush that has a never ending supply of paint. As you drag with the brush tool, what appears as a line flows from the end of the cursor. As with the freehand tool, Illustrator automatically assigns points, control handles, and segments that define the path after you complete the stroke. At first glance, the result may look like a thicker version of a path created with the freehand tool. But unlike the freehand tool, which must start and finish at the same point to form a closed path, the brush tool produces a closed path in a single drag, regardless of the final cursor position.

In Figure 5-22, the shape on the left was created with the brush tool. The shape on the right is an attempt to duplicate the left shape using the freehand tool. The gray arrows describe the motion of the associated tool. Notice the uniformity in width of the shape created with the brush tool compared with the relatively haphazard and wiggly outline created with the freehand tool.

Now recall the body of Groucho's cigar back in Figure 4-22. You can create this shape with any drawing tool, whether the freehand, brush, or pen tool (described later in this chapter). For an experienced user, the tool of choice for creating the cigar is a matter of preference, but novices will probably find that the brush tool produces the best results, offering the combined benefits of ease of use and speed.

Figure 5-22: A closed path created with the brush
tool (left) compared with one created with the
freehand tool (right).

The brush tool's width can range from 0 to 1296 points (that is,
18 inches or almost 46 centimeters). You set the width in the BRUSH
dialog box, shown in Figure 5-23. To display it, double-click on the
brush tool icon in the toolbox. In the BRUSH dialog box you can select
between a consistent width or one that varies between a specified
minimum and maximum. The variable width is applicable only to users that have a pressure-sensitive drawing tablet, as discussed later.

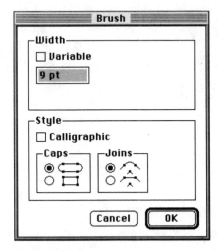

Figure 5-23: The Brush dialog box, displayed
by double-clicking on the brush tool slot, provides
control options for the brush tool.

The other options in the BRUSH dialog box deal with the style characteristics of the brush shape. You can select between round or flat *caps*, which affect the appearance of the ends of the shape. Similarly, you can select between round or beveled *joins*, which affect the appearance of corners. Select one radio button each from the "Caps" and "Joins" options according to your preference. Figure 5-24 demonstrates all four permutations. Lastly, you can opt for the brush tool to draw calligraphic shapes, as discussed in detail in the next section. Since the calligraphic option precludes caps and joins, the "Caps" and "Joins" options dim when you select the "Calligraphic" check box.

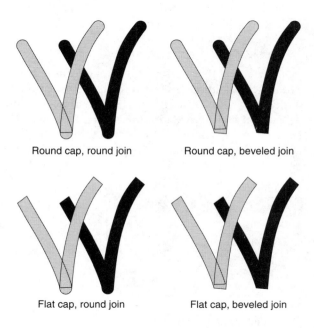

Round cap, round join   Round cap, beveled join

Flat cap, round join   Flat cap, beveled join

Figure 5-24: Each of the four possible caps and joins combinations outlined on left and filled on right.

The calligraphic option

With the brush tool you can create shapes that look like calligraphic pen strokes. Click on the "Calligraphic" check box to display the "Calligraphic angle" option box, as shown in Figure 5-25. The angle you enter here dictates the slant of the brush tool. This angle corresponds to the angle of the pen tip with respect to the page if you were using a real-world calligraphy pen.

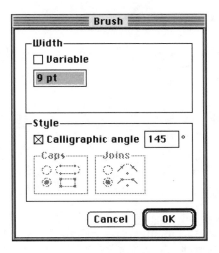

Figure 5-25: When the Calligraphic checkbox is checked, the Calligraphic angle option box displays.

For those who are unclear on how the "Calligraphic angle" option works, imagine that a small sundial with a round, transparent face is stuck on your monitor's screen with its face directed toward you. Think of the sundial's pointer as the calligraphic pen tip and the face as the circle that marks off the 360° through which the pen tip can rotate. The 0° mark on the circle is positioned at 3:00. So if the "Calligraphic angle" value is set to 0°, then the pointer will point directly to the right. If you move the sundial across the screen, the path of the pointer is similar to the top shape in Figure 5-26 on the next page. The shape is thinnest when you drag in the direction of the angle (as well as in the opposite direction of the angle, 180° or 9:00). As you move the brush away from the assigned angle, the shape widens. The maximum thickness occurs when you drag perpendicularly to the angle, which in this case would be either 90° or 270° (6:00 or high noon, respectively).

I created the bottom shape in the figure after assigning a angle of 135°, which is midway between 10:00 and 11:00 on the sundial face. The different angles produce dramatically different shapes.

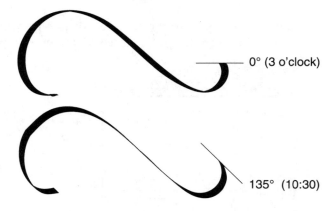

0° (3 o'clock)

135° (10:30)

Figure 5-26: When the "Calligraphic" option is activated, the widths of shapes vary depending on the angle of the pen tip with respect to the angle of your drag.

The thickness of a calligraphic shape produced with the brush tool varies from a minimum of 1 point to a maximum of the value entered in the WIDTH option box in the BRUSH dialog box. Since the direction that the brush tool moves dictates the width of the shape at a particular point, the width of the shape may not necessarily reach either of the two extremes. Consider Figure 5-27, in which the "Calligraphic angle" value was set to 45°. The thin diagonal shape on the left is the result of dragging in the direction of the angle. The thick diagonal shape on the right results from dragging perpendicularly to the angle. Since the middle shape results from dragging between the two extremes, its thickness is likewise more than the minimum and less than the maximum, never achieving either.

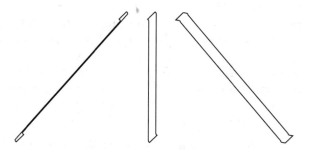

Figure 5-27: Three simple shapes drawn with the "Calligraphic angle" value set to 45°.

Pressure-sensitive drawing tablets

Not only is the brush tool new to Illustrator 5.0, it's the first Illustrator tool to support pressure-sensitive capabilities. This means that, provided you have a pressure-sensitive drawing tablet hooked up to your Mac, you can set the brush tool to respond to the amount of pressure you apply with the stylus to your drawing tablet. Once the drawing tablet is connected and its driver software is properly loaded, the BRUSH dialog box will provide access to the otherwise dimmed "Variable" check box. When the option is checked, the "Width" option box is replaced with the "Minimum" and "Maximum" option boxes, as shown in Figure 5-28. The first value defines the width that Illustrator assigns to the lightest stylus-to-tablet contact that your drawing tablet recognizes, and the second does the same for the strongest contact.

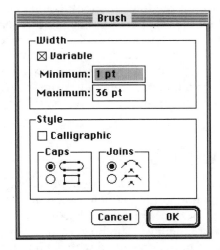

Figure 5-28: The Minimum and Maximum option boxes display when the Variable check box is checked.

Using the brush tool and a pressure-sensitive tablet together can greatly reduce the time and effort it takes to create complicated paths. For example, Groucho's nose from the Chapter 4 discussion could be produced with one quick swipe of the stylus. In fact, with a Wacom drawing tablet and the brush tool, it took me less time to create the school of snouts in Figure 5-29 on the next page than it took to create the original nose using a mouse with the pen tool.

Figure 5-29: With a pressure-sensitive drawing tablet and the brush tool, you can quickly create variations on a particular—and in this case, peculiar—theme.

As is the case for the freehand tool, you'll need to reshape paths created with the brush tool before they're quite ready for prime time, as Figure 5-29 attests. The brush tool is great for knocking out shapes quickly, especially when used in conjunction with a drawing tablet. Unfortunately, Illustrator usually assigns too many points and segments to a brush shape, resulting in undesirable ripples and wiggles. For complete information on reshaping, read Chapter 6.

Bézier paths

All paths in Illustrator are *Bézier* (pronounced bay-zee-ay) *paths*; that is, they rely on a handful of mathematical curve definitions, pioneered by Pierre Bézier, which have become an integral part of the PostScript printer language. The Bézier curve model allows for zero, one, or two levers to be associated with each point in a line or shape. These levers are called *Bézier control handles*. Each handle can be moved in relation to a point, bending and tugging at a curved segment like a piece of elastic taffy.

The geometric path tools and the freehand tool gloss over the nuts and bolts of path building. If you really want to understand how to draw in Adobe Illustrator, you must master the creation of lines and shapes on a point-by-point basis. The remainder of this chapter is devoted to a thorough examination of points, segments, and Bézier control handles. This all centers around a discussion of Illustrator's primary drawing tool—the *pen tool*.

The **Illustrator 5** Book

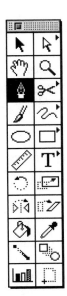

The pen tool

As discussed in Chapter 4, Illustrator defines lines and shapes as the combination of points. Each point determines how a segment in the path enters the point and how another exits it. The *pen tool*, the third tool on the right in your palette, works by defining a single point at a time. The way in which you operate the pen tool determines the identity of each point you create.

The pen cursors

If you're familiar with previous versions of Illustrator, you may find version 5.0's use of six different cursors somewhat surprising considering that, previously, two sufficed for all the same pen functions. Before, one cursor appeared while you were working on a path and another appeared before you started to draw. What could be simpler? Either you're drawing or you're not. So, why the additional cursors? The main reason is that, in addition to making a path, you can use the pen tool to close an open path, connect two open paths, or convert the identity of an endpoint. All this depends on what kind of point the pen cursor is positioned over. In adding cursors to Illustrator 5.0, Adobe is attempting to clarify which function the pen tool is about to execute. The following table shows the six cursors, both normal and precise, and lists their names. To access the precise cursors, select the "Precise cursors" option in the GENERAL PREFERENCES dialog box or press the CAPS LOCK key. The function of each cursor is described later in this chapter.

Table 5-1: The six kinds of pen cursor and their names

♦×	✕	The passive cursors
♦	-¦-	The active cursors
♦₀	-¦₀	The close cursors
♦ᴋ	-¦ᴋ	The convert cursors
♦/	-¦/	The connect cursors
♦□	-¦□	The reactivate cursors

Drawing straight segments

When you first select the pen tool and position the cursor in the drawing area, the cursor will appear as the icon in the pen tool slot with a small × to the right, for simply as an × if you are using precise cursors. This is the *passive cursor*, indicating that any point or path created at that spot will have no connection with any other part of your illustration.

Select the pen tool and click at some location on the screen to create a *corner point*, which shows up as a tiny black square, indicating that it is *selected*. Be careful only to click with the pen tool and not drag. If you drag more than two pixels while clicking with the pen tool, you will create a smooth point, as described later in this chapter.

The point you just created is *open ended*, meaning that it does not have both a segment coming into it and a segment going out from it. In fact, this new corner point—I'll call it point A—is associated with no segment whatsoever. It is a lone point, open ended in two directions.

If you again click with the pen tool at a new location on the screen, a straight segment will be drawn from the original corner point A to the new corner point B, as demonstrated by Figure 5-30. Notice that point A now appears hollow rather than black. This shows that point A is the member of a selected path but is itself *deselected*. The new corner point B is selected and open ended. A point always becomes selected immediately after it is created, thereby deselecting all other points.

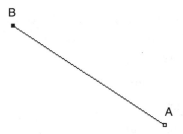

Figure 5-30: Create a straight line by clicking at two separate locations with the pen tool.

The plain pen tool cursor (or cross-shaped precise cursor) signifies that the selected path is *active*, meaning that it is ready to receive points. A segment will be drawn between the selected point and the next point you create. The pen cursor can also appear with an × in the lower right corner (or an ×-shaped precise cursor) indicating that all paths are *passive*. Even if a passive path includes an open-ended, selected point, no segment will be drawn between it and the next point you create.

If you click a third time with the pen tool, you create a new point, point C. As shown in Figure 5-31, point A remains open ended, since it is associated with only one segment, the one that attaches it to point B. Likewise, a segment goes from point B to point C. Because a point can be associated with no more than two segments, point B is no longer open ended. Such a point is called an *interior point*. Point C was just created, so it is selected and all other points are deselected. And because this last point is open-ended and the pen tool cursor still appears as the active cursor, the path remains active.

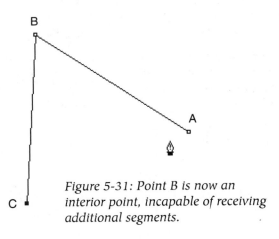

Figure 5-31: Point B is now an interior point, incapable of receiving additional segments.

Now *close* your path, changing it from a line into a shape and eliminating all open-ended points. Just click with the pen tool on point A, the first point in the path. When you position the pen cursor over point A, the cursor appears with a small circle in the lower right corner, signifying that you will convert the open path into a closed path when you click on the point. Since point A is open ended, it willingly accepts the segment drawn between it and point C, as shown in Figure 5-32 on the following page.

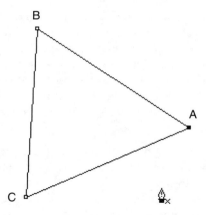

Figure 5-32: Closing a path deactivates it. The next point you create will begin a new path.

Illustrator now displays the passive pen cursor because no path is active. The moment you close a path, it becomes passive. So long as it remains closed , no segment will be drawn between the next point you create and any point in the selected shape.

Suppose you click again with the pen tool cursor. The triangle shape becomes deselected and a new point D is created (see Figure 5-33). Point D is open-ended in two directions and you again see the active cursor. The path-creation process has begun anew.

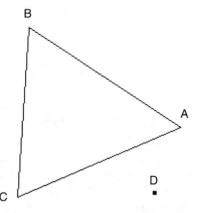

Figure 5-33: Creating a point D that is independent of the previous path deselects that path.

The **Illustrator 5** Book

To *deactivate* a path (make it passive) without closing or deselecting it, click the pen tool icon in the toolbox. The passive cursor will appear again even though the last path is still selected. Alternatively, you can press COMMAND to access the most recently used selection tool and click on a blank portion of the screen to deactivate and deselect the path.

Drawing perpendicular segments

To constrain a point so it is created at an angle that is a multiple of 45° from the selected, open-ended point, press SHIFT as you click with the pen tool. This technique allows you to create horizontal, vertical, and diagonal segments. In Figure 5-34, for example, the position of the active cursor shows the location at which I actually clicked with the pen tool. However, since the SHIFT key was pressed, the new point was constrained to a 0° angle from its neighbor, resulting in a horizontal segment.

Figure 5-34: Shift-click with the pen tool to create a horizontal, vertical, or diagonal segment.

You can alter the effects of pressing the SHIFT key by rotating the constraint axes using the "Constrain angle" option in the GENERAL PREFERENCES dialog box, as described in the *Geometric paths at an angle* section earlier in this chapter.

Drawing curved segments

Clicking with the pen tool creates a corner point, but if you drag with the pen tool, you create a *smooth point*, which ensures a smooth arc between one curved segment and the next. A smooth point sports two *Bézier control handles*, each of which appear as a tiny circle perched at the end of a hairline that connects the handle to its point (see Figure 5-35 on the next page). These handles act as levers, bending segments relative to the smooth point.

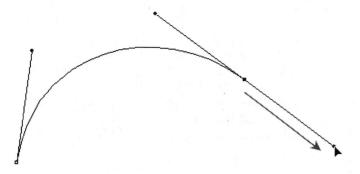

Figure 5-35: Here I've dragged twice with the pen tool (once on left and once on right) to create two smooth points each flanked by a pair of Bézier control handles.

The point at which you begin dragging with the pen tool determines the location of the smooth point; the point at which you release becomes a Bézier control handle that affects the next segment you create. A second handle appears symmetrically on the other side of the smooth point. This handle determines the curvature of the most recent segment, as demonstrated in Figure 5-35.

You can think of a smooth point as if it were the center of a small seesaw, with the Bézier control handles acting as opposite ends. Push down on one handle to make the opposite handle go up, and vice versa. Figure 5-36 shows four examples of dragging different distances from the same smooth point with the pen tool. Notice that the placement of both Bézier control handles is determined by the release location, since the second handle is symmetrical to the first around the smooth point. It is this seesaw quality that forces two segments to always form a continuous, seamless arc through a smooth point.

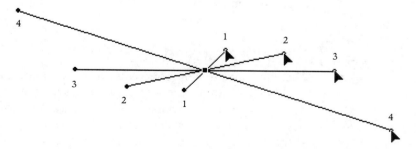

Figure 5-36: When dragging with the pen tool, the release location determines the placement of both Bézier control handles.

The **Illustrator 5** Book

Smooth points act no differently than corner points when it comes to building paths. Dragging with the pen tool creates a curved segment between the current smooth point and the previously selected, open-ended point in the active path. If no path is active, the smooth point becomes the first point in a new path. Clicking on the first point in an active path closes the path.

If the first point in a path is a smooth point, you should drag rather than click on the point with the pen tool to close the path. Otherwise, you run the risk of altering the identity of the point, as discussed in the next section.

Creating a cusp

As you've seen, a smooth point always has two Bézier control handles positioned on opposite ends of a seesaw. A corner point is much more versatile: It can have zero, one, or two handles. I've explained that clicking with the pen tool creates a corner point with no handle and that dragging with the pen tool creates a smooth point. To create a corner point that has one or two Bézier control handles—sometimes called a *cusp*—you must manipulate an existing corner or smooth point while creating its path. The following pages contain three examples of how this technique can work:

- **Option 1**: *Delete a handle from a smooth point*

The first two examples begin with the semicircle shown in Figure 5-37. You would create this path by dragging three times with the pen tool: First drag downward from the right point; then drag leftward from the bottom point; and finally drag upward from the left point, which is selected in the figure. The result is an active path composed of three smooth points.

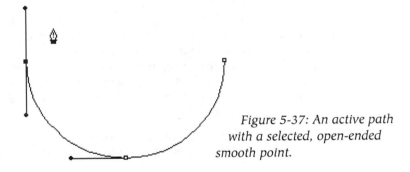

Figure 5-37: An active path with a selected, open-ended smooth point.

Illustrator allows you to alter the most recent point while you are in the process of creating its path. Suppose that you want to change the semicircle into a bowl-shaped path, like the one shown in Figure 5-38. This shape involves three segments, two of which meet to form a single large arc, and a third that is straight, flattening off the shape. Since smooth points may be associated only with curved segments, corner points must exist on both sides of this prospective straight segment. Therefore, you need to change the two topmost smooth points from Figure 5-38 to corner points, each with a single Bézier control handle that affects the curved segment below.

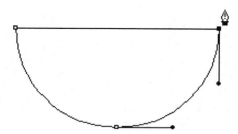

Figure 5-38: By clicking with the pen tool on the two top points, you change the existing smooth points to corner points with one Bézier control handle apiece.

After creating the left-hand smooth point shown in Figure 5-38, Illustrator displays the active cursor, indicating that a segment will be drawn between the selected, open-ended point and the next point you create. However, the bowl shape requires no new point, only a single new segment. So instead of clicking or dragging at a new location, click (do not drag) with the pen tool on the selected smooth point. When you position the cursor over this point, the cursor sports a small tilted caret in the lower left corner. This is the *convert cursor*, indicating that you will change the identity of the point when you click or drag on it. By clicking on a selected, open-ended smooth point with the pen tool, you amputate the control handle that does not currently control a segment. In Figure 5-38, the lower handle controls the left segment in the semicircular path, but the upper handle controls no segment. Therefore, clicking on the smooth point amputates this upper handle.

What's the result? A smooth point with only one control handle is an impossibility. This point must therefore be a corner point.

The **Illustrator 5** Book

You now have an open path composed of two smooth points and a corner point. You still need to close the path and to amputate a handle belonging to the first smooth point. Both maneuvers are accomplished in a single operation. Simply click on the first smooth point (the close cursor will appear). With one click, you close the path and amputate the Bézier control handle that would otherwise control the new segment. Hence, the new segment is straight, bordered on both sides by corner points with one Bézier control handle each. The result is the shape shown in Figure 5-39.

- **Option 2**: *Move one smooth point handle independently of the other*

The second example for creating a corner point with Bézier control handles also begins with the path shown in Figure 5-37. Suppose this time, however, that you wish to close the path with a rounded top, like the one shown in Figure 5-40 on the next page. All segments in this path are curved, and yet the upper segment meets with the lower segments to form two cusps. This means that we must change the two top smooth points to corner points with two Bézier control handles apiece—one controlling the upper segment and one controlling a lower segment.

In Illustrator, you can subtract a handle from a smooth point and add a new handle to the resulting corner point in one operation. To accomplish this, press the OPTION key and drag from the selected open-ended smooth point shown in Figure 5-37. The moment you drag from the smooth point while pressing the OPTION key, the point changes to a corner point. As you drag, a new handle emerges, as shown in Figure 5-39. This handle will control the next segment you create. Thus, you now have a corner point with two Bézier control handles, each fully independent of the other.

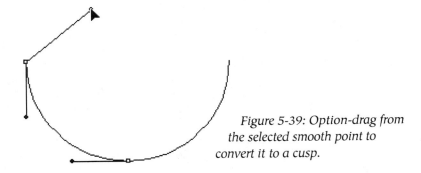

Figure 5-39: Option-drag from the selected smooth point to convert it to a cusp.

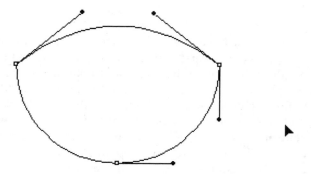

Figure 5-40: Close the shape by option-dragging on the first point in the path.

You can close the shape in the same manner. Press OPTION and drag with the pen tool from the first smooth point of the path. However, notice the location of the cursor as you drag, as illustrated by Figure 5-40. As you drag in one direction, the Bézier control handle emerges in the opposite direction. This is because when dragging with the pen tool, you always drag in the direction of the segment that *exits* the current point. The handle controlling the newly created segment—the segment that *enters* the current point—is positioned symmetrically to your drag, even if it is the only handle being manipulated.

- **Option 3**: *Add a handle to a corner point*

You have now seen how to subtract a handle from an existing open-ended smooth point to form a corner point with only one handle. You have also seen how to subtract a handle from a smooth point and add an independent handle to the resulting corner point at the same time. This third example demonstrates how you can add a handle to an existing open-ended corner point, one that is so far associated only with straight segments.

This time, suppose that you have created the straight-segment path by a series of clicks (do not drag, since we want all corner points) as shown in Figure 5-41 on the next page. By dragging from the selected, open-ended corner point in the figure, you can create a single Bézier control handle, as shown in Figure 5-42. Note that you do not convert the corner point to a smooth point by dragging at it. Although you can change a smooth point to a corner point, you cannot change a corner point to a smooth point using the pen tool.

The **Illustrator 5** Book

Figure 5-41: An active straight-segment path
with a selected, open-ended corner point.

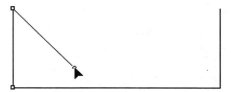

Figure 5-42: Drag from the selected corner point
to add a single Bézier control handle.

To close the path, drag at the first corner point in the path (the
top right point). Notice the location of the cursor during the drag, as
shown in Figure 5-43. Once again, you drag in the opposite direction of the emerging Bézier control handle. As in Figure 5-40, you
drag as if you were creating a handle controlling the segment that
exits the current point. The handle that actually exists controls the
segment that *enters* the current point; thus it moves symmetrically to
your drag.

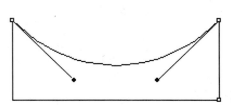

Figure 5-43: Close the shape by dragging on
the first corner point in the path.

Other uses for the pen tool

The pen tool can serve two other purposes. First, you can connect the active path that you are working on to an existing passive path in the same illustration. In Figure 5-44, I drew the wavy line on the right earlier with the freehand tool. This path is passive. I am in the process of creating the left path with the pen tool, so this path is active. When I position the cursor over one of the endpoints of the passive line, the *connect cursor* appears, indicating that when I click, the two paths will join into one. Figure 5-45 shows the resulting joined path.

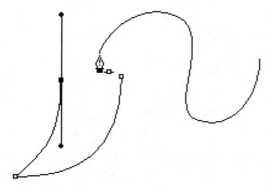

Figure 5-44: The connect cursor ready to connect the active path (left) with a passive path (right).

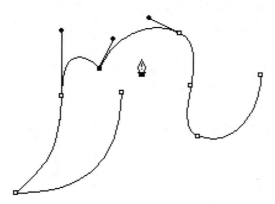

Figure 5-45: A single active path is the result.

Normally, clicking with the connect cursor produces a smooth point. To force a corner point, OPTION-click with the pen when connecting two paths.

The pen tool can also make a passive path active again. When no path is active, simply click on an endpoint in a passive path. When the pen tool is positioned over such an endpoint, Illustrator displays the *reactivate cursor*, which looks like a pen with a slash in the lower right corner. Click with the reactivate cursor and the path becomes active again.

Pen tool summary

Regardless of the tool used to create it, a path is made up of points and segments. The points determine the curvature of segments based on the positioning of Bézier control handles. In turn, the segments define the form of the path.

Although you can adjust the placement of points and Bézier control handles by reshaping a path created with any drawing tool, the pen tool is the only tool in Adobe Illustrator that allows you to exactly position points and handles while creating a path. And since any illustration is constructed by combining a series of lines and shapes, there is absolutely no illustration that you cannot create using the pen tool alone.

 Press the CONTROL key to temporarily access the pen tool when the freehand tool is selected. Unfortunately, in Illustrator 5.0, the reverse is no longer true.

The following items summarize the ways in which you can use the pen tool to create paths in Adobe Illustrator:

- To build a path, create one point after another until the path is the desired length and shape. As long as the path is *active* (the active cursor appearing), Illustrator will create a segment between each point.

- To close a path and in the process make the path *passive*, click on the first point in the active path (with the close cursor). Click again elsewhere with the passive cursor to begin a new path.

- To make an open path passive, COMMAND-click on an empty portion of the drawing area. Release the COMMAND key and click again with the passive cursor to begin a new path.

- To join an active path with another open path, click or drag with the connect cursor on an endpoint in the passive path. Illustrator automatically joins the two paths with a new segment and makes the path active.

- To reactivate a path, click or drag with the reactivate cursor on one of its endpoints. Remember that clicking or dragging on an existing endpoint may change the point's identity.

- To insert a bit of freehand drawing into an active path, drag from the selected point with the freehand tool. After you finish drawing, select the pen tool and click or drag from the selected point to continue adding points to the path.

The next items explain the specific kinds of points and segments that you can create with the pen tool:

- Click to create a *corner point*.

- Click at two separate locations to create a straight segment.

- Click at one location and SHIFT-click at another to create a diagonal or perpendicular segment (one that is a multiple of 45°).

- Drag to create a *smooth point* with two *Bézier control handles*.

- Drag at two separate locations to create a curved segment.

- Drag, press SHIFT, begin a new drag, and then release SHIFT while still dragging to create a curved segment whose smooth points align with respect to the constraint axes. Pressing SHIFT constrains the point; releasing SHIFT before you complete the drag allows you to move the Bézier control handles freely. An example of such a curve is shown in Figure 5-46.

- After beginning to drag, press SHIFT to constrain the Bézier control handles without affecting the placement of the smooth point. An example of this is shown in Figure 5-47.

- Press SHIFT and drag at two separate locations to create a perfect dome, as shown in Figure 5-48.

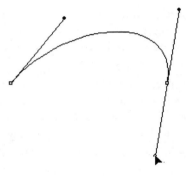

Figure 5-46: Press shift before dragging but then release to create a curve along the constraint axes. Notice how the points align horizontally.

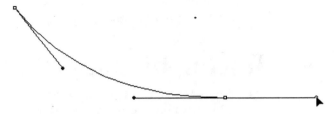

Figure 5-47: Begin the drag before pressing shift to align the Bézier control handles to the constraint axes without constraining the smooth point.

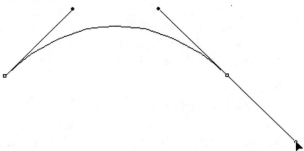

Figure 5-48: Shift-drag and shift-drag again to constrain both points and Bézier control handles to create a symmetrical dome.

- Click on a selected smooth point to delete a Bézier control handle, converting the smooth point to a corner point with one handle. Then click again at a different location to append a straight segment to the existing curved segment.

- Drag from a selected smooth point to change the length of the away-facing Bézier control handle. The two control handles will still obey the seesaw relationship but will no longer necessarily be the same length.

- Drag from a selected corner point to add a Bézier control handle. Then drag again at a different location to append a curved segment to the existing straight segment.

- Press OPTION and drag from a selected smooth point to redirect a Bézier control handle, converting the smooth point to a corner point with two independent handles. Then drag again at a different location to append a curved segment that meets the existing curved segment to form a cusp.

Tracing bitmapped images

Alas, not everyone can be a Rembrandt. Some of us are lucky to draw a straight line, much less triumph over the gamut of complex strategies inherent in the operation of the pen tool. Others can draw quite adequately with pencil and paper, but have problems making the transition to the computer-graphics environment.

If you fall into either of these categories, you can breathe a sigh of relief. Illustrator allows you to trace scanned images and artwork created in painting programs. It also automates the conversion process by providing a trace tool. Even skilled computer artists are well advised to sketch their ideas on paper or in a painting program before executing them in Adobe Illustrator.

Why trace a bitmap?

It is not easy to draw from scratch in Adobe Illustrator. Even if you draw exclusively with the freehand tool, you will frequently have to go back and edit your lines and shapes, point by point (as I'll discuss in the next chapter). Also, to build an image in Illustrator is to do just that: *build.* Heaps of mathematically defined lines and shapes must be combined and layered much like girders at a construction site.

On the other hand, the simple tools such as pencils and erasers that painting programs provide work just like their real-life counterparts. Your screen displays the results of your mouse movements instantaneously, letting you draw, see what you've drawn, and make alterations, all in the time it takes the appropriate neurons to fire in your brain.

But despite the many advantages of painting software, its single failing—the graininess of its output—is glaringly obvious, so much so that people who have never used a computer can immediately recognize a bitmapped image as computer-produced artwork. Object-oriented drawings, on the other hand, are smooth.

This jaggedness is particularly noticeable in black-and-white artwork. For example, the bitmapped fish in Figure 5-49 was fairly easy to create. It is well executed, but its jagged edges are far too obvious for it to be considered professional-quality artwork. Introducing shades of gray to the image softens much of its jaggedness, as shown in Figure 5-50 on the next page. But now the fish appears fuzzy and out of focus. No surprise, since grayscale scanning is more suited to photography than to line art.

Figure 5-49: A typically jagged black-and-white image created in MacPaint.

Figure 5-50: Gray pixels soften the edges, but make the image appear out of focus.

Figure 5-51: Tracing the bitmapped fish image lets me achieve this smooth, exemplary drawing.

The **Illustrator 5** Book

Only in a drawing application such as Adobe Illustrator can you create pristine line art. The fish in Figure 5-51, for example, required more time and effort to produce, but the result is a smooth, highly focused, professional-quality image.

By tracing a bitmapped image in a drawing program, you can have the best of both worlds. You can sketch your idea traditionally onto a piece of paper and then scan it into your computer, or you can sketch directly in a painting program. Either way, your sketch will be bitmapped. You can then import the sketch into Adobe Illustrator as a *tracing template* using the NEW... or OPEN... command, as discussed in the *Creating a new illustration* and *Swapping tracing templates* sections of Chapter 3. Then use Illustrator's drawing tools to convert the image to a collection of free-form lines and shapes.

The auto trace tool

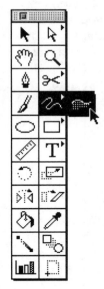

Illustrator's *auto trace tool*, which is accessible from the freehand tool slot, automates the process of tracing bitmapped artwork by outlining the borders of a template image with free-form paths. Typically, you operate the auto trace tool by clicking within six pixels of the portion of the template that you want to trace. Illustrator does the rest. The tool is easy to operate, certainly easier than tracing a template image by hand. But the results are predictably less precise and require more adjustments than paths created with the pen tool or even the freehand tool.

Figure 5-52: A black-and-white valentine image created in MacPaint.

Suppose that you used MacPaint or some other antiquated painting program to create the valentine shown in Figure 5-52. This image will act as your template. You can introduce the template to an illustration in either of two ways:

- Press the OPTION key and choose the NEW... command (⌘-⌥-N), select a template from the scrolling file list in the PLEASE OPEN TEMPLATE dialog box, and press RETURN.

- Choose the OPEN... command (⌘-O), select a template from the scrolling file list in the PLEASE OPEN ILLUSTRATION OR TEMPLATE dialog box, and press RETURN.

After you open the valentine template, it will appear grayed in the drawing area of the current window. The image is now ready to be traced with the auto trace tool. Click with the auto trace tool near the template image, as demonstrated by the location of the cross-shaped auto trace cursor in Figure 5-53. Notice that the cursor is within six pixels of the edge of the template. A few seconds after you click with the auto trace tool, Illustrator produces a closed path that traces the outline of the template. The auto trace tool always produces a closed path. Even if you were to click near the template image of a line, Illustrator will trace entirely around the line to create a long and very thin shape.

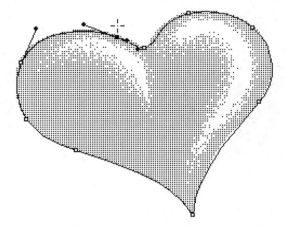

Figure 5-53: A point always appears at the location on the template nearest the spot at which you click.

The point on the template image nearest the place where you click with the auto trace tool becomes the first point in the traced path. Therefore, the location of your click plays a small but important role in determining how Illustrator traces your template. For instance, in Figure 5-53, the selected click point is an unnecessary point in the path. The valentine could be expressed without it. Also, if you look carefully, you will notice the auto trace path has not accurately traced the cleft in the top of the valentine. The cleft should be represented by a cusp (a corner point with two independent Bézier control handles); instead a smooth point occupies this spot. The auto trace path in Figure 5-54 is a truer representation of the template image. A corner point resides at the top of the shape and there are fewer un-necessary points. This is the result of repositioning the click point at the bottom of the shape (demonstrated by the location of the cursor the figure). Since the bottom of the valentine in the template forms a sharp tip, a corner point needs to exist there.

When tracing a template image, always click with the auto trace tool near a location on the template where a point is most likely to exist. In this way, you best aid Illustrator to produce the most efficient and accurate path possible.

Figure 5-54: Click near a corner of your template image to create the most accurate traced path.

File
New   ⌘N
Open...   ⌘O

Close   ⌘W
Save   ⌘S
Save As...

Place Art...
Import Styles...

Doc. Setup... ⌘⇧D
Page Setup...
Print...   ⌘P

Preferences   ▶

Quit   ⌘Q

Auto trace tolerance

Another way to create more accurate paths with the auto trace tool is to adjust the value for the "Freehand tolerance" option in the GENERAL PREFERENCES dialog box (⌘-K). This option affects the sensitivity of the auto trace tool in the same way that it affects the freehand tool. For example, a "Freehand tolerance" value of 0 instructs Illustrator to trace every single pixel of a bitmapped template. If you change the value to 10, the software ignores large jags in the outline of a template image and smooths out excessively imprecise portions of the template. Figure 5-55 shows the results of tracing a fish shape when the tolerance value is set to 0, 1, 2, 5, and 10. If you compare these images to those back in Figure 5-13 and 5-14, you will see that the tolerance value affects the performance of the auto trace and freehand tools very similarly. However, unlike with freehand tool tolerance, you should adjust the tolerance of the auto trace tool to compensate for inaccuracies in the image you are tracing, rather than inaccuracies in your personal drawing ability.

A "Freehand tolerance" value of 1 or 2 is best suited to most tracing template images. This is because when tracing it is better to have too many points than too few. Excessive points can always be deleted later, as explained in Chapter 6.

Tracing over gaps

The auto trace tool is most effective in tracing the borders between the black and white areas in a template. But it can also be used to trace gray areas and areas with broken or inconsistent outlines. Figure 5-56 on page 200 includes an enlarged view of the valentine template. Suppose this time that you intend to trace the white areas within the valentine that represent reflective highlights, giving the shape a three-dimensional quality. Click with the auto trace tool at each of the two cursor locations shown in the figure. (You may have to squint to see them. They're near the top of the valentine on either side.) Illustrator makes a valiant, though somewhat unattractive attempt to trace the template's loose pixels. This is a difficult task, since the auto trace tool normally looks for hard edges. Jumbles of dots are not conducive to point/path representation.

Figure 5-55: A bitmapped fish (top) and the results of tracing this image with tolerance values of 0, 1 (left side), 2, 5, and 10 (right side).

As luck and a little engineering would have it, Illustrator provides an "Auto trace over gap" option in the GENERAL PREFER-ENCES dialog box (see *Setting preferences* section of Chapter 3) that is designed specifically for tracing inconsistencies in the borders of a template image. To view this option, choose the GENERAL... command from the PREFERENCES submenu from the EDIT menu (⌘-K).

Figure 5-56: Tracing the loose pixels
inside the valentine template with the
"Auto trace over gap" option set to 0 pixels.

You can enter either 0, 1, or 2 in the "Auto trace over gap" option box. This value is measured in pixels. The default value 0 instructs Illustrator to trace around a template image from one black pixel to the next. If even a single white pixel separates one black area from another, the traced path will not pass over the gap. But as long as a corner of one black pixel touches the corner of another, both pixels will be traced. The path in Figure 5-56 was traced with an "Auto trace over gap" value of 0.

I produced the paths in Figures 5-57 and 5-58 by clicking at the same locations with the auto trace tool as in the previous figure. The only difference is in the "Auto trace over gap" value. In Figure 5-57, I set the gap value to 1. A gap distance of 1 specifies that black areas separated by no more than one white pixel are to be traced as a single shape. In Figure 5-58 the "Auto trace over gap" option has been raised to 2. This instructs Illustrator to ignore as many as two white pixels between any two black areas in a template.

The **Illustrator** 5 Book

Figure 5-57: Tracing the loose pixels inside the valentine template with the "Auto trace over gap" option set to 1 pixel.

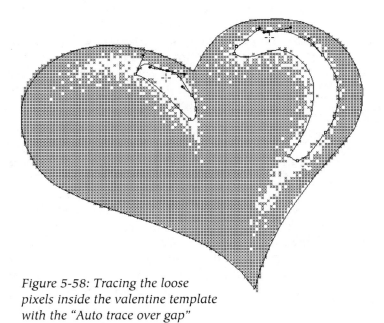

Figure 5-58: Tracing the loose pixels inside the valentine template with the "Auto trace over gap" option set to 2 pixels.

Like all PREFERENCES dialog box settings, both the "Freehand tolerance" and "Auto trace over gap" values are saved with the Adobe Illustrator 5.0 Prefs file. Each will affect all future illustrations until a new value is entered. Also, neither the tolerance value nor the gap value for a path can be altered after the path is created, since Illustrator calculates the points for a path only once, immediately after you click with the auto trace tool. Therefore, to create each path in Figures 5-57 and 5-58, I had to change the gap value and trace a new path.

Tracing a portion of an image

In addition to being able to click with the auto trace tool, you can also drag with the tool. By dragging, you specify that you want to trace only a fraction of a template image at a time.

The first example in Figure 5-59 on the following page is a new bitmapped image as it appears in MacPaint. The image is that of a large letter O. In the next few pages, I will demonstrate how to trace details from both the outer and inner borders of this template.

The lower left example in the figure shows how you can begin dragging outside and to the left of the image, as indicated by the location of the cross-shaped cursor. Then drag directly to the outer bottom side of the image—shown by the arrowhead cursor—and release. The location at which you begin dragging determines the location of the first point in the auto trace path; the release point determines the location of the last point. Only that portion of the image between the click and release points is traced.

The top right example in Figure 5-59 displays the portion of the image that was traced. This may come as a surprise, since the auto trace tool has produced a path that traces the longer of two distances around the O. Illustrator always traces the outside of an image in a clockwise direction; the opposite is true when it traces the inside of a template. For example, drag from the inside left edge of the image to the inside right edge of the image, as demonstrated by the click and release points shown in the third example of Figure 5-59. The final example in that figure shows the results. Because you traced the inside of a template image, the auto trace path was produced in a counterclockwise direction, running opposite to the outer path.

The **Illustrator 5** Book

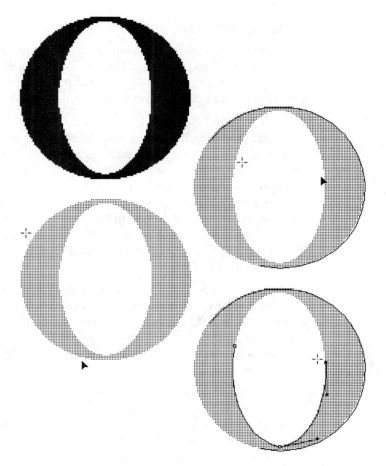

Figure 5-59: Tracing specific portions of a template image by dragging with the auto trace tool.

The auto trace tool traces gray areas (the template) surrounded by white (what's outside the template) in a clockwise direction; it traces white areas surrounded by black in a counterclockwise direction. If you forget this bit of wisdom, and a drag ends up producing the opposite effect you expected, just choose UNDO (⌘-Z) and reverse the direction of your drag.

Extending a line

As with the freehand tool, Illustrator allows you to extend an open path with the auto trace tool. This does not mean that you can extend any old line. A template image must exist within six pixels of the endpoint of the existing path from which you drag with the auto trace tool.

Extending a path with the auto trace tool is useful primarily for lengthening or closing paths that were originally created by dragging with the same tool, as described in the previous section. Suppose, for example, that you intend to trace half of a template image with the "Auto trace over gap" option set to 0, and the other half with a gap value of 2. You would drag with the auto trace tool to create the first half of the shape, change the gap value in the GENERAL PREFERENCES dialog box, and then drag from one endpoint in the auto trace path to the other to close the path.

The auto trace tool also creates smooth and corner points in the same manner as the freehand tool. Regardless of its original identity, an endpoint will be converted to a smooth point when you drag from it with the auto trace tool. This is true even when the point appears to be a corner, a fact that may affect future manipulations as discussed in the next chapter.

To make this point a corner point, press and hold the OPTION key before you begin your drag. If you are closing a path, the endpoint at which you release will also be a smooth point unless you press OPTION before ending your drag and hold the key down until after you release the mouse button.

Auto trace drawbacks

The auto trace tool is not a precise drawing tool. More often than not, you will have to spend a good deal of time reshaping your traced paths, as described in the next chapter. Perhaps the auto trace tool's greatest drawback, however, is that it can trace only one path at a time. In the rival drawing application Aldus FreeHand, for example, you can marquee a bitmapped image with the trace tool to create several paths at a time.

Well, as it turns out, Adobe markets a utility called Streamline that converts entire bitmapped images to object-oriented drawings at a much higher level of quality than either the FreeHand or Illustrator auto trace tools can match. For example, Streamline can trace several colors in a single pass and automatically fill paths after it creates them. Also, rather than always tracing with closed paths, Streamline can create and stroke open paths to repesent line art.

Adobe sometimes bundles Streamline with Illustrator 5.0. But if you didn't receive Streamline with your package, you can purchase version 3.0 through a discount house such as MacConnection, (800) 800-3333, MacWarehouse, (800) 255-6227, or MacZone, (800) 248-0800. When last I checked, all three were asking around $120. MacConnection is open during normal business hours; the other two are open 24 hours a day, seven days a week.

CHAPTER

RESHAPING PATHS THAT FRANKLY NEED HELP

After you create an object in Illustrator, it is by no means permanent. At any stage in the drawing process, you can adjust it to better suit your needs. If you do most of your drawing with the freehand, brush, and auto trace tools, nearly all your paths are going to need adjustment. If you draw primarily with the pen tool, adjustments will be less common. But either way, adjusting a path is like painting over the same area on a canvas—it's necessarily a fine-tuning process.

This chapter examines how to *reshape* both geometric and free-form paths. To reshape a path is to alter the placement or identity of its points and segments. The adjustment of whole paths is discussed later in Chapter 11, *Transforming and Duplicating Objects*.

Selecting elements

Before you can reshape a path, you must *select* one of more of its *elements*—a point, a segment, or just about any other small or large portion of an illustration. Selecting an element in Illustrator is not unlike selecting an element in some other object-oriented program on the Macintosh. Merely position your selection tool cursor over part of an image and click. Points and Bézier control handles display to indicate that the next action you perform will affect the selected element.

The selection tool

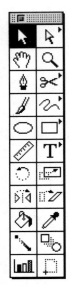

You can perform most manipulations covered in this chapter with one of the three *selection tools*—the selection (or arrow) tool, the direct-selection tool, and the group-selection tool. Clicking on a point or segment with any of these tools selects part or all of the path. The tools differ in the extent of the selection they make.

The standard *selection tool* is displayed in the first slot on the left side of the toolbox and is the most straightforward of the bunch. When this tool is active, you can click on any element of a path to select all points and segments in the path. In other words, if you click on any part of the path, you select the entire path. You can then move the entire path, apply a transformation, or perform several other manipulations that affect the path as a whole. You cannot reshape the segments in a path when selecting with the selection tool; therefore no Bézier control handles display, as shown in Figure 6-1. Clicking on a combined object, such as a group or compound path, selects all paths that make up the object.

Clicking on a path with the selection tool not only selects the path but also *deselects* all previously selected paths. To select multiple paths, click on the first path, then press SHIFT and click on each additional path you want to select.

The **Illustrator 5** Book

Figure 6-1: Click on any part of a path with the standard selection tool to select the entire path.

Another way to select multiple paths is to *marquee* them. Drag at an empty portion of your screen to create a rectangular marquee with a dotted outline. One corner of the marquee is positioned at the location at which you begin to drag; the opposite corner follows the movements of your cursor as you drag. All paths that fall within the boundaries of the marquee, even if only partially, will become selected when you release the mouse button. If any path in a combined object falls inside a marquee, the entire combined object becomes selected.

Marqueeing can be combined with SHIFT-clicking to select multiple paths. You can also marquee while pressing SHIFT, which adds the marqueed objects to an existing set of selected elements.

These and other ways to select elements with the selection tool are summarized in the following list:

- Click on a path, combined object, text block, or link to select that object and deselect the previous selection.

- Drag on an empty portion of the drawing area to create a marquee. All objects even partially inside the marquee become selected, and the previous selection becomes deselected.

- Press SHIFT and either click or marquee deselected objects to add them to the current selection. (If you SHIFT-click or SHIFT-marquee an object that is already selected, it will become deselected, as described in the *Deselecting elements* section.)

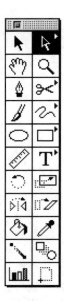

The direct-selection tool

The *direct-selection tool* is displayed by default in the first slot on the right of the toolbox. With the direct-selection tool selected, you can click on any element to select it. If you click on a point, you select the point; if you click on a segment, you select the segment. Click on any element of a group or combined object to select that element independent of the group.

Different elements have different ways of showing that they are selected with the direct-selection tool. For example, when you select a point, it appears as a small black square, as shown in the first example of Figure 6-2. All Bézier control handles associated with the selected point and the two neighboring segments also appear. Deselected points in the path appear as small hollow squares. When a segment is selected, only the Bézier control handles for that segment are visible. Unless some point in the path is also selected, all points appear as hollow squares.

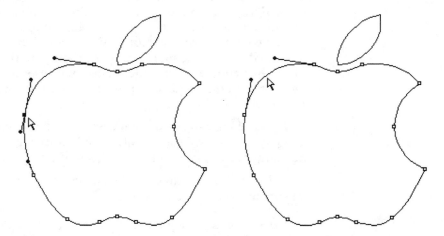

Figure 6-2: Select a single point (left) and a single segment (right) by clicking with the direct-selection tool. The location of each click is indicated by the hollow arrow tool cursor.

You can also drag with the direct-selection tool to marquee a number of elements. All points and segments that lie, at least partially, will become selected; while all points and segments completely outside the marquee will remain or become deselected, as shown in Figure 6-3.

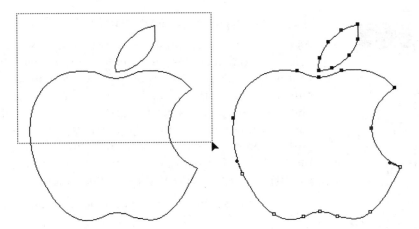

Figure 6-3: All elements that lie within the boundary of the marquee (left) becomes selected (right).

These and other ways to select elements with the direct-selection tool are summarized in the following list:

- Click on a point or segment to select it—even if the element is part of a group, combined object, text object, or link—and deselect the previous selection.

- Drag on an empty portion of the drawing area to create a marquee. All points and segments inside the marquee become selected, and the previous selection becomes deselected.

- Press SHIFT and either click or marquee deselected elements to add them to the current selection. (If you SHIFT-click or SHIFT-marquee an element that is already selected, it will become deselected, as described in the *Deselecting elements* section.)

- Press the OPTION key (to access the group-selection tool) and click on a point or segment to select a whole path in a group. Press OPTION and double-click to select a group within a group; OPTION-triple-click to select the group that contains that group, and so on.

- Press OPTION and marquee or SHIFT-OPTION-click elements to select multiple paths inside groups.

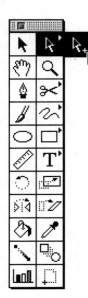

The group-selection tool

As noted in the preceding list, pressing OPTION while using the direct-selection tool accesses the *group-selection tool*. The group-selection tool is also the alternate tool for the top right tool slot. With it, you can select paths that are part of combined objects. For example, click once on a path within a group to select it. Click twice on the same path to select the group, compound path, or mask to which the path belongs. Each successive click will add the next larger group to the selection. For more information on selecting paths inside groups, see the *Selecting paths within groups* section of Chapter 11.

You can use the group-selection tool as follows:

• Click on a point or segment to select a whole path in a group. Double-click to select a group within a group. Click a third time to select the group that contains that group, and so on.

• Drag on an empty portion of the drawing area to create a marquee. All paths even partially inside the marquee become selected, and all previously selected objects become deselected.

• Press SHIFT and either click or marquee deselected paths to add them to the current selection. (If you SHIFT-click or SHIFT-marquee an path that is already selected, it will become deselected, as described in the *Deselecting elements* section.)

• Press the OPTION key (to access the direct-selection tool) and click on a point or segment to select it independently of its path and deselect the other stuff.

• Press the OPTION key and drag on an empty portion of the drawing area to create a marquee. All points and segments inside the marquee become selected independently of their paths, and the previous selection becomes deselected.

Selecting all elements

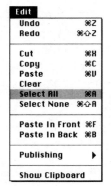

The only remaining selection method is the SELECT ALL command in the EDIT menu (⌘-A). When chosen, this command selects every point, segment, and other element in the current illustration (unless a text block is active with a text tool, in which case SELECT ALL highlights all text in the current story).

The **Illustrator 5** Book

Arbitrary selection notes

All those points and colored outlines that Illustrator uses to show an object is selected can really get in your face. Fortunately, in Illustrator 5.0, you can get rid of selection outlines by choosing the HIDE EDGES command from the VIEW menu (⌘-⇧-H). From that point on, no selection outline will appear, even if you select a different object. To again see the selection outlines, you have to choose SHOW EDGES from the VIEW menu or again press COMMAND-SHIFT-H.

I know it has nothing to do with what I was just talking about, but to temporarily access the most recently used of the three selection tools at any time, press and hold the COMMAND key. Releasing COMMAND returns you to the active tool. Press COMMAND-TAB to toggle between the standard selection tool and the tool currently displayed in the top right slot. If the tool in the top right slot isn't the one you want, just hold down the OPTION key and you're in business.

Deselecting elements

Sometimes you will want to *deselect* elements to prevent them from being affected by a command or mouse operation. To deselect all elements, simply click with one of the selection tools on an empty portion of the drawing area. Performing any one of the following actions also deselects all currently selected elements:

- Select an element that was not previously selected by clicking on it with one of the selection tools.

- Click or drag with one of the geometric path tools.

- Click or drag with a free-form drawing tool (freehand, brush pen, or auto trace) on an empty portion of the drawing area.

- Click or drag with the type tool on an empty portion of the drawing area.

- Click or drag with the graph tool.

- Place or paste any graphic element.

- Choose SELECT NONE (⌘-⇧-A) from the EDIT menu.

Deselecting individual elements

You don't have to deselect every element in an illustration. You can also deselect specific elements without affecting other elements in a selection.

To deselect a single selected element, SHIFT-click on it with the direct-selection tool. You can also deselect any selected elements by marqueeing them while pressing the SHIFT key.

If you SHIFT-click on a selected path with the selection or group-selection tool, you deselect every point and segment in that path. Likewise, SHIFT-marqueeing with either tool deselects all surrounded paths that are either partially or entirely selected.

Moving elements

The most common method for reshaping a path is to move one or more of its elements. Illustrator allows you to move selected points independently of deselected points in a path. You can also move segments, as well as the Bézier control handles associated with those segments, to alter the curvature of a path. The next few pages explain all aspects of moving and dragging elements in Adobe Illustrator.

Moving points

To move one or more points in a path, select the points you want to move and drag any one of them. All selected points will move the same distance and direction. When you move a point while a neighboring point remains stationary, the segment between the two points shrinks or stretches in length to accommodate the change in distance, as displayed in Figure 6-4.

When you move a point, any accompanying Bézier control handles move with it. Thus, a curved segment must not only shrink or stretch, but also bend to accommodate the movement of a point. Segments located between two deselected points or two selected points remain unchanged during a move, as demonstrated in Figure 6-5.

Figure 6-4: Dragging the selected point on left stretches the segments between the point and its deselected, stationary neighbors, as shown on right.

Figure 6-5: Dragging at any selected point in a shape (left) moves all selected points an identical distance and direction (right). Notice that a segment bordered on both sides by selected points is not reshaped.

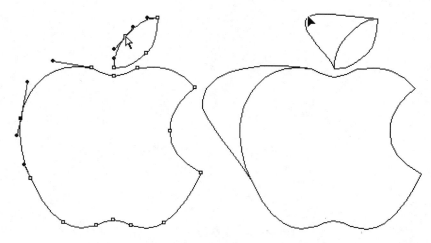

Figure 6-6: You can move multiple points even when selected points reside in different paths.

While you move an element, both its previous and current locations are displayed. This useful feature allows you to gauge the full effect of a move as it progresses. Also, when you drag a single selected point, Illustrator displays the point, the Bézier control handles associated with the two neighboring segments, and any neighboring deselected points, as shown in Figure 6-4. When dragging multiple points, no points or handles display, as demonstrated in Figures 6-5 and 6-6. This helps to avoid some of the confusion that might result from otherwise viewing hoards of Bézier control handles moving all over the screen during a complex reshaping maneuver.

Constrained movements

To constrain the movement of selected points to an angle that is a multiple of 45°, press the SHIFT key after beginning your drag and hold it down until after you release the mouse button. (If you press and hold SHIFT before beginning your drag, you will deselect the selected point on which you click, causing Illustrator to ignore your drag.) Horizontal, vertical, and diagonal movements are all multiples of 45°.

The effects of pressing the SHIFT key can be altered by rotating the *constraint axes* using the "Constrain angle" option in the PREF-ERENCES dialog box, introduced in the *Setting preferences* section of

⚛ The **Illustrator 5** Book

Chapter 3. The constraint axes, displayed in Figure 6-7, specify the eight directions in which an element can be moved. By default, these directions include the following:

- Right (0°)
- Diagonally up and to the right (45°)
- Straight up (90°)
- Diagonally up and to the left (135°)
- Left (180°)
- Diagonally down and to the left (225° or –135°)
- Straight down (270° or –90°)
- Diagonally down and to the right (315° or –45°).

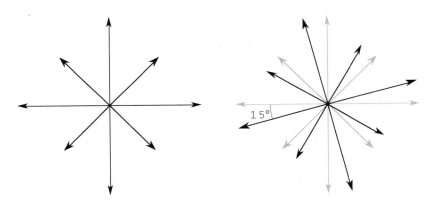

Figure 6-7: The default constraint axes (left) and the axes as they appear when rotated 15° (right).

Each direction differs from another by an angle of 45°. By entering a number between –360 and 360 for the "Constrain angle" option, you can rotate the contraint axes. The second example in Figure 6-7 displays the effect of rotating the axes 15°. If you SHIFT-drag an element under these conditions, your movements will be constrained to 15°, 60°, 105°, 150°, 195° (–165°), 240° (–120°), 285° (–75°), or 330° (–30°). Horizontal and vertical SHIFT-dragging will not be possible until you return the "Constrain angle" value to 0.

Exercise caution when altering the "Constrain angle" option, since doing so also affects the creation of geometric paths, text, and charts, as explained in the section *Geometric paths at an angle* in Chapter 5, as well as the performance of transformation tools, as explained in the section *Transforming rotated objects* in Chapter 11.

Snapping

While dragging an element, you may find that it has a tendency to move sharply toward another element. Called *snapping*, this effect is Illustrator's way of ensuring that elements belonging together are flush against each other to form a perfect fit. When you drag an element within two pixels of any point on your drawing area, your cursor will snap to the point, so that both point and cursor occupy an identical horizontal and vertical space. At the moment the snap occurs, your cursor will change from a filled arrowhead to a hollow arrowhead as in Figure 6-8. For example, you might drag the center point of a rectangle until it snaps to the center point of a deselected ellipse. In this way, both shapes would be centered about the same point.

Figure 6-8: Your cursor changes to a hollow arrowhead when snapping an element to a stationary point.

Your cursor will snap to stationary points as well as to the previous locations of points that are currently being moved. However, snapping occurs not only at points in a standard path or text block. Your cursor will also snap to any portion of a *guide object*, created using the MAKE command in the GUIDE submenu from the OBJECT menu (⌘-5) or by dragging from the horizontal or vertical ruler. Both guides and rulers are the subject of Chapter 11.

You can turn Illustrator's snapping feature on and off by clicking on the "Snap to point" check box in the GENERAL PREFERENCES dialog box. When this option is deselected, dragged elements will not snap to points or guides.

Dragging segments

You can also reshape a path by dragging at its segments. When you drag a straight segment, its neighboring segments stretch or shrink to accommodate the change in distance, as shown in the first example in Figure 6-9. However, when you drag a curved segment, you stretch only that segment. The effect is rather like pulling on a rubber band extended between two nails (see the second example below).

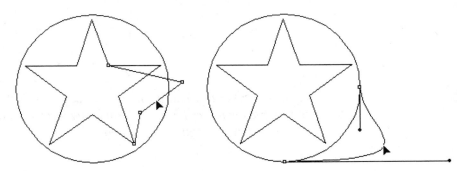

Figure 6-9: Dragging a straight segment (left) and a curved segment (right).

Figure 6-10 on the next page shows a single curved segment being stretched various distances and directions. The longer the drag, the more the segment has to bend. Notice that the Bézier control handles associated with the segment automatically extend and retract as you drag. Also, each handle moves along an imaginary line, constant with its original inclination. The angle of a Bézier control handle cannot be changed by dragging at a segment; this guarantees that the curved segment moves in alignment with neighboring stationary segments.

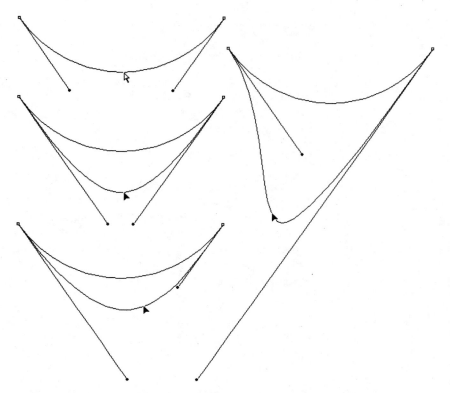

Figure 6-10: When you drag at a curved segment, each Bézier control handle moves back and forth along a constant axis determined by its original inclination.

To move a Bézier control handle out of alignment with its original orientation, you must drag the handle itself, as described in the *Dragging Bézier control handles* section, later in this chapter.

When dragging a segment, drag on the middle of the segment, approximately equidistant from both of its points. This method provides the best leverage and keeps you from distorting the segment in odd and unpredictable directions.

Using arrow keys

Another way to move a selected element is to press one of the four arrow keys (↑, ←, ↓, →). Each arrow key moves a selection in the direction of the arrow. The → key, for example, moves the selection to the right.

The distance that a single keystroke moves a selected element is determined by the "Cursor key" value specified in the GENERAL PREFERENCES dialog box, as introduced in the *Setting preferences* section of Chapter 3. The value that you enter is measured in centimeters, inches, or points, depending on the currently selected "Ruler units" option (also included in the PREFERENCES dialog box).

You can use arrow keys to move points as well as both straight and curved segments. Arrow keys cannot be used to move a Bézier control handle (as described in the *Dragging Bézier control handles* section later in this chapter), except in association with a curved segment, as described in the previous section.

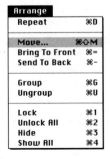 Unlike Canvas and FreeHand, Illustrator 5.0 provides no grid to regulate the movement of elements. You can fake a grid, however, by entering the desired grid increment into the "Cursor key distance" option. Then use the arrow keys to precisely position elements.

The arrow keys move the current selection in relation to the constraint axes. If you rotate the axes, as described in the *Constrained movements* section earlier in this chapter, you affect the direction at which a selected element moves. For example, if you enter 15° for the "Constrain angle" option in the GENERAL PREFERENCES dialog box, pressing the → key moves the selection in a 15° direction, pressing ↑ moves it in a 105° direction, and so on.

Using the Move dialog box

You can also specify the movement of selected elements numerically, via the MOVE dialog box shown in Figure 6-11 on the following page. Illustrator 5.0 provides two ways to access this dialog:

- Choose the MOVE... command from the EDIT menu (⌘-⇧-M).
- Press the OPTION key and click on the selection tool slot in the palette.

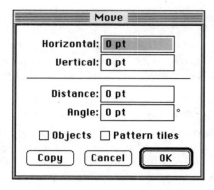

Figure 6-11: The Move dialog box allows you to specify a distance and a direction by which to move selected elements.

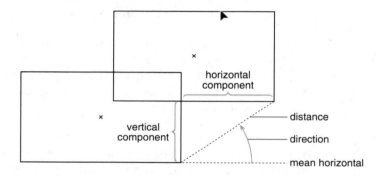

Figure 6-12: A diagram illustrating the distance and direction (angle) of a move.

To understand the options in this dialog, you need to understand the two basic components of a move: *distance* and *direction*. Distance is measured by tracking a specific point or other element in a selection. Figure 6-12 demonstrates the distance measured from a point in a rectangle at the shape's original location to the same point in the rectangle at its present location. Illustrator measures direction as an angle in degrees. As shown in the figure, this angle is measured between the *mean horizontal* and an imaginary distance line.

To use the MOVE dialog, enter values for *either* the "Distance" and "Angle" options *or* the "Horizontal" and "Vertical" options. The "Distance," "Horizontal," and "Vertical" values represent distances that are measured in centimeters, inches, or points, depending on the currently selected "Ruler units" option in the PREFERENCES dialog box. The "Angle" value represents the direction, measured in degrees. To move a selected element, enter a direct distance value in the "Distance" option box and a direction value in the "Angle" option box. A positive "Distance" value moves the selection in the direction specified; a negative value moves the selection in the opposite direction.

Unfortunately, figuring out the direction of a prospective move can be very difficult. After all, few of us have protractors pasted to our screens. You may find it easier to specify the horizontal and vertical components of a move, also displayed in Figure 6-12. You can enter positive and negative values for the "Horizontal" and "Vertical" options. As you do so, the "Distance" and "Angle" options will automatically update to reflect your changes.

Use the "Horizontal" and "Vertical" options as follows:

- Enter a positive "Horizontal" value to move the selection right.
- Enter a negative "Horizontal" value to move the selection left.
- Enter a positive "Vertical" value to move the selection upward.
- Enter a negative "Vertical" value to move the selection downward.
- Enter 0 in the "Horizontal" option to specify a purely vertical move.
- Enter 0 in the "Vertical" option to specify a purely horizontal move.

If a path in the current selection is stroked or filled with a tile pattern (as discussed in Chapter 8), select the "Pattern tiles" option to move the tile pattern along with the selection.

You can confirm your movement specifications by clicking on either the OK or COPY button. Clicking COPY retains any selected element at its original location while creating a *clone* at the location specified in the MOVE dialog. (For more information about clones, see the *Cloning objects* section of Chapter 11.)

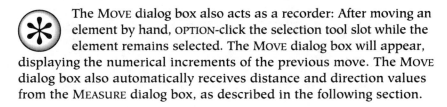 The MOVE dialog box also acts as a recorder: After moving an element by hand, OPTION-click the selection tool slot while the element remains selected. The MOVE dialog box will appear, displaying the numerical increments of the previous move. The MOVE dialog box also automatically receives distance and direction values from the MEASURE dialog box, as described in the following section.

The MOVE dialog moves the current selection in relation to the constraint axes. If you rotate the axes, as described in the *Constrained movements* section earlier in this chapter, you affect the direction in which a selected element is moved. For example, if you enter 15° for the "Constrain angle" option in the GENERAL PREFERENCES dialog box, a horizontal (0°) move becomes a 15° move, a vertical (90°) move becomes a 105° move, and so on.

Measuring a move

In general, you will probably find using the MOVE dialog box less convenient than moving elements by dragging and pressing arrow keys. Although these methods lack the degree of precision offered in the MOVE dialog box, they provide immediate on-screen reactions. Manual manipulations are more direct and thus more likely to produce aesthetic results.

Nonetheless, Illustrator provides a tool that makes the MOVE dialog box more useful by making it possible for you to precisely determine, and thereby predict, the dialog's results. This is the *measure tool*, by default the sixth tool on the left in your palette. The measure tool is used to measure the distance between two points. To operate it, select the tool and click at each of two different screen locations or drag between them. The INFO palette will display, as shown in Figure 6-13, listing the distance and direction between the two points, as well as the vertical and horizontal components of the measure. This information automatically appears in the MOVE dialog box if you immediately choose the MOVE... command (⌘-⇧-5) from the Arrange menu or OPTION-click the selection tool slot.

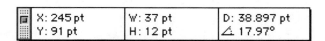

| X: 245 pt | W: 37 pt | D: 38.897 pt |
| Y: 91 pt | H: 12 pt | ∠ 17.97° |

Figure 6-13: The Info palette box displays the distance and direction between two points clicked with the measure tool.

For example, suppose that you want to move an element the exact distance and direction shown in Figure 6-11. With the measure tool, you first click on a selected element at its present location, then click at the location to which you want to move it. The INFO palette will display, listing the distance and direction between the first and second clicks of the measure tool. Also listed are the horizontal and vertical components of that distance. The INFO palette shown in Figure 6-13 tells us that if we were to move an element 37 points to the right and 12 points up, we would arrive at the same location as moving it 38.897 points in a 16.97° direction.

Incidentally, the MEASURE dialog works by first determining the horizontal and vertical components of the distance. The directional distance is then derived using the Pythagorean theorem:

$$a^2 + b^2 = c^2$$

where a and b are the horizontal and vertical components and c is the directional distance; hence the directional accuracy to $\frac{1}{1,000}$ of a point.

Having made a highly accurate measurement, you can now hide the INFO palette by choosing the HIDE INFO command from the WINDOWS menu (⌘-⋀-I) or clicking on the close box in the palette title bar. Then choose the MOVE... command (⌘-⇧-5) to display the same information in the MOVE dialog box. Press RETURN to initiate the measured movement.

The measure tool is best employed to measure the distance between existing points or guides in the drawing area. However, it will measure this distance only if the "Snap to point" check box in the GENERAL PREFERENCES dialog box is turned on. If this option is turned off, the measure tool measures the distance between your exact click locations, which may not accurately represent the distance between the points.

The INFO palette also displays the current position of your cursor in terms of the x and y coordinates. The x value is the horizontal distance from the bottom left corner of the artboard; the y value is the vertical distance from the same point.

Dragging Bézier control handles

The only element that I've so far neglected to move is the Bézier control handle. I save it until last because it is the most difficult element to manipulate. As I hope you recall from the previous chapter, Bézier control handles are the elements that define the arc of a segment as it exits or enters a point. Regardless of the identity of their points, you can move Bézier control handles in much the same way that you move points. To display a Bézier control handle, you can either select the point to which a handle belongs or select the segment it controls. You then drag the handle. Bézier control handles cannot be moved using an arrow key or the MOVE dialog box, except as a result of moving a selected curved segment.

Figures 6-14 through 6-18 feature four smooth points that are located in the exact same relative positions. From one figure to the next, only the numbered Bézier control handles have been moved. However, these simple adjustments have a dramatic impact on the appearance of each path. The handles have been numbered so you can see exactly how each handle is relocated from one path to the next. For the record, handle number 1 controls the left segment, handles 2 and 4 control the middle segment, and handle 3 controls the right segment.

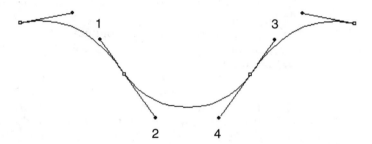

Figure 6-14: A path composed of four smooth points and three selected segments.

Moving one Bézier control handle for a smooth point causes the other handle for that point to move in the opposite direction. Hence, the two handles of a smooth point form a constant lever. Compare Figure 6-15 on the following page with Figure 6-14 above. In Figure 6-15, handles 3 and 4 have been moved only slightly. Handles 1 and 2, however, have been moved dramatically. I dragged handle 1 in a clockwise sweep, sending handle 2 upward. Figure 6-16 shows the path as it appears during the drag. I've inserted a gray line representing the motion of the drag to clarify the figure.

The **Illustrator 5** Book

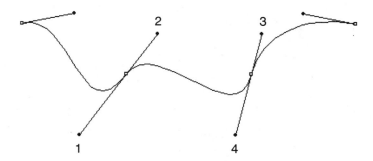

Figure 6-15: The same path after having dragged handle 1 in a clockwise sweep.

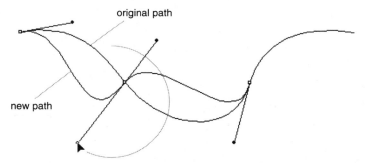

Figure 6-16: The act of dragging handle 1 shown in progress.

In Figure 6-15, handle 2 forces the center segment to ascend as it exits the left smooth point. But because of handle 4, the segment also ascends as it enters the right smooth point. So, somewhere between the two points, the segment has to change direction. Handles 2 and 4 pull at the beginning and at the end of the segment, respectively. The more the handles move from the center segment and away from each other, the more desperately the segment stretches to keep up, as is shown in Figure 6-17. Here, both handles 2 and 4 have been moved far away from each other. The result is a segment that bulges out in three directions—left, right, and downward. The final example in Figure 6-18, shows that there is essentially no limitation to the distance you can drag a Bézier control handle from its point, nor to how severely you can stretch a curved segment. The segment will always stretch to keep up, turning around only when necessary to meet the demands of the opposite point and its Bézier control handle.

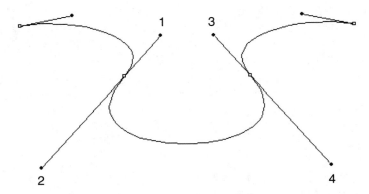

Figure 6-17: Dragging handles 2 and 4 far away from each other forces the center segment to bulge outward.

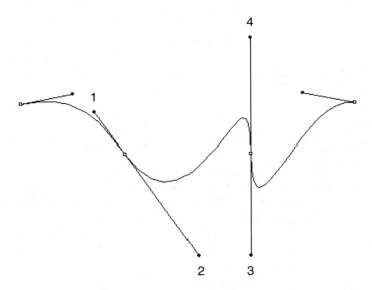

Figure 6-18: There is no limit to the extent that you can drag a handle or stretch a segment.

However, dragging Bézier control handles is not so much a question of what can you do as when you should do it. One of the most common problems new users have with Adobe Illustrator is trying to

The **Illustrator 5** Book

determine the placement of Bézier control handles. Several rules have been developed over the years, but the best are the *all-or-nothing rule* and the *30% rule*. The all-or-nothing rule states that every segment in your path should be associated with either two Bézier control handles or none at all. In other words, no segment should rely on only one control handle to determine its curvature. In the 30% rule, the distance from any Bézier control handle to its point should be approximately 30% the length of the segment.

The top path in Figure 6-19 violates the all-or-nothing rule. Its two curved segments are controlled by only one handle apiece, resulting in weak, shallow arcs. Such curves are to be avoided at all costs. The second example obeys the all-or-nothing rule. As the rule states, its straight segment is associated with no handle and the two curved segments have two handles apiece. The result is a full-figured, properly pumped-up dome, a credit to any illustration.

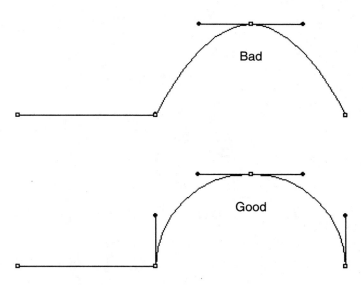

Figure 6-19: The all-or-nothing rule states that every curved segment should be controlled by two handles, one for each of its points.

The first path in Figure 6-20 violates the 30% rule. The handles for the central point are much too long, about 60% the length of their segments, and the two outer handles are too short, about 15% the length of their segments. The result is an ugly, misshapen mess. In the second example, the two handles belonging to the left segment are each about 30% of the length of the segment. The right segment is shorter, so its handles are shorter as well. This path is smooth and consistent in curvature, giving it a naturalistic appearance.

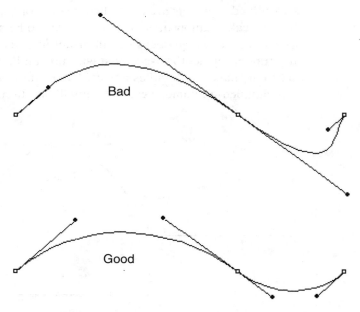

Bad

Good

Figure 6-20: The 30% rule states that every Bézier control handle should extend about 30% the length of its segment.

Moving points and adjusting control handles are fundamental ways to change the shape of a path. But sometimes, no matter how long you spend adjusting the placement of its points or the curvature of its segments, a path fails to meet the requirements of your illustration. In such a case, you may want to expand the path by adding points, or simplify the path by deleting points.

The **Illustrator 5** Book

Adding, deleting, and converting elements

The number and identity of points and segments in a path is forever subject to change. Whether closed or open, a path can be reshaped by adding, deleting, and converting points. In turn, adding or deleting a point forces the addition or deletion of a segment. The conversion of a point, from corner to smooth or from smooth to corner, frequently converts a segment, from curved to straight or from straight to curved. The following pages describe how all of these reshaping techniques can be applied to any existing path.

Adding elements to the end of a path

As discussed in Chapter 5, *Drawing and Tracing Paths*, a point associated with fewer than two segments is open-ended. Such a point is always located at one end or the other of a line. For this reason, an open-ended point is called an *endpoint*. An open path always has two endpoints. A closed path contains no endpoint, since each point in a shape is connected to another.

The selected endpoint in an active path is waiting for a segment to be drawn from it. To check if an open path is active, select the pen tool and move the cursor into the drawing area. If the active cursor appears, the selected path is active. If the passive cursor appears, all paths are passive. To *activate* an endpoint in a passive path so that a new segment can be drawn from it, click or drag the point with the pen tool, depending on the identity of the endpoint and whether you want the next segment to be straight or curved. (See the *Pen tool summary* section of Chapter 5 for more specific instructions.) Then, you can click or drag anywhere else on your screen to create a segment between the selected endpoint and the newly created point. Following this, your original endpoint will be bound by segments on both sides, no longer fit to be called an endpoint. It must relinquish this title to the newest point in the line.

You can also use this technique to close an existing path. Just select one endpoint, click or drag it with the pen tool to activate it, then click or drag on the remaining endpoint. A segment is drawn between the two endpoints, closing the path to form a shape and eliminating both endpoints by converting them to interior points.

You can also lengthen an open path by drawing from one of its endpoints with the freehand tool or, if the path touches a portion of a tracing template, the auto trace tool. You can close a path by dragging from one endpoint to the other with either tool.

Finally, you can join any two existing lines to form one longer line by activating an endpoint of the first path and then clicking or dragging with the pen tool on an endpoint of the second path. If you are using the freehand or auto trace tool, simply drag from an endpoint of one path to the endpoint of another.

Adding elements within a path

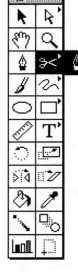

I have demonstrated how you can add points to the end of an existing line. But there will be many times when you want to add points in the middle of a path. This process requires a tool I have not discussed so far, the *add-anchor-point tool*. You can select the add-anchor-point tool, which appears as the pen tool with a plus sign, by dragging from the scissors tool slot in the toolbox.

First, select the path to which you want to add a point. Then click with the add-anchor-point tool on some segment in the path. (Do *not* click on a point.) A new point will appear at this location. The segment to which the point was added is broken into two segments.

Figure 6-21 on the following page shows an ordinary circle composed of four smooth points. Suppose that you want to change the circle into a crescent by adding points within the path. The following steps describe one way to perform this task:

1. Using the add-anchor-point tool, click at each of two similar locations on each of the right-hand segments. These points appear as selected in Figure 6-21.

2. Press and hold the COMMAND key to access the direct-selection tool (press COMMAND-TAB and/or OPTION if one of the other selection tools displays). Drag at the rightmost point, moving it toward and beyond the center of the shape, as shown in Figure 6-22.

3. Release COMMAND to redisplay the add-anchor-point tool cursor. Click in the middle of each of the two segments between the crescent tips and the dragged point. These points are shown as selected in Figure 6-23 on page 234.

The **Illustrator 5** Book

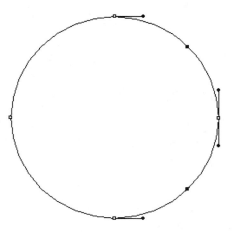

Figure 6-21: Add a point in the middle of each of the right-hand segments of an ungrouped circle.

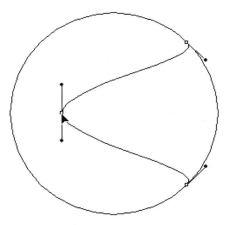

Figure 6-22: Drag the rightmost point toward the center of the shape.

4. Finally, move the most recently created points outward from the center of the shape, as shown in the first example in Figure 6-24. The Bézier control handles of the point at the center of the mouth will require some adjustment as well.

The completed image is displayed on the right side of Figure 6-24 on the next page.

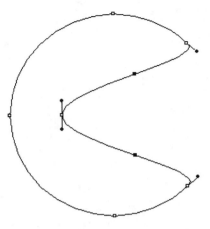

Figure 6-23: Add a point to the middle of each of the segments forming the mouth of the shape.

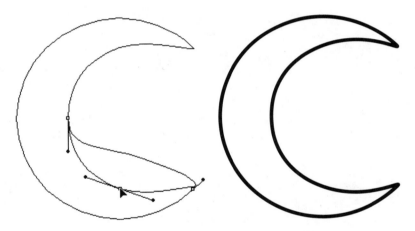

Figure 6-24: Drag the most recent points into position. The completed image is shown on right as it appears when printed from Illustrator.

All points added in Figures 6-21 though 6-24 happen to be smooth points. The identity of a point inserted into a segment using the add-anchor-point tool depends on the curvature of the segment. If the segment is straight, the inserted point will obviously be a corner point. If the segment curves in an even arc, like the segments in a circle, a smooth point will be inserted. However, if the segment curves slightly unevenly, as the majority of curved segments do, the

✺ The **Illustrator** 5 Book

identity of an inserted point becomes difficult to predict. I can only suggest that you adopt a trial-and-error attitude when using the add-anchor-point tool. If the identity of the inserted point does not match your needs, you can easily delete it using the delete-anchor-point tool or convert it using the convert-direction-point tool. Both of these tools are described in the upcoming pages.

KE Press the OPTION key to temporarily access the add-anchor-point tool when either the scissors or delete-anchor-point tool is selected. (To find out about the scissors tool, see *Splitting an element* later in this chapter.) When the pen tool is selected, press the CONTROL key.

You can click with the add-anchor-point tool on a segment in any existing path, even if the path is grouped, or combined or linked with other paths. However, Illustrator does not allow you to click with this tool directly on a point or at some empty location in the drawing area.

Deleting elements from a path

The simplest way to delete an element is to select it and press either BACKSPACE or DELETE. You can also choose the CLEAR command from the EDIT menu.

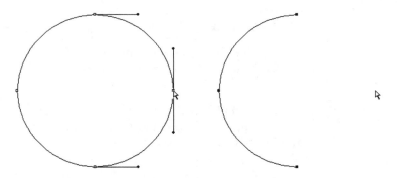

Figure 6-25: Selecting a point (left) and pressing the delete key deletes the point and its two segments from the path (right).

When you delete a selected point by pressing BACKSPACE or DELETE or choosing CLEAR, you also delete all segments associated with that point. The first example of Figure 6-25 shows a point selected in a

---

circular path. The second example shows the path after the point is deleted. Since both segments bordering a point become selected when you select a point, both segments are deleted along with the point. Deleting an interior point with the DELETE key therefore opens a closed path, as in the figure, or breaks an open path into two lines.

If you delete an endpoint from an open path, you delete the single segment associated with the point. Deleting an endpoint does not break a line in two.

You can also delete a single selected segment. Figure 6-26 shows a segment being selected and deleted from another circular path. Once again, this leaves a hole in the path. Therefore, deleting a segment also opens a closed path or breaks an open path into two separate lines. However, unlike a deleted point, a deleted segment takes no other element with it.

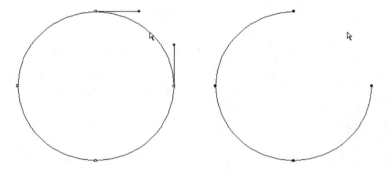

Figure 6-26: Selecting a segment (left) and pressing the delete key deletes the selected segment only (right).

You can also delete multiple points or segments, whether or not they belong to the same path. In this way, many paths can be opened and broken simultaneously.

Deleting a whole path

As shown in both Figures 6-25 and 6-26, deleting a point or segment from a path causes every remaining point and segment in that path to become selected. This means that if you press DELETE a second time, you will delete the entire path. And that means if, in the course of its creation, a path ends up deviating so drastically from your original

✦ The **Illustrator 5** Book

intention that there is no sense in attempting a salvage, you can delete the entire object by selecting any element in the path and pressing DELETE twice in a row.

You can also delete a path by selecting the entire path and pressing DELETE. I find that double-pressing the DELETE key is generally faster, because an element in a path is already selected if you just finished creating it, but feel free to use the method that works best for you. After all, the stark realization of one's own proclivity for error is not something most of us care to ponder for a prolonged period of time.

Deleting a point without breaking a path

If you want to delete an interior point from a path, but you do not want to open a closed path or to break an open path in two, use the *delete-anchor-point tool*. You can select the delete-anchor-point tool, which appears as the pen tool with a minus sign, by dragging from the scissors tool slot in the toolbox.

First, select the path from which you wish to delete a point. Then click with the delete-anchor-point tool on some point in the path. (Do *not* click on a segment.) The point you clicked will disappear, but rather than deleting both associated segments, Illustrator will draw a new segment between the two points that neighbored the deleted point.

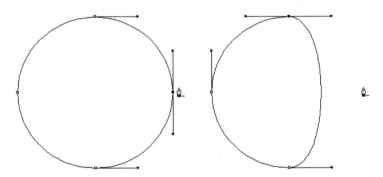

Figure 6-27: Click on an interior point with the delete-anchor-point tool, as indicated on the left, to delete the point but retain a segment (right).

The first example in Figure 6-27 shows the delete-anchor-point cursor poised to click on the rightmost point in the familiar circle path. The second example shows the path after the point is deleted. The two segments surrounding the deleted point are fused into a single segment, the curvature of which is determined by the remaining points in the path. The result is a path that remains closed.

You can click with the delete-anchor-point tool on a point in any existing path, even if the path is grouped, or combined or linked with other paths. However, Illustrator does not allow you to click with this tool on a segment or at some empty location in the drawing area.

 Press CONTROL to temporarily access the delete-anchor-point tool when the pen tool is selected, and position the cursor over a point you want to delete. The cursor will look like the add-anchor-point tool unless you position it over a point.

One last note: I advise that you do not delete a point from a line that consists of only two points. This will leave a single-point path, which is completely useless unless you intend to build on it immediately. Lone points clutter up the drawing area and needlessly increase the size of your illustration when saved to disk. Luckily, you can choose SELECT STRAY POINTS from the Select submenu under the FILTER menu to select all lone points and press the DELETE key to get rid of them.

Converting points

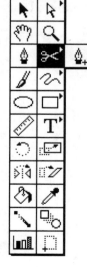

You can change the identity of an interior point in an existing path using the *convert-direction-point tool*. For example, you can convert a corner point to a smooth point by dragging on it. To select the convert-direction-point tool, which appears as an enlarged corner point flanked by two Bézier control handles, drag from the scissors tool slot in the toolbox.

Use the convert-direction-point tool as follows:

- Click on a smooth point to convert it to a corner point with no Bézier control handle.
- Drag one of the Bézier control handles of a smooth point to move it independently of the other Bézier control handle, thus converting the smooth point to a cusp.
- Drag from a corner point to convert it to a smooth point with two symmetrical Bézier control handles.

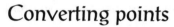

Figure 6-28 shows a circular path composed of four smooth points. Suppose that you want to convert the identity of one or more of these points to alter the form of the path. The following exercise demonstrates one way to proceed:

1. Select the convert-direction-point tool and click on the leftmost point in the circle. The smooth point immediately changes to a corner point with no control handle, as shown in Figure 6-29.

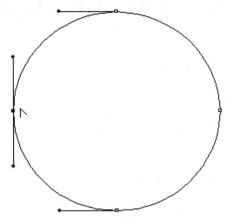

Figure 6-28: The convert-direction-point tool, poised to click on the left point in a circular path.

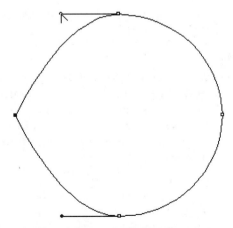

Figure 6-29: Drag the displayed Bézier control handle belonging to the top point.

2. Now drag the left-pointing Bézier control handle belonging to the top smooth point in the circle. The convert-direction-point tool allows you to drag one handle independently of another, immediately converting the smooth point to a cusp (a corner point with two handles).

3. Drag the handle all the way back to its point, as shown in Figure 6-30. When your cursor changes to a hollow arrowhead, indicating that it has snapped to the point, release the mouse button. You have now subtracted a Bézier control handle from the point, converting it to a corner point with only one handle.

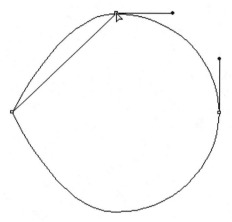

Figure 6-30: Drag the handle back to its point, subtracting the handle from the shape.

4. Press the COMMAND key to temporarily access the direct-selection tool and click on the bottom point to select it. (You may also need to press COMMAND-TAB and/or the OPTION key.) Release COMMAND and drag the left-pointing handle to the approximate position shown in Figure 6-31 on the following page.

5. Drag from the leftmost point that you converted to a corner point in step 1. This converts the point back to a smooth point. Drag the handle up and to the right as shown in Figure 6-32, bowing the bottom segment inward and the top segment outward.

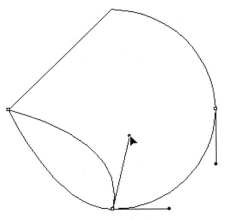

Figure 6-31: Drag the displayed segment for the bottom point up and to the right.

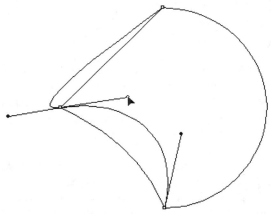

Figure 6-32: Drag from the left point to convert it back to a smooth point.

6. After releasing the mouse button, drag at the handle opposite the one you were just dragging, as shown in Figure 6-33. This time, drag the handle back to its point to subtract it. As this step and the previous one demonstrate, to add a handle to a corner point, you must convert it to a smooth point and then convert it back into a cusp.

The completed image is displayed on the right side of Figure 6-33, on the next page.

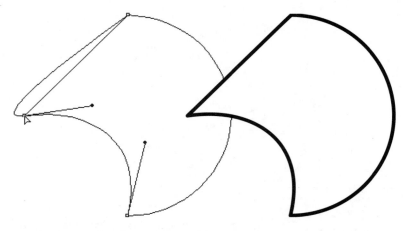

Figure 6-33: Drag the newest handle back to its point. Your cursor will snap to the point, as indicated by the hollow arrowhead cursor. The completed image is shown on the right as it appears when printed from Illustrator.

In between converting points, it is very tempting to adjust the placement of Bézier control handles using the convert-direction-point tool. If you do so, however, you will most certainly convert the point—to a corner point if the point is a smooth point, or to a smooth point if it is a corner point.

If you want to move a point or adjust a handle without converting a point, be sure to press the COMMAND key to temporarily access a selection tool before beginning your drag. Also, if you inadvertently convert a point, you can immediately choose the UNDO command from the EDIT menu (⌘-Z) to convert the point back to its original identity.

Press the CONTROL key to temporarily access the convert-direction-point tool when a selection tool is active. Press CONTROL-OPTION to temporarily access the convert-direction-point tool when the pen tool is selected. When almost any other tool is selected, press COMMAND-CONTROL to access the convert-direction-point tool; the scissors, add-anchor-point, delete-anchor-point, and freehand tools have no keyboard equivalent for accessing the convert-direction-tool.

The **Illustrator 5** Book

Joining and splitting elements

Almost all of the reshaping techniques described so far are available, in some form or another, in just about every drawing software available on the Macintosh. MacDraw, for example, although it provides no Bézier curve capacity, allows you to move elements, add and delete points, and convert straight segments to curved segments. Yet, MacDraw is commonly considered too primitive for tackling a complex illustration. This section discusses two areas where Illustrator stands head and shoulders above the common drawing crowd: the joining and splitting of points and segments, which make it possible to break up portions of various paths like pieces in a tailor-made puzzle, then assemble them in any way you see fit.

Joining endpoints with a straight segment

In the section *Adding elements to the end of a path* earlier in this chapter, I explained how you can join two lines into a single open path by drawing from one endpoint to another with the pen, freehand, or auto trace tool. But as it turns out, Illustrator offers a JOIN... command in the OBJECT menu (⌘-J) that makes the joining of endpoints less cumbersome while at the same time providing additional options and a greater degree of control.

First of all, the JOIN... command allows you to join two endpoints with a straight segment. Figure 6-34 on the next page displays two open paths. One endpoint in each path is selected. If you choose JOIN..., a straight segment will be drawn between the two selected endpoints, resulting in the path shown in Figure 6-35. When two endpoints are selected, whether they belong to the same path or not, and the two are separated by some distance, choosing JOIN... draws a straight segment between the two points. This segment is always straight, regardless of the identity of the points involved. In Figure 6-34, for example, the upper endpoint was a smooth point, as evident from the two symmetrical Bézier control handles. But in Figure 6-35, the point has been converted to a corner point to allow for the straight segment.

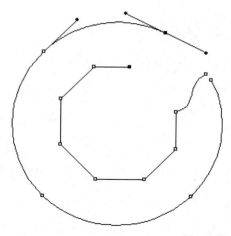

Figure 6-34: Two open paths with one selected endpoint each.

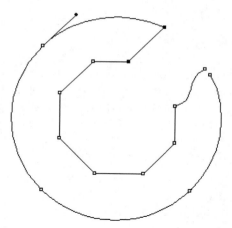

Figure 6-35: The Join... command draws a straight segment between the two selected endpoints.

Use the JOIN... command any time you want to draw a straight segment between two existing endpoints. For example, the JOIN... command would have simplified the creation of the semicircle shown back in Figure 5.38. Other images with straight edges can also make use of this feature.

🔅The **Illustrator 5** Book

Joining coincident endpoints

If two endpoints are *coincident*—that is, one point is positioned exactly on top of the other in the drawing area—the JOIN... command will fuse the two into a single interior point, whose identity you can specify by selecting options in the JOIN dialog box.

Joining coincident endpoints is a four-step process:

1. Drag one endpoint onto another with the direct-selection tool so the two points are coincident. Make sure they snap together, as verified by a hollow arrowhead cursor.

2. Marquee both points to select them. No other point should be selected.

3. Choose the JOIN... command to display the JOIN dialog box.

4. Select the desired kind of point (corner or smooth) and click the OK button or press RETURN.

Here is another example that demonstrates this process. Figure 6-36 shows one endpoint being dragged onto another in a single open path. Notice that the cursor appears as a hollow arrowhead, indicating that the dragged point has snapped to the stationary point, making them coincident.

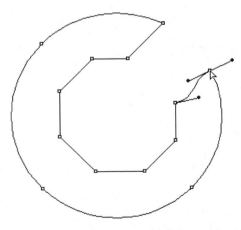

Figure 6-36: Dragging one endpoint in front of the other endpoint in the same path.

I next marquee the two points to select them. (Marqueeing is the only possible means of selection, since one point is inaccessible behind the other.) Figure 6-37 shows both endpoints as they appear when selected.

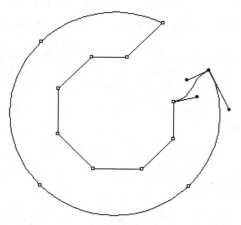

Figure 6-37: The two coincident endpoints as they appear when selected.

Figure 6-38: The Join dialog box allows you to specify the identity of the joined point.

After selecting the points, I choose the JOIN... command. If the endpoints are correctly positioned one directly in front of the other, the JOIN dialog box shown in Figure 6-38 will appear. If neither the JOIN dialog nor an error message appears, it means that Illustrator does not consider your endpoints to be exactly situated at the same location. The JOIN... command has therefore joined the two selected endpoints with a straight segment. Choose UNDO JOIN (⌘-Z) to delete the segment and then choose the AVERAGE... command from the AR-RANGE menu (⌘-L) to properly relocate the selected endpoints. (This command is discussed in detail in *Averaging points* later in this chapter.) The AVERAGE dialog box will appear, with the "Both" option selected by default. Press RETURN to initiate the command. Then choose JOIN... again to bring up the JOIN dialog box.

You can both average and join two selected points in one fell swoop by pressing COMMAND-OPTION-J. This will automatically average in both directions, and join the two into a corner point. If you want a smooth point instead, press COMMAND-OPTION-J, and then convert the point with the convert-direction-tool.

The examples in Figure 6-39 show the results of selecting various options in the JOIN dialog box. (In each example, the two coincident points and their adjoining segments have been enlarged to provide a better view.) The first example displays the selected points as they appear before joining. The second example is the result of selecting the "Corner" option in the JOIN dialog box. This is the default selection. The "Corner" option joins two selected endpoints to form a single corner point. The curvature of a bordering segment is never altered by selecting the "Corner" option.

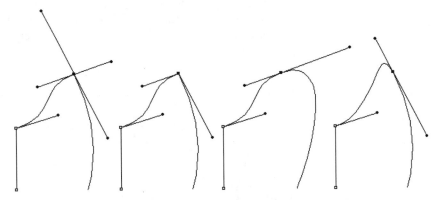

Figure 6-39: Two selected points before joining (left) followed by three ways to change the identity of a joined point using the Join dialog box.

The third and fourth examples in Figure 6-39 were produced by selecting the "Smooth" option in the JOIN dialog box. Selecting "Smooth," almost always alters the curvature of one of the segments associated with the coincident points. In this case, one segment curves from left to right and another curves from top to bottom. And yet, I have instructed Illustrator to surround the joined point with two segments that arc evenly into each other. Therefore, the form of at least one segment must be dramatically altered.

When joining any two points to form a smooth point in Illustrator, the curvature of the front segment remains intact while the rear segment curves to fit the requirements of the new smooth point. In the third example of Figure 6-39, the left-hand segment was the front segment. The right-hand segment has been substantially reformed to conform to its repositioned Bézier control handle. In the fourth example, the right-hand segment was the front segment and it is the left-hand segment that has been reshaped.

✳ If the segments of the two coincident points meet at an angle of less than 90° and you select the "Smooth" radio button, Illustrator will join the two points into a smooth point in which both handles appear on the same side of the point, as shown in the first example in Figure 6-40. This unnatural smooth-point configuration results in an extremely sharp corner, rather than a smooth arc. Dragging one of the handles with the direct-selection tool will not correct the problem. Instead, drag one of the segments until the handles appear on opposite sides of the point, as shown in the second example of Figure 6-40. Or drag at the point with the convert-direction-point tool.

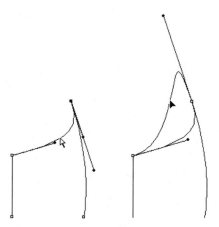

Figure 6-40: If the Bézier control handles for a smooth point become located on the same side of the point (left), drag one of the neighboring segments to relocate one handle to the opposite side of the point (right).

Two and only two points can be selected when you choose the JOIN... command. Otherwise, an error message will appear. If this occurs, press RETURN to hide the alert box. Then reselect your two points and retry the command.

Splitting an element

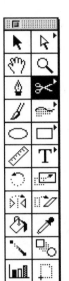

The *scissors tool*, displayed by default in the third tool slot on the right of the toolbox, is used to split a point or segment in two. By selecting the scissors tool and clicking at some location on a selected segment, you insert two endpoints into the segment, each associated with one segment. This means the segment is split into two segments. Clicking with the scissors tool on an interior point splits the point into two endpoints; once again, each is associated with a single segment. Therefore, you can click with the scissors tool to open a closed path or to split an open path into two segments.

Suppose you want to split an ordinary circle into the three shapes shown in the second example in Figure 6-43 on page 251. The following steps describe how to accomplish this using the scissors and pen tools:

1. Click with the scissors tool at two points on each of the right-hand segments in the circle. These points are shown as selected in Figure 6-41. The circle is now split up into four separate lines.

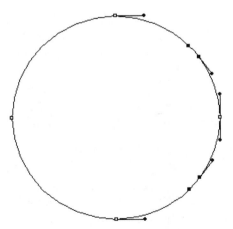

Figure 6-41: Each of the selected points in this circle was created by clicking with the scissors tool.

2. Select the direct-selection tool and click on the topmost of the single-segment lines to select the new path. Then SHIFT-click on the lower single-segment line to add it to the selection.

3. Drag both lines away from the remaining paths of the circle, as shown in Figure 6-42. Neither line is a part of the prospective final image, so press the BACKSPACE or DELETE key to delete them both. You are now left with two open paths.

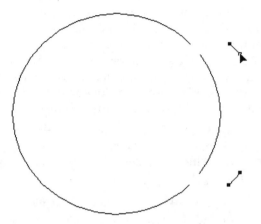

Figure 6-42: Drag the two single-segment lines away from the rest of the circle and delete them.

4. Select the pen tool. Press the OPTION key and drag from the top point in the right-hand path. This activates the path and converts the point from a smooth point to a cusp.

5. After releasing the OPTION key, drag again with the pen tool at a location that mirrors the center smooth point of the right-hand path.

6. Press OPTION again and drag at the bottom point in the right-hand path, closing the path to form a leaf-shaped path.

7. Close the second, larger path in a similar manner, adding to it two segments that are parallel to those that closed the right-hand shape. The result is the first example in Figure 6-43.

The **Illustrator 5** Book

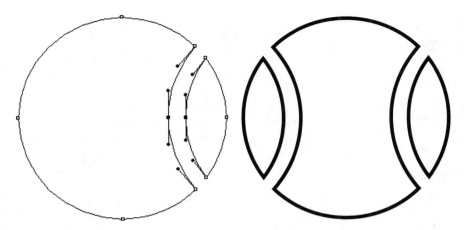

*Figure 6-43: Draw segments closing the two remaining paths.
Repeating the exercise on the left side of the shape results in the
image shown on right.*

The second example in Figure 6-43 shows the completed image
after repeating steps 1 through 7 on the left side of the circle.

You can click with the scissors tool on a point or segment in any
existing path, even if the path is grouped, or combined or linked with
other paths. However, Illustrator does not allow you to click with this
tool at some empty location in the drawing area.

Deleting split paths

Frequently, you will split off some portion of a path as a first step
to deleting it from your illustration, as demonstrated in the exercise.
When doing so, be careful to select the entire split portion before
pressing BACKSPACE or DELETE, or be sure to press the DELETE key
twice. For example, if you had selected the segment of only one of
the single-segment lines in Figure 6-41 and pressed DELETE only
once, you would have been left with two lone points, residing either
in front or in back of the endpoints of the paths you wanted to reshape. These lone points would have cluttered your drawing area
and might have gotten in the way when you tried to add segments
to the endpoints of the remaining paths.

Averaging points

Upon occasion you may find the need to align objects. In Figure 6-37, I could have aligned the two points to a coincident location, joined them, and then repositioned the final point. For this sort of alignment, Illustrator offers the AVERAGE... command in the OBJECT menu (⌘-L), which allows you to *average* the position of two or more selected points in the drawing area. For example, if two selected points are four inches apart, the AVERAGE... command will move the points two inches toward each other so they reside at the same location.

Choosing the AVERAGE... command from the OBJECT menu displays the AVERAGE dialog box shown in Figure 6-44. This dialog offers three "Average along" radio buttons. The options work as follows:

- **Both**. Select this radio button to average the location of all selected points to a single coincident location in the drawing area.

- **Horizontal only**. This radio button averages selected points horizontally along the constraint axes.

- **Vertical only**. This radio button averages selected points vertically along the constraint axes.

Select the desired radio button and click on the OK button or press RETURN to average the selected points.

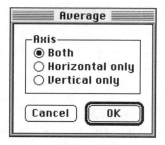

Figure 6-44: The Average dialog box allows you to average two or more selected points along the constraint axes.

Averaging in action

Figure 6-45 shows two shapes containing two selected points apiece (each of which is labeled so you can follow it from figure to figure). The following exercise demonstrates the results of averaging these elements:

1. After selecting the points shown in the figure, choose the AVER-AGE... command to display the AVERAGE dialog box. The "Both" option is selected by default. Select the "Horizontal only" option and press the RETURN key, which instructs Illustrator to relocate all selected points so they line up in a horizontal formation, as shown in Figure 6-46, on the next page.

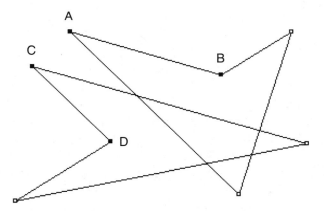

Figure 6-45: Two paths containing a total of four selected points (each circled and labeled).

2. All four selected points are aligned so that they occupy the same vertical space, while their horizontal positioning remains identical to that in Figure 6-45. Choose UNDO AVERAGE (⌘-Z) to return the points to their original locations.

3. Starting again from Figure 6-45, choose AVERAGE... but this time select the "Vertical only" radio button from the AVERAGE dialog and press RETURN. The points line up in vertical formation, as shown in Figure 6-47, on the next page. The four points now occupy the same horizontal space, while their vertical positioning remains unchanged.

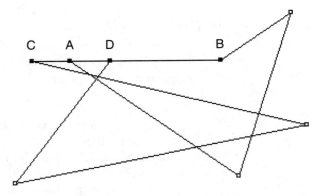

Figure 6-46: The four selected points averaged along the horizontal axis.

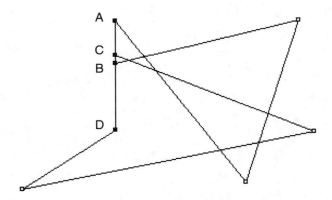

Figure 6-47: The four selected points averaged along the vertical axis.

4. Choose UNDO AVERAGE again.

5. Finally, choose AVERAGE..., check to see that the "Both" radio button is selected, and press RETURN. All four points become coincident, each occupying the same location as the three other selected points, as shown in Figure 6-48 on the next page.

The primary function for averaging points along both axes is to prepare two endpoints for a JOIN... command, as discussed in *Joining coincident endpoints* earlier in this chapter.

⚛ The **Illustrator 5** Book

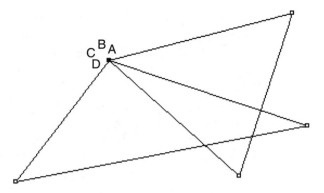

Figure 6-48: The four selected points averaged along both axes. All points are positioned at a coincident location.

Why average points?

The AVERAGE... command averages all selected points, whether in a group or in a combined or linked object. It does not average the location of segments or entire paths, except as a result of repositioning their points. For example, suppose you select two entire rectangles (all points in each) with the intention of positioning one rectangle directly in front of another. If you choose AVERAGE... and select the "Both" radio button, all points will become coincident, ruining the rectangles as recognizable objects.

So what the heck do you do with this command? For starters, you can make two endpoints coincident so they can be fused into a single point with the JOIN... command. This is not the command's only purpose, however. The list below includes all the functions (that I know of, anyway) to which AVERAGE... can be applied:

- Nothing looks worse than a straight segment that is only slightly angled; that is, *almost* horizontal or *almost* vertical, but not quite. Even when printed to a photo-imagesetter, a line that is off by as much as half a degree will appear jagged. To ensure a straight segment is perpendicular, select both points bordering the segment and apply the "Horizontal only" or "Vertical only" radio button.

- To join two separated points with a perfectly horizontal or vertical straight segment, apply the "Horizontal only" or "Vertical only" radio button before choosing the JOIN... command.

- If the JOIN dialog box does not appear after choosing the JOIN... command for what seem to be two coincident points, choose UNDO JOIN (⌘-Z) and apply the "Both" radio button to ensure the points are exactly coincident. Again choose the JOIN... command to display the JOIN dialog box.

- Applying the "Both" radio button may slightly rotate the angle of a horizontal or vertical segment. If a perpendicular segment is associated with any point being averaged with the "Both" radio button, you should go back and apply the "Horizontal only" or "Vertical only" option to the points that border the segment.

- Apply the "Horizontal only" option to selected points in different paths to align the bases of the paths, as shown in Figure 6-49, or the tops of the paths. Apply the "Vertical only" option to align the sides of the paths.

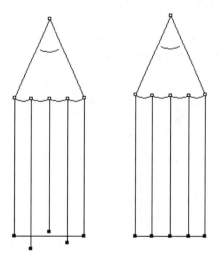

Figure 6-49: Align the bottoms of different paths by selecting the points at the bottom of the paths (left) and applying the "Horizontal only" option (right).

- Within grouped objects, the AVERAGE... command can be used to align the bottoms (see Figure 6-50 on the next page), tops, and sides of paths, so long as the specific points you want to align have been selected with the direct-selection tool.

The **Illustrator 5** Book

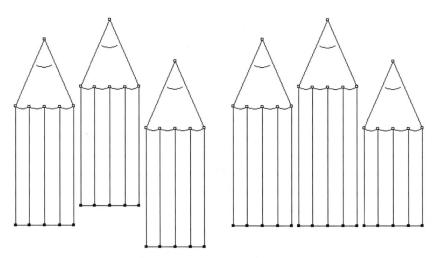

Figure 6-50: Align the bottoms of grouped objects by selecting the points at the bottom of the paths with the direct-selection tool (left) and applying the "Horizontal only" option (right).

Averaging along a rotated axis

Both the "Horizontal only" and "Vertical only" options average points in relation to the constraint axes. If you rotate the axes, as described in *Constrained movements* earlier in this chapter, you also rotate the axes along which points are aligned. For example, if you enter 30° for the "Constrain angle" option in the GENERAL PREFERENCES dialog box, the "Horizontal only" option in the AVERAGE dialog box will produce the effect shown in Figure 6-51. Since the "Both" option averages all points to a single location, it is not affected by the rotation of the constraint axes.

The AVERAGE... command can only be applied to points. At least two points must be selected when choosing the command; otherwise, an error message will appear. If this occurs, press RETURN to hide the alert box. Then reselect your points and try again.

If you want to align several whole objects, choose the ALIGN OBJECTS... command from the OBJECTS submenu under the FILTERS menu. This command is discussed in the *Aligning and distributing objects* section of Chapter 12.

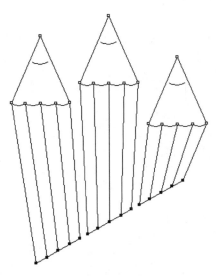

Figure 6-51: Averaging selected points along the horizontal axis when the "Constrain angle" option in the Preferences dialog box is set to 30°.

Undo and redo

Because we all make mistakes, especially when drawing and tracing complicated paths, Illustrator provides you with the ability to nullify the results of previous operations. In fact, Illustrator 5.0 provides you with a greater capacity to mull over past actions than its predecessor (finally catching up with FreeHand 1.0 in this respect). So when drawing anxiety sets in, remember this simple credo: *Undo, redo, relaxum.* That's Latin for "Chill, it's just a computer."

Edit	
Undo	⌘Z
Redo	⌘⇧Z
Cut	⌘H
Copy	⌘C
Paste	⌘U
Clear	
Select All	⌘A
Select None	⌘⇧A
Paste In Front	⌘F
Paste In Back	⌘B
Publishing	▶
Show Clipboard	

Undo

If you are familiar with other Macintosh or Microsoft Windows applications, such as PageMaker or CorelDraw, you are no doubt familiar with the UNDO command in the EDIT menu (⌘-Z). This command allows you to negate the last action performed. For example, suppose that you have added a point to a path and then decide that you don't like how it looks. Choose the UNDO PEN command and the new point will disappear. You will in fact be returned to the moment before you added the point. And unlike Illustrator 3.0 and its predecessors, you can *always* undo the last action, even if you have since clicked on screen or performed some minor action that the command does not recognize.

 Get this: You can even undo an operation performed prior to the most recent SAVE operation (although you cannot undo the SAVE command itself). For example, you can delete an element, save the illustration, then choose UNDO to make the element reappear. It's a real lifesaver.

The UNDO command, however, does have its limits. You cannot undo an operation performed in a previous Illustrator session.

Illustrator lists the name of the operation that you can undo under the EDIT menu following the word UNDO, so that you fully realize the consequences of choosing the command. Examples include UNDO MOVE and UNDO JOIN.

Multiple undos

In most applications, after you undo an operation, the UNDO command changes to a REDO command, providing a brief opportunity to reperform an operation, just in case you decide you didn't want to undo it after all. In Illustrator 5.0, the UNDO command remains available, so that you can undo the second-to-last operation, and the one before that, and so on. In fact, you can undo up to 200 consecutive operations. This power-user feature takes a great deal of the worry out of using Illustrator. Even major blunders can be reversed one step at a time.

You adjust the number of possible consecutive undos by entering any value from 1 to 99 for the "Undo Levels" option in the GENERAL PREFERENCES dialog box (introduced in the *Setting preferences* section of Chapter 3). The default value is 10. To make this value take effect, you have to quit Illustrator and relaunch the application, allowing the program an opportunity to create an adequately sized undo buffer in your computer's RAM.

After you undo the maximum number of operations, the UNDO command will appear dimmed in the EDIT menu. Pressing COMMAND-Z will produce no effect until you perform a new operation.

Redo

Just as you can undo as many as 200 consecutive actions, you can redo up to 200 consecutive undos using the REDO command in the EDIT menu (⌘-⇧-Z). You can utilize the REDO command only if an UNDO command was the most recent action performed; otherwise, the command will be dimmed. Also, if you undo a series of actions, perform a new series of actions, and then undo the new series of actions to the point where you had stopped undoing previously, you will not be allowed to go back and redo the first series of undos. Instead, you can simply continue to undo from where you left off.

Illustrator lists the name of the operation that you can redo under the EDIT menu following the word REDO, so that you fully realize the consequences of choosing the command. Examples include REDO MOVE or REDO JOIN.

PART 3
EMBELLISHMENTS

CHAPTER

CREATING AND EDITING TYPE

As you've seen in the preceding chapters, Illustrator 5.0 is quite the thing for creating and manipulating complex graphics. As if that weren't enough, the program also lets you add text to your illustration, either as an annotation or as part of the graphic itself. Text in Illustrator can be stroked, filled, transformed, employed as a clipping path, integrated into a compound path, and even converted into free-form paths. This chapter discusses how to create, modify, and manipulate text in Illustrator 5.0.

261

Creating text objects

Type in Illustrator is created and manipulated as a specific kind of element known as a *text object* (or *object d'text*). As I'll explain, text objects are in some ways like and in other ways unlike graphic objects. They are similar in that many of Illustrator's general commands—with the notable exception of those under the FILTERS menu—can be applied to text objects as easily as they are to graphic objects. Text objects differ from graphic objects in that a special set of tools, commands, and options is used to create and alter type.

Text objects are easier to view in the artwork mode than in the preview mode. In the preview mode, the text itself is always visible but the baseline on which the text sits is visible only when the text block or path is selected. This makes it difficult to select baselines, blocks, and text paths in the preview mode. In the artwork mode, the baselines and paths remain visible even when deselected, so text objects are easier to select. Unless otherwise noted, the figures in this chapter show text in the artwork mode.

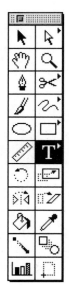

Creating point text

Use the *type tool* to create new text objects in the drawing area. This tool can be used to create type in a number of ways. First and most familiar to users of any application that has type capabilities, you can click with the type tool at any location in the drawing area. Clicking with the type tool creates the simplest kind of text object, the *point text block* (the first of three varieties of *text blocks*). An *alignment point* will appear as an × (in the artwork mode), along with a blinking *insertion marker*. The insertion marker always indicates the location at which type entered from the keyboard will appear in the current text object.

After clicking with the type tool, enter the desired text from your keyboard. Each letter will appear on the screen following the alignment point. The insertion marker moves right with each additional letter, as shown in the first example of Figure 7-1.

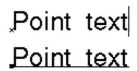

Figure 7-1: Point text as it appears when entering text (top) and after selecting a different tool (bottom).

When you have finished entering your text, select another tool in the toolbox or reselect the type tool. The text block will appear selected, as shown in the bottom example in Figure 7-1. The alignment point now appears as a small black box, like a selected point in a geometric or free-form path. You can drag the alignment point with the selection tool to move the text block in the drawing area, and other dragged objects will snap to this point when your cursor comes within two pixels of it. You can also drag a text block by its *baseline*, the line that runs under each row of type. The baseline is the imaginary line on which letters sit. Only a few lowercase characters—*g*, *j*, *p*, *q*, and *y*—descend below the baseline.

To add more text to a block of point text, select the type tool and click in the text block where you want the new text to appear. The baseline vanishes, the alignment point reverts to an × (in the artwork mode), and the insertion marker reappears at the location clicked.

When you enter text from the keyboard, keys perform the same function they do in a typical word-processing software. Most keys insert the character that appears on the key. Keys that perform other functions include the following:

- **Spacebar**. Inserts a standard space into a text block.
- **Delete, backspace, escape**, or **clear**. Pressing any of these keys deletes the character to the left of the insertion marker.
- **Caps lock**. Accesses uppercase letters when used with letter keys.
- **Shift**. Accesses uppercase letters when pressed with letter keys and special characters printed at the top of number keys.
- **Option**. Accesses special characters—such as £, ¢, ∞, §, ¶— when pressed with letter or number keys.
- **Shift** plus **option**. Accesses special characters—such as fi, fl, ‡, °—when pressed with letter or number keys.
- **Arrow keys**. ←, ↑, →, or ↓ moves the insertion marker.
- **Tab**. Moves the insertion marker, along with the text that follows it, to the opposite side of a wrapped graphic. See *Wrapping type around graphics* on page 319 for more information.
- **Return** or **enter**. Moves the insertion marker, along with any text to the right of the marker, to the next line of type.

Point text will not *wrap* to a lower row of text on its own. Letters will continue to accumulate to the edge of the drawing area (past which they still exist but are not visible) unless you insert *line breaks* as needed by pressing RETURN or ENTER.

Creating area text

Point text is the simplest kind of text object you can create, making it perfect for headlines, labels, captions, and other varieties of text that contain only a handful of letters. But because words do not wrap to new lines on their own, point text blocks are not well suited to paragraphs longer than a couple of sentences. For long documents, use the second variety of text block, the *area text block*.

In an area text block, type exists inside a geometric or free-form path. The most common path for this purpose is the rectangle, as shown in Figure 7-2. Rectangular columns of type ensure legibility, because readers are very familiar with them. However, you can also place text in unusual shapes, such as the one shown in Figure 7-3. In fact, you can fill any path with type in Illustrator 5.0.

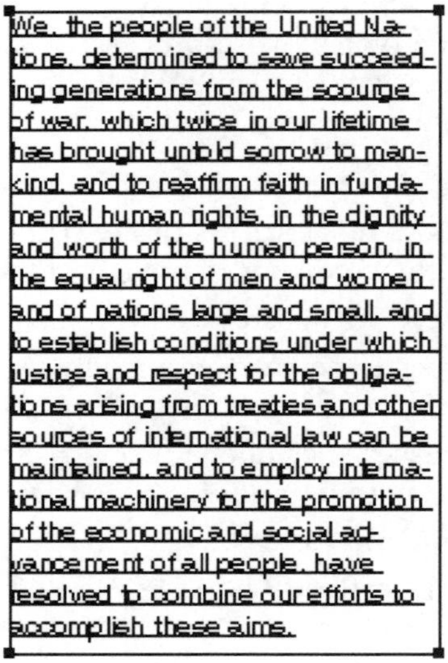

We, the people of the United Nations, determined to save succeeding generations from the scourge of war, which twice in our lifetime has brought untold sorrow to mankind, and to reaffirm faith in fundamental human rights, in the dignity and worth of the human person, in the equal right of men and women and of nations large and small, and to establish conditions under which justice and respect for the obligations arising from treaties and other sources of international law can be maintained, and to employ international machinery for the promotion of the economic and social advancement of all people, have resolved to combine our efforts to accomplish these aims.

Figure 7-2: The most common variety of area type is the rectangular column, shown here as it appears when selected (left) and when printed (right).

To create a column of type, drag with the type tool. The point at which you begin dragging determines one corner of the rectangular column; the point at which you release determines the opposite corner. After you complete your drag, a rectangle will appear with a blinking insertion marker in the upper left corner. Enter the desired text using your keyboard. Each letter will appear on the screen inside the column. As always, the insertion marker moves right with each additional letter, indicating the location at which the next letter you enter will appear. If a word threatens to extend beyond the edge of the column, it will automatically wrap to form a new line of type (unless "Auto hyphenate" is turned on in the PARAGRAPH palette, in which case the word may split).

After you finish entering text, select another tool in the toolbox or reselect the type tool. The text block will appear selected, as shown in the first example in Figure 7-2. The four points that make up the outline of the rectangle appear as small black dots like selected points in other paths. Baselines underscore the type to indicate that the letters themselves are selected. To reposition the text block, drag at either the rectangular path or one of the baselines with the selection tool.

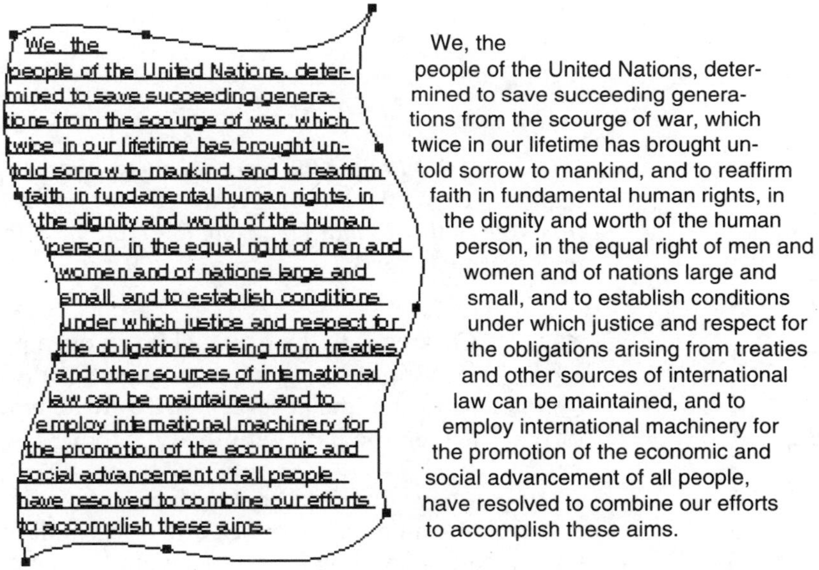

We, the
people of the United Nations, determined to save succeeding generations from the scourge of war, which twice in our lifetime has brought untold sorrow to mankind, and to reaffirm faith in fundamental human rights, in the dignity and worth of the human person, in the equal right of men and women and of nations large and small, and to establish conditions under which justice and respect for the obligations arising from treaties and other sources of international law can be maintained, and to employ international machinery for the promotion of the economic and social advancement of all people, have resolved to combine our efforts to accomplish these aims.

Figure 7-3: A free-form path can also contain text, shown here as it appears when selected (left) and when printed (right).

To create type inside a path, first create a closed path using one of the geometric path tools or the pen, freehand, brush, or auto trace tool. Then select the type tool and position your cursor over some portion of the outline of the path. Your cursor will change from an I-beam surrounded by a rectangular dotted outline to an I-beam surrounded by an oval dotted outline, as shown in Figure 7-4. As soon as this change occurs, click with the type tool. A blinking insertion marker will appear at the top of the path. As you enter text from the keyboard, it will appear inside the path. Words that would otherwise exceed the right edge of the shape will wrap to the next line (or break if the "Auto hyphenate" check box in the PARAGRAPH palette is turned on).

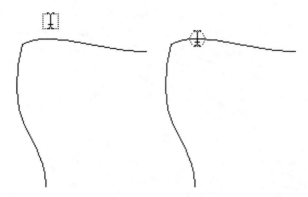

Figure 7-4: Positioning the type tool cursor over the outline of a closed path changes the cursor's appearance from that of the standard type tool (left) to that of the area-type tool (right).

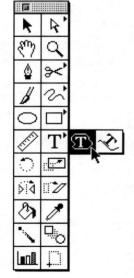

KE Clicking with the type tool on an open path rather than on a closed path creates type on a path (called *path text*), as described in the next section. To create type inside an open path, OPTION-click on the path with the type tool.

If you have difficulty positioning your cursor over a path when first creating an area text block and as a result find yourself inadvertently creating point text, or if you want to create area text in an open path, you may prefer to use the *area-type tool*, which guarantees that you will create an area text block. You can select this tool, which appears as a letter inside a lumpy shape, by dragging at the type tool slot. You create area text with the area-type tool by clicking on the outline of an existing path (open or closed), just as when using the standard type tool. If you miss the path, however, an error message will alert you of the fact, rather than simply creating a new block of point text as the standard type tool does.

✹ The **Illustrator 5** Book

You cannot drag with the area-type tool to create a column of type, as you can with the standard type tool. You can use the area-type tool only to click on existing paths.

 Press CONTROL to temporarily access the type tool when the area-type tool is selected. (Too bad there isn't a keyboard equivalent that lets you similarly access the path-type tool.)

When you finish entering text, select another tool in the toolbox or reselect the type tool to finish the text block. The text block will appear selected, as shown in the first example in Figure 7-3 on page 265. To reposition the text block, drag at the path or one of the baselines with the selection tool.

Creating path text

The third kind of text block you can create in Illustrator 5.0 is the *path text block*, also called type on a path, in which the baseline of a line of type is fixed to the outline of an existing path, as shown in Figure 7-5 on the following page.

To create type along the outline of a path, first create the path using one of the geometric path tools or the pen, freehand, brush or auto trace tool. If the path is closed, open it by deleting a segment or clicking on one of its points with the scissors tool. Then select the type tool and position your cursor over some portion of the outline of the path. Your cursor will change from an I-beam surrounded by a rectangular dotted outline to an I-beam with a small dotted diagonal line slicing through it, as shown in Figure 7-6 on the next page. As soon as this change occurs, click with the type tool. A blinking insertion marker will appear at the point on the outline of the path closest to where you have clicked. As you enter text from the keyboard, it will follow the contours of the path.

 Clicking with the type tool on a closed path rather than on an open path creates area text. To create path text along a closed path, OPTION-click on the path with the type tool.

Like point text, path text is ill-suited to long documents because the length of the path determines the length of your text. When a word extends past the end of an open path, it disappears from view like a ship sailing off the edge of the world. Long text simply wraps around and around a closed path, forcing words to overlap.

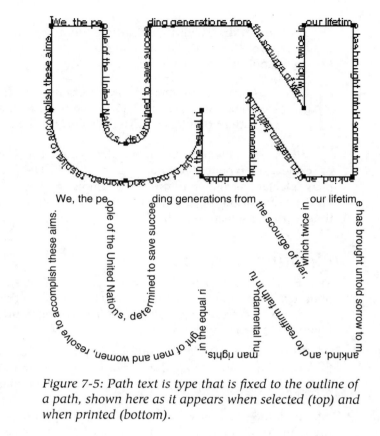

Figure 7-5: Path text is type that is fixed to the outline of a path, shown here as it appears when selected (top) and when printed (bottom).

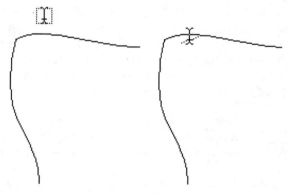

Figure 7-6: Positioning your type tool cursor over the outline of an open path changes the cursor's appearance from that of the standard type tool (left) to that of the path-type tool (right).

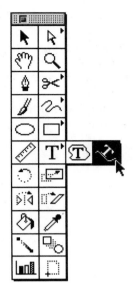

 Paths composed exclusively of smooth points—no corners—serve best for creating path text. When type has to flow around a corner, it may interrupt a word, as verified by several instances in Figure 7-5. Illustrator does not keep whole words together in path text. Also, type may overlap inside sharp corners. I avoided this in the figure by inserting spaces to spread overlapping letters apart, but the result still appears rather odd, and frequently illegible.

If you have difficulty positioning your cursor over a path when first creating a path text block and as a result find yourself inadvertently creating point text, or if you want to create path type along a closed path, you may prefer to use the *path-type tool*, which guarantees that you will create path text blocks. You can select this tool, which appears as a letter on a squiggly line, by dragging at the type tool slot. You create path text with the path-type tool by clicking on the outline of an existing path (open or closed), just as when using the standard type tool. If you miss the path, however, an error message will alert you of the fact, rather than simply creating a new block of point text as the standard type tool does.

KE Press the CONTROL key to temporarily access the type tool when the path-type tool is selected. Again, there's no keyboard equivalent for accessing the area-type tool.

When you finish entering text, select another tool in the toolbox or reselect the type tool to finish the text block. The text block will appear selected, as shown in the first example in Figure 7-5. To reposition the text block, drag at the path or one of the baselines with the selection tool.

Importing stories

Most of the text you use in Illustrator will be entered directly in Illustrator. But, there may be times when you'll want to create complete pages—especially now that the program accommodates multi-page layouts—or mix graphics with large amounts of text. When long documents (called *stories*) are called for, Illustrator allows you to import text documents created in the major word-processing programs. After all, word processors are faster for text entry and allow luxuries such as spell checking. Also, it's easier to edit text and apply formatting attributes in a word processor.

Preparing text

When importing text, Illustrator reads the file from disk and copies it to the current illustration. As this copy is being made, the text file passes through an *import filter* that converts the file's *formatting* commands, which specify typeface (Helvetica, Times), style (plain, bold, italic), and so on, into formatting commands recognizable to Illustrator. Illustrator 5.0 contains import filters for the following text formats:

- Microsoft Word, versions 3.0, 4.0, 5.0
- RTF (Rich Text Format).
- MacWrite, versions 4.5 and 5.0
- MacWrite II, version 1.0
- WriteNow, version 3.0
- ASCII (plain text, no formatting)
- WordPerfect, version 2.0
- DOS, Windows WordPerfect, version 5.0

Illustrator will not recognize word processor files for which an import filter does not exist. If you use a word processor other than Microsoft Word, MacWrite, WordPerfect, or WriteNow, try to save the file in one of the first four formats listed above. If your word processor does not support any of these formats, or if you want to use text created on a different model of computer, like the IBM PC, you may be able to convert the file using a file-conversion utility such as Apple File Exchange from Apple Computer, (408) 996-1010 or MacLink from DataViz, (203) 268-0030. Short of that, save the file as a text-only or *ASCII* document, which sacrifices all formatting. You will then have to reformat the text in Illustrator, as described in the *Formatting text* section later in this chapter.

Import filters may not be able to convert all formatting attributes correctly from a word processor file. The following list describes how Illustrator handles the most common formatting attributes and offers a few suggestions about the use of each:

- **Typefaces**. All text will retain the typeface, or *font*, specified in the word processor unless the required typeface is not found, in which case Illustrator substitutes Helvetica.
- **Type size and leading**. All text will retain the same type size and leading (line spacing) specified in the word processor. An automatic leading setting will select "Auto leading" in the CHARACTER palette, although the exact amount of leading may differ.

🌐 The **Illustrator 5** Book

- **Type styles**. Illustrator does not apply type styles in the way used by most word processors. Rather than letting you specify styles and fonts separately, Illustrator requires that you specify them together by choosing a stylized screen font from a sub-menu under the FONT menu. Styles for which stylized screen fonts do not exist—underline, outline, strikethru, small caps, and so on— cannot be accessed in Illustrator. Therefore, only bold and italic styles will convert successfully. *Baseline shifts*, on the other hand, will import, so imported superscript and subscript text will appear correctly.

- **Alignment**. Illustrator recognizes paragraphs that are aligned left, center, and right, as well as justified.

- **Indents**. All indents, including first-line indents, left indents, right indents, and hanging indents are transferred intact. Adjusting the margins in your word processor may also affect the indents of imported paragraphs.

- **Paragraph spacing**. Some word processors divide paragraph spacing into two categories: before spacing, which precedes the paragraph, and after spacing, which follows the paragraph. Illustrator combines them into a single "Leading before ¶" option in the PARAGRAPH palette, essentially retaining the same effect.

- **Carriage returns**. Each carriage return character (¶, accessed by pressing RETURN) in a word processor document will be successfully converted by Illustrator 5.0, which assumes each carriage return indicates the end of a paragraph. Line break characters (↵) are also converted into carriage returns. Therefore, try not to use carriage returns or line breaks to force breaks within a paragraph unless you intend to import the text into a point text block.

- **Tabs and tab leaders**. Tab characters convert incorrectly. Because Illustrator does not provide any way to set tab stops, and tabs function correctly only in wrapped text objects (as described in the *Wrapping text around graphics* section later in this chapter), Illustrator substitutes standard spaces for tabs.

- **Special characters**. Word processors provide access to special characters not included in the standard Apple-defined character set (ASCII values 32 through 255). These include em spaces, nonbreaking hyphens, automatic page numbers, and so on. Of these, only the discretionary hyphen character (accessed in Illustrator by pressing COMMAND-SHIFT-HYPHEN) transfers successfully.

will not transfer correctly

- **Page breaks**. Illustrator ignores page breaks in imported text.

- **Headers, footers, and footnotes**. Also ignored.

Formatting options not included in this list are most likely not supported by Illustrator and will therefore be ignored.

Importing text into columns

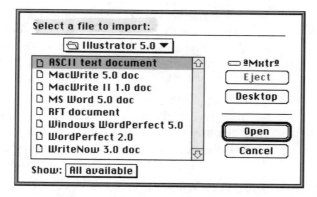

You can import text into a point text block, an area text block, or a path text block. However, because both point text and path text are so badly suited to long stories (path text does not even support carriage returns), you will probably want to import stories only into area text blocks.

To import a story, select the type tool and click on the closed path inside which you want the text to appear. (If you want to append an imported story inside an existing text block, click at the point in the text where you want to insert the story.) Then choose the IMPORT TEXT... command from the FILE menu to display the SELECT FILE TO IMPORT dialog box shown in Figure 7-7. (The IMPORT TEXT... command appears in place of the PLACE ART... command in the FILE menu only after you activate a text block using one of the type tools.)

Figure 7-7: The Select File to Import dialog box allows you to select a story to place into the current Illustrator text block.

The **Illustrator 5** Book

To import a story, select the proper file type from the "Show" pop-up menu, or pick the "All available" choice to display all importable files. Double-click on the desired file name in the scrolling file list, or select the file and click the OPEN button or press RETURN. The DESKTOP and EJECT buttons, folder bar, and keyboard equivalents operate in the same way described in the section *Creating a new illustration* in Chapter 3. Click the CANCEL button or press COMMAND-PERIOD to cancel the import operation.

Shortly after confirming a text file, the SELECT FILE TO IMPORT dialog box will disappear and the imported story will appear in the current text block. If the story is too long to fit inside the current path, a small plus sign is appended to the text block. To display the rest of the story, you can enlarge the path or *flow* the story into additional paths as described in the following section.

Adjusting area text

Like any path-based objects in Adobe Illustrator, you can adjust area text and path text objects in a variety of ways. For one, the paths in which or on which the text resides can be reshaped using the direct-selection tool to allow more or fewer words to display in a text block. In the case of path text, you can move the text along the path to determine exactly how the text sits. Finally, you can *link* a story over several area text blocks, creating both multi-column and multi-page articles. Reshaping, linking, and related topics are explained in the course of the following pages.

Reshaping area text paths

When you enter type inside a path, one of three problems may occur as a result of the size and shape of the path:

- The path may be too narrow to accommodate a word.
- The path may be too small to hold an entire story.
- You may simply dislike the shape of the text block.

When a path is too narrow to hold any one word on a single line, the word is broken onto two lines. A minus sign appears in a small box to the right of the broken word and slightly outside the path, as shown next to the word *determined* in Figure 7-8. This problem generally occurs only if the path is very narrow or the type is very big. To remedy the problem, you can: 1) reduce the type size (as described in the *Formatting text* section later in this chapter), 2) click on the AUTO HYPHENATION check box in the PARAGRAPH palette, 3) manually hyphenate the word by inserting a discretionary hyphen (COMMAND-SHIFT-HYPHEN) or regular hyphen, or 4) increase the width of the text block.

We, the
people
of the
United
Nations,
determin
ed to

Figure 7-8: A boxed minus sign indicates a word cannot fit on a single line; a boxed plus sign indicates the path is too small to hold the story.

When a path is too small to hold an entire story, the words that exceed the lowest segment in the path disappear from view. Such a path is called an *overflow text block*. A plus sign appears in a small

The **Illustrator** 5 Book

box slightly outside the lower right corner of the path, also shown in Figure 7-8. Because stories can be very long, this problem occurs fairly frequently. To remedy the problem, you can: 1) reduce the size of the type to allow more text to fit in the path, 2) edit the text until it fits in the path, 3) enlarge the path until all text is visible, or 4) *flow* the text into multiple paths (as described in the *Flowing area text* section later in this chapter).

Reshaping a path allows you to fit long words on a single line, include more or less text in a path, or simply change the appearance of a block of area text. To reshape any text object, you must use the direct-selection tool to select the path without selecting the text. The following steps describe how to reshape a rectangular column of type.

1. After creating or editing a text block, select the direct-selection tool from the selection tool slot. The path will appear selected, as shown in Figure 7-9.

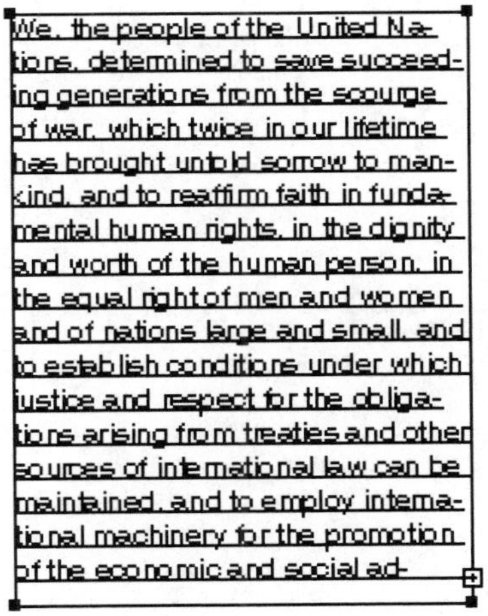

We, the people of the United Nations, determined to save succeeding generations from the scourge of war, which twice in our lifetime has brought untold sorrow to mankind, and to reaffirm faith in fundamental human rights, in the dignity and worth of the human person, in the equal right of men and women and of nations large and small, and to establish conditions under which justice and respect for the obligations arising from treaties and other sources of international law can be maintained, and to employ international machinery for the promotion of the economic and social ad-

Figure 7-9: Text and path appear selected when you initially select the direct-selection tool after entering the text.

2. Click on an empty portion of the drawing area to deselect the text block.

3. Click on a segment of the path you want to reshape. Make sure you click between two lines of text so that you don't accidentally click a baseline and select the text inside the path. The path will appear selected and the text deselected, as shown in Figure 7-10.

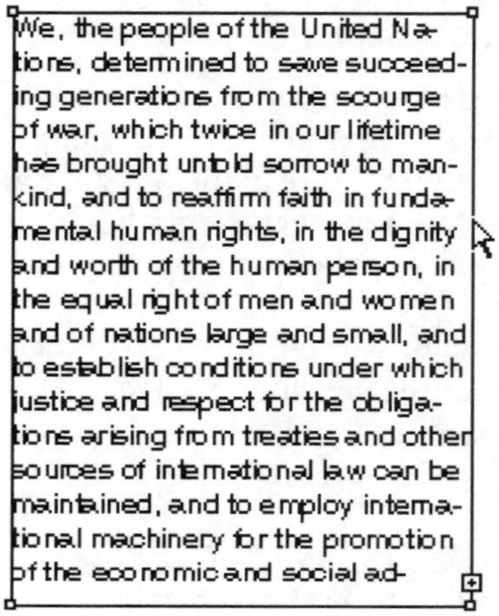

We, the people of the United Nations, determined to save succeeding generations from the scourge of war, which twice in our lifetime has brought untold sorrow to mankind, and to reaffirm faith in fundamental human rights, in the dignity and worth of the human person, in the equal right of men and women and of nations large and small, and to establish conditions under which justice and respect for the obligations arising from treaties and other sources of international law can be maintained, and to employ international machinery for the promotion of the economic and social ad-

Figure 7-10: Clicking on the deselected path with the direct-selection tool selects the path without selecting its type.

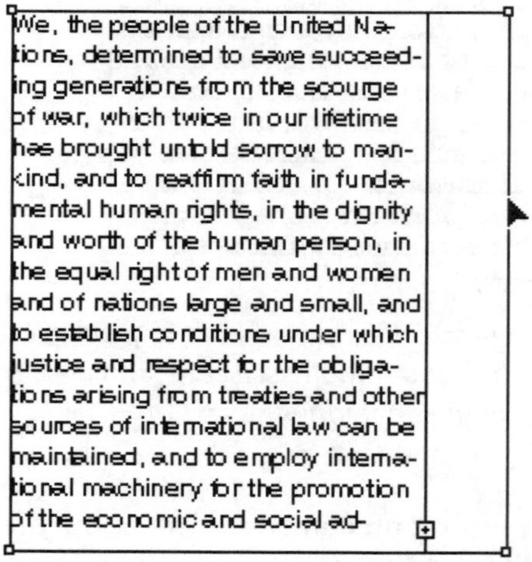

We, the people of the United Nations, determined to save succeeding generations from the scourge of war, which twice in our lifetime has brought untold sorrow to mankind, and to reaffirm faith in fundamental human rights, in the dignity and worth of the human person, in the equal right of men and women and of nations large and small, and to establish conditions under which justice and respect for the obligations arising from treaties and other sources of international law can be maintained, and to employ international machinery for the promotion of the economic and social ad-

Figure 7-11: Shift-drag a vertical segment to widen the text block.

4. To widen the text block, drag one of the vertical segments away from the text, as shown in Figure 7-11. To maintain perpendicular margins, press the SHIFT key while dragging to constrain your move.

5. To lengthen the text block, drag one of the horizontal segments. Press SHIFT to constrain your drag along the vertical axis.

6. To distort the text block, drag a segment without pressing the SHIFT key. You can also drag a point, as shown in Figure 7-12.

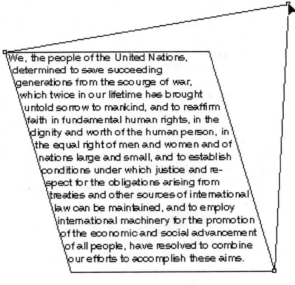

Figure 7-12: Drag a point in a rectangular text path to distort the text block.

You can reshape an area text path using most of the techniques discussed back in Chapter 6. In addition to moving points and segments by dragging, pressing arrow keys, or using the MOVE dialog box, you can drag Bézier control handles; extend an open path using the pen, freehand, and auto trace tools; alter points with the add-anchor-point, delete-anchor-point, and convert-direction-point tools; split segments in a closed path with the scissors tool; join the two endpoints of the same path with the JOIN... command; and average points with the AVERAGE... command.

Some reshaping techniques, however, are not applicable to text paths. These include the following:

- You cannot split an open text path into two separate paths using the scissors tool.

- You cannot join an open text path to a separate open path using the JOIN... command.

- You cannot use the delete-point tool or the DELETE key to delete a point from a text path that contains only two points.

- You cannot select a segment in an open path and press the DELETE key, although you can delete a segment from a closed path, the result of which is shown in Figure 7-13. Also, you cannot delete the entire path if it is the only path for that text block.

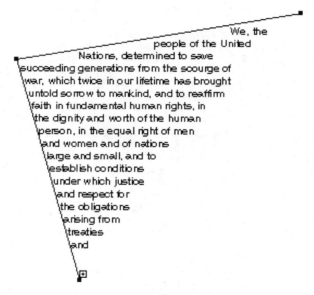

Figure 7-13: You can delete a segment from a closed path to create an open path filled with text.

Similarly, you can reshape a path associated with path text, as discussed in the section *Reshaping path text* later in this chapter.

The **Illustrator 5** Book

Flowing area text

If a story contains more than a couple of paragraphs, you'll probably want to do more than simply reshape it to make the entire story visible in the drawing area. Long stories can be *flowed* across text blocks to create multiple columns or even multiple pages of text. Figure 7-14 shows a story flowed between three paths. Such a story is called a *linked object*, because each text block in the story is linked to another.

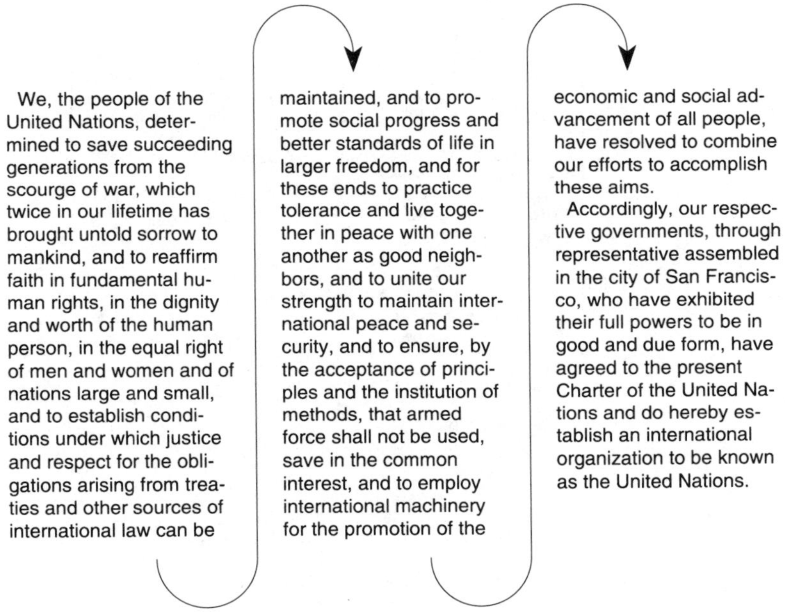

We, the people of the United Nations, determined to save succeeding generations from the scourge of war, which twice in our lifetime has brought untold sorrow to mankind, and to reaffirm faith in fundamental human rights, in the dignity and worth of the human person, in the equal right of men and women and of nations large and small, and to establish conditions under which justice and respect for the obligations arising from treaties and other sources of international law can be maintained, and to promote social progress and better standards of life in larger freedom, and for these ends to practice tolerance and live together in peace with one another as good neighbors, and to unite our strength to maintain international peace and security, and to ensure, by the acceptance of principles and the institution of methods, that armed force shall not be used, save in the common interest, and to employ international machinery for the promotion of the economic and social advancement of all people, have resolved to combine our efforts to accomplish these aims.

Accordingly, our respective governments, through representative assembled in the city of San Francisco, who have exhibited their full powers to be in good and due form, have agreed to the present Charter of the United Nations and do hereby establish an international organization to be known as the United Nations.

Figure 7-14: A single story flowed between three area text blocks.

You can link a text block in one of two ways. The simplest also provides the advantage of guaranteeing that all columns are the same size. First select the group-selection tool and click—click once only—the path of an area text block that displays a boxed plus sign. This selects the entire path without selecting the text inside. Next, drag the path to a new location that does not overlap the current path, as demonstrated in Figure 7-15. While still dragging, press the OPTION key, release the mouse button, then release the OPTION key. This creates a *clone* of the first path (as discussed in the *Cloning objects* section of Chapter 11). The clone automatically fills with the overflow type from the first path, as shown in Figure 7-16. If this new path also displays a boxed plus sign, additional text still exists. Choose the REPEAT TRANS-FORM command from the ARRANGE menu (⌘-D). A third path will be created the same distance and direction from the second path as the second path is from the first. Continue choosing this command until no plus sign displays outside the newest text block.

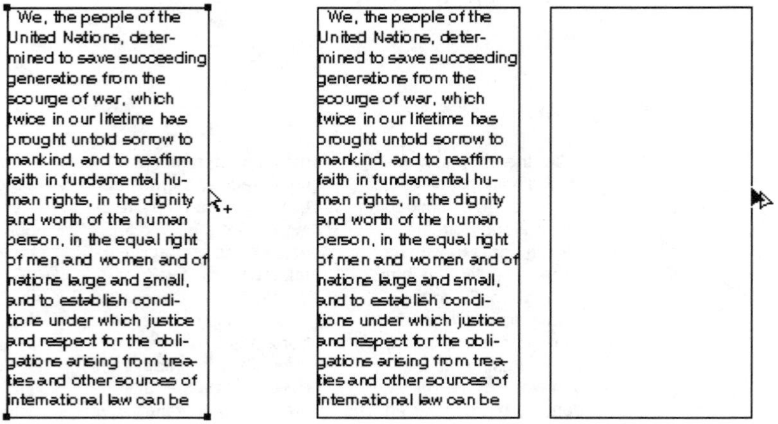

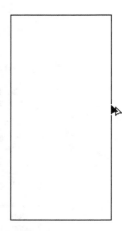

We, the people of the United Nations, determined to save succeeding generations from the scourge of war, which twice in our lifetime has brought untold sorrow to mankind, and to reaffirm faith in fundamental human rights, in the dignity and worth of the human person, in the equal right of men and women and of nations large and small, and to establish conditions under which justice and respect for the obligations arising from treaties and other sources of international law can be

Figure 7-15: Click the path of an overflow text block to select the entire path without selecting its text (left); then option-drag the path to a new location in the drawing area (right).

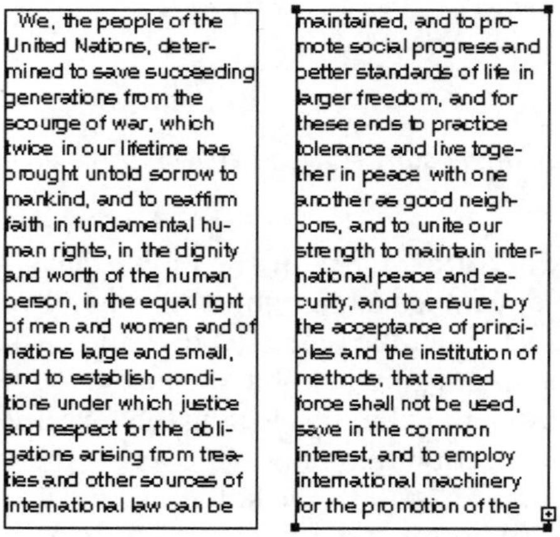

We, the people of the United Nations, determined to save succeeding generations from the scourge of war, which twice in our lifetime has brought untold sorrow to mankind, and to reaffirm faith in fundamental human rights, in the dignity and worth of the human person, in the equal right of men and women and of nations large and small, and to establish conditions under which justice and respect for the obligations arising from treaties and other sources of international law can be

maintained, and to promote social progress and better standards of life in larger freedom, and for these ends to practice tolerance and live together in peace with one another as good neighbors, and to unite our strength to maintain international peace and security, and to ensure, by the acceptance of principles and the institution of methods, that armed force shall not be used, save in the common interest, and to employ international machinery for the promotion of the

Figure 7-16: The overflow text from the first path flows into the new, cloned path.

The **Illustrator 5** Book

You can also clone a path, and hence flow a story into an additional text block, by choosing MOVE… from the EDIT menu and clicking the COPY button in the MOVE dialog box. Or you choose the COPY command from the EDIT menu (⌘-C) and then choose PASTE IN FRONT (⌘-F) to create a duplicate filled with overflow type directly in front of the original path. All of these commands are discussed in detail in Chapter 11, *Transforming and Duplicating Objects*.

If, after flowing all the text in a story, you click any one of the paths with the selection tool, all text blocks associated with the story will become selected, as will their contents. This indicates that all text blocks are linked. You can manipulate individual paths in a linked object using the direct-selection tool.

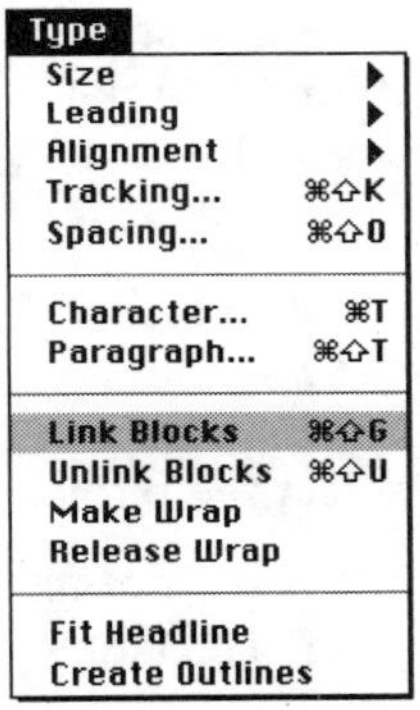

The second way to link text blocks involves using the LINK BLOCKS command in the TYPE menu (⌘-⇧-G). First select the path of an overflow text block with the selection or the direct-selection tool. Then press SHIFT and click on a second existing path—one that does *not* currently contain text—to add it to the selection. Press SHIFT and click on as many additional paths as you think will be required to contain the current story. Then choose the LINK BLOCK command. All paths will fill with as much overflow type as is available, as shown in Figure 7-17.

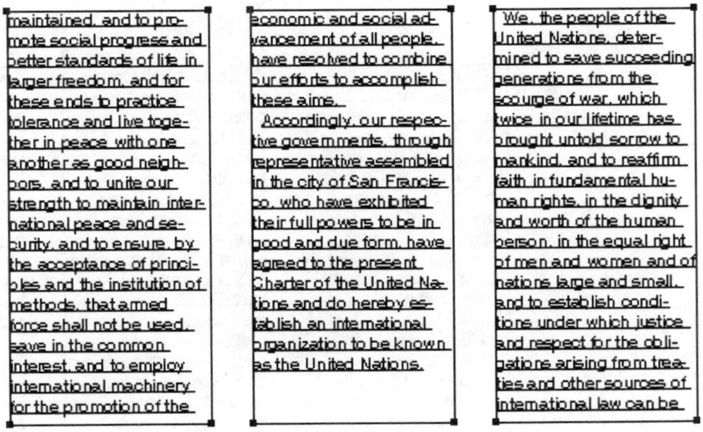

Type	
Size	▶
Leading	▶
Alignment	▶
Tracking...	⌘⇧K
Spacing...	⌘⇧O
Character...	⌘T
Paragraph...	⌘⇧T
Link Blocks	**⌘⇧G**
Unlink Blocks	⌘⇧U
Make Wrap	
Release Wrap	
Fit Headline	
Create Outlines	

maintained, and to promote social progress and better standards of life in larger freedom, and for these ends to practice tolerance and live together in peace with one another as good neighbors, and to unite our strength to maintain international peace and security, and to ensure, by the acceptance of principles and the institution of methods, that armed force shall not be used, save in the common interest, and to employ international machinery for the promotion of the

economic and social advancement of all people, have resolved to combine our efforts to accomplish these aims.
   Accordingly, our respective governments, through representative assembled in the city of San Francisco, who have exhibited their full powers to be in good and due form, have agreed to the present Charter of the United Nations and do hereby establish an international organization to be known as the United Nations.

We, the people of the United Nations, determined to save succeeding generations from the scourge of war, which twice in our lifetime has brought untold sorrow to mankind, and to reaffirm faith in fundamental human rights, in the dignity and worth of the human person, in the equal right of men and women and of nations large and small, and to establish conditions under which justice and respect for the obligations arising from treaties and other sources of international law can be

Figure 7-17: Choose the Link command to fill all selected paths with a single story. The story flows in the order that the paths are layered.

To create evenly sized, evenly spaced rectangular columns of type, you may want to establish a series of guide, as described in the *Creating guides* section of Chapter 11. You can also use the AVERAGE… command to even up the tops and bottom of text blocks, as described in the *Why average points?* section of Chapter 6.

Reflowing a story

Regardless of how it was created, a story flows through a linked text object in the order that its paths are layered (as discussed in the *Layering objects* section of Chapter 11), starting with the rearmost path and working its way forward. This is known as the *linking order*. In Figure 7-17, the right path is the rear path, the middle path is the front path, and the left path is in between. Therefore, the story starts in the right path, flows into the left path, and ends in the middle path; despite the fact that the story started in the left path before the LINK BLOCK was chosen.

If you want to rearrange the order in which a story flows in a linked object, you can relayer the paths by following these steps:

1. Click an empty portion of the drawing area to deselect the paths.

2. Using the direct-selection tool, select the path that you want to contain the first text block in the story. Choose SEND TO BACK from the ARRANGE menu (⌘--, COMMAND-HYPHEN).

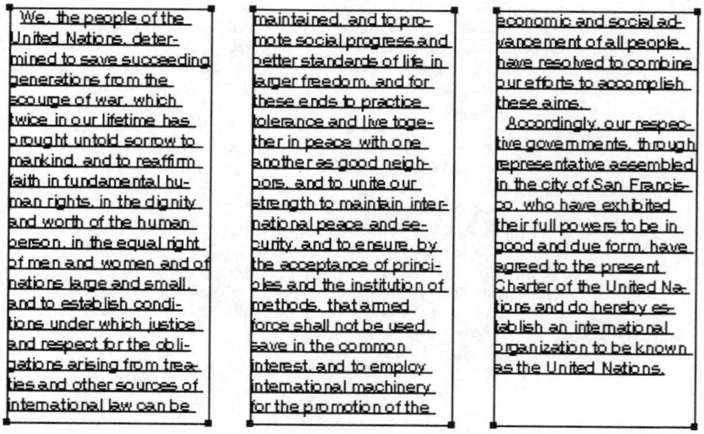

We, the people of the United Nations, determined to save succeeding generations from the scourge of war, which twice in our lifetime has brought untold sorrow to mankind, and to reaffirm faith in fundamental human rights, in the dignity and worth of the human person, in the equal right of men and women and of nations large and small, and to establish conditions under which justice and respect for the obligations arising from treaties and other sources of international law can be

maintained, and to promote social progress and better standards of life in larger freedom, and for these ends to practice tolerance and live together in peace with one another as good neighbors, and to unite our strength to maintain international peace and security, and to ensure, by the acceptance of principles and the institution of methods, that armed force shall not be used, save in the common interest, and to employ international machinery for the promotion of the

economic and social advancement of all people, have resolved to combine our efforts to accomplish these aims.
    Accordingly, our respective governments, through representative assembled in the city of San Francisco, who have exhibited their full powers to be in good and due form, have agreed to the present Charter of the United Nations and do hereby establish an international organization to be known as the United Nations.

Figure 7-18: Layering and relinking a story reflows it in the correct order.

3. Press SHIFT and click the path that will contain the second text block, adding it to the selection. Choose SEND TO BACK again.

4. Keep adding one path after another to the selection in sequential order, choosing SEND TO BACK after the addition of each path.

5. When all but the last path have been sent to the back of the current illustration, SHIFT-click the last path and again choose the LINK BLOCK command from the TYPE menu (⌘-⇧-G). The story is reflowed in the selected paths, as demonstrated in Figure 7-18.

Unlike a grouped object, which can be grouped within other groups, a single linked object cannot be linked more than once. Applying the LINK command to an already linked object does not double-link it; it simply reflows the story.

Other ways to reflow text inside a linked object include the following:

- Reduce the size of a path in the linked object to flow text out of that path and into the next path in the linking order.

- Enlarge the size of a path in the linked object to flow text into that path and out of the next path in the linking order.

- Delete a path in the linked object by clicking on the path with the group-selection tool and pressing DELETE or BACKSPACE to flow all text out of that path and into the next path.

We, the people of the United Nations, determined to save succeeding generations from the scourge of war, which twice in our lifetime has brought untold sorrow to mankind, and to reaffirm faith in fundamental human rights, in the dignity and worth of the human person, in the equal right of men and women and of nations large and small, and to establish conditions under which justice and respect for the obligations arising from treaties and other sources of international law can be

maintained, and to promote social progress and better standards of life in larger freedom, and for these ends to practice tolerance and live together in peace with one another as good neighbors, and to unite our strength to maintain international peace and security, and to ensure, by the acceptance of principles and the institution of methods, that armed force shall not be used, save in the common interest, and to employ international machinery for the promotion of the

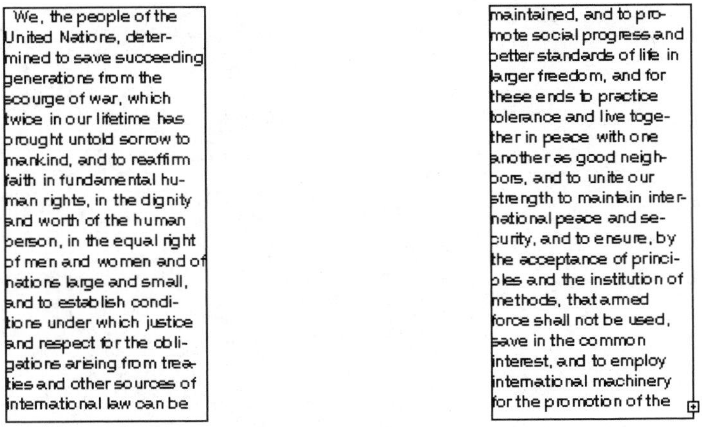

Figure 7-19: Deleting the middle path reflows the text into the last path.

Figure 7-19 on the previous page demonstrates the effect of deleting the middle path from Figure 7-18. Notice that all of its text flows into the last column. The text from the last column now becomes overflow text. (You cannot delete a path if it is the only path in the story.)

Deleting a text block from a story

Deleting a path from a linked object reflows the story. But if you select an entire text block, both path and text, and then delete it, you subtract that portion of the text from your story. You can select an entire text block, independently of other text blocks in a linked object, in one of two ways:

- Click on the baseline of one of the lines of type in the text block with the direct-selection tool.

- Double-click on the path of the text block with the group-selection tool.

In either case, both path and text will be selected, as shown in Figure 7-20. Pressing DELETE under this circumstance will delete text and path from the story. The remaining paths will remain linked.

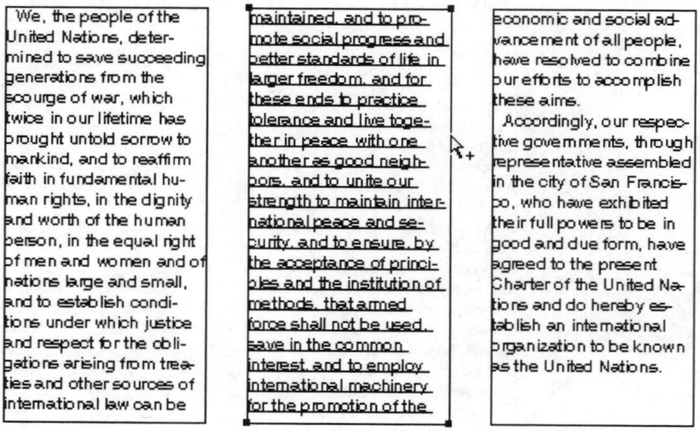

We, the people of the United Nations, determined to save succeeding generations from the scourge of war, which twice in our lifetime has brought untold sorrow to mankind, and to reaffirm faith in fundamental human rights, in the dignity and worth of the human person, in the equal right of men and women and of nations large and small, and to establish conditions under which justice and respect for the obligations arising from treaties and other sources of international law can be maintained, and to promote social progress and better standards of life in larger freedom, and for these ends to practice tolerance and live together in peace with one another as good neighbors, and to unite our strength to maintain international peace and security, and to ensure, by the acceptance of principles and the institution of methods, that armed force shall not be used, save in the common interest, and to employ international machinery for the promotion of the economic and social advancement of all people, have resolved to combine our efforts to accomplish these aims. Accordingly, our respective governments, through representative assembled in the city of San Francisco, who have exhibited their full powers to be in good and due form, have agreed to the present Charter of the United Nations and do hereby establish an international organization to be known as the United Nations.

Figure 7-20: Double-click its path to select a single whole text block within a story.

Press SHIFT and click the baseline of one of the lines of type in the selected text block to deselect the text while leaving the path selected. You can then press DELETE to delete the path and reflow the text as described in the previous section.

Unlinking text blocks

To unlink text blocks in a linked object, choose the UNLINK BLOCK command from the TYPE menu (⌘-⇧-U). This command isolates the paths so that each text block is its own story. Use this command only when you are happy with the way text appears in each column of type and you want to prevent it from reflowing under any circumstance. (To reflow type, do *not* choose UNLINK BLOCK, make changes, and choose LINK BLOCK. Simply make your changes with the direct-selection tool and reapply the LINK BLOCK command, as described in the previous section.)

Adjusting path text

Like an area text block, a path text block can be adjusted to change the way its type is displayed. However, certain different rules apply. For example, you cannot flow path text onto another path. Nor can you create a block of path type that is more than a single line long (although the one line can be as long and winding as you like). But with these limitations come opportunities. Path text includes an *I-beam handle* that you can drag to determine the point at which type aligns on the path. If you flip the handle, the type will flip to the underside of the path. Also, you can combine multiple path text blocks to create special effects.

Reshaping path text paths

When entering type along a path, you may encounter many of the same problems as when entering type inside a path. If the path is too short to accommodate all its text, for example, a plus sign will appear in a small box located on the last point in the path, as shown in Figure 7-21 on the next page. In path text blocks, Illustrator makes no distinction between a single word that cannot fit and an entire story. Since path type cannot wrap to a second line, it either fits on the path or it doesn't.

Figure 7-21: Any amount of overflow text will prompt the boxed plus sign to appear in a block of path type. Type may break in the middle of a word, as shown here.

Because you cannot flow path text onto another path, you have only three choices for fixing the appearance of type along an inadequate path: 1) reduce the size of the type (as described in the *Formatting text* section later in this chapter), 2) edit the text down until it fits on the path, or 3) lengthen the path until all text is visible.

To lengthen a path of path text, you can drag both segments and points with the direct-selection tool in any way that you want. After each drag, the text will refit to the path, so you can see your progress. Suppose, for example, that you want to lengthen the lower line shown in Figure 7-21. The following steps demonstrate a few reshaping methods:

1. Using the direct-selection tool, drag the right endpoint as shown in Figure 7-22. The type will immediately refit to the path, as shown in Figure 7-23.

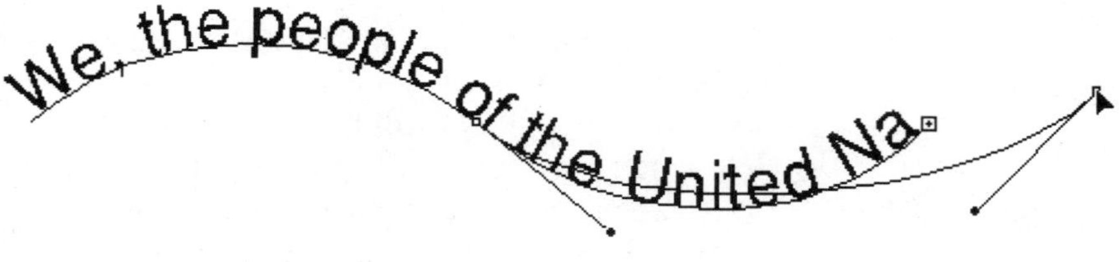

Figure 7-22: Drag the endpoint of an open path independently of its type, using the direct-selection tool.

Figure 7-23: The type refits to the path immediately following the drag.

2. Notice that the line no longer curves as fluidly nor as symmetrically as it did in Figure 7-21. To compensate, drag down on the right segment or adjust the Bézier control handles as shown in Figure 7-24.

Figure 7-24: You can also move the Bézier control handles of a path text block using the direct-selection tool.

3. If your path needs to be lengthened dramatically, you might prefer to use one of the drawing tools. In this case, use the pen tool to lengthen the path. Drag up and to the right from the right-hand endpoint to activate the path. Then drag at desired locations to create additional smooth points. With each additional segment, more text becomes visible until eventually no overflow text remains. The boxed plus sign will disappear to verify that the path is now long enough to accommodate its text, as shown in Figure 7-25 on the next page.

You can also add points, delete points, convert points, and split segments (in a closed path only) using the tools available from the scissors tool slot. However, the same restrictions apply to reshaping path text as apply to area text (refer to the list on page 278).

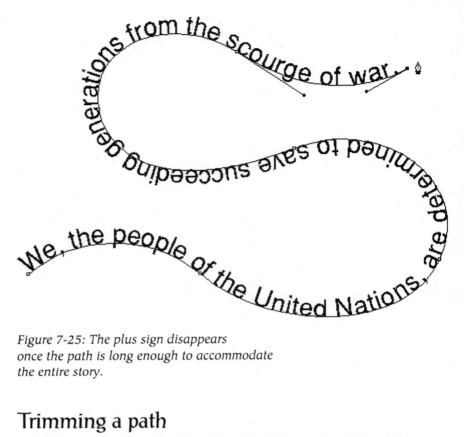

*Figure 7-25: The plus sign disappears
once the path is long enough to accommodate
the entire story.*

Trimming a path

What if instead of being to short, your path is too long? Certainly you can enlarge the type size, edit the text so it's longer, or decrease the dimensions of a closed path. But what if you want to simply trim a little slack off the end of the path? You can't split it off using the scissors tool, because Illustrator won't allow you to split any open path associated with a text object into two separate paths.

Normally, you don't need to worry about excess path. As shown if Figure 7-26, the path is hidden by default when previewing or printing an illustration. Only if you want to *stroke* the path separately of its text—as described in Chapter 9, *Stroking Graphic Objects and Type*—does shortening a path become an issue.

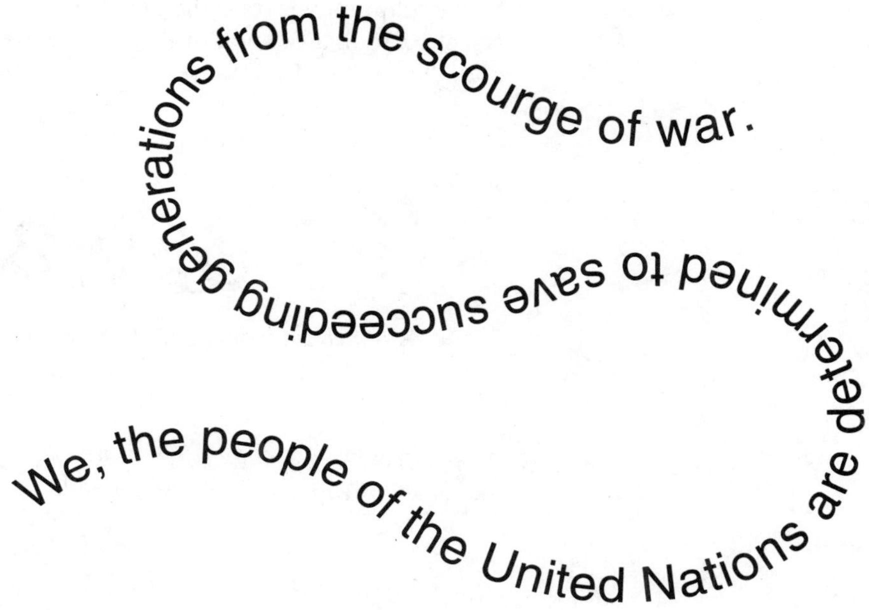

...from the scourge of war.

...generations

...determined to save succeeding

We, the people of the United Nations are

Figure 7-26: The path text block from the previous figure as it appears when printed.

If you do intend to stroke your path, follow these steps to trim away any excess segments:

1. Click at the point at which you want the path to end with the add-anchor-point tool (or OPTION-click with the scissors tool), as shown in Figure 7-27.

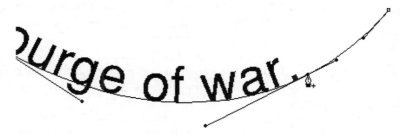

Figure 7-27: Insert a point at the location where you want the path to end (just to the right of the period).

2. Select all points beyond the newly added point with the direct-selection tool, as shown in Figure 7-28. (Do not select the added point itself.)

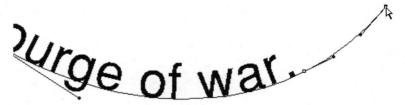

Figure 7-28: Select all points to the right of the newly added point.

3. Press DELETE or BACKSPACE. The selected points and their segments will disappear, making the added point the new endpoint.

Moving type along its path

When both path and type are selected in a block of path text—by clicking the path with the selection tool or double-clicking with the group-selection tool—a special *I-beam handle* displays, as shown in Figure 7-29. This handle allows you to adjust the placement of the story on its path in any of the following ways:

- Drag the handle with any of the selection tools to slide the text back and forth on its path.

- Drag the handle across the path to flip the text to the other side of the path, causing it to change directions.

- Double-click the handle to flip the text to the other side of the path, causing it to change directions.

Using the I-beam handle is a straightforward process. Suppose, for example, that you want to adjust the type shown in Figure 7-29. The following exercise demonstrates how this might work:

1. Select the path text block with the selection tool to display the I-beam handle. The current position of the I-beam is determined by the location that you clicked on the path with the type tool or path-type tool when you originally created the text block.

We, the people of the United Nations...

*Figure 7-29: The I-beam handle (on
the left end of the path) displays when the
whole path-text block is selected.*

2. Drag the handle to some random position in the middle of the
   path, such as the position shown in Figure 7-30. As you drag,
   the new position of type will appear to overlap the original position, making the text illegible. After you release, the original
   position will disappear, allowing you to easily view the results
   of your adjustment. If your story no longer fits on the path, as
   in Figure 7-30, a boxed plus sign will appear over the endpoint.

We, the people of the U

*Figure 7-30: Drag the I-beam handle
to move the text toward the middle of the path.*

3. Drag the type back to the left endpoint in the path until your
   cursor snaps into place, as demonstrated in Figure 7-31 by the
   hollow cursor. Generally, you will want your text to begin at
   the left endpoint in an open path to take fullest advantage of
   the path.

We, the people

*Figure 7-31: Drag the handle back to
the left endpoint in the path until it snaps.*

4. Now drag the handle down to the other side of the path. A copy of the text will flip to face the opposite direction, as shown in Figure 7-32. Drag the handle to the middle of the path so that there is enough room to display some text. If any overflow type exists, the boxed plus sign will appear on the endpoint opposite its usual location, as shown below.

Figure 7-32: Drag the handle (which is invisible during the drag) across the path to flip the text. The boxed plus sign now appears on the left endpoint.

5. Double-click the I-beam handle. The type will immediately jump to the opposite side of the path. The location of the handle relative to the path, however, will remain constant. In Figure 7-33, for example, the handle merely scoots to the other side of the path.

Figure 7-33: Double-click the I-beam handle to flip the text across the path. The boxed plus sign also flips to the opposite endpoint.

You can display the I-beam handle only by clicking on the path of the text block. Do not try to click at the location where you expect the handle to be when the text block is not selected.

The **Illustrator 5** Book

Moving type up and down on a path

When you flip text across a path by dragging or double-clicking the I-beam handle, you also flip the direction of the text when you move it to the other side of the path. But what if you want to move the text without flipping its direction? This is a job for *baseline shift* (or vertical shift). In Illustrator, baseline shift is a formatting feature that allows you to raise or lower type with respect to the baseline. With path text, the baseline is the path itself, so baseline shift allows you to raise and lower type with respect to the path.

You can access baseline shift by selecting text and choosing the CHARACTER... command from the TYPE menu (⌘-⇧-T). However, the easiest way, especially when adjusting type along a path, is to press the SHIFT and OPTION keys along with the up or down arrow key. Press SHIFT-OPTION-↑ to raise the selected type; press SHIFT-OPTION-↓ to lower selected type. The following exercise demonstrates how this feature might be applied:

1. Suppose that you want to create a logo using the old title of this book, *Mastering Adobe Illustrator*. Begin by drawing a circle that measures about 3 inches in diameter.

2. Select the type tool. Position the tool over the topmost point in the path so that the cursor changes to that of the area-type tool. Press the OPTION key to display the path-type tool cursor and click.

3. Type the word *MASTERING*, in capital letters.

4. Press COMMAND-A to highlight the text. Choose the CHARAC-TER... command from the TYPE menu to format the text (as explained in the *Formatting text* section, later in this chapter). Our type is 40-point Helvetica Inserat, but you can select anything you want, so long as it's remotely similar. Choose the HIDE CHARACTER command from the WINDOW menu or click on the close window button in the title bar to exit the CHARACTER palette.

5. Press COMMAND-SHIFT-C to center the type on the path. (Alignment is also discussed in the *Formatting text* section.)

6. Click on the path with the selection tool. Press OPTION and drag the I-beam handle for the text block around to the bottom point in the path; then, without releasing, drag it across the path. Be sure to release the OPTION key *after* releasing the mouse button. A clone of the type moves and flips to the interior of the circle, as shown in Figure 7-34.

Figure 7-34: Option-drag the type to the inside bottom portion of the circle.

7. Click inside the cloned text with the type tool. Press COMMAND-A to select it. Type *ADOBE ILLUSTRATOR* in capital letters, replacing the highlighted text, as shown in Figure 7-35.

Figure 7-35: Enter new text for the cloned type.

8. The upper and lower text blocks do not align properly. You need to move the lower text outward to the outer edge of the path, without flipping it. While the blinking insertion marker still appears in the text, press COMMAND-A to highlight the lower text

block. Since you want to lower the type with respect to its path, press SHIFT-OPTION-↓ to move the type downward. Notice it scoot slightly? It moves only two points (assuming that you have not changed the "Baseline shift" value in the GENERAL PREFERENCE dialog box). After pressing SHIFT-OPTION-↓ a total of eight times, your text will appear as shown in Figure 7-36.

Figure 7-36: Highlight the lower text block and press shift-option-↓ eight times.

9. Now click in the upper text block with the type tool and press COMMAND-A to highlight it. Press SHIFT-OPTION-↓ eight times to achieve the result shown in Figure 7-37 on the following page.

Figure 7-38 displays the finished text as it appears when printed. To add the bullets shown in the figure, I added bullet characters (≋-8) to the beginning and end of the upper text block. I had to do some additional baseline shifting to match the placement of the bullets to that of the upper and lower text blocks.

If you click on the circle with the selection tool, you will notice that two I-beam handles display. This is not because both lines of type adhere to the same path, as you might expect. In fact, no more than one text block can be fitted to a path in Illustrator 5.0. Instead, Illustrator automatically grouped the two paths when you created the clone, assuming that you wanted to manipulate the two paths together in any future transformation.

Figure 7-37: Highlight the upper text block and press shift-option-↓ eight times again.

Figure 7-38: The two text blocks as they appear when printed with bullets.

Each time you press SHIFT-OPTION-↓, you moved the type downward two points. Altogether, you moved the upper and lower text blocks 16 points each. Therefore, 32 points of baseline shift was required to align two blocks of 40-point text.

As a rule of thumb, when creating type along a circle, figure on shifting type a total of 70 to 80 percent of its point size to move the baselines into alignment.

Unlike FreeHand, Illustrator *still* can't alter the orientation of type on a path. In other words, you cannot create text that is at all times vertically oriented despite the shape of the path, as shown in Figure 7-38. If this were an option in Illustrator, you could create cool dimensional effects, like the type around a globe shown in Figure 7-39. Alas, you will have to use FreeHand to achieve this effect.

PIA VO NA DNUORA SEOG TI$
AHH TYPE THAT IS VERTICAL AP

Figure 7-38: Aldus FreeHand allows you to create type that remains vertical as it goes around a path. Illustrator should offer this feature, but doesn't.

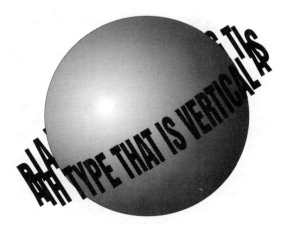

Figure 7-39: Vertically oriented type can be useful for creating type around a globe. If you want to create this effect, you must use FreeHand.

Don't start thinking you bought the wrong software, though. In all other ways, Illustrator's path-type feature outscores FreeHand's. You can edit the text directly on screen, you can adjust the placement of the type simply by dragging a handle, and Illustrator automatically *tracks* type along a path to ensure consistent spacing between letters. In FreeHand, you have to kern characters manually to eliminate inconsistent and amateurish letter spacing.

Formatting text

Text editing features can be broken into two categories: those that are applied to characters of type and those that are applied to whole paragraphs. It is important to understand the distinction and to know what features fall into which category to properly apply formatting commands.

- **Character-level formatting** includes options such as typeface, size, leading, kerning and tracking, baseline shift, and horizontal scaling. To change the formatting of one or more characters, you first select the specific characters and then apply the desired options. Only the selected characters will be modified.

- **Paragraph-level formatting** includes indentation, alignment, paragraph spacing, letter spacing, and word spacing. To change the formatting of a single paragraph, you need only position the blinking insertion marker inside that paragraph. To change the formatting of multiple paragraphs, select at least one character in each of the paragraphs you want to modify.

You may also change character-level or paragraph-level formatting for a new text block before typing it. After clicking with the type tool in the drawing area or on the outline of an existing path, specify the desired formatting options and then begin typing.

To alter the *default formatting options* for an illustration, specify the desired options while no text block is active; that is, the blinking insertion marker does not appear anywhere on screen, nor is any text highlighted. Default formatting changes will apply to all future text blocks; existing text blocks will remain unaffected.

Selecting and editing text

You can select text in Illustrator using the selection tool or one of the type tools. Clicking on a text block with the selection tool selects all type in the object. Any formatting changes will therefore affect all characters. Selecting multiple text blocks with the selection tool lets you format multiple text objects at a time.

If you select text with a type tool, you may only format text within a single text object. However, you can also select individual characters and paragraphs of type, something that you can't do using any of the selection tools.

The following items explain how you can use any type tool to select type in any text object:

- Select a text tool and drag over the characters that you want to select. Drag to the left or to the right to select characters on the same line of type; drag upward or downward to select characters on multiple lines; and drag across columns in a linked object to select large portions of a story, as shown in Figure 7-40. The selected text becomes highlighted.

We, the people of the United Nations, determined to save succeeding generations from the scourge of war, which twice in our lifetime has brought untold sorrow to mankind, and to reaffirm faith in fundamental human rights, in the dignity and worth of the human person, in the equal right of men and women and of nations large and small, and to establish conditions under which justice and respect for the obligations arising from treaties and other sources of international law can be maintained, and to promote social progress and better standards of life in larger freedom, and for these ends to practice tolerance and live together in peace with one another as good neighbors, and to unite our strength to maintain international peace and security, and to ensure, by the acceptance of principles and the institution of methods, that armed force shall not be used, save in the common interest, and to employ international machinery for the promotion of the economic and social advancement of all people, have resolved to combine our efforts to accomplish these aims. Accordingly, our respective governments, through representative assembled in the city of San Francisco, who have exhibited their full powers to be in good and due form, have agreed to the present Charter of the United Nations and do hereby establish an international organization to be known as the United Nations.

Figure 7-40: Drag across columns in a linked text object with the type tool to select large portions of a story.

- Double-click on a word to select that word. Hold down the mouse button on the second click and drag to select more words.

- Triple-click inside a paragraph to select that paragraph. Hold down the mouse button on the third click and drag to select additional paragraphs.

- Click to set the insertion marker at one end of the text you want to select, then SHIFT-click at the opposite end of the desired selection. All text between the first click and the SHIFT-click will become highlighted.

- Click anywhere in a text block and choose SELECT ALL from the EDIT menu (⌘-A) to select all text in the current story, including type linked to the current text block.

- Click to set the insertion marker at one end of the text you want to select and extend the selection using the following keyboard equivalents:

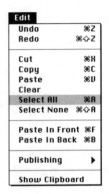

To extend selection	Keystroke
One character to the left	⇧-←
One character to the right	⇧-→
One word to the left	⌘-⇧-←
One word to the right	⌘-⇧-→
One line up	⇧-↑
One line down	⇧-↓
To beginning of paragraph	⌘-⇧-↑
To end of paragraph	⌘-⇧-↓

Highlighted text can be formatted, as discussed in the following pages, or replaced by entering new text from the keyboard. You may also delete selected text by pressing the DELETE or BACKSPACE key. You can copy selected text to the Macintosh Clipboard by choosing the COPY command from the EDIT menu (⌘-C). Or you can delete the selected text and at the same time send a copy to the Clipboard by choosing CUT from the EDIT menu (⌘-X). Finally, you can replace the selected text with some type that you copied earlier to the Clipboard by choosing PASTE from the EDIT menu (⌘-V). Pasted text always retains its original character formatting, although it will assume the paragraph-level formatting of the paragraph into which it is pasted.

The **Illustrator 5** Book

Choosing a font

Font
Chicago
Courier ▶
Geneva
✓Helvetica ▶
Lucida Sans ▶
Monaco
New York
Palatino ▶
Symbol
Times ▶

The FONT menu lists all *typefaces* (also called *fonts*) available to your system software. Choosing a font command designates both the typeface and *type style* (plain, bold, italic) for the selected text. Unlike most Macintosh software, Illustrator lacks specific style options to allow you to embellish plain screen fonts with bold, italic, outline, shadow, underline, and other fabricated styles. Instead, Illustrator relies strictly on *stylized fonts*, which provide separate font information for each type style in a *family*. Illustrator 5.0 automatically combines stylized versions of all PostScript fonts into submenus for quick and easy access. This results in a more organized and manageable FONT menu.

For example, the PostScript family Times includes the stylized fonts Times-Roman, Times-Bold, Times-Italic, and Times-BoldItalic. So long as you are using the PostScript version of the font, each of these styles is available as a command in the TIMES submenu. By allowing you to choose from these font options exclusively, Illustrator ensures that no styles are created for which matching PostScript printer fonts are not available. On the other hand, if you want to apply a style to a TrueType font, you're out of luck. No submenu of stylized fonts appears next to the name of a TrueType typeface. Some TrueType fonts—namely Chicago, Geneva, and Monaco—don't appear in the FONT menu at all.

To guarantee the best use and accuracy in all of your Macintosh typography, you should always *attach* complete font families, including a separate screen font for each style available in the type family. For the Times family, for example, you should load the screen fonts Times, B Times Bold, I Times Italic, and BI Times BoldItalic.

Thanks to improvements in the latest version of Adobe Type Manager (ATM), you can add fonts that are presently not in use to the Extensions or Fonts folder inside the System Folder at the Finder level under System 7 while Illustrator is running. The added fonts will become immediately available in the FONT menu; you don't have to quit Illustrator and restart as in the old days. For more information about loading and attaching screen fonts, see the description of Adobe Type Manager in Appendix A.

Choosing a type size

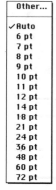

The SIZE command allows you to control the *type size* of the currently selected text, measured in points from the top of an ascender (such as an *f* or *l*) to the bottom of a descender (such as a *g* or *p*). The SIZE submenu provides access to several common sizes and the OTHER... command. To select a size that is not displayed in the SIZE submenu, choose OTHER... (⌘-⇧-S) to display the CHARACTER palette, shown in Figure 7-41. Any value between 0.1 and 1296 in (0.001-point increments) can be entered in the "Size" option box.

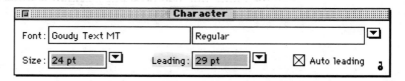

Figure 7-41: The upper portion of the Character palette allows you to specify custom type size and leading values (plus much more).

You can adjust type size from the keyboard by the amount specified in the "Size/Leading" option in the GENERAL PREFERENCES dialog box (⌘-K). Press COMMAND-SHIFT-< to decrease the type size; press COMMAND-SHIFT-> to make the selected type larger.

Choosing a leading

The LEADING command allows you to control the *leading* of the selected text, which determines the distance between a selected line of type and the line above it, as measured in points from one baseline to the other. The LEADING submenu provides access to several common leading values, as well as to an AUTO command and an OTHER... command. Choose the AUTO command to make the leading 120 percent of the current type size (rounded off to the nearest half-point). To select a leading that is not displayed in the LEADING pop-up menu, choose the OTHER... command (⌘-⇧-S), which displays the CHARACTER palette shown in Figure 7-41. Any value between 0.1 and 1296 in (0.001-point increments) can be entered in the "Leading" option box. You may also opt for automatic leading by click on the "Auto leading" check box in the CHARACTER palette.

You can adjust leading from the keyboard by the amount specified in the "Size/Leading" option in the GENERAL PREFERENCES dialog box (⌘-K). Press OPTION-↑ to decrease the space between lines of type; press OPTION-↓ to increase the leading.

Any time that one line of text contains characters with two different leading specifications, the larger leading will prevail. When making a large initial capital letter, for example, you might have a 24-point character on the same line as 12-point characters. If both the 24-point character and the 12-point character use auto leading, then the entire line will be set at 29-point leading (120% the 24-point type size).

Changing the alignment

The lines of type in a paragraph can be aligned along their left edges (*flush left*) their right edges (*flush right*), or both (*justified*), with or without the last line in each paragraph justified as well. Lines of type can also be centered with respect to each other. Text alignment is adjusted relative to the width of the paragraph's text block. Choosing the ALIGNMENT command displays a submenu containing the following five commands:

- LEFT (⌘-⇧-L) aligns lines of type flush left.

- CENTERED (⌘-⇧-C) centers the lines of type.

- RIGHT (⌘-⇧-R) aligns lines of type flush right.

- JUSTIFY (⌘-⇧-J) aligns all lines of type in a paragraph *except* the last line to so they fill the full column width.

- JUSTIFY LAST LINE (⌘-⇧-B) aligns all lines of type in a paragraph *including* the last line so they fill the full column width.

Each ALIGNMENT command will affect all lines of type in a partially selected paragraph.

Kerning and tracking

The fourth position in the Type menu toggles between the Kern... command and the Tracking... command. The Kern... command appears when the insertion marker is positioned between two characters of type; the Tracking... command appears when one or more characters are selected. Both kerning and tracking control the amount of space between each selected pair of characters.

To determine the position of each character in a text block relative to the characters immediately before and after it, Illustrator relies on information that is included with the screen font. As determined by the font's designer, this information specifies the width of a character as well as the amount of space that should be placed before and after the character, known as the left and right *side bearings*, as shown in Figure 7-42. In most cases, the space between any two characters is determined by the right bearing of the first character plus the left bearing of the second.

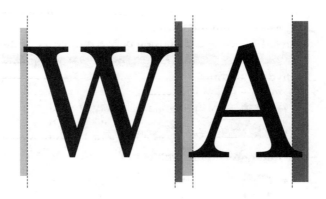

Figure 7-42: Each character has a width (demonstrated by the dotted lines) as well as right and left side bearings (shown as the light and dark gray areas). Together, these elements constitute the horizontal space a letter occupies.

However, font designers can specify that certain pairs of letters, called *kerning pairs*, should be kerned closer together than the standard character spacing would allow. Whenever the two characters of a kerning pair appear next to each other, they are spaced according to the special information provided with the font, as illustrated by Figure 7-43.

Figure 7-43: Certain pairs of letters are defined as kerning pairs. Their screen font includes special spacing information, regardless of their normal widths and side bearings.

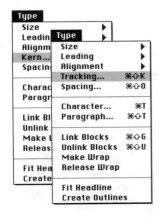

If you are not satisfied with the default amount of kerning between two characters of type, Illustrator allows you to adjust the amount of kerning. Click between two characters and choose the KERN... command from the TYPE menu (⌘-⇧-K). Or if you are dissatisfied with the kerning between multiple characters, select those characters and choose the TRACKING... command (also ⌘-⇧-K). In either case, the fully extended CHARACTER palette will appear containing either a "Kerning" or "Tracking" option box, as shown in Figure 7-44. The value in this option box is measured in ¹⁄₁,₀₀₀ *em space*, which is a character as wide as the type size is tall. For example, an em space in a block of 12-point type is 12 points wide. Enter any number between –1,000 and 10,000 for this option. A negative value will squeeze letters together; a positive value will spread them apart.

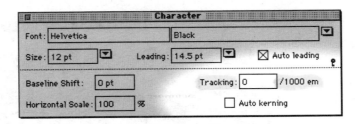

Figure 7-44: This option allows you to change the horizontal spacing between selected characters of type.

Select the "Auto kerning" check box to instruct Illustrator to take advantage of the default kerning information built into the font definition. If no text is selected, this option is dimmed.

If you're a type savant, you will notice that Illustrator's idea of tracking is not the real thing. There is no automatic spacing variation between large and small type sizes. Illustrator's tracking is uniform.

KE Both tracking and kerning can be adjusted from the keyboard by the increment specified in the GENERAL PREFERENCES dialog box (⌘-K). Press OPTION-← to squeeze letters together; press OPTION-→ to spread them apart. To adjust letters by five times the increment specified in the GENERAL PREFERENCES dialog box, press COMMAND-OPTION-← or COMMAND-OPTION-→.

When kerning small type, you may not be able to see a visible difference as you add or delete space because the display is not accurate enough. In such a case, use the zoom tool to magnify the drawing area while kerning or tracking characters from the keyboard. Assuming you have installed the Adobe Type Manager, large characters display spacing adjustments more accurately than small characters.

Spacing letters and words

You can control the amount of space that is placed between characters in a text block by adjusting the *letter spacing*. You can also control the amount of space between words in a text block by changing the *word spacing*. To access these spacing options, choose the SPACING... command from the TYPE menu (⌘-⇧-O), which displays the fully extended PARAGRAPH palette shown in Figure 7-45. Spacing attributes are considered paragraph-level formatting options; your modifications will affect any partially selected paragraph.

There are two primary reasons for manipulating spacing:

- To give a paragraph a generally tighter or looser appearance. This general spacing is controlled using the "Desired" options.

- To determine the range of spacing manipulations Illustrator can use when justifying a paragraph. Some lines must be tightened to fit exactly inside the column; others must be loosened up. You can specify limits using the "Minimum" and "Maximum" options.

Type	
Size	▶
Leading	▶
Alignment	▶
Tracking...	⌘⇧K
Spacing...	⌘⇧O
Character...	⌘T
Paragraph...	⌘⇧T
Link Blocks	⌘⇧G
Unlink Blocks	⌘⇧U
Make Wrap	
Release Wrap	
Fit Headline	
Create Outlines	

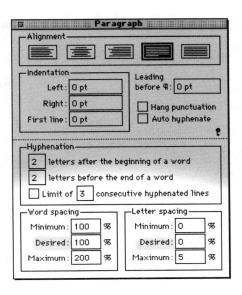

*Figure 7-45: These options control the amount
of space between letters and between words
in a partially selected paragraph.*

When spacing flush left, centered, or flush right paragraphs, Illustrator relies entirely on the values in the "Desired" options. The other options will be dimmed. All values are measured as a percentage of a standard space, as determined by the information contained in the current font. For example, a desired "Word spacing" value of 100% inserts the width of one space character between each pair of words in a paragraph. Reducing or enlarging this percentage makes the space between words bigger or smaller than one normal space character. A desired "Letter spacing" of 10% inserts 10% of the width of a space character between each pair of letters. Negative percentages squeeze letters closer together.

If one or more justified paragraphs are selected, the "Minimum" and "Maximum" options become available. These options will be dimmed if even one flush left, centered, or flush right paragraph is partially selected.

The values for these options may range as follows:

- Minimum word spacing: 0% and ≤ Maximum
- Desired word spacing: ≥ Minimum and ≤ Maximum
- Maximum word spacing: ≥ Minimum and ≤ 1000%
- Minimum letter spacing: –50% and ≤ Maximum
- Desired letter spacing: ≥ Minimum and ≤ Maximum
- Maximum letter spacing: ≥ Minimum and 500%

Word: 75%, 100%, 150%

We, the people of the United Nations, determined to save succeeding generations from the scourge of war, which twice in our lifetime has brought untold sorrow to mankind, and to reaffirm faith in fundamental human rights, in the dignity and

Letter: –5%, 0%, 10%

We, the people of the United Nations, determined to save succeeding generations from the scourge of war, which twice in our lifetime has brought untold sorrow to mankind, and to reaffirm faith in fundamental human rights, in the dignity and

Word: 25%, 50%, 100%

We, the people of the United Nations, determined to save succeeding generations from the scourge of war, which twice in our lifetime has brought untold sorrow to mankind, and to reaffirm faith in fundamental human rights, in the dignity and worth of the

Letter: –25%, –15%, 0%

We, the people of the United Nations, determined to save succeeding generations from the scourge of war, which twice in our lifetime has brought untold sorrow to mankind, and to reaffirm faith in fundamental human rights, in the dignity and worth of the human person,

Word: 150%, 150%, 200%

We, the people of the United Nations, determined to save succeeding generations from the scourge of war, which twice in our lifetime has brought untold sorrow to mankind, and to reaffirm faith in fundamental human rights, in

Letter: 0%, 25%, 50%

We, the people of the United Nations, determined to save succeeding generations from the scourge of war, which twice in our lifetime has brought untold sorrow to mankind, and to reaffirm faith in fundamental human rights,

Figure 7-46: Examples of different word and letter spacing values. In the left column, letter spacing is constant. In the right column, word spacing is constant.

The **Illustrator** 5 Book

Figure 7-46 shows a single justified paragraph under various letter spacing and word spacing conditions. In the first column of paragraphs, only the word spacing changes; all letter spacing values remain constant at 0%. In the second column, only the letter spacing changes; all word spacing values remain constant at 100%. Above each paragraph is a headline stating the values that have been changed. The percentages represent the values entered for the "Minimum," "Desired," and "Maximum" values respectively.

How is letter spacing any different than kerning or tracking? First, the system of measurement is different: percentages of standard space versus $\frac{1}{1,000}$ em space units. But more notably, kerning and tracking affect selected characters only; letter spacing and word spacing affect entire paragraphs.

Automatic hyphenation

Despite its many typographic abilities, the old Illustrator 3.0 provided no automatic hyphenation feature. What exactly was life like back in those days? Well, you had to insert your own hyphens where they appeared necessary. If you are a fan of antiquity, you can still place hyphens by hand. But inserting a standard hyphen character can cause problems. If you edit the text later on, you'll end up with stray hyphens between words that no longer break at the ends of lines. A better idea is to insert a *discretionary hyphen*, which disappears any time it is not needed. You can access the discretionary hyphen by pressing COMMAND-SHIFT-HYPHEN. If no hyphen appears when you enter this character, it simply means that the addition of the hyphen does not help Illustrator to break the word. You can try inserting the character at a new location, or tighten the word and letter spacing slightly to allow room for the word to break.

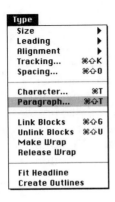

But while discretionary hyphens are useful, wouldn't it be wonderful if somehow Illustrator automatically hyphenated words where necessary in a text block? Well, as you've probably guessed from the title of this section, version 5.0 can. Select a paragraph with a selection or type tool and choose the PARAGRAPH command from the TYPE menu (⌘-⇧-T) to display the PARAGRAPH palette. Then select the "Auto hyphenate" check box. Illustrator will add hyphens and break words across lines as it deems necessary.

Illustrator provides three hyphenate options in the middle portion of the PARAGRAPH palette, as shown in Figure 7-47. Use the top two option boxes to specify the minimum number of letters that come between the hyphen and the beginning and end of a word. As the options stand in Figure 7-47, Illustrator could split the word *apple* as *ap-ple* since both the first and last syllables are at least 2 letters long. On the other hand, if the options were set to 2 "letters after the beginning of a word" and 4 "letters before the end of a word", the word apple could not be split because, although the first criterion is met, the second syllable contains one letter less than needed for an hyphen. You can also decide whether there is a limit to the number of consecutive lines that can end in hyphens and what that limit is.

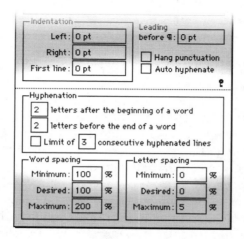

Figure 7-47: The middle portion of the Paragraph palette, in which you can specify how and when Illustrator automatically hyphenates words.

In addition to the hyphenation options in the PARAGRAPH palette, you can instruct Illustrator that you want certain words to remain un-hyphenated regardless of where they fall in a paragraph. Choose the HYPHENATION OPTIONS... command in the PREFERENCE submenu from the FILE menu. The HYPHENATION OPTIONS dialog box will display, as shown in Figure 7-48. Simply type the word you want never to hyphenate in to the ENTRY box and click on the ADD button. To remove a word, select it in the scrolling list and click on the DELETE button. Click on the DONE button when you are through.

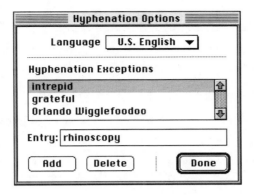

=================== **Hyphenation Options** ===================

Language [U.S. English ▼]

. . . .

Hyphenation Exceptions

intrepid
grateful
Orlando Wigglefoodoo

Entry: [rhinoscopy]

(Add)   (Delete)   (**Done**)

*Figure 7-48: Enter words that you don't want
Illustrator to hyphenate in this dialog box.*

If you add a word in the HYPHENATION OPTIONS dialog box
that already exists in a text block, it won't unhyphenate without a little help from you. Select the text block, then deselect
and reselect the "Auto hyphenate" check box in the PARAGRAPH palette to make Illustrator reapply its automatic hyphenation.

The Character palette

Type	
Size	▶
Leading	▶
Alignment	▶
Tracking...	⌘⇧K
Spacing...	⌘⇧O
Character...	⌘T
Paragraph...	⌘⇧T
Link Blocks	⌘⇧G
Unlink Blocks	⌘⇧U
Make Wrap	
Release Wrap	
Fit Headline	
Create Outlines	

Choosing CHARACTER... from the TYPE menu (⌘-T) brings up the
CHARACTER palette shown in Figure 7-49 on the next page. This dialog
box provides access to every character-level formatting function discussed so far, as well as one other function. This dialog box is useful
when you need to alter the horizontal scale or baseline shift of the
currently selected text or when you simply want to access several
character level formatting options at a central location.

Notice that the CHARACTER palette can appear in a contracted or
expanded form. You can toggle between these two forms by clicking
on the little black mailbox flag located on the right side of the CHAR-
ACTER palette in Figure 7-49. The following pages describe how each
option in this palette works:

- **Font**. Click and hold on the down-pointing arrow icon to the far
  right of this option to display a pop-up menu listing all available typefaces. You can also enter the first few characters in the
  name of the typeface and style into the two option boxes.

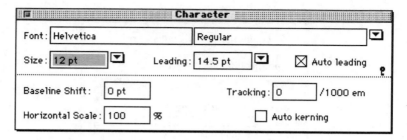

Figure 7-49: The Character palette provides access to all character-level formatting option at a central location.

- **Size**. You can click and hold on the down-pointing arrow icon to the right of this option to display a pop-up menu of type size options. Or simply enter any value between 0.1 and 1296 (in 0.001-point increments) into the option box. The "Size" option will appear empty if the selection is set to more than one type size.

- **Leading**. You can click and hold on the down-pointing arrow icon to the right of this option to display a pop-up menu of possible leading values. Or simply enter any value between 0.1 and 1296 (in 0.001-point increments) into the option box. Select the "Auto leading" check box to make the leading approximately 120% of the current type size. The "Leading" option will appear empty if the selection uses more than one leading value.

  Click on the word "Leading" to change the "Leading" value to match the current "Size" value. Unfortunately, you can no longer click on the word "Size" to change the "Size" value to match the current "Leading" value like you used to be able to do in version 3.0.

- **Baseline shift**. The value in this option box determines the distance between the selected type and its baseline. You can use this option to create superscripts and subscripts, or to adjust type along a path. Enter any value between –1296 and 1296 points (roughly –18 inches and 18 inches) or the equivalent, which is measured in centimeters, inches, or points, depending on the currently selected "Indent/Shift units" option in the GENERAL PREFERENCES dialog box.

KE You can adjust the baseline shift from the keyboard by the amount specified in the GENERAL PREFERENCES dialog box (⌘-K). Press SHIFT-OPTION-↑ to raise the selected text above its baseline; press SHIFT-OPTION-↓ to lower the text below its baseline.

✱ To create a perfect fraction in Illustrator, enter the fraction using the real fraction symbol (⇧-⌥-1) rather than the standard slash. Select the numerator, make it about half its current type size, and enter a baseline shift value equal to about one-third the original type size. Then select the denominator and match its type size to that of the numerator, but do not adjust the baseline shift. The result will be a fraction such as the one shown in Figure 7-50.

$$^{35}\!\!\big/_{38}$$

Figure 7-50: You can make any fraction by varying type size and baseline shift. The fraction above was first set in 100-point type. The numerator (35) was then changed to 50-point and shifted 33 points up. The denominator (38) was also changed to 50-point type but not shifted.

- **Horizontal scale**. The value in this option determines *horizontal scale* of the selected type, which is its width as measured as a percentage of its normal width. In this way, you can expand or condense type to any extent between 1% and 10,000% (100 times its normal width). The "Horizontal scale" option is used primarily to achieve special graphic effects with type. Take care not to modify any type so severely that its legibility is compromised, as shown in Figure 7-51 on the next page.

Condensed to 30%

Expa nded 400%

Figure 7-51: Decreasing the horizontal scaling of a text block may result in fat horizontal character strokes and skinny vertical strokes. Increasing the option may result in fat vertical strokes and skinny horizontal strokes. Both effects decrease the legibility of the text.

Incidentally, if you have scaled a text block disproportionately using the scale tool (as described in *Scaling objects* section of Chapter 11), the "Horizontal scale" option will change to reflect the discrepancy between the current width and the normal width of the selected type. You can reset the type to its normal width by changing the option to 100%.

- **Kerning/Tracking**. If the insertion marker is positioned between two characters of type, the fourth option will be labeled "Kerning." If several characters are selected or no type at all, the option is labeled "Tracking." Enter any value between –1000 and 10,000 for this option, measured in $\frac{1}{1,000}$ em space. Select the "Auto kerning" option to activate the default kerning defined by the screen font for the current selection. This check box will appear dimmed when the option box is labeled "Kerning."

You can click on the names of many character-level options to reset their values. Clicking the word "Kerning," "Tracking," or "Baseline shift" will reset the corresponding option to 0. Clicking the word "Horizontal scale" resets its value to 100%.

The Paragraph palette

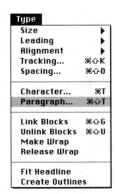

Choosing PARAGRAPH... from the TYPE menu (⌘-⇧-T) brings up the PARAGRAPH palette as shown in Figure 7-52. This dialog box provides access to every paragraph-level formatting function discussed so far, as well as three others. These options affect any partially selected paragraphs.

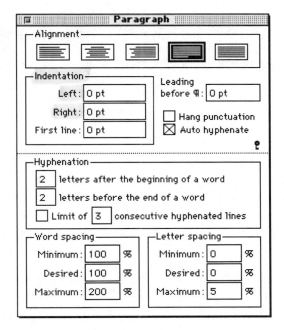

Figure 7-52: The Paragraph palette provides centralized access to all paragraph-level formatting options.

- **Alignment**. The five "Alignment" icons allow you to change the alignment of the lines of type in a partially selected paragraph. Select the first icon (▤) to align the paragraph flush left; select the second icon (▤) to center the paragraph; select the third icon (▤) to align the paragraph flush right; select the fourth icon (▤) to justify the paragraph; and select the fifth icon (▤) to justify the paragraph and *force justify* the last line of the paragraph. Forced justifying the last line works well only when the last line is almost the length of text block.

- **Indentation**. The "Left" indent option specifies the positioning of the left edge of each line in the paragraph relative to the left edge of the text block. The "Right" option specifies the positioning of the right edge of each line relative to the right edge of the text block. The "First line" option specifies the position of the left edge of the first line of type in a text block relative to the left edge of the *other lines* in the paragraph (as specified in the "Left" option). A positive "First line" value results in a standard paragraph indent, as shown in the first example of Figure 7-53. A negative "First line" value creates a *hanging indent*, as shown in the second example in the figure. Enter any value between –1296 and 1296 points (–18 inches and 18 inches) or the equivalent, which is measured in centimeters, inches, or points, depending on the currently selected "Indent/Shift units" option in the GENERAL PREFERENCES dialog box.

　　We, the people of the United Nations, determined to save succeeding generations from the scourge of war, which twice in our lifetime has brought untold sorrow to mankind, and to re-

1.　We, the people of the United Nations, determined to save succeeding generations from the scourge of war, which twice in our lifetime has brought untold sorrow to mankind,

Figure 7-53: A paragraph with a positive "First" indent value and a "Left" value of 0 (top) and a paragraph with a positive "Left" value and a negative "First" value.

If you're familiar with creating hanging indents in a word processor, you may have a tough time creating them in Illustrator, since there is no way to set tab stops to align the first line with those that follow. A tip for creating perfect hanging indents is included in the section *Using tabs with wrapped objects*, which starts on page 323.

The **Illustrator 5** Book

- **Leading before ¶** . Enter a value in this option to insert some extra space before one or more selected paragraphs. *Paragraph leading* helps separate paragraphs from each other, making them more identifiable and in some cases more legible. The paragraphs of body text in this book, for example, are separated by 6 points of paragraph leading. Enter any value between –1296 and 1296 for this option, which is measured in points.

- **Hanging punctuation**. Select this check box to make punctuation such as commas, quotation marks, hyphens, and so on, hang outside the edge of a selected paragraph, as shown in Figure 7-54. As the period and closing quote in the second example of the figure demonstrate, if two adjacent punctuation symbols occurs at the beginning or end of a line, only the first or final symbol hangs outside the paragraph. This option can be applied to flush left, flush right, or justified paragraphs.

"We, the people of the United Nations, are determined to save succeeding generations from the scourge of war, which twice in our lifetime has brought untold sorrow to mankind."

"We, the people of the United Nations, are determined to save succeeding generations from the scourge of war, which twice in our lifetime has brought untold sorrow to mankind."

Figure 7-54: The quotation mark hangs outside the flush left paragraph (top). The closing quotation mark and some commas hang outside the flush right paragraph (bottom).

✳ You can click on the names of any paragraph-level option box to reset its value. Clicking the word "Left," "Right," "First line," or "Leading before ¶" will reset the corresponding option to 0.

- **Auto hyphenate**. Click on this check box if you want the words in a particular text block to hyphenate when they extend beyond the right edge of the text block. Otherwise, such words on the edge will automatically drop in their entirety to the beginning of the next line.

- **Hyphenation**. The first two option boxes allow you to specify the minimum number of letters that must exist in the first and last syllables of a word to allow it to hyphenate. The last option box limits the number of consecutive lines that can end in hyphens. For example, in this book, you never see more than two lines in a row ending in hyphens.

- **Word spacing**. Enter a number between 0 and 1,000 to determine the percent of a full space that should separate each word in the paragraph. If you select either of the justified alignment options, you can enter a range of spacing values that allow the spaces to vary depending on the requirements of each line of type. The three values must obey the relationship: 0% ≤ "Minimum" ≤ "Desired" ≤ "Maximum" ≤ 1,000%.

- **Letter spacing**. Enter a number between –50 and 500 to determine the percent of a space character that should separate each letter in the paragraph. Again, if you select either of the justified alignment options, you can enter a range of spacing values that allow the spaces to vary depending on the requirements of each line of type. The three values must obey the relationship: –50% ≤ "Minimum" ≤ "Desired" ≤ "Maximum" ≤ 500%.

✳ You can click on the names of any paragraph-level option box to reset its value. Clicking the word "Left," "Right," "First line," or "Leading before ¶" resets the corresponding value to 0. Click on the word "Minimum" to make it match the "Desired" value.

You can undo any changes made in either the CHARACTER or PARAGRAPH palettes by choosing the UNDO command from the EDIT menu (⌘-Z).

Wrapping type around graphics

Illustrator was the first drawing program to provide a *text wrapping* feature, previously virtually unique to page-layout programs such as Aldus PageMaker and QuarkXPress. The wrapping feature instructs type to flow around the boundaries of one or more graphic objects, as shown in Figure 7-55. Using the "Indentation" options in the PARA-GRAPH palette, you can even determine the amount of space between type and graphic objects.

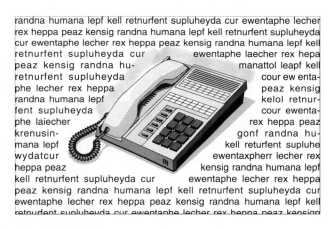

randna humana lepf kell retnurfent supluheyda cur ewentaphe lecher rex heppa peaz kensig randna humana lepf kell retnurfent supluheyda cur ewentaphe lecher rex heppa peaz kensig randna humana lepf kell retnurfent supluheyda cur ewentaphe laecher rex hepa peaz kensig randna hu- manattol leapf kell retnurfent supluheyda cour ew enta- phe lecher rex heppa peaz kensig randna humana lepf kelol retnur- fent supluheyda cour ewenta- phe laiecher rex heppa peaz krenusin- gonf randna hu- mana lepf kell returfent supluhe wydatcur ewentaxpherr lecher rex heppa peaz kensig randna humana lepf kell retnurfent supluheyda cur ewentaphe lecher rex heppa peaz kensig randna humana lepf kell retnurfent supluheyda cur ewentaphe lecher rex heppa peaz kensig randna humana lepf kell retnurfent supluheyda cur ewentaphe lecher rex heppa peaz kensign

Figure 7-55: In Illustrator, you may wrap type around the boundaries of one or more graphic objects.

Wrapping text around a graphic is a five-step process in Illustrator:

1. Determine which text block you want to wrap. Only area text can be wrapped around graphics in Illustrator.

2. Select the graphic objects around which you want your text to wrap. For safety's sake, first group the objects by choosing the GROUP command from the ARRANGE menu (⌘-G).

3. Drag the group into position in front of the text block. Choose the BRING TO FRONT command from the EDIT menu (⌘-=). The graphic must be in front of the text block to wrap properly.

4. Select both text block and graphic object and choose the MAKE WRAP command from the TYPE menu to fuse the selection into a single *wrapped object*. The type will wrap automatically.

5. Use the PARAGRAPH palette to adjust the indentation between type and graphic boundaries.

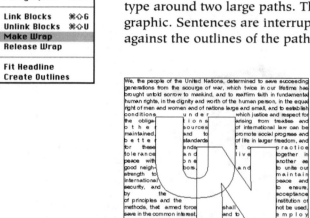

The MAKE WRAP command is completely automatic. After you choose the command, the selected text will wrap to every nook and cranny of a selected graphic, regardless of how irregular the boundary. Keep in mind, however, that irregular text wrapping can make for illegible text. In Figure 7-56, for example, we have wrapped some type around two large paths. The type appears riddled inside the graphic. Sentences are interrupted by enormous gaps, and text butts against the outlines of the paths.

Figure 7-56: Text wrapped around an irregular graphic boundary (left) and the same text as it appears when selected (right).

In the right example of the figure, the entire text block has been highlighted with the type tool. This allows you to see exactly how the paths cut into the text block. Notice that there are several large gaps in sentences where the graphic does not interrupt the type. These gaps are caused by the paragraph formatting. Each segment in the graphic is treated as another edge to the text block. Because the text in the figure is justified, words are forced flush to the boundaries of the wrapped paths just as they are to the sides of the column.

Most forms of any paragraph formatting will affect the appearance of wrapped type. The paragraph formatting options that produce the most dramatic effects are:

- **Indentation**, which determines the amount of room, called *standoff*, between the graphic and the text.

- **Alignment**, which determines the way words align between the sides of the column and the boundaries of the paths.

- **Word spacing and letter spacing**, which determine how much text fits on each line and how well the text matches the contour of the graphic.

For example, the only difference between the examples in Figure 7-56 and those in Figure 7-57 is the paragraph formatting. In the first example, the type has been aligned flush left. In the second example, the word spacing has been tightened from 100% to 70% and the letter spacing has been reduced from 0% to –5%.

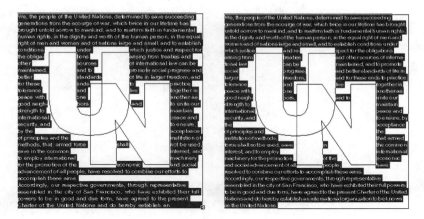

Figure 7-57: The same text block aligned flush left (left) and subjected to tighter word and letter spacing (right).

The most powerful paragraph formatting feature, however, is indentation. The following section explains how you can use both left and right indents to increase or decrease the amount of standoff between type and graphic objects.

Adjusting standoff

There are two ways to adjust the amount and the shape of the stand-off around a graphic object. The simplest method is to use indentation. The outline around a graphic is treated as another side to the column surrounding a text block, which makes for several left and right margins. Therefore, both the left and right paragraph indents can be used to create a standoff. In Figure 7-58, both the left and right indents have been increased to 9 points, or ⅛ inch. I also inserted several discretionary hyphens to lend the story a more consistent appearance.

Figure 7-58: Adding left and right indents creates a standoff between type and graphics. The right example shows the image as it appears when printed.

You can also establish a standoff by creating a special path to act as a dummy for the actual graphic object. This path should have no fill and no stroke (as described in Chapters 8 and 9) so that it becomes invisible when previewed or printed. You then wrap the type around the invisible path rather than around the graphic image. After creating the wrapped object using the MAKE WRAP command, position the graphic object as desired. This technique offers more flexibility, because you can reshape the invisible path at any time to adjust the boundaries of the standoff. An example of such a wrapped object is displayed in Figure 7-59.

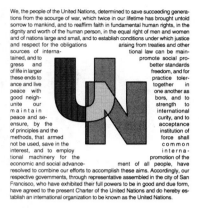

Figure 7-59: The selected path on the left is an unfilled, unstroked dummy path that has been made part of the wrapped object. The actual graphic objects are separate. The right example shows how the dummy path disappears when printed, creating a clear standoff around the graphic.

Using tabs with wrapped objects

You may already have toyed with inserting tab characters into text blocks in Illustrator. If so, you no doubt discovered that a tab knocks the insertion marker down to the next line of type. What actually happens is the tab character moves the insertion marker to just beyond the next path segment that it encounters. It's probably an error on Adobe's part, but it's an error that you can exploit in a unique and useful manner.

Consider the wrapped object in Figure 7-59. The type in the middle portion of the graphic is divided into two pockets—one on the left side of the graphic and one on the right. If you were to click with the type tool someplace in the left pocket of text and press the TAB key, you move the insertion marker and all type following it past the next edge in the graphic and into the right pocket. The following exercise demonstrates how this use of tabs in a wrapped object can be used to create paragraphs with perfect hanging indents:

1. Drag on an empty portion of the drawing area with the type tool to create a column.

2. Enter the text shown in Figure 7-60 on the following page. Press the TAB key at the point indicated by the ➡| symbol.

```
1. ➡|
We, the people of the United Nations,
determined to save succeeding
generations from the scourge of war,
which twice in our lifetime has brought|
```

*Figure 7-60: Create the column of type shown
above (or something to that effect). The ➡| symbol
indicates where you should press the tab key.*

3. Click and SHIFT-click with the pen tool to create a vertical line
   at least as tall as the text block.

4. Drag the line a quarter to a half inch inside the text block.

5. Select both line and column and choose MAKE WRAP from the
   TYPE menu. The result will be the text block shown in Figure 7-61.

```
1. We, the people of the United Na-
   tions, determined to save succeed-
   ing generations from the scourge of
   war, which twice in our lifetime has
   brought
```

*Figure 7-61: The type after the tab wraps to the
opposite side of the vertical line.*

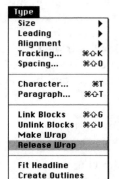

6. Use the "Indentation" options in the PARAGRAPH palette to determine the amount of spacing between the type and the vertical line. The final image is the same as that shown back in the
   second example of Figure 7-53.

Unwrapping text blocks

To split type and graphic objects, choose the RELEASE WRAP command
from the TYPE menu. Choosing this command returns text block and
graphic objects to their original states and allows the type to flow over
the graphic.

Fitting large text

Type
Size ▶
Leading ▶
Alignment ▶
Tracking... ⌘⇧K
Spacing... ⌘⇧O

Character... ⌘T
Paragraph... ⌘⇧T

Link Blocks ⌘⇧G
Unlink Blocks ⌘⇧U
Make Wrap
Release Wrap

Fit Headline
Create Outlines

New to Illustrator 5.0 is the ability to exactly fit a line of type across the width of a text block. Simply select a text block that contains type that either falls short of filling the first line or spills over slightly onto the second line, and choose the FIT HEADLINE command from the TYPE menu. The type will expand or contract to fit the length of the block, somewhat analogous to a column's headline in a newspaper.

In Figure 7-62, the top two lines of type show what the lower lines looked like before the application of the FIT HEADLINE command. The next two lines show the results. "But hey," you might say, "these two lines look like someone simply adjusted the tracking so that the type fits the first line. In fact, I'd say they look like doggie yak!" Okay, so *you* wouldn't call it doggie yak, but however you put it, you'd be absolutely correct. But, don't despair, because the FIT HEADLINE command is not designed with regular old run-of-the-mill fonts in mind. Like usual, Adobe has envisioned something better.

Regular old Type 1 fonts

| United Nations | United |
| United Nations | United Nations |

Multiple master fonts

| United Nations | **United** |
| **United Nations** | United Nations |

Figure 7-62: The results of applying the Fit Headline command to type that is two narrow for its text block (left) and type that is too wide (right).

The truth is, FIT HEADLINE is designed for use with *multiple master fonts*. Multiple-master technology, a recent Adobe invention, allows an application to consult two master designs that represent extremes in font characteristics and blend them into a unique style. Thousands

---

of blends are possible. When the FIT HEADLINE command is applied to a multiple master font, Illustrator does not change the tracking, as it does with a normal font, but rather blends the font characteristics between the master designs. For example, it might increase the width of the letters on one hand or the thickness of the stems and serifs on the other until the type just fits on the first line of the text block. In other words, the FIT HEADLINE command creates a whole new type style that exactly works within the confines of your text block.

Converting type to paths

The final type ability in Illustrator 5.0 is both the best and the easiest. By choosing the CREATE OUTLINES command from the TYPE menu, you can convert any selected text block into a collection of editable paths. The only catch is that the type must be selected with the selection tool (it cannot be highlighted with the type tool). But this will seem like a small inconvenience when you see how quickly and powerfully this command performs.

The left example in Figure 7-63 shows a three-character text block selected using the selection tool. The second example shows the characters after choosing CREATE OUTLINES. The characters are now standard paths, composed of Illustrator-compatible points and segments.

Of the three characters converted in the figure, notice that the *T* and *G* have been converted into a single path apiece, but the ampersand has been converted into three paths. To make interior paths transparent, such as those in the ampersand, Illustrator converts all characters to *compound paths*. In this way, it lets you see through the character to the objects behind it, as discussed in the *Making holes* section of Chapter 8. However, to perform complex manipulations, such as joining part of one path to another, it may be necessary to separate the character into one or more normal paths by choosing the RELEASE command in the COMPOUND PATHS submenu from the OBJECT menu (⌘-9).

After you choose the CREATE OUTLINES and RELEASE commands, you can reshape, transform, duplicate, and otherwise manipulate converted type in any manner, as demonstrated by the fantastic example in Figure 7-64. It may not be art, but at least it's possible.

🪐 The **Illustrator 5** Book

Figure 7-63: Select the text block with the selection tool (top) and choose the Create Outlines command to produce a collection of fully editable points and segments (bottom).

Figure 7-64: And to think, this was once Helvetica.

The text filters

Illustrator 5.0 provides two commands under the FILTERS menu that deal specifically with type: the EXPORT... and FIND... commands under the TEXT menu. These are the only two filters that are discussed outside Chapter 12, *The Hodgepodge World of Filters*. The reason I discuss them here is that—with the exception of a couple of commands under the SELECT submenu—these are the only filters that are applicable to text.

Very quickly, filters are external files that Illustrator loads into memory during the startup process. These files are found in the Plug-Ins folder inside the same folder that contains the Illustrator application. They represent functions that Adobe felt you might not need on a daily basis and thus did not merit incorporation into the basic Illustrator application. For more information on the whole filter scene, read the introduction to Chapter 12.

The Export filter

The EXPORT filter allows you to export text from Illustrator to any application that supports one of several word-processing file formats. Simply select one or more characters of type from any text block with the type tool; you cannot select the text with the selection tool. Then choose EXPORT... from the TEXT submenu under the FILTERS menu. The EXPORT dialog box will display, as shown in Figure 7-65. Name the file and specify the destination folder as you would in the SAVE ILLUSTRATION dialog box. Near the bottom is the "Export file" pop-up menu. Click on it to display a number of file formats that you can assign to your exported file. For the most part, these are the same file formats described on page 270 of this chapter.

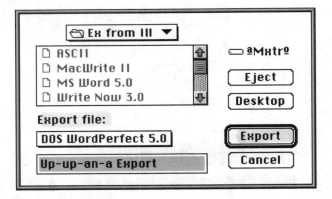

Figure 7-65: The Export dialog box lets you export selected text so you can open it in a word processor.

The **Illustrator** 5 Book

Keep in mind that when you export text from Illustrator to another application, you save only the type and its formatting attributes. No path information is included. For example, if you export a line of path type that surrounds a circle and then import it into a word processor, the type will appear like any other line of type, laid out from left to right along a straight baseline. Not so much as a trace of a circle in sight. If you want to export fancy type including paths and everything, export the illustration in the EPS format, as discussed in Chapter 14, *Importing and Exporting Artwork*.

The Find filter

The FIND... filter allows you to locate all occurrences of a particular string of type and, if you want, replace each occurrence with a different string of type. The string of type can consist of as many characters as you like, including spaces. Click with the type tool at the location where you want to begin the search process and choose FIND... from the TEXT submenu under the FILTERS menu. The TEXT FIND dialog box will display, as shown in Figure 7-66. Enter the string you want to search for in the "Find what" option box and the replacement string (if needed) in the "Replace with" option box. Then select the desired check boxes and click the button that reflects your needs.

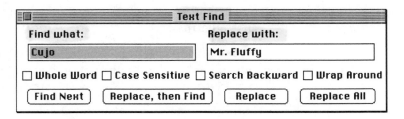

Figure 7-66: The Find... filter allows you to search for a particular string of type and then replace each occurrence with another string of type.

If none of the check boxes are selected, the search will start at the insertion marker and continue to the end of the text block. The search will find any occurrence of the string including those that happen in the middle of a word. For example, if I were to use the string shown in Figure 7-66 in a search, then Illustrator would find both the words *Cujo* and *concujoration* (not that the latter is a word, of course). The check boxes let you limit the search as well as the manner in which the search is executed.

The check boxes in the TEXT FIND dialog box work as follows:

- **Whole Word** limits the search to whole words that exactly match the string that appears in the "Find what" option box.

- **Case Sensitive** limits the search to portions of the text block that exactly match the uppercase and lowercase letter scheme of the string that appears in the "Find what" option box.

- **Search Backwards** begins the search at the insertion marker and proceeds back towards the beginning of the text block.

- **Wrap Around** begins the search at the insertion marker and proceeds to the end of the text block, starts over at the beginning of the text block, and continues to the insertion marker again.

The four buttons along the bottom of the dialog box work like so:

- **Find** searches for the next occurrence of the string that appears in the "Find what" option box. Click again to find the occurrence after that.

- **Replace, then Find** replaces the selected text with the contents of the "Replace with" option box and then looks for the next occurrence of the "Find what" string.

- **Replace** replaces the selected text with the contents of the "Replace with" option box. That's it. If you want to search around some more, you'll have to click on the FIND button again.

- **Replace All** looks for every occurence of the "Find what" string from the insertion marker to the end of the text block and replaces it with the contents of the "Replace with" option box. If you want to search from the insertion marker to the beginning of the text block, select the "Search Backwards" check box and click on the REPLACE ALL button. If you want to replace every last occurence of the "Find what" string throughout the entire text block, select the "Wrap Around" check box and click on the REPLACE ALL button.

A beep will sound when the TEXT FIND dialog box finishes its duly appointed rounds.

CHAPTER

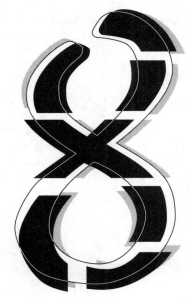

FILLING GRAPHIC OBJECTS AND TYPE

In the artwork display mode, all paths have transparent interiors surrounded by thin, solid black outlines. All type is black. But now that Illustrator 5.0 lets you work in the preview mode, color and other object attributes become more accessible and easier to use than ever before. The interior of a graphic object or a character of text can be black or red, or it can fade from blue to yellow with green in between. Outlines can be as thick or thin as you like, dashed or solid, orange or purple,

333

series of many colors and gray values. One of Illustrator's greatest strengthens is the complete freedom it allows you to determine the appearance of a path or text object.

The qualities you can assign to type and graphic objects are called *fills* and *strokes*. Fill determines the appearance of the interior of an object, and is the subject of this chapter. Stroke is applied to the outline of an object, and is covered in Chapter 9, *Stroking Graphic Objects and Type*.

How fill affects an object

In Illustrator, any path or text block can be filled. If a closed path is filled, its entire interior is affected. Figure 8-1 shows a closed path as it appears in the artwork mode and the same path as it appears when printed. The shape is a kind of malleable water balloon, with the fill seeping into every nook and cranny.

Figure 8-1: In the artwork mode, the fill of a closed path is invisible (left). But when you preview or print the path, its fill seeps into every nook and cranny in the shape (right).

Following that same logic, you might think that the fill would quickly flow out of an open path. Instead, an imaginary straight segment connects the two endpoints of the line. The first example in Figure 8-2 is an open path with a thick stroke. The path in the second example is filled with light gray. No part of the fill exceeds the boundaries of the imaginary straight segment between the endpoints. The imaginary segment is not stroked; it acts as an invisible barrier between the fill path and the unfilled background.

Figure 8-2: Generally, an open path is stroked and not filled (left). If you do fill an open path, an imaginary straight segment between the two endpoints defines the boundary of the fill (right).

Filled open paths can be very useful for creating indefinite boundaries in a graphic. The cartoon plane in Figure 8-3 is an example of this technique. Notice that the front and rear wings are not stroked at the bases where they join the body of the plane. This is because these are the locations of the endpoints of two open paths. Imaginary straight segments define the boundary of the white fills. If either path were closed, a stroke following the closing segment would appear at the junction of the wing with the plane. Without such a stroke, the joint between wing and plane is less defined, more naturalistic.

Figure 8-3: The wings on this plane were created as filled open paths, creating the effect of indefinite boundaries.

Filling text

Text objects can also be filled. Illustrator 5.0 has made filling type easier than it was in the previous version. If you select a text block with the selection tool and apply a fill, the fill will affect all the type in the text object only and leave the associated path unchanged. For example, the first item in Figure 8-4 shows an area text block selected with the standard selection tool. If you fill the object with a light gray, the type becomes filled, as shown in the second item in the figure. The result is gray letters against a white background.

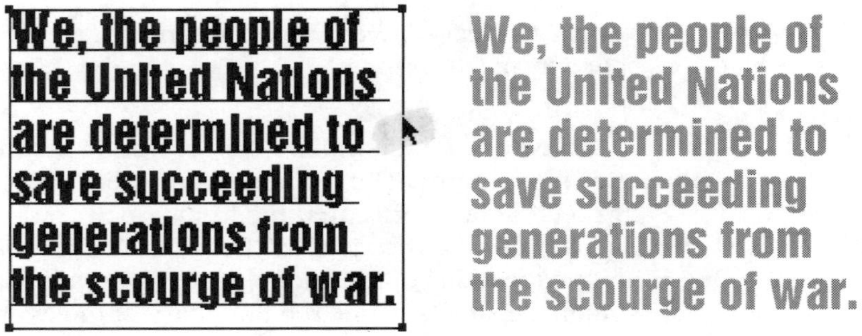

Figure 8-4: If you fill a text block selected with the selection tool (left), only the type will become filled (right).

However, Illustrator also allows you to fill the path. If you select the path with the direct-selection tool, you can apply a fill that affects only the path, leaving the text as is, as demonstrated in Figure 8-5.

You can also fill type separately of its path by selecting it with a type tool. Simply click inside the text block with a type tool and choose the SELECT ALL command (⌘-A) to select the entire story. Then apply the desired fill.

To fill single words and other collections of specific characters, you have to use a type tool. Like any character-level formatting attribute, such as font or type size, fill affects only highlighted characters, as demonstrated in Figure 8-6. In this way, Illustrator allows you to apply several different fills to a single text object.

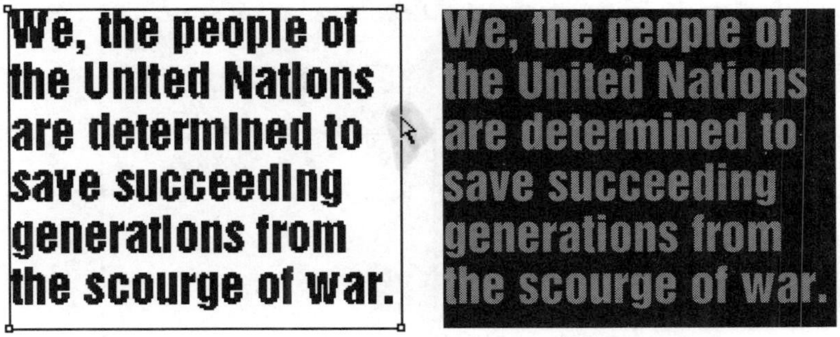

Figure 8-5: *If you use the direct-selection tool to select the path associated with a text block (left), only the path will become filled (right).*

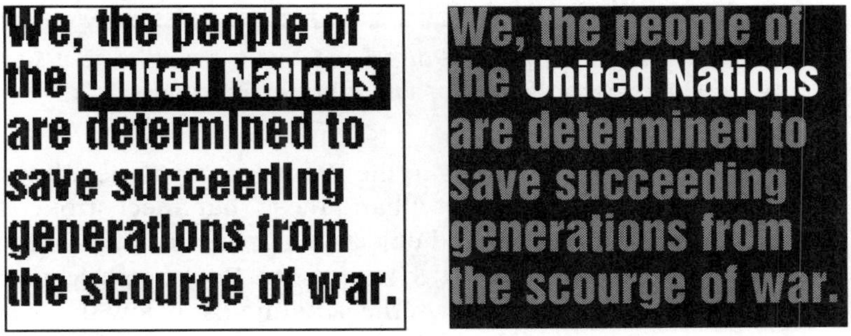

Figure 8-6: *By selecting text with the type tool (left), you fill only the highlighted text (right).*

Object

Paint Style... ⌘I
Custom Color...
Pattern...
Gradient...
Attributes... ⌘^A

Join... ⌘J
Average... ⌘L

Guides ▶
Masks ▶
Compound Paths ▶
Cropmarks ▶
Graphs ▶

Painting the fill

To fill or stroke any object, you must select the object and choose the PAINT STYLE... command from the OBJECT menu (⌘-I). The PAINT STYLE palette will display, as shown in Figure 8-7 on the next page. Almost every characteristic of a fill or a stroke can be determined or manipulated within this dialog box.

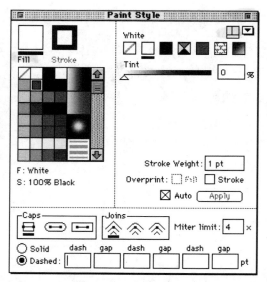

Figure 8-7: The Paint Style palette provides access to most of Illustrator's fill and stroke features.

The options in the PAINT STYLE palette fall into two categories: those that affect fill and those that affect stroke. To apply a fill to one or more selected objects, click on the "Fill" box in the upper left corner of the PAINT STYLE palette. You then select a fill by clicking on any of the swatches in the scrolling list below the "Fill" box, or by clicking on any of the seven fill type boxes to the far right of the "Fill" box. Illustrator applies the color, tile pattern, or gradation to the interior of the selected objects. The name of the fill (such as Process White, Grass Green, Parquet Floor, or Steel Bar), or the process-color scheme that makes up the fill color (such as 23C 14M 80Y 10K) appears directly below the scrolling list.

The PAINT STYLE palette can expand or contract to four different sizes to best accommodate your needs. Fully expanded, as shown in Figure 8-7, it displays all fill and stroke options. The bottom portion of the dialog box displays only those attributes that deal with the outline of an object, and needs not be displayed if you are working with the fill only. To hide that portion, click and hold on the down-pointing arrowhead that appears in the top right corner of the PAINT STYLE palette. Four size icons will display in a pop-up menu. Select any one of the bottom three icons that represent the palette with the lower portion hidden.

The last three icons in the pop-up menu allow you to display both the left and right sides of the PAINT STYLE palette, or the left or right side by itself, respectively. If you have organized all the colors, tile patterns, and gradations that you want to use in the scrolling list, you can get away with displaying the left side of the palette only. If you have no desire to take advantage of the scrolling list, you can display the right side of the palette only. In any of these cases, the bottom portion of the palette remains hidden.

You can also switch palette views by clicking on portions of the thumbnail representation of the palette in the upper right corner (just left of the pop-up menu). Or click on the toggle box on the far right side of the title bar to switch between the full palette view and another view of your choosing.

Other notable options

The PAINT STYLE palette contains an "Auto" check box and an APPLY button. When the "Auto" check box is checked, selected objects automatically adopt the fill displayed in the "Fill" box. In other words, as soon as you select a new color, tile pattern, or gradation or edit the existing fill, all selected objects update immediately to reflect your change.

When the "Auto" check box is deselected, you will have to click on the APPLY button to manually apply your settings to the selected objects.

Some fills provide access to an "Overprint: Fill" check box. This option applies strictly to color illustrations that are printed using the Adobe Separator utility. When selected, overlapping colors in different separations are allowed to blend with each other. Colors cannot overprint within a single separation or composite print. See Chapter 10, *Filling and Stroking in Color*, for a complete description of the "Overprint" option. I discuss the Adobe Separator utility in Chapter 15, *Printing Your Illustrations*.

All other options—including the "Stroke Weight," "Caps," "Joins," "Miter limit," "Solid," and "Dashed" options—represent stroking attributes. See the following chapter for complete information on these options.

Coloring a fill

Click on one of the seven *fill type boxes*—labeled in Figure 8-8—to select a color, tile pattern, or gradation for the fill of selected objects. Only one of the boxes can be selected at a time. A thick black line appears under the selected box and the fill type name appears over the far left box.

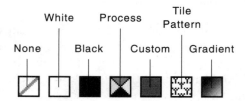

Figure 8-8: The seven fill type boxes and their names.

The fill type options work as follows:

- **None**. When this box is selected, the interior of selected objects will be transparent. This is useful when you want only the stroke of paths or type to be visible. You can also assign both a transparent fill and stroke to create an entirely transparent object that remains visible in the artwork mode but will neither preview nor print. You can use such an object for alignment purposes or as the boundary of a wrapping object, as described in the section *Adjusting standoff* in Chapter 7. The "Overprint: Fill" check box is dimmed when this option is selected.

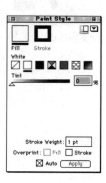

- **White**. Selecting this box makes the fill of a selected path white. A white interior is generally used to partially hide an element in back of the selected path. You can also create white type against a colored background.

    When "White" is selected, a "Tint" bar and percent option box appear under the fill type boxes, indicating the tint of the fill. Moving the bar's triangular indicator to the right increases the amount of black in the fill, presenting a shade, or *tint*, of gray. You can also adjust the tint of a gray fill by altering the percentage value in the percent option box that appears just to the right of the "Tint" bar. A value of 0% is solid white; 100% tint produces solid black. Values between 0% and 100% produce

The **Illustrator 5** Book

progressively darker shades of gray. Figure 8-9 displays several gray values when printed to a standard imagesetter with a default *screen frequency* of 90 lines per inch (as described in Chapter 15, *Printing Your Illustrations*). Because density readings vary from one output device to another, your gray values may print differently. Each printed shade of gray is expressed as a series of tiny black dots, or *halftone cells*. Light shades of gray are made up of small dots; darker shades contain larger dots.

The "Overprint: Fill" check box option is available when the "White" fill type box is selected and the "Tint" value is set higher than 0%.

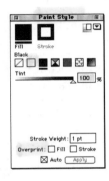

- **Black**. When the "Black" fill type color box is selected, the same "Tint" bar and percent option box appears as when "White" is selected, and you can achieve the same shades of gray that are shown in Figure 8-9.

The "Overprint: Fill" check box option is available when the "Black" fill type box is selected and the "Tint" value is set higher than 0%.

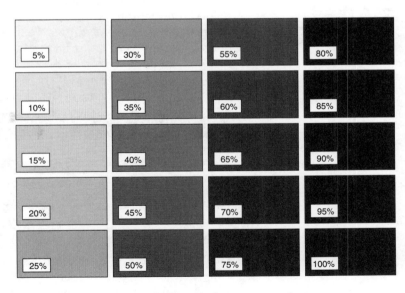

Figure 8-9: Various gray values as they appear when printed to a typical imagesetter.

- **Process Color.** Selecting this box displays the "Cyan," "Magenta," "Yellow," and "Black" bars and corresponding percent option boxes. By moving the triangular indicator along the bars, you determine the percentage of each primary printing color that is combined to create a specific *process color*, which is displayed in the "Fill" box. The composite name will appear under the scrolling list on the left of the PAINT STYLE palette. For example, 50C 25M 75Y 10K indicates a process color made up of 50% cyan, 25% magenta, 75% yellow, and 10% black. Chapter 10, *Filling and Stroking in Color*, contains an in-depth discussion of process colors.

  The "Overprint: Fill" check box option is available when the "Process" fill type box is selected, provided that at least one of the four color bars is set to a value higher than 0%.

- **Custom Color.** Selecting this fill type box produces a scrolling list of custom colors defined using the CUSTOM COLOR... command under the OBJECT menu. When you launch Illustrator, the program loads all predefined custom colors contained in the Adobe Illustrator Startup file (located inside the Plug-Ins folder) into the scrolling list. Illustrator comes with a number of optional custom color files that contain thousands of predefined colors from Pantone, Trumatch, and others that you can open or import into your illustration. To import a custom color library, choose IMPORT STYLES... from the FILE menu. In the OPEN dialog box that appears, locate the Color Systems folder inside the same folder that contains the Illustrator application, and double-click on the name of the file you want to import.

  To simply open a custom color file, choose the OPEN... command from the FILE menu and select a color system file. The advantage of opening rather than importing is that you can close the colors that you decide not to use and avoid cluttering your scrolling list with a bunch of unwanted junk.

  The "Tint" bar and percent option box under the scrolling list allow you to lighten the shade of a custom color to any percentage value between 0% (white) and 100% (the solid color).

  The "Overprint: Fill" check box option is available when this or either of the two following boxes—"Pattern" and "Gradient"—are selected. The name of the custom color, tile pattern, or gradation appears under the scrolling list on the left side of the PAINT STYLE palette.

✦ The **Illustrator** 5 Book

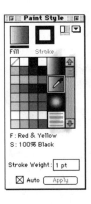

- **Pattern**. Selecting this box produces a scrolling list of tile patterns defined using the PATTERN... command under the OBJECT menu (as discussed in the *Tile patterns* section, which begins on the next page). Illustrator loads all predefined patterns contained in the Adobe Illustrator Startup file into the scrolling list. The Gradients & Patterns folder inside the Illustrator folder contains files of predefined tile patterns and gradations that you can import or open.

- **Gradient**. Selecting this box produces a scrolling list of gradations defined using the GRADIENT... command under the OBJECT menu (as discussed in the *Gradient fills* section, which begins on page 357). Illustrator loads all predefined gradients contained in the Adobe Illustrator Startup file into the scrolling list.

More about the palette

The PAINT STYLE palette always displays the attributes of the selected object. If several objects with different fill attributes are selected, the palette will display only the information that is common to all selected objects and leave differing options blank or deselected. For example, suppose you've selected two paths, identical in all respects but one: One path is filled with black, the other is filled with 35% gray. The "Black" fill type box will be selected since both fills are variations on black, but the "Fill" box will contain a question mark and the "Tint" option box will be empty. In this way, Illustrator lets you alter the shared attributes without affecting the dissimilar gray values.

Before I embark on more exciting matters, I should explain one last item, namely the scrolling list on the left-hand side of the PAINT STYLE palette. Divided into four columns of little *swatches* and one column of big ones, the list serves as a reservoir for fill and stroke styles that you use on a regular basis. Here how it works:

- To add a style to the list, scroll down to where the blank swatches start. Then drag from the "Fill" box into an empty swatch. Or just OPTION-click on the swatch to transfer the color from the "Fill" box, provided that "Fill" is selected. You can add any fill style to either a big or little swatch.

- Click on a swatch to transfer the style to the "Fill" box, provided that "Fill" is selected.

- Press COMMAND and click on a swatch to delete its style.

Tile patterns

In Illustrator, both type and graphic objects can be filled with *tile patterns*, which are object-oriented patterns or designs composed of other stroked and filled objects. Like the surface of a kitchen linoleum, a single rectangular *tile* is repeated over and over throughout a specified area. Illustrator allows you to create libraries of tile patterns that can be used to fill or stroke any element. This is the first of two techniques that allows you to achieve the appearance of one object being set within another; the other one, *masking*, is described in the *Clipping paths* section later in this chapter.

Creating a tile pattern

Pattern tiles are always rectangular. This is very important to understanding and creating patterns in Illustrator. The appearance of a pattern can be far from rectangular, of course, but when you create a tile, it must exist fully within a rectangular boundary. A tile pattern cannot contain a clipping path or an object painted with a tile pattern. Sometimes, it is advisable to first create a rectangle to represent the perimeter of the pattern tile and then create your pattern objects within this perimeter.

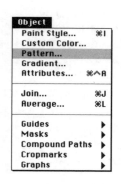

After you have filled and stroked all objects that will make up your pattern (including the bounding rectangle) and correctly positioned the rectangle in relation to the rest of the objects, select the rectangle and choose the SEND TO BACK command from the EDIT menu (⌘--, COMMAND-HYPHEN). Next, select the rectangle and its objects and choose the PATTERN... command from the OBJECT menu to display the PATTERN dialog box. Click the NEW button and a preview of your tile will appear in the top right corner of the dialog box, as shown in Figure 8-10.

If an error message appears, it is probably because the rearmost object in your selection is not a rectangle. Click the CANCEL button, relayer your objects or choose the RELEASE command in the MASKS menu from the OBJECT menu, and again choose the PATTERN command from the OBJECT menu.

Enter a name for your pattern into the "Change name to" option box. The name will take the place of *New Pattern 1* in the scrolling pattern list when you next open the dialog box. Click the OK button or press RETURN to confirm the creation of your new tile pattern.

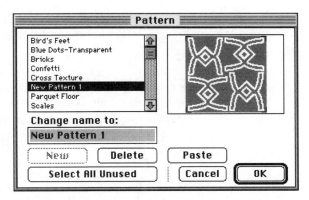

Figure 8-10: The Pattern dialog box allows you to create new tile patterns and organize existing ones.

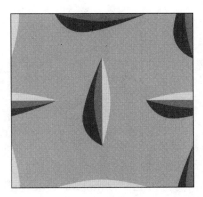

Figure 8-11: This tile produces a pattern resembling the metal ridges on a metal plate.

The following exercise demonstrates how to create a pattern that looks like the raised ridges of a metal non-slip surface, like on a fire engine bumper, as shown in Figure 8-11. Although the exercise is rather long and involved, the procedure is not particularly difficult:

1. First, draw the three paths on the left of Figure 8-12 on the next page, each of which is roughly 1.25 inches tall. Overlap the three paths to achieve the middle example in the figure, so that the largest of the three paths is in back. Finally, fill each path with a different shade of gray to impart a sense of depth and shadow, as shown in the third example in the figure.

2. Select the three paths and choose the GROUP command from the ARRANGE menu (⌘-G) to create one ridge.

3. Press OPTION and click on the selection tool icon in the toolbox to display the MOVE dialog box. Enter 1 for the "Horizontal" option and 0 for the "Vertical" option, then click the COPY button. (This assumes you are working in inches. If you are using picas and points, enter 72 and 0, respectively.) A cloned ridge will appear an inch to the right of the original.

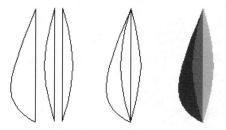

Figure 8-12: The three shapes that make up the ridge shown apart (left) and together (middle) in the artwork mode, followed by the filled shapes in the preview mode (right).

4. Choose the REPEAT TRANSFORM command from the ARRANGE menu (⌘-D), to create a second clone of the group. You now have three ridges, spaced equidistantly.

5. Select the middle group. Using the reflect tool, OPTION-click at the center of the selected group, or double-click on the reflect tool slot. In the REFLECT dialog box, select the "Angled axis" radio button, enter 45 in the corresponding option box, and press RETURN. The object will flip and rotate, as shown in Figure 8-13. (For complete information about the reflect tool and the REFLECT dialog box, see the *Flipping objects* section of Chapter 11.)

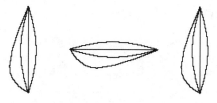

Figure 8-13: Clone two additional ridges and reflect the middle one around a 45° axis.

🜉 The **Illustrator** 5 Book

6. The first row of ridges is now complete. Select the three ridges and OPTION-click the selection tool icon in the toolbox to display the MOVE dialog box. Enter 1 (72 points) for the "Horizontal" option and –1 (–72 points) for the "Vertical" option, then click the COPY button. A set of cloned ridges will appear below and to the right of the first, creating the beginning of a second row.

7. Select the two right ridges in the second row and SHIFT-OPTION-drag them to the left from the top point in the selected vertical ridge. Release the mouse button when this point snaps to the similar point (assuming that the "Snap to point" check box in the GENERAL PREFERENCE dialog box is checked) in the stationary vertical ridge in the same row, as shown in Figure 8-14. By snapping, you ensure that the space between all ridges is constant.

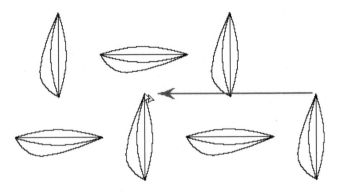

Figure 8-14: Move and copy the first row down and right, and clone the last two ridges of the new second row over to the left to tack-on an additional ridge.

8. You now have two coincident vertical ridges in the middle of the second row, one in front of the other. Select the front one and press DELETE or BACKSPACE to get rid of it. The right vertical ridge is also extraneous, so delete it as well.

9. To create a third row of ridges, select the three grouped objects in the top row and OPTION-click on the selection tool icon to again display the MOVE dialog box. Enter 0 for the "Horizontal" option and –2 (–144 points) for the "Vertical" option, then click the COPY button. Figure 8-15 on the next page shows the third row of ridges.

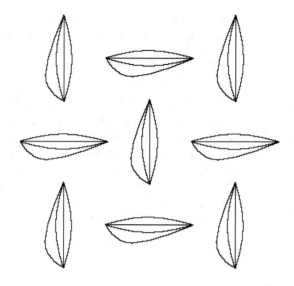

Figure 8-15: Clone the top row of ridges and move the clones down 144 points, or 2 inches.

Figure 8-16: Draw a square to determine the boundaries of the tile.

10. Draw a square surrounding the portions of the ridge objects that you want to repeat in the pattern, as shown in Figure 8-16. This square determines the boundaries of the tile.

11. The square must always be the rearmost object in the tile. While the square remains selected, choose the SEND TO BACK command from the EDIT menu (⌘--, COMMAND-HYPHEN).

> ✳ When you draw your rectangle around the tile objects, try to visualize how the pattern will look when it is repeated. Objects that touch the left edge of the rectangle will be flush with the objects that touch the right edge. Likewise, objects that touch the top of the rectangle will meet with the objects that touch the bottom. Figure 8-17 shows six copies of the metal tile (with dotted lines representing the rectangular boundaries) arranged in a pattern. Each object flows continuously through one tile and into another.

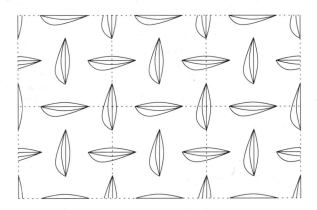

Figure 8-17: When drawing the boundary rectangle, visualize how the tiles will fit together.

12. Fill the square with a medium shade of gray to act as a background for the ridges.

13. Select the square and the ridge objects in front of the rectangle and choose the PATTERN... command from the OBJECT menu to display the PATTERN dialog box.

14. Click on the New button to instruct Illustrator to designate the selected objects as a pattern tile. A preview of the prospective pattern tile will appear in the bottom right corner of the Pattern dialog box. If the preview does not match the one shown in Figure 8-18, click the Cancel button, manipulate the pattern elements as necessary, and try again. Enter the name *Metal non-slip plate* into the "Change name to" option box and press Return to complete the creation of your new pattern.

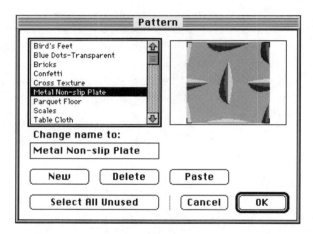

Figure 8-18: The Pattern dialog box previews the selected pattern tile.

You have now produced a simple tile pattern. The next section describes how to fill a text block or graphic object with a tile pattern and how to transform tiles within an object.

Filling objects with tile patterns

To fill selected objects with a pattern, choose the Paint... command from the Object menu (⌘-I). Select the "Pattern" color type box along the top of the Paint Style palette. Then select a tile pattern from the scrolling list that appears. A preview of the tile will appear in the "Fill" box at the upper left of the dialog box.

The **Illustrator 5** Book

Transforming patterns within objects

After filling a selected object with a tile pattern, you can move, scale, rotate, reflect, or slant a tile pattern inside the object. To do this, choose MOVE... from the OBJECT menu or double-click on one of the transformation tool icons in the toolbox to display the MOVE, SCALE, ROTATE, REFLECT, or SHEAR dialog box, each of which allows you to apply a transformation to objects and their fills (as discussed in Chapter 11, *Transforming and Duplicating Objects*), as well as transform the patterns independently of their objects. To do the latter, be sure that the "Pattern tiles" check box is selected and the "Objects" check box is deselected. The five dialog boxes contain the following options:

- **Move**. This dialog box allows you to move a pattern inside an object. Enter the desired values into the "Horizontal" and "Vertical" option boxes or enter the distance and direction of the move into the "Distance" and "Angle" option boxes. These values are measured in centimeters, inches, or points.

- **Scale**. This dialog box allows you to enlarge or reduce a pattern inside an object. To scale the pattern proportionally, select the "Uniform" radio button and enter a percentage in the corresponding option box. Values less than 100% will reduce the pattern; values greater than 100% will enlarge it. If you want to scale the horizontal and vertical dimensions of the pattern differently, select the "Non-Uniform" option and enter values into the "Horizontal" and "Vertical" option boxes.

- **Rotate**. This dialog box allows you to rotate the pattern. The "Angle" value is measured in degrees. Positive values rotate the tile pattern counterclockwise; negative values rotate the pattern clockwise.

- **Reflect**. This dialog box allows you to flip a pattern inside an object. To flip the pattern head-to-toe, select the "Horizontal" option (because you are flipping around the horizontal axis). If you want to flip the pattern side-to-side, select "Vertical." To flip the pattern across a rotated axis, select the "Angled" radio button and enter a value in the corresponding option box.

- **Shear**. This dialog box allows you to slant a pattern inside an object. Enter the degree of the slant into the "Angle" option box. Select the direction of your slant from the "Horizontal," "Vertical," or "Angled" option. If "Angled," enter a directional value into the corresponding option box.

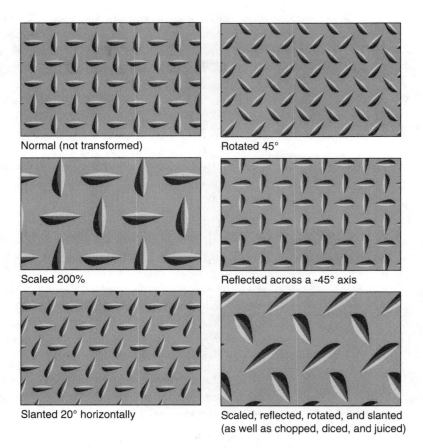

Normal (not transformed)

Rotated 45°

Scaled 200%

Reflected across a -45° axis

Slanted 20° horizontally

Scaled, reflected, rotated, and slanted (as well as chopped, diced, and juiced)

Figure 8-19: The metal plate pattern subjected to various transformations.

Figure 8-19 shows the results of transforming the metal plate pattern within the fill of a rectangle. The first example in the figure shows the pattern as it appears normally, prior to any transformation. The

The **Illustrator** 5 Book

second example on the left shows the pattern scaled to 200%; the third example on the left shows the slanted 20°. On the right-hand side of the figure, the first example shows the pattern rotated 45°; the second example shows the pattern reflected across a –45° axis along a horizontal axis; and in the third example, all four transformation tools have been applied to the pattern.

Notice that when the "Object" check box is deselected in each of these dialog boxes, the transformations apply only to the pattern tiles within the selected object and not to the object itself. Also, a pattern is transformed only within the current selection. Transforming a pattern within one object does not transform that pattern within other deselected objects filled or stroked with the same pattern.

As with other kinds of transformations, the REPEAT TRANSFORMATION command under the ARRANGE menu (⌘-D) is sensitive to pattern transformations. For example, if you move the pattern inside a selected object 3 points to the right, you can immediately move it 3 more points by pressing COMMAND-D.

Transforming objects with patterns

Finally, you can use the MOVE, SCALE, ROTATE, REFLECT, and SHEAR dialog boxes to transform a tile pattern along with a filled object. Simply select both the "Object" and the "Pattern tile" check boxes in any of these dialog boxes.

These options do not affect manual transformations. For example, when the "Transform pattern tiles" check box in the PREFERENCES dialog box is selected, dragging an object filled with a pattern will cause the pattern to move as well. When the option is deselected, you can drag the object independently of the pattern. This is especially useful when you want a tile pattern to run seamlessly through several different objects. With "Transform pattern tiles" turned off, you can transform the objects as much as you like without ruining the effect.

You cannot manually transform a pattern independently of the path it fills. In other words, to apply a transformation to a pattern while leaving its object unchanged, you have to use a dialog box; you cannot transform by dragging with a tool. For more information on the whole crazy transformation scene, see Chapter 11.

Organizing tile patterns

It's now time to return to the PATTERN dialog box, displayed back in Figures 8-10 and 8-18 (take your pick). In addition to allowing you to create new patterns, the PATTERN dialog box provides options for organizing and editing existing tile patterns.

The central part of the dialog box is the scrolling pattern list. You can add a pattern name to the scrolling list by clicking the NEW button. The list also contains the names of all the patterns that appear in the Adobe Illustrator Startup file, any patterns defined previously in the current document, and patterns created in other open documents. If you create a new pattern in one file, it immediately becomes available to every other open file.

To create a library of patterns that is available every time you use Illustrator, add the patterns to the Adobe Illustrator Startup file. Keep in mind, however, that patterns consume space in the application memory and may very well slow or hamper Illustrator's performance.

You can manipulate patterns in the scrolling list using other buttons in the PATTERN dialog box as well. These buttons include the following:

- **Delete**. Click this button to delete a selected pattern name from the scrolling list. The selected pattern is removed from the current document *as well as from any other open document*. Any object that was filled or stroked with the deleted pattern will be painted with black. Extreme caution should be exercised when deleting patterns. Whenever possible, delete a pattern only when the current illustration is the only file open. You can retrieve deleted patterns by clicking on the CANCEL button.

  If you delete a pattern name and click the OK button to confirm the deletion, you can regain the pattern by immediately choosing the UNDO PATTERN CHANGES command from the EDIT menu (⌘-Z).

- **Paste**. Sometimes you may wish to revise a pattern for which the objects that make up the pattern tile are not readily available. It may be a pattern from another document, or you may have discarded the objects in the drawing area after creating the pattern with the NEW button. Click the PASTE button to

The **Illustrator 5** Book

paste the objects of the selected pattern to the center of the current window. Click the OK button to confirm the paste. These objects can then be manipulated as you see fit.

After changing the pattern objects, you can define them as a new pattern. You can also redefine an existing pattern, assigning an existing pattern name to a new or altered set of objects. To accomplish this, select the objects (with rectangle in back), choose PATTERN... from the OBJECT menu, and select the name of the pattern that you want to redefine from the scrolling pattern list. Then click the OK button, or press RETURN. Don't be put off by the fact that Illustrator shows no sign of acknowledging the redefinition. All elements filled or stroked with that pattern will now be painted with the new pattern, as will elements in *any other open document*. You must use the same discretion when redefining patterns as you would when deleting them.

- **Select All Unused**. This button selects all patterns in the scrolling list that are not applied to objects in any open illustration. Since patterns consume a great deal of disk space, RAM space, and space in your printer's memory, it is often advisable to delete patterns that you are not currently using, provided that they exist in some other illustration that is not currently open. To delete unused patterns, click the SELECT ALL UNUSED, click DELETE, and then click OK or press RETURN.

You can rename a pattern by selecting it from the scrolling list and entering a new name in the "Change name to" option box. This will change its name in all open illustrations.

Viewing patterns

Patterned fills and strokes can be viewed on screen only in the preview mode. However, patterns take a long time to preview, comparatively longer than any other fill effect. To increase previewing speed, select just those specific objects you want to preview and choose PREVIEW SELECTION from the VIEW menu (⌘-⌥-Y). Alternatively, you can simply prevent patterns from previewing at all by deselecting the "Preview and print patterns" option in the DOCUMENT SETUP dialog box (first introduced in the *Document Setup* section of Chapter 3). Keep in mind, however, that this option also prevents patterns from printing. Pattern fills and strokes will appear gray.

One last note—Figure 8-20 displays a small sampling of additional patterns that you can create in Adobe Illustrator. Some patterns are shown exactly as they were created; others have been slanted or rotated. But they all demonstrate that both man-made and natural images repeat themselves and can therefore be expressed as a series of repeated tiles.

Figure 8-20: A selection of tile patterns created in Adobe Illustrator.

Tile patterns can also be applied to type, as shown in Figure 8-21. The pattern fill will appear only when printed and will display as a gray fill in preview mode. Generally, large sans serif type is best suited to this purpose.

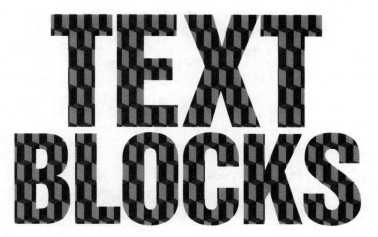

Figure 8-21: A printed text block with a pattern fill.

Patterns can be beautiful to look at, but they take a lot of effort to create and they eat up disk space and printer memory like you would not believe. The rectangles in Figure 8-20 took over 15 minutes to print to an imagesetter with the newest ROMs available. For a more efficient filling technique that doesn't restrict you to using repeating images, create a clipping path as described later in this chapter.

Gradient fills

A new feature to Illustrator 5.0 is the ability to create automatic *gradient fills* (also called *gradations*), in which one color fades continuously into another color. For example, if the left side of a shape is filled with black and the right side is filled with blue, the two colors will fade together throughout the middle of the shape. Gradations can be *linear*, which means that the color transition follows a straight line, or *radial*, which starts in the center with one color and fades outward in a circle to another color.

To create a gradient fill, choose the GRADIENT... command from the OBJECT menu. Alternatively, you can double-click on the name of a gradation in the scrolling list that appears in the right half of the PAINT STYLE palette when you select the "Gradient" fill type box. The GRADIENT palette will display, as shown in Figure 8-23. Along the top of the palette is the *gradient fade bar*. The starting color appears as a triangular *color stop* on the left and the ending color is the triangle on the right. The diamond in the middle, called the *midpoint marker*, marks the spot where the two colors mix in exactly equal amounts. You can change the location of a stop or marker by dragging it or by selecting it and entering a value into the percent option box on the right. A value of 0% corresponds to the far left end of the fade bar; 100% corresponds to the far right.

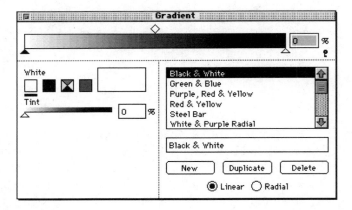

Figure 8-23: In the Gradient palette you can create new gradient fills or modify existing ones.

Below the percentage option box is a flag that allows you to contract the GRADIENT palette so that just the fade bar and percent box are visible. At the bottom of the GRADIENT palette are two radio buttons that determine whether the gradient fill is linear or radial. The options in the lower left portion of the GRADIENT palette work just like their counterparts in the PAINT STYLE palette.

The **Illustrator 5** Book

Creating gradients

To create a gradient, click on the NEW button below the scrolling list in the GRADIENT palette. Enter a name for your gradient into the option box below the scrolling list. The name will take the place of *New Gradient 1* in the list. The default linear white-to-black gradation will appear in the gradient fade bar. You are now ready to create your gradient fill.

Click on the left-hand color stop to specify the first color in the gradation. When a color stop is selected, the triangle appears black. The details of the color marked by a selected color stop display in the lower left portion of the GRADIENT palette. In this case, the color is white, so the familiar "Tint" bar displays below the four color type boxes. Select your desired starting color. Just as in the PAINT STYLE palette, click on the appropriate color type box and then mix the color using the "Tint" or CMYK bars or select a predefined color from the "Custom" color list. When you have finished, select the right-hand color stop and repeat the process to specify the ending color in your new gradation.

Two color stops make for a two-color gradation. But unlike other drawing programs, Illustrator lets you assign as many as 32 colors to a gradation. To add a color stop, click along the bottom of the fade bar. A new triangle will appear. You can assign any color to the new color stop just as before.

To remove a color stop, drag the triangle down into the lower portion of the GRADIENT palette. The triangle will vanish and the fade bar will automatically adjust as defined by the remaining color stops.

Drag a color stop right or left to reposition it along the gradient fade bar. If you position a color stop near another color stop, you create a quick transition between the two colors. If you allow more room between the neighboring color stops, you create a more gradual color transition.

For each pair of color stops, one midpoint marker appears along the top of the gradient fade bar. By default, a midpoint marker appears at the halfway point between the two neighboring color stops, producing the most homogeneous fade possible. Drag the midpoint marker between its two color stops to force the midpoint color to a different position. This changes the rate at which the neighboring colors mix in the fade bar. When the midpoint marker is closer to, say, its left-hand color stop, the resulting gradation fades faster toward the beginning of the color transition than toward the end. Figure 8-24 shows the results of three different midpoint marker positions applied to two sets of white-to-black gradations.

The last thing to determine is whether your gradient is going to be linear or radial. Simply click on the corresponding button at the bottom of the GRADIENT palette. Examples of both appear in Figure 8-24.

Figure 8-24: Six white-to-black gradations, with midpoint markers set to 50% (left), 25% (middle), and 75% (right).

Modifying old gradient fills

To change an existing gradation, simply click on its name in the scrolling list in the GRADIENT palette. The gradation will appear in the fade bar. You can change the colors of the color stops, add new color stops or remove existing ones, reposition any color stop or midpoint marker, and change the gradation from linear to radial or vice versa. To change the name, highlight the name in the option box that appears below the scrolling list and enter a new name. If the gradient is currently being used in your illustration, any changes made to the gradient will update automatically (provided that the "Auto" check box in the PAINT STYLE palette is selected).

To switch the colors of any two color stops, click and drag one color stop onto another. The colors will swap positions, and Illustrator will automatically update the fades between any other color stops accordingly. Note that the midpoint markers will not reposition when color stops are swapped.

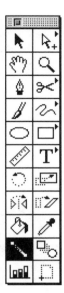

Moving the gradation in a shape

The *gradient-vector tool*, the second-to-last tool on the left of the tool-box, allows you to change the center and direction of a gradation in-side a filled object. If a selected object is filled with a linear gradation, you can change its direction and length by dragging inside the object with the gradient-vector tool. The color gradation will begin at the point where you start your drag, follow along the direction of your drag, and end where you release the mouse button, as demonstrated in Figure 8-25.

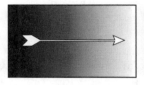  

Figure 8-25: Three different examples of the effect of the gradient vector tool on a black-to-white linear gradation. The arrows show the directions and lengths of my drags.

Notice that the portions of the shape that fall outside the drag are filled with solid color. In Figure 8-25, for example, the area beyond the tail of the arrow—which represents the beginning of the drag—fills with black, the first color in the gradation. The area beyond the head of the arrow—the end of the drag—fills with white, the grada-tion's last color.

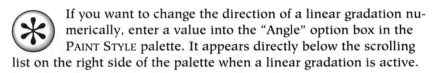 If you want to change the direction of a linear gradation nu-merically, enter a value into the "Angle" option box in the PAINT STYLE palette. It appears directly below the scrolling list on the right side of the palette when a linear gradation is active.

Using the gradient-vector tool on an object filled with a radial gra-dation changes the balance of the gradation and repositions the cen-ter. Drag on a selected object that has a radial gradient fill. The gradation will center at the point where you start dragging and extend to where you end your drag, as demonstrated in Figure 8-26 on the next page. The center color is the first color in the gradation. Illustra-tor fills the area of the selected object outside the drag with the last color in the gradation.

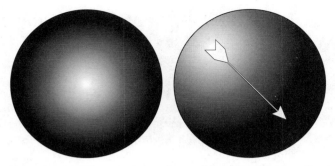

Figure 8-26: The starting point and length of the gradient tool drag, as shown by the arrow, dictate the center and radius of the radial gradation of a selected object

You can click with the gradient-vector tool on a selected object that has a radial gradient fill to offset the *focus point*, which is the point where the intensity of the starting color is the greatest. If you have ever played with a magnifying glass—back in the days when you thought pest control might be fun—you have probably seen a similar image. Suppose that you position a magnifying glass over a piece of paper. When the magnifying glass is perpendicular to the rays of the sun, a homogenous gradation appears on the paper with the point of greatest light intensity appearing in the center of the image. Tilt the glass and the point of greatest intensity shifts from the center. Clicking on a radial gradation similarly repositions the focus point by moving the center independently of the outer ring of the gradation. The gradation spreads heterogeneously around the new focus point, as shown in the second example of Figure 8-27.

Figure 8-27: Click on a radial gradation to shift the position of the focus point.

Finally, the gradient tool allows you to apply a continuous gradation across multiple selected objects. In this way, all objects appear lit by a single light source. To accomplish this effect, select the objects, fill them with a gradation, and drag across them with the gradient-vector tool.

Figure 8-28 shows this effect applied to multiple characters of type. Since Illustrator does not let you apply gradations to type, I had to first convert the characters to free-form paths using the CREATE OUTLINES command under the TYPE menu. I then applied the gradation and dragged with the gradient-vector tool.

Figure 8-28: After converting the type to paths, I filled them with a gradation and used the gradient-vector tool to apply the fill continuously across all paths.

Clipping paths

Clipping path is the PostScript term for a path that is created specifically to be filled with other objects. It is also called a *masking object*, or simply a *mask*, after the airbrushing technique where masking tape is laid down to define the perimeter of a spray-painted image.

The basic concept behind the clipping path is simple: Rather than filling an object with a color or gradation, you fill it with other objects, known as *masked elements*. Any graphic object created in Illustrator can serve as a clipping path. You can even use a text block as a clipping path without first converting it to paths. Any number of paths and text blocks can fill a clipping path. And as if that weren't enough, one clipping path can be a masked element inside another. Masking is among the most flexible of Illustrator's capabilites.

Creating a clipping path

Object	
Paint Style...	⌘I
Custom Color...	
Pattern...	
Gradient...	
Attributes...	⌘⌃A
Join...	⌘J
Average...	⌘L
Guides	▶
Masks	▶
Compound Paths	▶
Cropmarks	▶
Graphs	▶

Creating a clipping path is similar to creating a pattern, except that it involves no dialog boxes. After filling and stroking all objects, assemble the prospective mask and the masked elements. Then select the mask and choose the BRING TO FRONT command from the ARRANGE menu (⌘-=). Select all objects by marqueeing or SHIFT-clicking with the selection tool and choose the MAKE command in the MASKS submenu under the OBJECT menu. The frontmost object in the selection masks all objects behind it.

Figure 8-29: The following exercise demonstrates how to color the bomb-pop (left) with the stripes (right).

Figure 8-29 shows a popsicle next to some stripes. The following exercise demonstrates how to set the stripes inside the body of the popsicle to create a . . . a whatchamacallit, a *bomb-pop,* or as Webster's calls it, "colored water frozen in a rectangular shape on a flat handle." Yum. Ah, come on, you know, it's one of those three-color frozen treats kids like to rub all over their faces and drip on their shirts and so on. Well, anyway, the problem is this: How do you set the stripes inside the bomb-pop body without affecting the drip or the stick?

As if in answer to that very question, here's how it works:

1. To create the clipping path, you must first move the prospective masked elements—the stripes—into position relative to the bomb-pop. Figure 8-30 shows the proper relative locations of masked elements and clipping path, as viewed in the artwork mode. This positioning will determine the exact manner in which the elements will fill the mask.

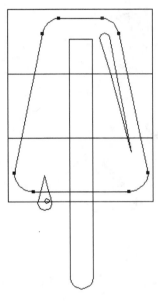

Figure 8-30: Mask and masked elements assembled, as viewed in the artwork mode.

2. A clipping path masks only those selected elements that are in back of it. From Figure 8-29, you can surmise that the layering order for the popsicle before adding the stripes was something like this: The stick was at the back, the bomb-pop body was in front of that, and the paths that make up the drip were at the forefront. To mask the stripes, they must be layered behind the body. To make sure this is the case, select the three stripes and choose the CUT command from the EDIT menu (⌘-X). Then select the bomb-pop body path and choose PASTE IN BACK from

the EDIT menu (⌘-B). The stripes are now directly in back of the body in layering order. (For a complete description of the PASTE IN BACK command, see the *Layering objects* section of Chapter 11.)

3. Select both the stripes and bomb-pop body and choose the MAKE command in the MASKS submenu under the OBJECT menu. The result is shown in Figure 8-31.

Figure 8-31: Choosing the Make (Masks) command clips away the rear selected elements along the path of the frontmost selected shape.

The clipping path loses its stroke and fill when you apply the MAKE (MASKS) command. To retain the stroke around a clipping path, select the masking object with the selection tool, copy it (⌘-C), click somewhere else to deselect the mask (⌘-⇧-A), paste the object in front of the clipping path (⌘-F), and give it the proper stroke color and weight. This adds a stroke that is not masked in front of the path.

The final steps in the exercise demonstrate how you can apply this technique to the popsicle:

4. Select the bomb-pop body with the selection tool and choose COPY from the EDIT menu (⌘-C) to copy it to the Clipboard.

5. Choose SELECT NONE from the EDIT menu (⌘-⇧-A) to deselect the mask.

6. Choose the PASTE IN FRONT command (⌘-F) to paste the copy of the body in front of the mask.

7. While the copy remains selected, apply a black stroke using options in the PAINT STYLE palette. First click on the "Stroke" box (next to the "Fill" box), then select the "Black" option from the row of six stroke type boxes. Finally, enter 2 in the "Stroke Weight" option box. Figure 8-32 shows the finished drawing.

Figure 8-32: The finished image with original stroke restored.

For complete information on applying a stroke, read the following chapter, *Stroking Graphic Objects and Type*.

Creating multiple masks

Only one clipping path can mask a set of masked elements. In other words, one masked element cannot be distributed over multiple clipping paths. (For an exception to this, see the tip on the facing page.)

However, if you want to create the appearance of shared masked elements, you can duplicate a set of masked elements, one for each of several clipping paths.

Figure 8-33: The graphic portion of this logo comprises four clipping paths filled with continuous masked elements.

For example, Figure 8-33 displays a logo made up of four similar clipping paths. Each path is shaped differently. However, each path masks what appears to be part of one large pattern of objects. To accomplish this, I created a set of masked elements that was as large as all four clipping paths combined. I then grouped these elements independently of their clipping paths, sent the group to back, and copied it. Next, I selected the first clipping path and the group of masked elements and chose the MAKE (MASKS) command. The left-hand portion of the logo was complete. To create the second portion of the logo, I selected the second path and chose the PASTE IN BACK command to produce another group of masked elements, SHIFT-clicked on the second logo path to reselect it, and again chose MAKE (MASKS). I then repeated the process for the third and fourth paths in the logo. The final illustration creates a sort of puzzle-like effect, where the contents of one clipping path flow into the contents of its neighbor.

Actually, there is a simpler way to create the effect shown in Figure 8-33, but it involves establishing a compound path, a process I discuss in detail in the upcoming *Making holes* section. Illustrator treats a compound path like one continuous path even though it comprises several objects. To create Figure 8-33, for example, I would select all four logo shapes and choose the MAKE command from the COMPOUND PATHS submenu under the OBJECT menu (⌘-8). Now the paths will share the same contents, whether a tile pattern, gradation, or a bunch of masked elements.

Masking endnotes

In previous versions of Illustrator, you grouped the clipping path with the masked elements to contain the mask. This is no longer necessary. In fact, in version 5.0, you can use a group as a clipping path. Just group the paths, layer them in front of the masked elements, select group and masked elements, and choose MAKE (MASKS). The result is that only those portions of the paths inside the group that overlap each other fill with the masked elements.

In other news, you may recall how I mentioned that text can also be a clipping path. However, only whole text blocks selected with a selection tool can mask other objects. You cannot select specific characters with the type tool to make them masking objects.

Finally, you can break apart a selected mask by choosing the RELEASE command from the MASKS submenu under the OBJECT menu. All masked elements will become entirely visible in the preview mode. (Note that both clipping path and masked elements are always visible in the artwork mode.)

Making holes

Object

Paint Style...	⌘I
Custom Color...	
Pattern...	
Gradient...	
Attributes...	⌘⌃A
Join...	⌘J
Average...	⌘L
Guides	▶
Masks	▶
Compound Paths	▶
Cropmarks	▶
Graphs	▶

Another way to display objects within objects is to create one or more holes in the middle of a path by applying the MAKE command in the COMPOUND PATHS submenu under the OBJECT menu (⌘-8). For example, consider the handsome devil shown in Figure 8-34. The first example in the figure displays his full face. But suppose you need to add a ski mask to the drawing. A real-life ski mask has holes cut into it for the eyes. This allows you to see where you're going when holding up convenience stores. Therefore the cartoon ski mask must also have holes for the eyes, as shown in the second example in the figure. The holes in the cartoon ski mask are actually paths that have been combined with the ski mask path using the MAKE (COMPOUND PATHS) command.

Figure 8-34: A cartoon face (left) and the same face dressed to apply for a non-qualifying, interest-free loan (right). Compound paths can contain holes through which you can see underlying objects.

The eye holes and mask together constitute a *compound path*, because in a few key respects, Illustrator treats the object as a single path. All objects included in the compound path must be filled and stroked identically using options available in the PAINT STYLE palette. And, like a group or a linked object, selecting any part of a compound path with the selection tool selects the entire compound path. But as with a group, you can use the direct-selection tool to manipulate objects independently within a compound path.

Creating a compound path

Compound paths are about the easiest special effect you can create in Illustrator. First assemble the objects that you want to combine in their desired relative positions. One path will act as the background path and one or more other paths will act as the holes. For best results, all holes should overlap some portion of the larger background path. Select the background path and choose the SEND TO BACK command from the EDIT menu (⌘- –, COMMAND-HYPHEN). Then select all paths—background path and all holes—and choose the MAKE command in the COMPOUND PATHS submenu from the OBJECT menu (⌘-8). Background and holes are now combined.

To change the fill or stroke of all objects in a compound path, select any one of the objects using the selection tool or direct-selection tool and change the settings in the PAINT STYLE palette.

The obvious doughnut exercise

Figure 8-35 on the next page shows a doughnut on a checkered napkin. Unfortunately, it does not look much like a doughnut because the doughnut hole has not yet been removed. You can save this doughnut from a heartbreaking existence on the Island of Misfit Pastry by completing the following exercise. You will also create a shadow beneath the doughnut that is itself a compound path:

1. Draw the doughnut as a combination of two circles by SHIFT-dragging with the oval tool a couple of times.

2. A doughnut is a simple drawing, consisting of a background shape and a single hole. To ensure that the larger circle will act as the background, select the shape and choose the SEND TO BACK command (⌘- –, COMMAND-HYPHEN).

Figure 8-35: This doughnut would look more like a doughnut if you could see through its center.

Figure 8-36: Send the large circle to the back of the illustration.

3. The large circle now appears in back of the napkin, as shown in Figure 8-36. That's a little too far back, but the problem will take care of itself. Select both circles and choose the MAKE (COM-POUND PATHS) command (⌘-8). The doughnut now has a hole, as shown in Figure 8-37. Notice that the large circle is in front

⚛ The **Illustrator** 5 Book

of the napkin. The MAKE (COMPOUND PATHS) command always moves all selected objects to directly in back of the frontmost object in the selection, which in this case is the hole.

4. To create the shadow shown in Figure 8-38, clone the doughnut by OPTION-dragging it with the selection tool about a half inch down and to the right. (Cloning is explained in the *Cloning objects* section of Chapter 11.)

Figure 8-37: Combining the circles makes a hole and brings the large circle in front of the napkin.

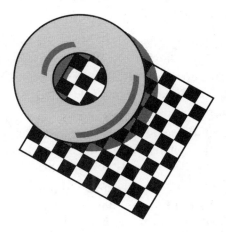

Figure 8-38: The finished doughnut with shadow.

5. Send the clone to the back of the illustration by choosing SEND TO BACK (⌘- –, COMMAND-HYPHEN).

6. In the PAINT STYLE palette, click on the "Fill" box, select the "Black" fill type box, and enter 50 into the "Tint" percent option box. Then click on the "Stroke" box and select the "None" stroke type box. The finished illustration appears as shown in Figure 8-38 on the previous page.

In case you're wondering, the shadow appears to shade the napkin because the napkin is filled with a partially transparent tile pattern. The pattern contains only black squares. The appearance of white squares is created by an absence of black squares. Therefore, you can see through the "white" squares to the shadow at the back of the illustration.

Compound masking

In Illustrator 5.0, a compound path can double as a clipping path, as I described in the tip on page 369. But in addition to flowing masked elements between multiple objects, you can create a path that is filled with masked elements and has holes punched out of it. After creating a compound path, layer the masked elements in back of the compound path, and choose the MAKE (MASKS) command.

In Figure 8-39, I've added several stripes of icing in front of the doughnut. The following exercise describes how to use the doughnut to mask the icing:

1. Select either path in the doughnut with the selection tool and choose the SEND TO FRONT command (⌘- =, COMMAND-EQUAL). This ensures that the clipping path (the doughnut) is in front of the masked elements (the icing).

2. Press the SHIFT key and click on each of the icing stripes so that both the icing and the pasted donut are selected. Choose the MAKE command from the MASKS submenu under the OBJECT menu. The mask is now complete.

3. Unfortunately, the stroke and fill have disappeared from the doughnut. All you have is a bunch of masked stripes. Luckily Illustrator provides a filter that will reapply the fill and stroke. But first, choose SELECT NONE (⌘-⇧-A) to deselect everything.

4. Click on a circle with the selection tool to select the doughnut. Using the options in the PAINT STYLE palette, select the fill and stroke attributes that you want to apply to the doughnut. Don't be discouraged when they seem to have no effect whatsoever.

5. To make the attributes take hold, choose the FILL & STROKE FOR MASK command from the CREATE submenu under the FILTER menu. The finished doughnut is shown in Figure 8-40.

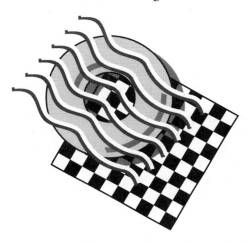

Figure 8-39: The next exercise demonstrates how to fill the doughnut with these stripes of icing.

Figure 8-40: The finished doughnut with icing.

Compound paths and text

Unhappily, type cannot be associated with a compound path. However, you can convert a block of type to paths using the CREATE OUTLINES command from the TYPE menu and then combine these paths with other graphic objects using the MAKE (COMPOUND PATHS) command. You should note, however, that type is automatically converted to compound paths when you choose the CREATE OUTLINES command. You may therefore find it helpful to break the paths apart using the RELEASE (COMPOUND PATHS) command (⌘-9) before combining them with other paths.

Who gets to be the hole?

```
Object
 Paint Style...      ⌘I
 Custom Color...
 Pattern...
 Gradient...
 Attributes...      ⌘⌃A
 Join...             ⌘J
 Average...          ⌘L
 Guides           ▶
 Masks            ▶
 Compound Paths   ▶
 Cropmarks        ▶
 Graphs           ▶
```

If one object doesn't cut a hole in another in a compound path, it's because the two paths progress in the same direction. (For the whole story on the subject of path direction, see the *Filling theory* section that follows.) To change the direction of a single object in a compound path, select it with the direct-selection tool, choose the ATTRIBUTES... command from the OBJECT menu, and select or deselect the "Reverse path direction" check box in the ATTRIBUTES dialog box according to the following rules:

- If a background path is selected, the "Reverse path direction" check box should be turned off, indicating that the current object is not a hole.

- If a foreground path is selected, the "Reverse path direction" check box will be selected, indicating the current object *is* a hole.

Usually, you won't have to worry about this option because Illustrator does the work automatically. But if ever it doesn't do what you want, now you know how to fix it.

Filling theory

Now I'll mention one last bit of information that concerns the method by which Illustrator fills paths with overlapping segments, including overlapping portions of different objects within a compound path. The question is: When is part of a path considered to be outside the path and when is it considered inside? To determine the answer, Illustrator uses a PostScript routine known as the *non-zero winding number rule* to determine the fill of a shape. To save paper, I'll just call it the *Ø-rule*.

To demonstrate this rule, I've drawn the complex path shown in Figure 8-41. I have designed this path so that every segment overlaps at least two other segments in the path. In Figure 8-42, I have enhanced the shape with directional arrows. These arrows demonstrate the direction in which each segment in the shape progresses from point to point. If you start at any point in the path and trace along the path in the direction indicated by the arrows, you will eventually arrive back at the point at which you started, having traced every segment exactly one time. Therefore, the arrows represent the consistent progression of the path through its points.

Figure 8-41: Every segment in this path overlaps at least two and as many as five segments.

The manner in which I have drawn the path divides it into 19 *subsections*, which are portions of the path separated from other portions by part of a segment. If a subsection is bordered entirely by other subsections, then I say it is *encompassed*. Any subsection that is *not* encompassed is obviously inside the path and will be filled just like a path whose segments do not overlap. In Figure 8-42, the four encompassed subsections are identified by flagpoles, labeled 1 through 4. These are the subsections that are subject to the Ø-rule.

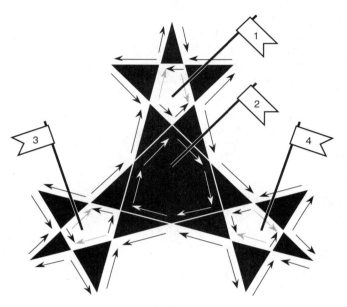

Figure 8-42: A filled version of the same path notated with arrows and flags.

Each flagpole begins inside an encompassed subsection and extends to a location outside of the path. Each pole crosses two or more segments. Each segment, according to its arrows in the figure, progresses at least partially in a rightward or leftward direction. To illustrate the winding number rule, we will use the metaphor of raising flags up the flagpoles. Before I begin raising the flag, I have a "flag variable" of zero. As I raise the flag, it will cross a number of segments. For each rightward-progressing segment that it crosses, I add 1 to the flag variable. For each leftward-progressing segment crossed, I subtract 1 from the flag variable. Once the flag is raised beyond all crossing segments, I compute the total.

The **Illustrator 5** Book

This final flag variable leads me to one of two conclusions:

- If it is zero, then the encompassed subsection from which the flagpole emanates is *outside* of the shape, and will *not* be filled.

- If it is not equal to zero, the encompassed subsection is *inside* the shape and will be filled.

Flag 1 in Figure 8-42 crosses both a rightward- and leftward-progressing segment. The flag variable is 0+1−1=0, so its subsection is outside the shape by the Ø-rule. The same is true for flags 3 and 4. However, flag 2 crosses two rightward-progressing segments. Its flag variable is 0+1+1=2. Therefore, its subsection is inside the shape.

The conclusion: Of all the encompassed subsections, only the center one is filled, as shown in the figure.

Perhaps an easier way to think of this rule is this:

- If all directional arrows surrounding an encompassed subsection do *not* progress in a consistently clockwise or counterclockwise formation, the subsection is considered by Illustrator to be *outside* the shape.

- If all directional arrows *do* progress in a consistently clockwise or counterclockwise formation, the subsection is considered by Illustrator to be *inside* the shape.

The arrows surrounding the subsection containing flag 2 establish a consistently clockwise order; thus the subsection is filled. The subsections containing flags 1, 3, and 4, however, each have one or more dissenting arrows that flow against the majority direction. These dissenting arrows are grayed in Figure 8-42.

Keep in mind, this rule affects only paths with overlapping segments or compound paths composed of multiple objects. Standard paths with no overlapping segments are always filled according to your directions, as described in previous sections of this chapter. If you do have to create an overlapping path (very rare) and this rule seems too complex (very common), just preview the path and take your chances. You can always go back and fix it later.

CHAPTER

STROKING GRAPHIC OBJECTS AND TYPE

Like the fill attribute, *stroke* is applied to both type and graphic objects to determine the appearance of your printed artwork. While fill is applied to the interior of an object, stroke is applied to its outline. Strokes share many similarities with fills: They can be colored with gray values, process colors, and even as tile patterns. Or they can be transparent, so that only the fill is visible. If you also apply a transparent fill, you can create an invisible object, which can be used for aligning other objects. On the other hand, unlike with fills, a gradation cannot be used for a stroke. Also, you cannot subject a stroke to masking or hole making—features that can be applied only to the interior of a shape. By the same token, some options that apply to stroke are irrelevant to fill: line weight, dash patterns, caps, joins, and so on, all of which are explained in this chapter.

How stroke affects objects

Stroke can be applied to any object in Adobe Illustrator. Applying a stroke to a path is a straightforward process. If you want to see a path's outline, apply a stroke. Otherwise, do not.

Figure 9-1 shows an identical stroke applied to an open path and a closed path. In both cases, I have drawn in the path in white to show how the stroke always centers on the path. This is important to keep in mind when trying to determine the amount of space a stroke will take when you print your artwork. You can also exploit this feature to create useful effects, as described in the section *Mixing stroke attributes* later in this chapter.

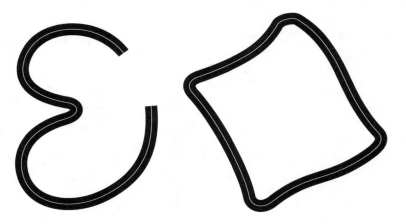

Figure 9-1: An open path (left) and a closed path (right), each stroked with a heavy line. The paths themselves are displayed in white.

Stroking text

You can also stroke text objects. If you select a text block with the selection tool, applying a stroke will affect all type along the path. The first example in Figure 9-2 shows a selected path text block. In the second example, you can see how stroking the object affects the type but does not affect the path. (Note that in each of the next three figures, the first line of type is displayed in artwork mode while the second shows how the first would print.)

If you select the path with the direct-selection tool, you can apply a stroke to the path only, leaving the text as is, as in Figure 9-3.

Figure 9-2: If you stroke a text block selected with the selection tool (top), only the text will become stroked (bottom).

Figure 9-3: If you select the path with the direct-selection tool (top), only the path will become stroked (bottom).

You can also stroke single words and other collections of specific characters without affecting the path by selecting the text with the type tool. Like any character-level formatting option, such as font or type size, stroke affects only highlighted characters, as demonstrated in Figure 9-4. In this way, Illustrator allows you to apply several different strokes to a single text object.

Figure 9-4: By selecting text with the type tool (top), you stroke only the highlighted type (bottom).

Painting the stroke

To stroke an object, you must select it and choose the STYLE... command from the OBJECT menu (⌘-I). The PAINT STYLE palette will display, as shown in Figure 9-5. You can determine and manipulate every characteristic of a stroke within this dialog box.

As you might expect, all the options selected or changed when the "Stroke" box, just to the right of the "Fill" box, is selected affect the stroke of a selected object. The entire lower portion of the PAINT STYLE palette contain options that relate to stroke. These options include the following:

- **Weight**. This option determines the thickness, or *line weight*, of the current stroke, as measured in points. You can enter any value between 0 and 1296 (18 inches) for this option.

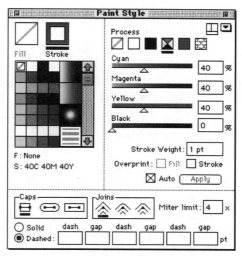

Figure 9-5: The Paint Style palette provides access to all of Illustrator's stroking options.

- **Caps**. This option allows you to select from three radio buttons that control the appearance of a stroke at the end of an open path. Represented by icons, these options include the *butt cap* (⬛), *round cap* (⬛), and the *square cap* (⬛). When selected, the butt cap option instructs the stroke to end exactly at an endpoint. The round cap option appends a semicircle to the endpoints of a path. The square cap extends the stroke half the line weight past each endpoint. The "Caps" options do *not* affect the appearance of closed paths or text unless a dash pattern is used (as described in the *Dash patterns and line caps* section, later in this chapter).

- **Joins**. This option allows you to select from three radio buttons that control the appearance of a stroke at each corner or cusp in the current object. Represented by icons, these options include the *miter join* (⬆), *round join* (⬆), and the *bevel join* (⬆). When selected, the miter join option forces the stroke to form a single, crisp corner. The round join option smooths off corners to give paths a soft appearance. The bevel join severs the stroke abruptly at the corner point.

- **Miter limit**. The value in this option box tells Illustrator at what point to slice off an overly long miter join to form a bevel join. The value, which can be between 0 and 10, is measured in multiples of the current line weight. For example, when the value is 4, the default, Illustrator allows the miter join to extend a distance from its corner point equal to four times the current line weight. If the miter join is any longer (due to a very sharp corner in the path), the stroke is severed at the corner point to form a bevel join.

- **Dash pattern**. The very bottom of the PAINT STYLE palette contains two radio buttons: "Solid" and "Dashed." When solid is selected, the current stroke will be solid, free of interruptions, except those inherent in a tile pattern, if the "Pattern" option is selected in the "Stroke" box. Select "Dashed" to interrupt the stroke at regular intervals to create a *dash pattern*. Enter the length of each dash and gap in the option boxes to the right of the "Dashed" option. The first, third, and fifth option boxes determine the dashes; the second, fourth, and sixth option boxes determine the gaps. All values are measured in points.

All other options control aspects of painting an object, as described in the *Painting the fill* section of Chapter 8.

Coloring a stroke

Select one of the six stroke type boxes in the PAINT STYLE palette to color the stroke of one or more selected objects. These are the same as the first six of the fill type boxes shown back in Figure 8-8. Only one of the boxes can be selected at a time. Upon selecting one of the boxes, additional options that request specifications for determining the color of a stroke will display. Each stroke type box and its related options are discussed in the following items:

- **None**. This option is selected by default the first time you enter the PAINT STYLE palette. It makes the outline of the selected path transparent. The "None" option is useful for stroking type and paths when you want only the fill to be visible. You can also assign both a transparent stroke and a transparent fill to a path. An entirely transparent path remains visible in the artwork mode but will neither preview nor print. Such a path can be used for alignment or as the boundary in a wrapping object, as described in the section *Adjusting standoff* in Chapter 7.

The **Illustrator 5** Book

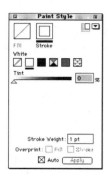

When "None" is selected, the "Stroke Weight" option box and all options at the bottom of the PAINT STYLE palette will become dimmed. Therefore, "None" may not be used in conjunction with any option described in future sections of this chapter.

- **White**. Selecting this box makes the fill of a selected path white. A white outline is generally used to partially hide an element or a similar stroke in back of the selected path. You can also create type with a white outline against a colored background.

When "White" is selected, a "Tint" bar and percent option box appear under the stroke type boxes, indicating the tint of the stroke. Moving the bar's triangular indicator to the right increases the amount of black in the stroke, presenting a shade of gray. You can also adjust the tint of a gray stroke by altering the percentage value in the percent option box that appears just to the right of the "Tint" bar. A value of 0% is solid white; 100% tint produces solid black. Values between 0% and 100% produce progressively darker shades of gray.

The "Overprint: Stroke" check box option is available when the "White" stroke type box is selected and the "Tint" value is set higher than 0%.

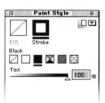

- **Black**. When the "Black" stroke type box is selected, the same "Tint" bar and percent option box appears as when "White" is selected, and you can achieve the same shades of gray.

The "Overprint: Stroke" check box option is available when the "Black" stroke type box is selected and the "Tint" value is set higher than 0%.

- **Process Color**. Selecting this box displays the "Cyan," "Magenta," "Yellow," and "Black" bars and corresponding percent option boxes. By moving the triangular indicator along the bars, you determine the percentage of each primary printing color that is combined to create a specific *process color*, which is displayed in the "Stroke" box. The composite name will appear under the scrolling list on the left side of the PAINT STYLE palette. For example, 50C 25M 75Y 10K indicates a process color made up of 50% cyan, 25% magenta, 75% yellow, and 10% black. Chapter 10, *Filling and Stroking in Color*, contains an in-depth discussion of process colors.

The "Overprint: Stroke" check box option is available when the "Process" stroke type box is selected, provided that at least one of the four color bars is set to a value higher than 0%.

- **Custom Color**. Selecting this stroke type box produces a scrolling list of custom colors defined using the CUSTOM COLOR... command under the OBJECT menu. When you launch Illustrator, the program loads all predefined custom colors contained in the Adobe Illustrator Startup file (located inside the Plug-Ins folder) into the scrolling list. Illustrator comes with a number of optional custom color files that contain thousands of predefined colors from Pantone, Trumatch, and others that you can open or import into your illustration. To import a custom color library, choose IMPORT STYLES... from the FILE menu. In the OPEN dialog box that appears, locate the Color Systems folder inside the same folder that contains the Illustrator application, and double-click on the name of the file you want to import.

To simply open a custom color file, choose the OPEN... command from the FILE menu and select a color system file. The advantage of opening rather than importing is that you can close the colors that you decide not to use and avoid cluttering your scrolling list with a bunch of unwanted junk.

The "Tint" bar and percent option box under the scrolling list allow you to lighten the shade of a custom color to any percentage value between 0% (white) and 100% (the solid color).

The "Overprint: Stroke" check box option is available when the "Custom" stroke type box is selected. The name of the custom color appears under the scrolling list on the left side of the PAINT STYLE palette.

- **Pattern**. Selecting this box produces a scrolling list of tile patterns defined using the PATTERN... command under the OBJECT menu. Illustrator loads all predefined patterns contained in the Adobe Illustrator Startup file into the scrolling list. The Gradients & Patterns folder inside the Illustrator folder contains files of predefined tile patterns that you can import or open.

The "Overprint: Stroke" check box option is available when the "Pattern" stroke type box is selected. The name of the tile pattern appears under the scrolling list on the left side of the PAINT STYLE palette.

The **Illustrator** 5 Book

Specifying a line weight

To the right of the "Stroke" box are a series of options that affect the stroke of a selected path. The first of these is the "Weight" option box, which controls the thickness, or *line weight*, of a stroke. Regardless of the selected "Ruler Units" option in the GENERAL PREFERENCES dialog box (introduced in the *Setting preferences* section of Chapter 3), line weight is always specified in points. Also, unlike some programs that allow you to choose only from a predetermined set of line weights, Illustrator gives you total control, allowing you to enter any value between 0 and 1296, the latter being equal to the width of the entire drawing area.

Generally, I advise against specifying a line weight value smaller than 0.15. A 0.3-point weight is commonly considered a *hairline* weight, so 0.15-point is only half as heavy as a hairline. As an example, suppose you specify a 0-point line weight, which instructs Illustrator to print the thinnest line available from the current output device. The thinnest line printable by a 300-dpi laser printer is 0.24-point thick ($\frac{1}{300}$ inch). However, higher-resolution printers, such as Linotronic and Compugraphic imagesetters, easily print lines as thin as 0.03 point, or 10 times thinner than a hairline. Nonetheless, because any line thinner than 0.15-point is almost invisible to the naked eye, such a line will probably drop out when reproduced commercially.

Specifying a line cap

Another set of options that affect stroke are the "Caps" options. Inside the "Caps" box, you can select from three *line caps*, which determine the appearance of a stroke at an endpoint. Line caps are generally useful only when stroking an open path. The only exception to this is when line caps are used in combination with dash patterns, as described in the *Dash patterns and line caps* section, later in this chapter.

The "Caps" options function as follows:

- **Butt cap**. The first radio button in the "Caps" box is the *butt cap* option, the default setting and by far the most commonly used line cap. Notice the black line that runs through the center of each of the icons in the "Caps" box. This line denotes the position of the path relative to the stroke. When the butt cap option is selected, the stroke ends immediately at an endpoint and is perpendicular to the final course of the path, as its icon suggests.

- **Round cap**. The second radio button is a *round cap* option. Giving a stroke a round cap is like attaching a circle to the end of a path. The endpoint acts as the center of this circle, and its radius is half the line weight, as demonstrated by Figure 9-6. For example, suppose you have a 4-point line weight with round caps that follows a horizontal path. A 2-point portion of the stroke is on top of the path and the other 2-point portion is underneath. Since the path is itself invisible, the two halves of the stroke meet with no break between them. Upon reaching the end of the path, the top half of the stroke wraps around the endpoint in a circular manner to meet with the bottom half of the stroke; hence a semicircle with a 2-point radius.

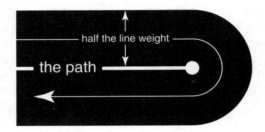

Figure 9-6: When the round cap option is selected, the stroke wraps around the endpoints in a path to form semicircles.

We, the people
We, the people

Figure 9-7: Two lines of type composed of open paths, one stroked with square caps (top) and one with round caps (bottom).

The **Illustrator** 5 Book

When combined with round joins (described in the next section), round caps can be used to give an open path an informal appearance. Figure 9-7 shows several letters composed of open paths. The first example is stroked with square caps (described below), the second is stroked with round caps. Which do you think looks friendlier? If you're not sure, ask some preschoolers which one they think Barney would like better.

- **Square cap**. The third radio button is the *square cap* option. Here, a square is attached to the end of a line; the endpoint is the center of the square. It is similar to the rounded cap in the sense that the size of this square is dependent on the line weight. The width and height of the square are equal to the weight of the stroke, so that the square projects from the endpoint a distance equal to one half the weight of the stroke. If the path in Figure 9-8 has a 4-point line weight, for example, the upper corner of the stroke would be located 2 points above and 2 points to the right of the endpoint.

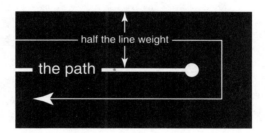

Figure 9-8: When the square cap option is selected, the stroke wraps around the endpoints in a path to form perpendicular corners.

Specifying a line join

Next to the "Caps" box in the PAINT STYLE palette are the "Joins" options. Inside the "Joins" box, you can select from three *line joins*, which determine the appearance of a stroke at places in a path where two segments meet at a corner point. Line joins have no affect on the appearance of stroked smooth points.

The "Joins" options function as follows:

- **Miter join**. The first radio button in the "Joins" box is the *miter join* option, which is the default setting. If a corner has a miter join, the outside edges of a stroke extend until they meet. Notice the first example of Figure 9-9. A corner with a true miter join will always form a single crisp corner. Miter joins can, however, be cut short using the "Miter limit" option, explained in the next section.

Figure 9-9: Three corners and three joins: from top to bottom, a miter join, a round join, and a bevel join.

- **Round join**. The second radio button is the *round join* option, which is identical in principle to the round cap. Half of the line weight wraps around the corner point to form a semicircle. In fact, rounded joins and rounded caps are so alike that they are almost exclusively used together. I recommend that you do not use round joins in combination with butt caps, especially if any dash pattern is involved, because round joins actually form complete circles around corner points. See the *Dash patterns and line joins* section later in this chapter for more information.

- **Bevel join**. The third and last radio button is the *bevel join* option. The bevel join is very similar to a butt cap. Instead of allowing the edges of a stroke to meet, as in the case of a miter join, the stroke is sheared off at the corner point. The result is what appears to be two very closely situated corners. Unlike a butt cap, however, a bevel join is not sheared perpendicularly to any path segment. Since two segments meet at a corner point, a compromise is struck. As you can see in the last example of Figure 9-9, the angle at which the bevel join's sheared edge meets with one segment is identical to the angle at which it meets the other.

Bevelling excessive miter joins

Directly to the left of the "Joins" box in the PAINT STYLE dialog is the "Miter limit" option box, which allows you to bevel excessively long miter joins. This option works by establishing a relationship between the current line weight and the maximum width of a stroke at any corner point, called the *miter limit*. If a miter join is longer than the line weight times the value entered in the "Miter limit" option box, the join is converted into a bevel join at that corner point only.

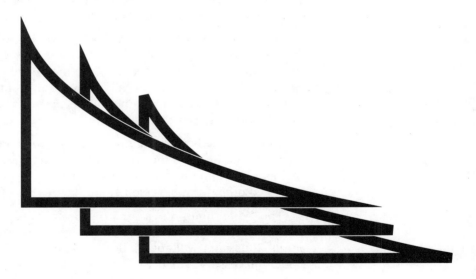

Figure 9-10: Three versions of a path stroked with miter joins but with different miter limits: from top to bottom, the "Miter limit" value is 10, 5, and 3.

The top path in Figure 9-10 includes two pairs of segments that meet to form sharp corners. The stroke of this path includes miter joins. The top and right-hand corners are so sharp that the joins must extend an extreme distance before the two edges of the stroke can finally meet. Occasionally, you will discover that excessively long tips at the corners of a path may protrude into other paths or simply appear unattractive. Unfortunately, Illustrator does not allow you to combine different line joins in a single path. But it does allow you to do the next best thing.

Using the "Miter limit" option, you can specify that if the mitered stroke of a path extends beyond any corner point to form a tip that is longer than a specified multiple of the line weight, then that corner is converted to a bevel join. The line weight of each path in Figure 9-10 is 10 points. The miter limit of the top path has been set to 10, which is Illustrator's maximum miter limit value. This means that if the stroke of the path extends from any corner point to form a tip that measures more than ten times the 10-point line weight, or 100 points long, the miter join at that point will be sliced off completely. Since none of the segments in the figure meet to form such a sharp corner, the top path contains only miter joins.

In the middle path of Figure 9-10, however, the miter limit has been decreased to 5. Since the stroke at the right corner measures more than 50 points from the inside to the outside of the "elbow" of the path, Illustrator automatically converts this miter join to a bevel join. The stroke at the top corner of this path remains a miter join, since its tip is shorter than 50 points.

To create the bottom path in the figure, the miter limit has been changed to 3. Because the strokes at both the top and right-hand corners measure more than 30 points from inner to outer tip, both joins are sliced off to form bevel joins.

The "Miter limit" value can range from 1 to 500, provided that the miter limit multiplied by the stroke weight doesn't exceed 1800 points. Illustrator will automatically compensate the "Miter limit" value if necessary. The default value is 4. A miter limit of 1 specifies that every corner in a path should be beveled, and is therefore identical to selecting the bevel join option from the "Joins" box. The "Miter limit" option is useful only with miter joins. If either the round join or bevel join is selected in the "Joins" box, the "Miter limit" option will be dimmed.

Choosing between a huge corner tip and no tip at all is a harsh compromise. If you want to preserve the attractive quality of a miter join without allowing it to take over too large a portion of your drawing, you may prefer to adjust your path to increase the angle between a pair of segments, thus decreasing the length of the tip formed by the stroke. A miter limit should be used only as a last resort.

Creating a dash pattern

The only remaining options in the PAINT STYLE palette that affect the stroke of a path are those in the "Dash pattern" box. *Dash patterns* are variations in the manner in which a stroke follows its path. Most often, this results in repetitive interruptions in a stroke. For example, a standard coupon border in a newspaper advertisement is a dash pattern.

The "Solid" option, selected by default, is by far the most common dash pattern. A solid stroke simply means that a stroke remains constant throughout the length of its path. If you select the "Dashed" option, six previously dimmed option boxes become available, each representing an interval, measured in points, during which a dash will be "on" or "off" in the course of stroking a path. "On" values determine the length of the dashes; "off" values determine the length of the gaps between the dashes. Odd option boxes (first, third, and fifth) turn the dash on; even option boxes (second, fourth, and sixth) turn it off.

Suppose that you want to create a dashed line composed of a series of 8-point dashes followed by 4-point gaps. After selecting the "Dashed" radio button, enter 8 in the first option box and 4 in the second. Leave the remaining four option boxes blank. If a series of consecutive "Dashed" options are blank, Illustrator simply ignores them. Once Illustrator has created the first 8-point dash and accompanying 4-point gap, it repeats the sequence over and over throughout the length of the selected path.

This same pattern can be indicated in many different ways. For example, instead of leaving the last four options blank, you might fill them with 8/4/8/4. Alternatively, the first four options could contain zeros, and the last two could contain the 8 and the 4. Many other variations will produce the same effect.

All sorts of line patterns can be created, since every on and off indicator may contain a different value. You can create a pattern that repeats one, two, or three dash/gap combinations. Also, you need not specify an off value for every on value. A solid stroke, for example, is all dashes and no gaps. Its dash pattern may contain any positive number for its first option value while the remaining options may be left blank. However, a blank "Dashed" option cannot exist between two option boxes that contain values. If you want to skip a dash or gap in a stroke, enter a zero for that option.

Dash pattern values can range from 0 to 1296 and are accurate to $\frac{1}{1000}$ of a point. They are always specified in points, regardless of the selected "Ruler units" option in the GENERAL PREFERENCES dialog (introduced in the *Setting preferences* section of Chapter 3).

Dashed strokes are most popularly used to indicate cut-out lines. They surround mail-in coupons, paper dolls, and any number of other items that are specifically created to be clipped from a page. Dash patterns may also indicate a ghostly or translucent image.

Mixing stroke attributes

Stroking effects are created by mixing dash patterns with caps, joins, and line weights. More complicated effects can be achieved by layering duplicates of an object, one copy in front of another, each with a slightly different stroke. Provided that the line weight of each stroke is thinner than the line weight of the stroke behind it, portions of each stroke will show through to create unusual effects.

Layering strokes

The simplest stroking effect is the result of layering duplicate paths stroked with increasingly thinner line weights. The following exercise demonstrates how to use this technique to change the block of standard outline type shown in Figure 9-11 into a block of *inline* text, as shown in Figure 9-13 on page 398:

1. Start with something large, really large, something you could see from a couple of miles off on the side of a Winnebago, like a line of 120-point type. This will act as the first object in the stroking effect.

The **Illustrator** 5 Book

2. For best results, the backmost object in a layer should always be stroked with a thick line weight. In this case, select the text block, choose the PAINT STYLE… from the OBJECT menu (⌘-I), and enter 6 for the "Weight" option in the PAINT STYLE palette.

3. While the PAINT STYLE palette remains displayed, select "None" from the "Fill" box and "Black" from the "Stroke" box. The result is the text block similar to the one shown in Figure 9-11.

4. Copy the selected text block (⌘-C) and paste the copy directly in front of the original (⌘-F).

Figure 9-11: A block of 120-point type painted with a 6-point line weight and no fill.

5. Display the PAINT STYLE palette again (⌘-I). Select "White" from the stroke type box and enter 4 into the "Weight" option box. Then press RETURN. The result is the type shown in Figure 9-12.

Figure 9-12: Copy the type, paste it in front, and apply a thinner, white stroke.

6. Choose PASTE IN FRONT again (⌘-F). Display the PAINT STYLE palette and change the stroke to a black, 2-point line weight. The finished image is shown in Figure 9-13 on the next page.

Figure 9-13: Paste it in front again and apply an even thinner, black stroke. Ta da, inline type.

Other stroking effects can be accomplished by layering duplicated objects with progressively reduced line weights. If you lighten the color of a line each time you reduce the line weight, you can create neon type. In Figure 9-14, for example, the backmost text block is stroked with a 100% black, 6-point line weight. The text block front of that is stroked with a 90% black, 5.5-point line weight, and so on, until the frontmost text block, which is stroked with a white, 0-point line weight. I added round joins to all paths to emulate the curves associated with real-life neon tubes.

Figure 9-14: Neon type is made up of duplicated text blocks, each stroked with a thinner, lighter colored stroke than the object behind it.

Dash patterns and line caps

Forget layering duplicate objects for a moment. Even if you are stroking only a single object, you can achieve interesting effects by combining dash patterns with line caps. This is because Illustrator treats the beginning and ending of each dash in a pattern as the beginning and ending of a stroke. Therefore, both ends of a dash are affected by

The **Illustrator 5** Book

the selected line cap, allowing you to create round dashes as well as rectangular ones.

Suppose that you have created a black stroke that contains round caps and a 12-point line weight. You add to this by selecting the "Dashed" option in the PAINT STYLE palette and entering 0 for the dash value and 16 for the gap. The resulting line is shown in Figure 9-15. The diagram in Figure 9-16 shows how each dash is constructed. When you specify the length of each dash to be 0, you instruct Illustrator to allow no distance between the center of the round cap at the beginning of the dash and the center of the round cap at the end of the dash. The two round caps are coincident, implying that a series of black circles exist, the centers of which are 0-point dashes (shown as small white circles in Figure 9-16). Each circle has a 6-point radius (half the 12-point line weight), which makes a 12-point diameter. Because 12 points of each 16-point dash/gap sequence are consumed by a round cap circle, a distance of only 4 points remains between each circle. In conclusion, a dash pattern that is essentially never on, but rather always off in 16-point intervals appears to be on for 12 points and off for only 4 points when a stroked with a 12-point line weight and rounded caps.

Figure 9-15: A dash pattern with a 0-point dash, a 16-point gap, a 12-point line weight, and round caps.

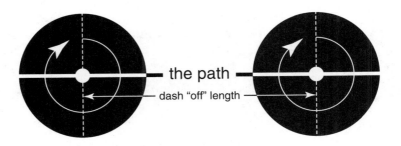

Figure 9-16: Round caps wrap around the ends of each dash in a dash pattern. If the dash value is 0, the round caps form perfect circles.

The first, third, and fifth "Dashed" option boxes in the PAINT STYLE dialog must contain zeros (or remain blank) if you want to create a stroke with perfectly round dashes. Also, the second, fourth, and sixth "Dashed" options must contain gap values (if any) larger than the line weight to prevent the round dashes from touching each other.

Layering dash patterns and line caps

Even more interesting results can be achieved by layering dash patterns in front of other dash patterns. As when layering solid strokes, the line weight of each path should be thinner than the line weight of the path behind it. Also, although you can vary the line caps, you will generally want to keep the dash pattern constant throughout all layered paths; that is, the length of each dash and length of each gap— what I call the *periodicity* of the pattern—should not vary.

The following example begins with the line shown in Figure 9-15 on the preceding page. The periodicity of this line is 16 points— a 0-point dash plus a 16-point gap. In the exercise, you will layer two additional paths in front of this line to create a pattern of inline circles.

1. Copy the line (⌘-C) and paste it directly in front of the original (⌘-F).

2. Using the PAINT STYLE palette (⌘-I), change the color of the stroke to white and decrease the line weight to 10 points. The result is displayed in Figure 9-17. The frontmost white circles all but cover up the larger black circles of the original line. Since the periodicity of the dash pattern remains constant, the circles of the white line exactly fit within the circles of the black line, producing a series of outlined dots.

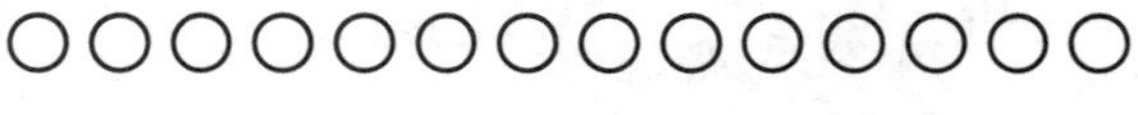

○ ○ ○ ○ ○ ○ ○ ○ ○ ○ ○ ○ ○

Figure 9-17: The pattern from Figure 9-15 after adding a 10-point white stroke in front of it.

3. To create the line shown in Figure 9-18, paste another copy of the original path in front of the existing ones. Change the color

of the stroke to black and decrease the line weight to 6 points. The effect is a series of black dots surrounded by white outlines, which are themselves surrounded by black outlines.

Figure 9-18: Layering a 6-point, black line in front of the other paths makes an inline effect.

If you are familiar with line weights, you might notice that the outlines around the circles in Figure 9-17 are 1 point thick. This may seem incongruous with the fact that the first line is stroked with a 12-point line weight and the second line is stroked with a 10-point line weight. After all, the difference between the strokes is two points, not one. However, recall that it is the radius of a rounded cap that wraps around the end of a dash. Therefore, you must subtract the radius of the smaller round cap from that of the larger round cap to determine the amount of the original stroke that remains exposed. Since the radius of a round cap circle is equal to half its line weight, the outline of each dot appears to be 6 minus 5, or one point thick.

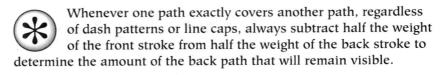 Whenever one path exactly covers another path, regardless of dash patterns or line caps, always subtract half the weight of the front stroke from half the weight of the back stroke to determine the amount of the back path that will remain visible.

Dash patterns and line joins

Dash patterns can also produce unusual effects when combined with line joins. The stroke of the path in Figure 9-19 on the following page, for example, is made of a 32-point line weight with round joins and a lively dash pattern. The path itself is demonstrated as a thin, white line. Each corner point in the path is numbered. Notice that corners 1 and 2 coincide with gaps in the dash pattern so that they appear to be cut off, or beveled—not what you might expect from a line with round joins. By contrast, corners 3 and 4 meet with dashes in the pattern. Due to constraints of the PostScript language, Illustrator is forced to represent the round joins at these corners as black circles, interrupting the flow of the pattern. This problem is less noticeable in paths with smaller line weights, although a high-resolution printer will uncover these mistakes, even with narrow lines.

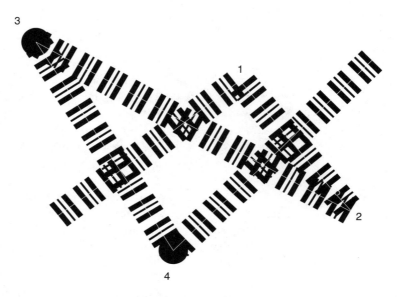

Figure 9-19: When combined with a lively pattern, round joins form circles at corners that coincide with dashes (3 and 4) and bevel at corners that coincide with gaps (1 and 2).

 To avoid the problem shown in Figure 9-19, you can either select beveled or miter joins, or move the corner points of a path so they coincide with gaps, rather than dashes.

CHAPTER

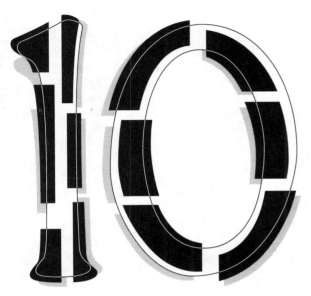

FILLING
AND
STROKING
IN COLOR

There was a time when the Macintosh computer was seen as a strictly monochrome machine. Only a few years ago, most users worked on SEs or older model Macs, computers with built-in monitors that display only black and white pixels. Today, color is the standard, complete with color machines, color monitors, and color output. Every major application on the market now offers color capabilities of some kind. And somewhere near the top of the list is Illustrator, chock-full of some of the best color controls available in any software, including support for four-color process colors, custom spot colors, and the four commercial color-matching libraries. If you don't use a color display device, you can still access Illustrator's color capabilities; you just have to become a little more adept at predicting the results.

The benefits of Illustrator's color abilities include increased quality and control as well as cost savings over traditional color-separation techniques. The price for these benefits is additional complexity, demanding technical requirements, and the expense of printing color proofs and color-separated film negatives. But with a little understanding of how to work with color, in addition to the help of your commercial printer, you can master the color capabilities of Illustrator 5.0.

Displaying colors

Illustrator's color abilities are available to anyone who can run the software; they are not limited by the monitor on which you are working or by the printer on which you proof your work. When you work on a monochrome monitor, specified colors appear in corresponding shades of gray. If you have a color monitor, however, Illustrator takes full advantage of it, displaying up to 16 million colors at one time, depending on the capacity of your monitor and video card.

Preparing your color monitor

If you work with a color monitor, you want your screen to display colors that match the commercially printed results as closely as possible. Since the color display varies widely from one brand of monitor to another, and even between monitors from the same manufacturer, Illustrator 5.0 includes the ability to reset the color definitions used by your display.

When using Illustrator in color, you will generally want to set your Monitors *control panel* to display as many colors as possible—256 colors if you are using an 8-bit video card, "Thousands" if you are using a 16-bit video card, and "Millions" if you are using a 24-bit video card. Control panels, also known as *cdevs* (pronounced see-devs), are accessed by choosing the Control Panel folder from the APPLE menu. To display the Monitors cdev, double-click on its icon, as shown in Figure 10-1. However, there may be times during the creation of your color document when you wish to reduce the number of colors displayed or even turn off the color entirely in order to speed up the preview of your illustration. These changes will not affect the color definitions used for your illustration, and you can safely change the color settings as often as you desire. You can even use a color-switching utility that allows you to toggle between display modes. My favorite is Switch-A-Roo, a free Fkey from Bill Steinberg available over CompuServe (where Bill's account number is 76703,1027) and other national bulletin board systems.

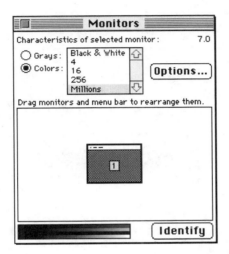

Figure 10-1: The Monitors Control Panel allows you to set the number of colors that can be displayed simultaneously on your monitor.

Any adjustment to the Monitors cdev affects the colors used by all Macintosh software. You can also customize your screen display strictly for Illustrator from within the application. This color-adjustment process serves to alter certain key screen colors to match printed samples as closely as possible. For best results, you need to obtain a sample color bar from the commercial printer who will be reproducing your illustrations. This sample should include a separate color square for each of the four process colors—cyan, magenta, yellow, and black—plus combinations of each pair and of all three process colors, excluding black.

General...	⌘K
Color Matching...	
Hyphenation Options...	
Plug-ins...	

To begin the color adjustment, choose the COLOR MATCHING... command in the PREFERENCE submenu from the EDIT menu. The COLOR MATCHING dialog box appears, as shown in Figure 10-2, which shows the current appearance of each primary color and primary-color combination. The goal is to adjust each of the colors so that it is as close as possible to the appropriate printed color sample. Be aware, however, that monitors do not create colors in the same way that colors are created in the printing process—so perfect matches will be unlikely. To adjust the on-screen representation of a color, click on the color you wish to adjust. The APPLE COLOR WHEEL dialog box will be displayed, as shown in Figure 10-3.

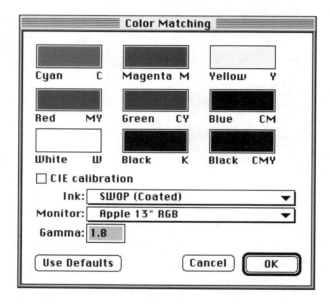

Figure 10-2: Click a color box in the Color Matching dialog box to adjust the color to better match a printed sample.

The APPLE COLOR WHEEL dialog box provides specific control over the display of the selected primary color. To alter a color, you can use one of two color models: *RGB* (red, green, blue) or *HSB* (hue, saturation, brightness). Each model is explained in the following sections.

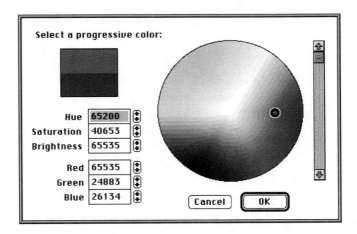

Figure 10-3: The Apple Color Wheel dialog box allows
you to edit colors according to two different models.

Coloring with light

The RGB color model defines colors by mixing two or more *primary
hues*. The amount of each hue mixed is called its *intensity*, as measured between 0 (no hue) and 65,535 (full intensity). The RGB model
is also called the *additive primary model*, because a resulting color becomes lighter as you add higher intensities of primary hues. All monitors and other devices that transmit or filter light—TVs, movie
projectors, even stained glass—rely on the additive model.

The additive primary model consists of three hues—red, green,
and blue—from which all colors in the visible spectrum are derived.
These primary hues can be mixed as follows:

- Full-intensity red and green mix to form yellow. Subtract some
red to make chartreuse; subtract some green to make orange.

- Full-intensity green and blue mix to form cyan. Subtract some
green or blue to produce more shades of turquoise, jade, sea
green, and sky blue than you could hope to use in a lifetime.

- Full-intensity blue and red mix to form magenta. Subtract some
blue to make rose; subtract some red to make purple.

- Full-intensity red, green, and blue mixed together make white,
the brightest color in the visible spectrum.

- Low intensities plunge the color into blackness.

The color wheel

The APPLE COLOR WHEEL dialog box also provides a second model for adjusting the amount of light in a color. The HSB color model, as it is called, makes use of the properties of hue, saturation, and brightness. The *hue* of a color is measured on a color wheel representing the entire visible spectrum. The wheel is divided into 65,535 sections. Some of the most popular hues are found at the following numeric locations:

- Red is 0
- Orange is 5,500
- Yellow is 11,000
- Chartreuse is 16,500
- Green is 22,000
- Cyan is 33,000
- Blue is 44,000
- Violet is 49,000
- Magenta is 54,500
- Rose is 60,000

Saturation represents the purity of a color. A saturation of 0 is always gray; a saturation of 65,535 is required to produce the most vivid versions of each of the colors listed above. You can think of the saturation value as the difference between a black-and-white television and color television. When the saturation value is low, all information about a color is expressed except the hue itself. Most natural colors require moderate saturation values. Highly saturated colors appear vivid.

Brightness is the lightness or darkness of a color. A brightness of 0 is always black; a brightness of 65,535 is used to achieve each of the colors listed above. For example, if the hue is red, a brightness value of 65,535 will produce bright red; 49,152 produces medium red; 32,768 produces dark red; and 16,384 makes a red so dark, it almost appears black.

Changing screen colors

To change a color using the RGB color model, enter values between 0 and 65,535 in the "Red," "Green," and "Blue" option boxes. Alternatively, you can click on the up or down arrow next to each option box to raise or lower the corresponding value. Press TAB to advance from one option box to the next.

To change a color using the HSB model, alter the values in the "Hue," "Saturation," and "Brightness" options. Or you can reposition the *color-adjustment dot* inside the *color wheel* on the right side of the dialog box. The color wheel works in association with the nearby scroll bar. The color wheel and scroll bar can be adjusted as follows:

- Move the color-adjustment dot around the perimeter of the wheel to change the hue.

- Move the color-adjustment dot between the perimeter and center of the wheel to alter the saturation. Colors along the perimeter equate to a saturation value of 65,535; the center color equates to a saturation value of 0.

- Move the scroll box within the scroll bar to change the brightness. The top of the scroll bar equates to a brightness value of 65,535; the bottom equates to 0.

After you press the TAB key or complete an adjustment to the color wheel or scroll bar, the new color displays in the *new color box* above the option boxes. Directly below the new color box is the *original color box*, which shows the color as it appeared prior to the new changes, for comparative purposes.

Click on the OK button or press RETURN when you are satisfied with your color adjustment, or click on the CANCEL button to close the dialog box and revert to the previous color settings. When you have satisfactorily adjusted all the colors presented in the COLOR MATCHING dialog have been satisfactorily adjusted, click on the OK button or press RETURN.

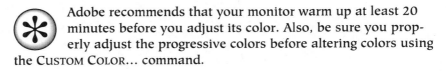 Adobe recommends that your monitor warm up at least 20 minutes before you adjust its color. Also, be sure you properly adjust the progressive colors before altering colors using the CUSTOM COLOR... command.

CIE Calibration

At the bottom of the COLOR MATCHING dialog box, Illustrator provides three calibration options. Traditionally, *calibrating* a system means synchronizing the machinery. However, in the context of Illustrator, it means adjusting or compensating for the color displays on the monitor to match the colors of the printing device so that what you see on screen is what you get in your finished product. In other words, from one device to the next, colors match. Empirically speaking, this is impossible—a yellow image on screen won't look exactly like the yellow printed from a set of color separations—but calibrating is designed to make the colors look as much alike as possible, taking into account the fundamental differences in hardware technology. Expensive hardware-calibration solutions seek to change the configuration of monitor and printer. Less expensive software solutions—including Illustrator—account for the differences between devices. When the "CIE Calibration" check box is selected, Illustrator allows you to select the printing system you use to print your illustration, the monitor you are working on, and the *gamma* value that best suits your needs.

- **Ink**. Select the specific variety of inks and paper stock that you will use to reproduce the current image. If you aren't sure, consult your commercial printer for this information.

- **Monitor**. Select your monitor from this pop-up menu. Illustrator will automatically change the value in the "Gamma" option box in accordance with the recommendations of the monitor's manufacturer. If you can't find your exact model, look for a model from the same manufacturer whose only difference is screen size.

    Do not assume all monitors from the same vendor are basically alike. Most vendors sell screens manufactured by different companies. For example, SuperMac sells 19-inch monitors manufactured by Sony and Ikegami. More important, the screens use different display technology (Trinitron versus shadow-masked tridot). Select a different monitor only if its name is identical except for screen size.

- **Gamma**. This value represents the brightness of medium colors on screen. Low values (down to 0.75) darken the image to compensate for an overly light screen; high values (up to 3.00) lighten the image to compensate for an overly dark screen.

Generally speaking, 1.8 is the ideal value for Macintosh RGB screens. When using an NTSC television monitor—as when editing video images using TrueVision's NuVista+ video board—set the gamma to 2.2.

Coloring illustrations

You can apply colors to the objects in an illustration using the "Fill" and "Stroke" options in the PAINT STYLE dialog box, as described in Chapters 8 and 9. You can use two types of colors to fill or stroke an object: *process colors* and *custom colors*.

Creating process colors

To apply process color to any Illustrator object, select the object with the selection tool and choose the PAINT STYLE... command from the OBJECT menu (⌘-I). Click on either the "Fill" or "Stroke" box inside the PAINT STYLE palette and then click on the "Process Color" box. If you select this option, the four process-color bars and corresponding option boxes—"Cyan," "Magenta," "Yellow," and "Black"—will display. These are the *primary hues,* which you can use to create any color on a printed page.

As when adjusting colors on your monitor, you define colors on the printed page by mixing two or more primary hues. However, colors on paper behave differently than colors on a computer screen. They use an entirely different color model, known as the *subtractive primary model*, in which a color becomes darker as you add higher concentrations of primary hues.

Coloring with pigments

Most naturally occurring colors are the results of the subtractive color model, which works like this: Sunlight contains every visible color found on earth. When sunlight is projected on an object, the object absorbs (subtracts) some of the light and reflects the rest. This reflected light is the color that you see. For example, a fire engine is red because it absorbs all other colors not meant specifically for fire engines—you know, in the grand scheme of things—from the white light spectrum.

Pigments on a sheet of paper work the same way. A purple crayon absorbs all non-purple colors; green ink absorbs all colors that aren't green. Every child learns that you can make any color using red, yellow, and blue. Red and yellow mix to create orange, yellow and blue make green, and so on. This is the subtractive primary model.

Unfortunately, what you learned in elementary school is a rude approximation of the truth. Did you ever try mixing a vivid red with a bright yellow, only to produce a disappointingly drab orange? And the very idea that deep blue and vivid red make purple is almost laughable. The true result is more a washed-out gray.

The true subtractive primary model used by commercial artists and printers consists of four hues: cyan (a very pale greenish blue), magenta (a bright purplish pink), yellow, and black, each of which is applied to white paper. These primary hues can be mixed as follows:

- Full concentrations of cyan and magenta mix to form a deep blue. Subtract some cyan to make purple; subtract some magenta to make a dull medium blue.

- Full concentrations of magenta and yellow mix to form a brilliant red. Subtract some magenta to make vivid orange; subtract some yellow to make rose.

- Full concentrations of yellow and cyan mix to form a medium green. Subtract some yellow to make a deep teal; subtract some cyan to make chartreuse.

- Full concentrations of cyan, magenta, and yellow make a muddy brown.

- Black pigmentation added to any other pigment darkens the color.

- No pigmentation results in white (assuming the paper is white).

To create a process color, enter percentage values between 0% (no concentration) and 100% (full concentration) in the "Cyan," "Magenta," "Yellow," and "Black" option boxes. The resulting color is displayed in the "Fill" or the "Stroke" box, whichever is selected.

The **Illustrator** 5 Book

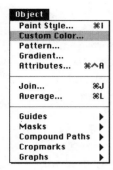

Creating custom colors

Process colors are defined "on-the-fly" for each instance in which they are used. However, Illustrator also allows you to create *custom colors*, which you define only once and then save with the current illustration, enabling you to access them again and again. You define custom colors in Illustrator by choosing CUSTOM COLOR... from the OBJECT menu, which displays the CUSTOM COLOR dialog box, shown in Figure 10-4.

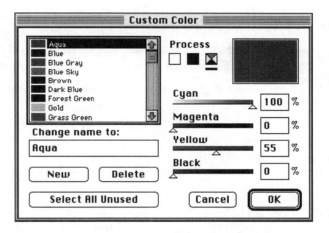

Figure 10-4: The Custom Color dialog box allows you to create colors that you intend to use several times throughout an illustration.

The scrolling color list in the CUSTOM COLOR dialog box lists all the custom colors included in the Adobe Illustrator Startup file as well as those that you have defined previously in the current document or in any other open document. Custom colors in Illustrator are always shared among all open documents. If you create a new color in one open document, it immediately becomes available to the others.

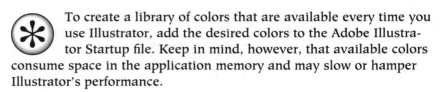

To create a library of colors that are available every time you use Illustrator, add the desired colors to the Adobe Illustrator Startup file. Keep in mind, however, that available colors consume space in the application memory and may slow or hamper Illustrator's performance.

You can manipulate colors in the scrolling list using the buttons in the CUSTOM COLOR dialog box. These buttons include the following:

- **New**. To create a new color, click on the NEW button, and the name "New Color 1" appears in the scrolling color list. This name is also selected in the "Change name to" option box, making it easy for you to rename your color as desired. Color names can be up to 31 characters long, including any alphanumeric characters and spaces. After naming your color, you can define it by sliding the triangular indicator along the "Cyan," "Magenta," "Yellow," and "Black" color bars or by entering percentage values into the corresponding option boxes. As you change these values, the resulting color will display in either the "Fill" or "Stroke" box, whichever is selected.

- **Delete**. Click on this button to delete a selected color name from the scrolling list. The selected color is removed from the current document *as well as from any other open document*. Any object that was filled or stroked with the deleted color will be painted with black. Exercise caution when deleting colors. Whenever possible, delete a color only when the current illustration is the only file open. Deleted colors can be returned by clicking on the CANCEL button.

- **Select All Unused**. This button selects all colors in the scrolling list that are not applied to objects in any open illustration. Since colors consume some space on disk and in your computer's RAM, it is often advisable to delete colors that you are not currently using, provided that they exist in some other illustration that is not currently open. To delete unused colors, click on the SELECT ALL UNUSED option, click on DELETE, and then click on OK or press RETURN. Deleted colors can be restored by clicking on the CANCEL button.

If you delete one or more custom color names and click on the OK button to confirm the deletion, you can regain the colors by immediately choosing the UNDO CUSTOM COLOR command from the EDIT menu (⌘-Z). All objects that previously contained the colors will regain them.

You can rename a color by selecting it from the scrolling list and entering a new name in the "Change name to" option box. This changes its name in all open illustrations. You can also edit the color by changing the positions of the triangular markers along the "Cyan," "Magenta," "Yellow," and "Black" color bars or by entering new values in the corresponding option boxes. Altering a custom color changes the color of all objects that use that color in any open illustration.

Brand-name colors

Illustrator provides access to literally thousands of other predefined custom colors that belong to four brands—Focoltone, Pantone, Toyo, and Trumatch, all of whom get a big kick out of capitalizing their names in dialog boxes. I honestly think one of these companies would stand out better if its name *wasn't* capitalized. Anyway, at the risk of offending a few of these companies, you're likely to find certain brands more useful than others.

The colors are grouped in families, and each family is contained in a separate file in the Color Systems folder in your Adobe Illustrator folder (assuming you installed the Color Systems folder). You can either open or import the file that contains the color family that you want to use. In either case, choose the appropriate command (OPEN... or IMPORT STYLES...) from the FILE menu. The colors in the file then appear in the scrolling lists in both the CUSTOM COLOR dialog box and PAINT STYLE palette. If you open the file, in addition to the colors contained in the file, a document displays, providing you with additional information about the color file. When you close the document, all the colors from the file that are not currently in use also close. This is comparable to clicking on the SELECT ALL UNUSED and DELETE buttons in the CUSTOM COLOR dialog box. Importing colors does not open a document.

The following sections briefly introduce the brands in order of their impact on the American market—forgive me for being ethnocentric in this regard—from smallest impact to greatest.

- **Focoltone and Toyo**. Both Focoltone and Toyo fall into the negligible-impact category. Both are foreign color standards with followings abroad. Focoltone is an English company that used to have a branch office in Kansas, but it recently up and left the United States, having made very little impression in this market. Toyo is very popular in the Japanese market but has next to no subscribers outside Japan.

- **Trumatch**. Designed entirely using a desktop system especially with desktop publishers in mind, the Trumatch file features over 2,000 process colors, organized according to hue, saturation, and brightness or by name. You can purchase a swatch book, the *Trumatch Colorfinder*, that shows you exactly which colors you can attain using a desktop system.

As if the Colorfinder weren't enough, Trumatch provides the ColorPrinter Software utility, which automatically prints the entire 2,000-color library to any PostScript-compatible output device. The utility integrates EfiColor and PostScript Level 2, thereby enabling design firms and commercial printers to test out the entire range of capabilities available to their hardware. Companies can provide select clients with swatches of colors created on their own printers, guaranteeing that what you see is darn well what you'll get.

The *Colorfinder* swatchbook retails for $85; the ColorPrinter Software costs $98. Together, swatchbook and utility sell for $133. Support for Trumatch is built into Illustrator and Photoshop, FreeHand, PageMaker, QuarkXPress, Cachet, as well as Corel Draw and Micrografx Designer in the Windows environment.

- **Pantone**. Prior to Trumatch, Pantone had a virtual monopoly on the desktop market, and the company acted like it. It was unresponsive to criticism, condescending to service bureaus and desktop designers alike, and slow to improve its product. Since Trumatch came along, Pantone has acted like a different company.

On the heels of Trumatch, Pantone released a 3,006-color *Process Color System Guide* priced at $75, $10 less than the Trumatch Colorfinder. Pantone also produces the foremost spot-color swatchbook, the *Color Formula Guide 1000*, and the *Process Color Imaging Guide* which enables you to quickly figure out whether you can closely match a Pantone spot color using a process-color blend, or whether you ought to just give it up and stick with the spot color (defined in Chapter 15). Furthermore, Pantone is supported by every computer application that aspires to the color prepress market. So long as it retains the old competitive spirit, you can most likely expect Pantone to remain the primary color-printing standard for years to come.

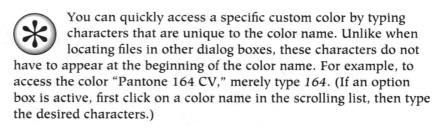 If you use one of the color files in the Color Systems folder on a consistent basis, you will probably want constant access to it. At the Finder level, rename the desired color file *Adobe Illustrator Startup*. If you have already created a special Adobe Illustrator Startup file or if you want the content of the original Startup file, copy the contents of that file, paste them into the desired color file, and rename the color file. As always, keep in mind that available colors consume space in the application memory, and additional colors can slow or hamper Illustrator's performance.

Using custom colors

To apply a custom color to any Illustrator object, select the object with the selection tool and choose the PAINT STYLE... command from the OBJECT menu (⌘-I). Select either the "Fill" or "Stroke" box inside the PAINT STYLE palette and click on the "Custom Color" box. If you select this option, a scrolling list appears, displaying all the custom colors currently available, in alphabetical order. The color is displayed to the left of each color's name. To select a custom color, click on its name. Use the scroll bar arrows to view custom colors that are not displayed. When selected, the color is displayed in the "Fill" or "Stroke" box.

You can quickly access a specific custom color by typing characters that are unique to the color name. Unlike when locating files in other dialog boxes, these characters do not have to appear at the beginning of the color name. For example, to access the color "Pantone 164 CV," merely type *164*. (If an option box is active, first click on a color name in the scrolling list, then type the desired characters.)

The "Tint" bar and percentage option box below the scrolling color list allows you to create a *tint* for any custom color. Tints are lightened variations of custom colors, specified as percentage values between 0% (white) and 100% (the solid color). When used in *spot-color printing* (as defined in Chapter 15, *Printing Your Illustrations*), tints are an inexpensive way to create shades of a single ink to achieve the effect of using multiple colors.

Overprinting colors

The "Overprint" option check box—available in the PAINT STYLE dialog box when the "White," "Black," "Process Color," "Custom Color," "Gradient" radio button is selected—controls whether a specific color prints on top of another color that is directly behind it in an illustration. When this option is selected, an object is allowed to *overprint* the object behind it, provided the other color is printed to a different *separation* (as defined in Chapter 15, *Printing Your Illustrations*). For example, if your drawing consists of two custom colors—orange and blue—then orange can overprint blue, blue can overprint orange, and either may overprint or be overprinted by black, because orange, blue, and black are printed to their own separations during the printing process. However, a 30% tint of blue cannot overprint a 70% tint of blue, because all blue objects are printed to the same separation.

If the "Overprint" option is deselected, as by default, portions of an object covered by another object will be *knocked out* when they appear on different separations. Knocked out portions do not print on a separation.

For example, imagine that the faces in Figure 10-5 are filled and stroked in tints of orange, and that the hats are painted in tints of blue. In the first example, the portion of the orange object under the hat has been knocked out. In the second example, the objects overprint, allowing the colors to blend, giving the hat a transparent appearance.

Figure 10-5: An orange face with a blue hat as it appears when the "Overprint" option is deselected (left) and selected (right). I'm afraid you have to use a little imagination on this one.

Process color versus custom color

Although it is not difficult to define a fill or stroke as either a process color or a custom color, it can be difficult to determine which technique is more appropriate for the current object. With most software, the printing method used to reproduce an illustration determines which type of color should be used. Process colors should be applied in an illustration that contains many colors and will therefore be separated as a four-color process image. Custom colors are better suited to spot-color printing situations, in which only two or three specific inks are required.

These generalizations are untrue when working with Adobe Illustrator. As explained in Chapter 15, the Adobe Separator utility is capable of separating custom colors into their process-color components, rendering custom colors as appropriate to process-color printing as they are to spot-color printing.

As it turns out, custom colors are preferable in almost all situations. They provide accessibility, ready exchange among documents, and the benefits of global editing, and they can be output as either spot colors or four-color process separations. Process colors are best used in situations where a color is used only once and will be output on a color printer or separated for four-color process printing.

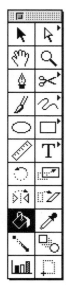

Applying colors with tools

Illustrator 5.0 introduces two new tools for applying colors: the *paint bucket tool* and the *eyedropper tool*. The paint bucket tool applies the fill and stroke attributes displayed in the PAINT STYLE palette to graphic objects and text blocks. The eyedropper tool is the paint bucket's opposite, lifting fill and stroke attributes from objects and displaying them in the PAINT STYLE palette.

To use the paint bucket tool, specify the fill and stroke attributes that you want to apply in the PAINT STYLE dialog box and then click on the target object that you want to fill and stroke. Not only does Illustrator fill and stroke the object, it also selects it. You can even SHIFT-click with the paint bucket tool to fill, stroke, and select multiple objects (though you can't marquee with the tool). When using the paint bucket tool on text blocks, you must click on the alignment point, baseline, or text path to apply the paint attributes. Clicking on the letters themselves will not work.

Press the OPTION key to temporarily access the paint bucket tool when the eyedropper tool is selected. Likewise, you can press OPTION to access the eyedropper tool when the paint bucket tool is selected.

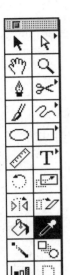

To use the eyedropper tool, simply click on a graphic object or on the alignment point or baseline of a text block. The eyedropper cursor will become partially black to show that you are lifting colors. Illustrator then displays the fill and stroke attributes of the object on which you clicked in the PAINT STYLE palette.

Double-click on an object with the eyedropper tool to both lift the paint attributes assigned to the object *and* apply the attributes to all selected objects and text blocks. This enables you to quickly apply a fill and stroke to multiple objects at one time.

Double-click on either the paint bucket or eyedropper tool icon in the toolbox to display the PAINTBUCKET/EYEDROPPER dialog box, which allows you to adjust the specific attributes that are applied and lifted with the paint bucket and eyedropper tools. The options are grouped according to fill and stroke attributes. A selected checkbox indicates that the corresponding tool will either apply or lift the attribute in question. For example, if you want the eyedropper tool to lift only the line weight and dash pattern attributes from an object, select the "Stroke," "Weight," and "Dash Pattern" check boxes and deselect all others on the "Eyedropper picks up" side of the dialog box.

The "Fill" and "Stroke" check boxes in the PAINTBUCKET/EYEDROPPER dialog box may prove confusing to some folks, thanks to the fact that they serve no real function. For example, if you deselect both the "Color" and "Overprint" options below the "Fill" check box, then it doesn't matter whether you select or deselect the "Fill" check box; either way, no fill will be applied or lifted. As a result, if you want the paint bucket tool to apply the fill in the PAINT STYLE palette, it is not sufficient to select the "Fill" checkbox alone. You must select it as well as the specific fill attributes that you want the tool to apply.

The **Illustrator** 5 Book

PART 4
SPECIAL EFFECTS

CHAPTER

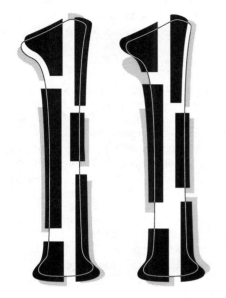

TRANS-
FORMING
AND
DUPLICATING
OBJECTS

In Chapter 6, I discussed manipulation techniques that change the form of paths. These techniques apply to points, segments, and entire paths, but their scope is limited to graphic objects; you can't reshape type.

In this chapter, I discuss two categories of manipulation techniques—*transforming* and *duplicating*—that do not necessarily alter the form of a path and apply to both graphic

421

objects and type. I also examine Illustrator's limited collection of precision drawing features, and how you can use these features to control the transformation and duplication of objects.

We end the chapter with a detailed discussion of *blending*, a special feature that both transforms and duplicates objects at the same time. This is the only feature covered in this chapter that cannot be applied to type, unless the type is converted to paths using the CREATE OUTLINES command.

Grouping

Most of the time, you'll apply transformations to whole paths rather than to individual points or segments. You may even want to transform multiple objects at a time. So imagine that, instead of thinking in terms of paths and objects, you could manipulate whole images. This is the beauty of *grouping*, which allows you to assemble throngs of elements into a single object.

Suppose, for example, that you have created an image made up of several paths. You want to rotate the image, but you're afraid of upsetting the fragile relationship between the paths during the transformation. To safeguard the basic appearance of the image, select the objects in the image and choose GROUP from the ARRANGE menu (⌘-G). The rotation affects the whole image, as shown in Figure 11-1.

Arrange	
Repeat Transform	⌘D
Move...	⌘⇧M
Bring To Front	⌘=
Send To Back	⌘-
Group	⌘G
Ungroup	⌘U
Lock	⌘1
Unlock All	⌘2
Hide	⌘3
Show All	⌘4

Figure 11-1: Before transforming a collection of complex paths, group the paths into a single object.

🔬 The **Illustrator 5** Book

When you choose the GROUP command, you accomplish the same goal, whether you select only a single point or segment or a whole path. All objects that are even partially selected become grouped in their entirety.

You apply the GROUP command to a single path to retain the relationship between points and segments. You can even group multiple groups. In fact, the GROUP command can be applied to any graphic object or text block that you create inside of or import into Illustrator.

You select a whole group by clicking on it with the selection tool or by clicking multiple times with the group-selection tool. To reshape a path in a group, you can use the direct-selection tool to select and manipulate individual elements. You can also select individual objects in a group to fill or stroke them without affecting other grouped objects. Or you can transform an object independently without affecting other objects in a group.

 If you duplicate an object within a group using the direct-selection tool, the duplicate will become part of the group as well. To duplicate an object separately of its group, select the object with the direct-selection tool, choose COPY (⌘-C), click on an empty portion of the drawing area to deselect the group, and choose any one of the PASTE commands (⌘-V).

Selecting paths within groups

Click with the group-selection tool or OPTION-click with the direct-selection tool to select whole paths in a group. Click two or more times to select groups within groups. Each successive click selects the group that includes the current group. The following exercise demonstrates how this works:

1. Draw four rectangles with the rectangle tool. Draw a fifth rectangle that surrounds the others.

2. Select two of the inner rectangles and choose GROUP (⌘-G). Select the other pair of inner rectangles and group them as well.

3. Select both grouped pairs and choose GROUP. Finally, select all five rectangles and group them. The result is two groups combined into a group that is itself a member of another group.

4. Using the group-selection tool, click on one of the inner rectangles. This selects that rectangle alone.

5. Click on the selected rectangle a second time. This selects both of the rectangles in the grouped pair.

6. Click on the selected rectangle a third time. This selects both grouped pairs. All inner rectangles are now selected.

7. Click on the selected rectangle a fourth time. The most senior of the groups—the one that includes all five rectangles—is now selected.

Ungrouping

Arrange	
Repeat Transform	⌘D
Move...	⌘⇧M
Bring To Front	⌘=
Send To Back	⌘-
Group	⌘G
Ungroup	⌘U
Lock	⌘1
Unlock All	⌘2
Hide	⌘3
Show All	⌘4

You can ungroup any group by choosing the UNGROUP command from the ARRANGE menu (⌘-U). Multiple groups can be ungrouped simultaneously, but only one level at a time. In other words, if a group contains groups, then the most recently created group must be ungrouped first. The member groups can then be ungrouped by again choosing UNGROUP.

Ungrouping is sometimes an essential part of the reshaping process. Most notably, you can not join two endpoints if the endpoints are in paths that are not in the same group. For example, one endpoint may be in a grouped path, and the other endpoint may be in an ungrouped path. The only solution in this case is to ungroup the path, choose the JOIN... command, and the regroup the path.

Distinguishing groups from non-groups

What if ungrouping a path doesn't produce the desired effect? Perhaps the object wasn't grouped in the first place. Illustrator 5.0 allows you to create various kinds of collective objects, including compound paths, linked objects, and wrapped objects. Groups are generally easily distinguished from links and wrapped objects because the latter two contain type. (See the *Flowing area text* and *Wrapping type around graphics* sections of Chapter 7 for complete descriptions of both objects.) Compound paths, however, may be difficult to distinguish from groups. Letters that have been converted to paths are always expressed as compound paths. However, if you want to find out for sure, display the COMPOUND PATHS submenu under the OBJECT menu. If the RELEASE command is dimmed, the selected object is not a compound path. If the command is available, then the object is a compound path.

Controlling movements

Illustrator allows you to move objects in the same way you move elements, as described in the *Moving elements* section of Chapter 6. In fact, moving is the primary and most common means for transforming objects in Illustrator. Give one of the following techniques a try:

- Using any of the selection tools, drag the object by any of its points, segments, or—in the case of a text object—baselines.

- Press the SHIFT key and drag the object to move it along the constraint axis.

- Drag the object over the point of a stationary object to snap the object into place (provided the "Snap to point" check box is checked in the GENERAL PREFERENCE dialog box).

- Press an arrow key (↑, →, ↓, or ←) to move a selected object by the amount specified in the "Cursor key distance" option in the GENERAL PREFERENCES dialog box.

- Press OPTION and click on the selection tool icon in the toolbox to display the MOVE dialog box. Enter the desired movement values and press RETURN.

- Use the measure tool to measure the distance between the current location of an object and its prospective location. Then OPTION-click on the selection tool icon to display the MOVE dialog box, which will contain the measured values.

Pressing the SHIFT key, snapping, using arrow keys, and the MOVE and MEASURE dialog boxes all represent means for making precise, controlled movements in an illustration. Illustrator 5.0 provides two additional control features that we have not discussed previously. These are *rulers* and *guides*, both of which are discussed in the following sections.

Using the rulers

Illustrator provides access to one vertical and one horizontal ruler that you can use to track the movement of your cursor. By choosing the SHOW RULERS command from the VIEW menu (⌘-R), you display these rulers, which appear at the bottom and right-hand edges of the current illustration window. Once the rulers are visible, the SHOW RULERS command changes to a HIDE RULERS command (⌘-R), thus allowing you to put the rulers away at any time.

View	
✓Preview	⌘Y
Artwork	⌘E
Preview Selection	⌘⌥Y
Hide Template	
Show Rulers	⌘R
Hide Page Tiling	
Hide Edges	⌘⇧H
Hide Guides	
Zoom In	⌘]
Zoom Out	⌘[
Actual Size	⌘H
Fit In Window	⌘M
New View...	⌘⌃V
Edit Views...	

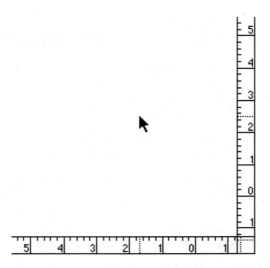

Figure 11-2: The horizontal and vertical rulers as they appear when the current unit of measure is centimeters.

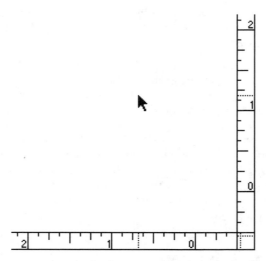

Figure 11-3: The horizontal and vertical rulers as they appear when the current unit of measure is inches.

The unit of measure used by both rulers can be centimeters, inches, or picas—each of which is displayed in Figures 11-2, 11-3, and 11-4—as determined by the selected "Ruler units" pop-up menu in the GENERAL PREFERENCES dialog box. To change the current unit

The **Illustrator** 5 Book

of measure, choose the GENERAL... command in the PREFERENCES sub-menu from the EDIT menu (⌘-K). The GENERAL PREFERENCES dialog box displays, containing three entries in the "Ruler units" pop-up menu: "Centimeters," "Inches," and "Picas/Points." The last option is selected by default. Select the desired option and press RETURN.

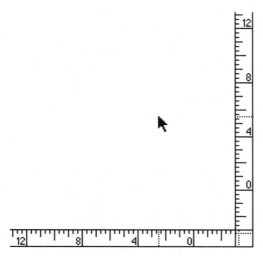

Figure 11-4: The horizontal and vertical rulers as they appear when the current unit of measure is picas.

As on traditional rulers, whole centimeters, inches, or picas are indicated by long tick marks; fractions are indicated by short tick marks. As you magnify the view size, the units on the rulers become larger and more detailed. As you zoom out, units become smaller and less detailed. Numbers on each ruler indicate the distance from the *ruler origin*, the location on your drawing area at which the horizontal and vertical coordinates are both zero. All ruler measurements are made relative to this origin.

At all times, you can track the movement of your cursor on the horizontal and vertical rulers. Figures 11-2 through 11-4 each show a small dotted *tracking line* that moves along the horizontal ruler and another that moves along the vertical ruler, indicating the present location of your cursor in the drawing area. For example, the cursor in Figure 11-4 is 5 picas and 6 points (5½ picas) above and 2 picas and 6 points to the left of the ruler origin.

Unlike rulers in some other programs, which track the movement of an object, Illustrator's rulers always track the location of the cursor. This is even true, for example, when you are moving a text block or graphic object.

Changing the ruler origin

By default, the ruler origin for an illustration is located at the bottom right corner of the primary page. The number of this page depends on the selected "Artwork board" option in the PREFERENCES dialog box. If the "Single full page" or the "Tile full pages" radio button is selected, the primary page is page 1. If "Tile imageable areas" is selected, it is page 5.

You can relocate the ruler origin by dragging from the *ruler origin box*, the square created by the intersection of the horizontal and vertical rulers. Figure 11-5 demonstrates this process. The dotted lines that extend from the + cursor indicate the prospective position of the new origin. Notice that even the movement of the ruler origin is tracked by the rulers. At the end of the drag, the ruler origin moves to the location occupied by the cursor. All ruler measurements are now made from this new ruler origin.

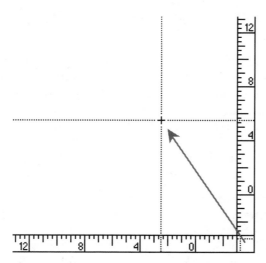

Figure 11-5: Drag from the ruler origin box to relocate the ruler origin.

The **Illustrator 5** Book

Creating guides

Illustrator 5.0 allows you to create *guides* to assist in positioning and aligning objects in the drawing area. Guides appear dotted in the artwork mode and the preview mode, but they don't print. If the "Snap to point" check box in the GENERAL PREFERENCES dialog box is selected, your cursor snaps to an existing guide if you drag within two pixels of the guide while moving or otherwise transforming an object. Also, your cursor snaps to any portion of the outline of a guide, not just to the points as it does when snapping to stationary objects.

You can create a guide in one of the following ways:

- Drag upward from the horizontal ruler to create a horizontal *ruler guide* the width of the entire drawing area.

- Drag to the left from the vertical ruler to create a vertical ruler guide the height of the entire drawing area.

- Select an existing object in the drawing area and choose MAKE from the GUIDE submenu under the OBJECT menu (⌘-5).

You create ruler guides by dragging from either the horizontal or vertical ruler, as demonstrated in the first example of Figure 11-6. The second example in the figure shows that the guide appears as a dotted line after it is created, allowing you to easily distinguish it from objects that make up your illustration. Ruler guides are used to mark a specific horizontal or vertical location inside the drawing area. You can then align the sides or center points of objects to the ruler guide to create perfect rows or columns of objects.

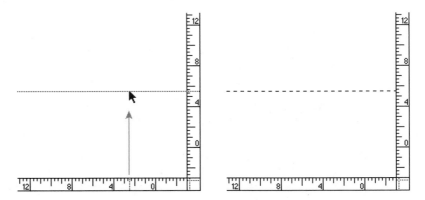

Figure 11-6: Dragging from one of the rulers (left) creates a ruler guide (right).

In the course of dragging a guide from the horizontal ruler, press the OPTION key to rotate it 90°, toggling a vertical guide. Likewise, OPTION-dragging from the vertical ruler toggles a horizontal guide.

Object

Paint Style...	⌘I
Custom Color...	
Pattern...	
Gradient...	
Attributes...	⌘⌃A
Join...	⌘J
Average...	⌘L
Guides	▶
Masks	▶
Compound Paths	▶
Cropmarks	▶
Graphs	▶

Choose the MAKE command from the GUIDE submenu under the OBJECT menu (⌘-5) to turn one or more selected objects into *guide objects*. Only graphic objects can be subjected to the MAKE (GUIDE) command. If you select a text block and choose MAKE (GUIDE), an error message appears, alerting you that the selected objects could not be converted to guides. After pressing RETURN to exit the alert box, you can deselect all text objects and choose the MAKE command in the GUIDE submenu again. Figure 11-7 shows how different objects convert into guides; the text object remains unchanged.

To create a guide object without sacrificing the selected graphic object, copy the object (⌘-C), paste it in front (⌘-F), and then choose the MAKE (GUIDE) command (⌘-5) to convert the duplicate object only.

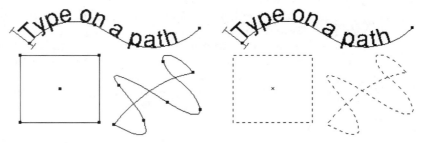

Figure 11-7: Only selected graphic objects (left) can be converted into guide objects (right). Selected text objects remain unaffected.

Manipulating guides

By default, all guides are *locked*. You cannot select a locked guide by clicking on it, thus preventing you from moving, transforming, or manipulating it. To unlock all guide in an illustration, choose the LOCK command in the GUIDE submenu from the OBJECT menu (⌘-7). The check mark in front of the LOCK command will disappear. Choose LOCK again to lock all guides.

Once a guide is unlocked, you can select and manipulate it as you can any other graphic object. Use the direct-selection tool to reshape a guide. Press SHIFT and click or marquee with a selection tool to select and manipulate multiple guides at a time. You can press an arrow key or use the MOVE dialog box to move a selected guide. Press DELETE or BACKSPACE to delete a selected guide. Use the scale, reflect, rotate, or shear tool as described later in this chapter to transform a selected guide.

 It is not absolutely necessary to unlock a guide to select it. To select a locked guide, press SHIFT and CONTROL while clicking on it with one of the selection tools. As usual, any previously selected objects become deselected.

The following items describe ways to manipulate a locked guide:

- With one of the selection tools in use, press SHIFT and CONTROL and drag a locked guide to move it to a new location. After beginning the drag, release the SHIFT key to move the guide without constraint.

- With any other tool selected, press SHIFT, CONTROL, and COMMAND and drag a locked guide to move it to a new location. Again, release the SHIFT key after beginning the drag to move the guide without constraint.

- Press OPTION along with the other keys described above to clone a locked guide. Release SHIFT during the drag to move the guide without constraint, but do not release OPTION until after you complete the drag.

You cannot reshape a locked guide, since no element can be selected independently of another within a locked guide. Also, you cannot select or manipulate multiple locked guides at a time unless they are members of the same group.

Incidentally, you can convert a single object within a group to a guide without converting other objects in the group. The guide remains a member of the group. Any manipulations performed on the group also affect the guide.

Converting guides to objects

To convert a selected guide in the current illustration to an object, choose the RELEASE command in the GUIDE submenu from the OBJECT menu (⌘-6). The guide will be converted into a selected object provided that the guide is not locked. If the guide is locked, first unlock the guide by choosing the LOCK command in the GUIDE submenu from the OBJECT menu (⌘-7). Ruler guides convert into lines that extend the entire width or length of the pasteboard.

To convert any single guide back into a graphic object (locked or otherwise), press SHIFT and CONTROL and double-click on the guide with any selection tool. Press COMMAND as well if you are using a tool other than a selection tool.

Protecting objects

There are times in the course of working on an illustration when you will have positioned an object, call it object A, exactly where you want it. Your illustration may be very complicated, containing several objects that overlap and are overlapped by object A but are not yet properly formed or located. In the process of reshaping and transforming these objects, you may find yourself accidentally selecting and altering object A. This can be exceedingly frustrating, requiring you to fix an object that was previously correct. The more complicated your drawing becomes, the greater the likelihood of disarranging one or more perfectly positioned objects.

To protect text blocks and graphic objects from being upset or altered, Illustrator provides *locking* and *hiding* features, which are the subjects of the following sections.

Locking objects

Locking an object prevents it or any of its points or segments from being selected. This means you can neither delete the object nor transform it in any manner. In addition, you cannot change its fill or stroke. Once an object is locked, it immediately becomes deselected. If you attempt to click on a locked object with a selection tool, you will instead select some nearby unlocked object or select no object at all. Likewise, neither marqueeing nor choosing the SELECT ALL command (⌘-A) will select a locked object.

Arrange

Repeat Transform	⌘D
Move...	⌘⇧M
Bring To Front	⌘=
Send To Back	⌘-
Group	⌘G
Ungroup	⌘U
Lock	**⌘1**
Unlock All	⌘2
Hide	⌘3
Show All	⌘4

You lock objects by selecting them and choosing the LOCK command from the ARRANGE menu (⌘-1). You cannot lock a single point or segment independently of other points and segments in a path. If you specifically select one point in a path and choose the LOCK command, the entire path will become locked.

When you are working on a very specific detail in an illustration, you may find it helpful to lock every object not included in the detail. This may be hundreds of objects, possibly making it difficult and time consuming to select each object by marqueeing, SHIFT-clicking, SHIFT-marqueeing, and so on. Instead, simply select the objects that you *don't* want to lock and press the OPTION key while choosing the LOCK command. All objects that are *not* selected will become locked.

Press ⌘-⌥-1 to lock all objects that are not selected. This is the same as pressing the OPTION key while choosing the LOCK command from the ARRANGE menu.

Unlike the LOCK command in the GUIDES submenu, the LOCK command in the ARRANGE menu allows you to lock individual text blocks and graphic objects, including guides. However, know that if you lock a guide with the LOCK (ARRANGE) command, you can't unlock it with the LOCK (GUIDES) command.

Unlocking objects

Arrange

Repeat Transform	⌘D
Move...	⌘⇧M
Bring To Front	⌘=
Send To Back	⌘-
Group	⌘G
Ungroup	⌘U
Lock	⌘1
Unlock All	**⌘2**
Hide	⌘3
Show All	⌘4

Because a locked object cannot be selected, there is no way to indicate that you wish to unlock only one or more specific objects. Therefore, you must unlock *all* locked objects at the same time. Upon choosing the UNLOCK ALL command from the ARRANGE menu (⌘-2), all previously locked objects become unlocked and selected. In this way, previously locked objects are called to your attention, allowing you to easily relock them if you so desire.

Locking is saved with the illustration. Therefore, when you open an existing file, all objects that were locked during the previous session are still locked.

Hiding objects

If an object is really in your way, you can do more than just lock it: you can totally *hide* it from view. A hidden object cannot be viewed in any display mode nor does it appear when an illustration is printed. Since a hidden object is always invisible, it cannot be selected or manipulated.

Arrange

Repeat Transform	⌘D
Move...	⌘⇧M
Bring To Front	⌘=
Send To Back	⌘-
Group	⌘G
Ungroup	⌘U
Lock	⌘1
Unlock All	⌘2
Hide	**⌘3**
Show All	⌘4

You hide objects by selecting them and choosing the HIDE command from the ARRANGE menu (⌘-3). You cannot hide a single point or segment independently of other points and segments in a path. If you specifically select one point in a path and choose the HIDE command, the entire path will be made invisible.

When you are working on a very specific detail in an illustration, you may find it helpful to hide every object not included in the detail. This may be hundreds of objects, possibly making it difficult and time-consuming to select each object by marqueeing, SHIFT-clicking, SHIFT-marqueeing, and so on. Instead, simply select the objects that you *don't* want to hide and press the OPTION key while choosing the HIDE command. All objects that are *not* selected will become hidden.

 Press ⌘-⌥-3 to hide all objects that are not selected. This is the same as pressing the OPTION key while choosing the HIDE command from the ARRANGE menu.

Showing objects

Arrange

Repeat Transform	⌘D
Move...	⌘⇧M
Bring To Front	⌘=
Send To Back	⌘-
Group	⌘G
Ungroup	⌘U
Lock	⌘1
Unlock All	⌘2
Hide	⌘3
Show All	**⌘4**

Because a hidden object cannot be selected, there is no way to indicate that you wish to make only one or more specific objects visible. Therefore, you must display *all* hidden objects at the same time. Upon choosing the SHOW ALL command from the ARRANGE menu (⌘-4), all previously hidden objects reappear in the drawing area and become selected. In this way, previously hidden objects are called to your attention, allowing you to easily rehide them if you so desire.

Unlike locking, hiding is *not* saved with the illustration. Therefore, when you open an existing file, all objects that were hidden during the previous session reappear.

Hiding unpainted objects

Illustrator 3.0 provided a command that hid only those objects that were neither filled nor stroked. Illustrator 5.0 has dropped this command since you can now work in the preview mode, where such objects are invisible. If you prefer to work in the artwork mode, you can still hide just the unpainted objects by clicking on one such object, choosing the SAME PAINT STYLE command from the SELECT submenu under the FILTER menu, and then choosing the HIDE command. For complete information on filters, read the following chapter.

Scaling objects

A *transformation* is any manipulation that permanently alters the appearance of an object without affecting its basic form. In Illustrator, transformations include moving an object—as discussed in the *Controlling movements* section of this chapter—as well as scaling, flipping, rotating, and slanting an object. These latter transformations are accomplished in Illustrator using special tools, each of which is discussed in this chapter. The first tool I discuss is the *scale tool*.

Using the scale tool

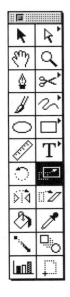

The scale tool, seventh tool on the right side of the toolbox, is used to reduce and enlarge text blocks and graphic objects. The scale tool, like all transformation tools, is operated by *both* clicking *and* dragging, each done at a separate location. The following steps explain how to use this tool:

1. Select the object or objects that you wish to scale. Then select the scale tool. Your cursor will appear as a small cross.

2. Click with the scale tool at some location in your drawing area relative to the selected object. This location will act as the *scale origin*, the core of a reduction or enlargement.

3. After establishing a scale origin, your cursor will change to an arrowhead. Drag toward the origin to reduce the selected object; drag away from the origin to enlarge it.

   To better understand the concept of the scale origin, consider the example shown in Figure 11-8 on the next page. Here are a series of circles enlarged one about the other. All circles have been enlarged about a single scale origin, shown in the figure as a small cross from which the four directional lines emanate. These lines follow the progression of the points in the enlarged paths. The fact that the points progress outward in straight lines demonstrates that the scale origin marks the center of any reduction or enlargement.

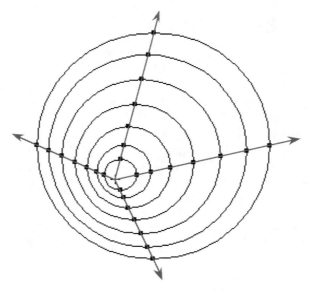

Figure 11-8: Enlarging a circle several times about a single scale origin.

Figure 11-9 displays two paths representing a telephone. The path of the receiver is entirely selected. Suppose that you want to scale the receiver without affecting the telephone carriage. The following exercise demonstrates how:

1. Select the scale tool and click at the location displayed as a small cross in Figure 11-9. This establishes the scale origin.

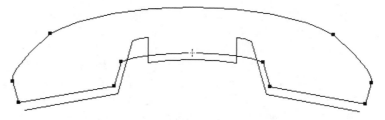

Figure 11-9: Click with the scale tool near the middle of the selected shape to establish a scale origin.

The **Illustrator 5** Book

2. By creating a scale origin, you establish imaginary horizontal and vertical axes, which divide the drawing area into four *quadrants*. In Figure 11-10, these axes are displayed as two dotted lines. For best results, you should always begin dragging with the scale tool well within one of these quadrants. In this case, begin your drag at a point on the right side of the top segment in the selected path.

3. Drag up and to the right, as demonstrated by the arrow in Figure 11-10. As you drag away from the scale origin, the path of the receiver grows larger and larger. Both the previous and current size of the selected path are displayed throughout your drag, allowing you to gauge the full effect of the enlargement.

4. Release the mouse button to complete the enlargement. Choose UNDO SCALE (⌘-Z) to return the path to its original size.

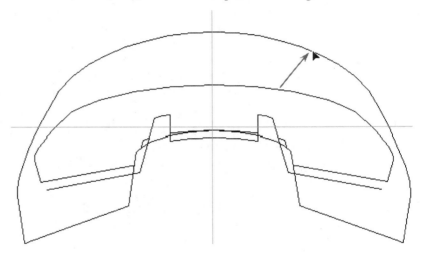

Figure 11-10: Drag away from the scale origin to enlarge the selected object. Begin your drag well within one of the quadrants defined by the origin.

5. Click again at the location of the small cross in Figure 11-9 to establish the scale origin. Begin dragging at the point on the right side of the top segment in the selected path, just as before.

6. Drag down and to the left, as demonstrated by the arrow in Figure 11-11 on the next page. As you drag toward the scale origin, the selected path grows smaller and smaller.

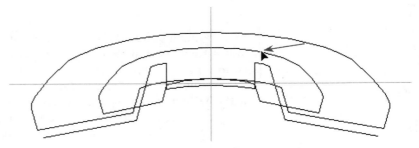

Figure 11-11: Drag toward the scale origin to reduce the selected object.

7. Release your mouse button to complete the reduction. Choose UNDO SCALE (⌘-Z) to return the path to its original size.

8. In the previous steps, the horizontal and vertical proportions of your drags have been almost identical. Thus, the height and width of the selected object were affected very similarly, resulting in one proportional enlargement and one proportional reduction. This time, however, you will stretch the height of the path but barely change its width. To begin, click on the lower left-hand corner of the object with the scale tool to establish the origin.

9. Figure 11-12 shows how the new origin has redefined the imaginary axes and quadrants. Begin dragging with the scale tool somewhere inside the left side of the selected object.

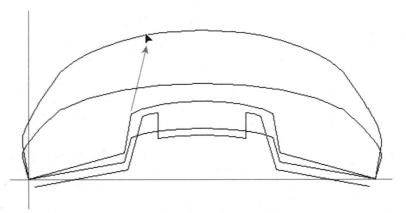

Figure 11-12: Drag directly upward to stretch the object vertically while barely affecting its width.

The **Illustrator 5** Book

10. Drag directly upward from the scale origin to increase the height of the shape while only slightly altering its width, as shown in Figure 11-12.

Drag vertically to affect the height of a selected object; drag horizontally to affect its width. Drag away from the scale origin to enlarge an object; drag toward the origin to reduce the object. In part, this explains why it is so important to begin your drags well within one of the quadrants defined by the origin. If you drag from a location that is either on or very close to the origin, you will have very little chance of reducing the size of the selected object, since there is so little room to maneuver. Also, a slight movement away from the origin will dramatically enlarge the object.

There is no maximum size beyond which you can no longer enlarge a selected object. The object may even exceed the confines of the drawing area, although you will no longer be able to view the entirety of such an image. You can also drag so close to the scale origin that you reduce an object to virtual invisibility. If you drag *past* the scale origin, you will flip the selected object, as shown in Figure 11-13. This little-known feature of the scale tool allows you to flip and scale objects at the same time.

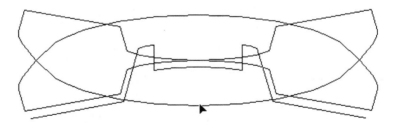

Figure 11-13: Drag past the origin with the scale tool to flip the selected object.

You can flip objects only vertically and/or horizontally with the scale tool. To flip an object across an angled axis, use the reflect tool as described in the next section *Flipping objects*.

Constrained scaling

To constrain an enlargement or reduction so that the height and width of the selected object are affected equally, press the SHIFT key while dragging diagonally with the scale tool. If you SHIFT-drag vertically or horizontally, you scale the object's height or width exclusively.

The effects of SHIFT-dragging with the scale tool can be altered by rotating the constraint axes using the "Constrain angle" option in the PREFERENCES dialog box. For more information, see *Transforming rotated objects,* later in this chapter.

Scaling partial paths

Illustrator allows you to scale whole selected objects. But you may also scale specific elements within objects independently of their deselected neighbors. Simply select the desired points and segments that you wish to scale, and use the scale tool as directed in the previous sections.

For example, only six points are selected in the skyline path shown in Figure 11-14. The segments that border each of these points are the only segments that will be affected by the scale tool.

1. Click with the scale tool at the location indicated by the small cross cursor in Figure 11-14.

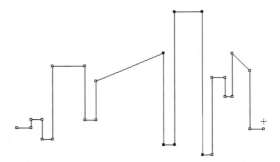

Figure 11-14: Position the scale origin to the right of the partially selected object.

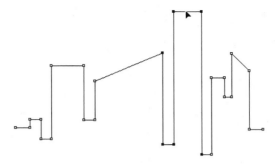

Figure 11-15: Begin your drag at the top of the tallest building.

2. Begin dragging at the selected segment along the top of the tallest building, as demonstrated by the arrowhead cursor in Figure 11-15.

3. Drag downward, toward the origin, as shown in Figure 11-16. Only the selected points and segments are affected. Release when you are satisfied with the scaling.

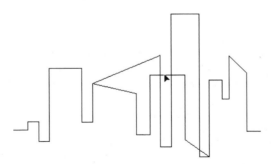

Figure 11-16: Drag downward to reduce the size of the selected elements while leaving deselected elements unchanged.

Dragging points with the scale tool can be remarkably like dragging them with a selection tool. The only difference is that each selected point is moved slightly differently, depending on its proximity to the scale origin. If you look closely at Figure 11-16, you'll notice that points close to the scale origin move much less than those farther away. This results in various reductions in the length of the each selected segment, depending on the orientation of each segment relative to the drag.

The scale tool can prove very useful for moving specific points in ways that the selection tool does not allow. For example, to move two selected segments equal distances in opposite directions about a central point, click at this point and drag the segments as shown in Figure 11-17.

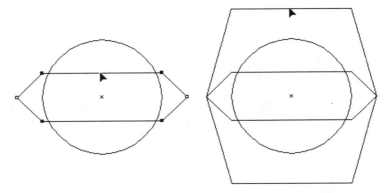

Figure 11-17: After clicking at the center point of the circle with the scale tool, we drag up from the top selected segment (left) to move both selected segments an equal distance in opposite directions (right).

Scaling a clone

You may see both the previous and current size of any selected object while dragging with the scale tool. A reason for this that we have not yet mentioned is that both versions of the object can be retained by OPTION-dragging; that is, press the OPTION key after beginning a drag and holding the key down until after the drag is completed. This creates a *clone* of the selected object that can be manipulated independently of the original. (A more complete discussion of cloning is included in the section *Cloning objects*, later in this chapter.) After OPTION-dragging with the scale tool, the cloned object remains selected, but its original is deselected.

The **Illustrator** 5 Book

Using the Scale dialog box

If you press the OPTION key before clicking with the scale tool, the cross-shaped cursor gains an ellipsis in the lower right corner and the information bar changes to read "Scale: click to choose origin." This shows that once you click, the SCALE dialog box will display.

Press OPTION and click with the scale tool to simultaneously determine the location of the scale origin and display the SCALE dialog box, shown in Figure 11-18. This dialog box allows you to scale one or more selected objects numerically.

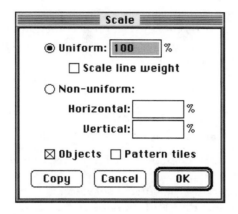

Figure 11-18: The Scale dialog box allows you to specify the percentage by which a selected object is enlarged or reduced.

To scale the width and height of an object proportionally, select the "Uniform" value and enter a value in the option box. Values less than 100% will reduce the size of selected objects; values greater than 100% will enlarge selected objects; a 100% value will leave the size of selected objects unaltered.

When "Uniform" is selected, you can opt to have the line weights scale proportionally with the object or to remain unaffected by the scaling. If the "Scale line weight" check box is not selected, the proposed scaling has no effect on the line weights associated with the selected object. This means that if you reduce a path stroked with a 4-point line weight to 25% of its original size, the reduced path will still have a 4-point line weight. If the "Scale line weight" check box is selected, the line weight will be affected by the scaling. In this case, reducing a path stroked with a 4-point line weight to 25% of its original size will reduce the stroke to a 1-point line weight ($4 \times 0.25 = 1$).

The "Scale line weight" check box in the SCALE dialog box corresponds to the "Scale line weight" check box in the GENERAL PREFERENCES dialog box. Selecting or deselecting either option changes the default setting for the other option as well. Future proportional scalings performed by SHIFT-dragging with the scale tool are also affected by the new setting.

To scale the width and height of an object independently, select the "Non-uniform" option. When this option is selected, the radio buttons in the box above the option become dimmed and two option boxes appear in the box below: these are "Horizontal" and "Vertical." Use these options as follows:

- A "Horizontal" value less than 100% makes the selection thinner.

- A "Horizontal" value greater than 100% makes the selection wider.

- A "Vertical" value less than 100% makes the selection shorter.

- A "Vertical" value greater than 100% makes the selection taller.

If some object in the current selection is filled or stroked with a tile pattern, select the "Pattern tiles" option to transform the tiles along with the selection. If you wish to scale the pattern and not the object itself, deselect the "Object" check box and only the pattern will scale, as discussed in the *Transforming objects with patterns* section of Chapter 8. If none of the selected objects has a pattern fill, these check boxes will be dimmed.

You can confirm your scaling specifications by clicking on either the OK or COPY button. Clicking COPY retains any selected object at its original size, as well as creating a clone scaled to the dialog specifications.

You can also access the SCALE dialog box by double-clicking on the scale tool icon in the toolbox. Illustrator automatically scales the object with respect to its exact center. If multiple objects are selected, Illustrator scales the objects with respect to the center of the selection. Use this technique when you can't figure out where the center point is.

Flipping objects

In the previous section, I mentioned how dragging past the scale origin with the scale tool will flip a selected object. Illustrator also provides a dedicated *reflect tool* for those times when you want to flip an object without scaling it. The reflect tool flips an object around a *reflection axis*, which acts like a pivoting mirror. The selected object looks into this mirror; the result of the flip is the image that the mirror projects.

Using the reflect tool

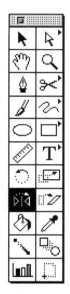

The reflect tool, eighth tool on the left side of the toolbox, is used to flip text blocks and graphic objects. It is operated by clicking at each of two different locations *or* by both clicking and dragging, each at a separate location. The following steps explain how to use this tool:

1. Select the object or objects that you wish to flip. Then select the reflect tool. Your cursor will appear as a small cross.

2. Click with the reflect tool at some location in your drawing area relative to the selected object. This location will act as the first point in the reflection axis.

3. After you establish the first point in the axis, your cursor changes to an arrowhead. Click or drag relative to the first point to determine the angle of the reflection axis, about which the selected objects will flip.

Figure 11-19 on the next page displays two paths representing a telephone. They are identical to those in Figure 11-9 except that a cord has been added to the selected path. This addition makes the path asymmetrical to better demonstrate the reflection operation. Suppose that you want to flip the path around an angled axis. The following exercise explains how:

1. Select the reflect tool and click at the location displayed as a small cross in Figure 11-19, establishing the first point in the reflection axis (sometimes called the *reflection origin*).

2. Drag with the arrowhead cursor. As you drag, the invisible reflection axis continually rotates so that it runs in a straight line between the cursor and the origin.

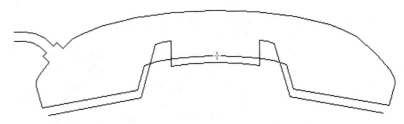

Figure 11-19: Click with the reflect tool near the middle of the selected path to establish a reflection origin.

3. Drag the cursor above and to the left of the origin, as shown in Figure 11-20. Illustrator displays both original and current positions on screen. In the figure, a gray line has been added to indicate the angle of the reflection axis.

4. Release your mouse button to complete the flip.

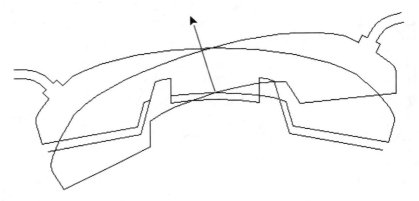

Figure 11-20: Drag up and to the left to tilt the reflection axis about 15° from vertical.

If you prefer, you can simply click with the arrowhead cursor, instead of dragging, to flip a selected object. After establishing a reflection origin, clicking a second time immediately creates a reflection axis between the two click points, and the selected object is flipped accordingly.

Constrained flipping

To constrain a reflection so that the selected object is flipped about a vertical, horizontal, or diagonal axis, press the SHIFT key while clicking a second time or dragging with the reflect tool. Constraining limits the angle of the reflection axis to some multiple of 45°.

The effects of pressing SHIFT while operating the reflect tool can be altered by rotating the constraint axes using the "Constrain angle" option in the GENERAL PREFERENCES dialog box. For more information, see the section *Transforming rotated objects*, later in this chapter.

Flipping partial paths

Just as you can flip whole objects, you can flip selected elements within objects independently of their deselected neighbors. Simply select the desired points and segments that you wish to flip, and use the reflect tool as directed in the previous sections.

For example, suppose that you want to flip the selected elements in the skyline path shown back in Figure 11-14:

1. Click with the reflect tool to the right of the path, at the same location indicated by the small cross cursor in Figure 11-14.

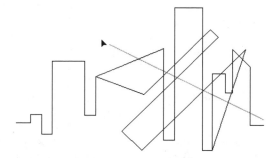

Figure 11-21: Drag up and to the left with the reflect tool to flip the selected elements across an angled axis.

2. Drag up and to the left with the reflect tool arrowhead cursor. Figure 11-21 shows how all selected points pivot to the opposite side of the invisible reflection axis, rotating many selected segments and stretching those that are bordered by a deselected point.

Flipping a clone

You can retain both the original and current position of a flipped object by OPTION-dragging with the reflect tool; that is, press the OPTION key after beginning a drag and hold the key down until after the drag is completed. You may also press OPTION before clicking a second time with the tool to create a *clone* of the selected object that can be manipulated independently of the original. (A more complete discussion of cloning is included in the *Cloning objects* section later in this chapter.) After OPTION-dragging or OPTION-clicking with the reflect tool, the cloned object remains selected, but its original is deselected.

Using the Reflect dialog box

If you press the OPTION key before clicking with the reflect tool the first time, the cross-shaped cursor gains an ellipsis in the lower right corner and the information bar changes to read "Reflect: click to choose origin." This shows that the REFLECT dialog box will display once you click with the mouse.

Press OPTION and click with the reflect tool to simultaneously determine the location of the reflection origin and display the REFLECT dialog box, shown in Figure 11-22, which allows you to flip one or more selected objects around a numerically tilted axis.

The "Axis" box contains three radio buttons, any one of which you can select to specify the angle of the reflection axis. These options produce the following results:

- Select "Horizontal" to flip an object on its head.

- Select "Vertical" to flip an object onto its side.

- Select "Angle" and enter a value between –360 and 360 in the corresponding option box to flip an object around an angled axis.

The value in the "Axis" option box is measured in degrees from the mean horizontal (0°). Because the axis extends to either side of the reflection origin, values over 180° are repetitious. (For an explanation of degrees, see the *Constrained movements* section of Chapter 6.)

If some object in the current selection is filled or stroked with a tile pattern, select the "Pattern tiles" option to transform the tiles along with the selection. If you wish to reflect the pattern and not the object itself, deselect the "Objects" check box and only the pattern will scale, as discussed in Chapter 8. If the none of the selected objects has a pattern fill, these check boxes are dimmed.

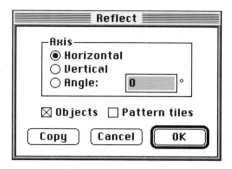

Figure 11-22: The Reflect dialog box allows you to specify the angle of the reflection axis.

You can confirm your reflection specifications by clicking on either the OK or COPY button. Clicking COPY retains any selected object at its original position while creating a clone reflected across the specified axis.

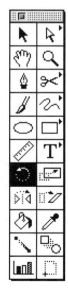

You can also access the REFLECT dialog box by double-clicking on the reflect tool icon in the toolbox. Illustrator automatically flips the object with respect to its exact center. If multiple objects are selected, Illustrator flips the objects with respect to the center of the selection. Use this technique when you can't figure out where the center point is.

Rotating objects

In Illustrator, any text block or graphic object can be rotated to any degree imaginable. This allows you to create angled type and other tilted images. You accomplish rotations with the *rotate tool*.

Using the rotate tool

The rotate tool, seventh tool on the left side of the toolbox, is operated by *both* clicking *and* dragging, each at a separate location. The following steps explain how to use this tool:

1. Select the object you wish to rotate. Then select the rotate tool. Your cursor will appear as a small cross.

2. Click with the rotate tool at some location in your drawing area relative to the selected object to establish the *rotation origin*, the center of the rotation.

3. After you establish a rotation origin, the cursor changes to an arrowhead. Drag the selected object about the origin to rotate it.

In principle, the rotation origin is much like the scale origin. Figure 11-23 shows an ellipse in various stages of rotating around a single origin, displayed as a small cross. The original location of the ellipse is the rightmost shape in the figure. All other ellipses are the results of many separate drags, each of which has rotated the shape by 45°. During the drags, all points in the ellipse remain equidistant from the rotation origin. A gray arrow demonstrates the course of each drag. Together, these arrows form a large circle whose center is the rotation origin.

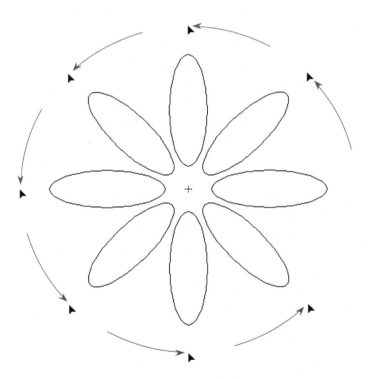

Figure 11-23: Rotating an ellipse in 45° increments around a single rotation origin.

The rotate tool offers the most control when the distance between the rotation origin and the point at which you begin your drag is greater than or equal to the length of the selected object.

I will demonstrate this tip in the following exercise, which offers various ways to approach the rotation of the selected path shown in Figure 11-24:

1. Select the rotate tool and click on the bottom left-hand corner point of the selected path, indicated by the small cross in Figure 11-24. This establishes the rotation origin.

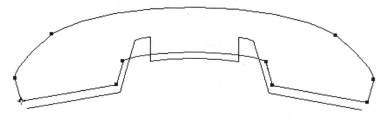

Figure 11-24: Click with the rotate tool on the bottom left point in the selected shape to establish a rotation origin.

2. Move the arrowhead cursor to a location about ⅓ inch to the right of the origin and drag slightly upward, as shown in Figure 11-25 on the next page. The distance of the drag in the figure is only 10 points (less than ⅙ inch), but the shape rotates dramatically, approximately 24° counterclockwise.

3. Release your mouse button to complete the rotation. Choose UNDO ROTATE (⌘-Z) to return the receiver to its original position.

4. Click again at the location of the small cross in Figure 11-24 to establish the origin. This time, begin dragging at the bottom right-hand corner point on the opposite side of the selected path, approximately 16 times the distance from the origin as the previous drag.

5. As also shown in Figure 11-25 on the next page, you have to drag 160 points from this location to achieve the same result as your previous 10-point drag. If you drag upward only 10 points, as shown in Figure 11-26, the selected shape rotates less than 2°. Thus, beginning your drag far from the rotation origin provides you with more fine-tuning control.

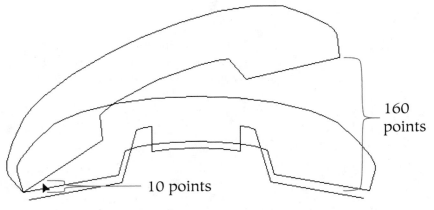

160
points

10 points

Figure 11-25: If you begin dragging close to the rotation origin, small movements will produce dramatic results.

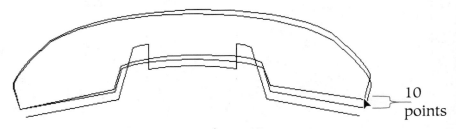

10
points

Figure 11-26: Begin dragging far from the rotation origin to better control the result.

Constraining rotations

To constrain a rotation so that the selected object is rotated by a multiple of 45° from its original position, press the SHIFT key while dragging with the rotate tool.

Unlike other transformation tools, the effects of pressing SHIFT while operating the rotate tool are *not* altered by rotating the constraint axes using the "Constrain angle" option in the GENERAL PREFERENCES dialog box.

Rotating partial paths

Just as you can rotate whole objects, you can rotate selected elements within objects independently of their deselected neighbors. Simply select the desired points and segments that you wish to rotate and use the rotate tool as directed in the previous sections.

For example, suppose that you want to rotate the selected elements in the skyline path shown in Figure 11-27:

1. Click with the rotate tool on the bottom right selected point, as indicated by the small cross cursor in Figure 11-27.

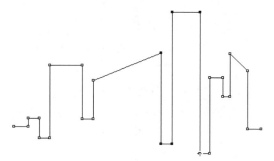

Figure 11-27: Position the rotation origin at the bottom right selected point in the path.

2. Begin dragging at the point on the left side of the segment along the top of the tallest building.

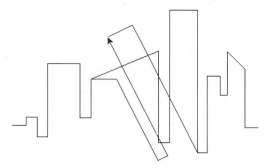

Figure 11-28: Drag to the left to rotate the selected elements counterclockwise around the origin.

3. Drag to the left with the rotate tool, as shown in Figure 11-28. All selected points remain equidistant from the origin during their moves, causing the rotation of all segments surrounded by selected points.

Rotating a clone

You can retain both the original and current positions of a rotated object by OPTION-dragging with the rotate tool; that is, press the OPTION key after beginning a drag and hold the key down until after the drag is completed. This creates a *clone* of the selected object that can be manipulated independently of the original. (A more complete discussion of cloning is included in the *Cloning objects* section, later in this chapter.) After you OPTION-drag with the rotate tool, the cloned object remains selected, but its original is deselected.

Using the Rotate dialog box

If you press the OPTION key before clicking with the rotate tool the first time, the cross-shaped cursor gains an ellipsis in the lower right corner and the information bar changes to read "Rotate: click to choose origin." This shows that once you click with the mouse, the ROTATE dialog box will display.

Press OPTION and click with the rotate tool to simultaneously determine the location of the rotation origin and display the ROTATE dialog box, shown in Figure 11-29. This dialog box allows you to rotate one or more selected objects numerically.

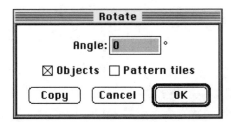

Figure 11-29: The Rotate dialog box allows you to specify the number of degrees a selected object will be rotated.

Enter any value between –360 and 360 in the "Angle" option box. The value is measured in degrees and is accurate to 0.01 degree. A negative value rotates an object clockwise; a positive value rotates an object counterclockwise.

If some object in the current selection is filled or stroked with a tile pattern, select the "Pattern tiles" option to transform the tiles along with the selection. If you wish to rotate the pattern and not the

⚛ The **Illustrator 5** Book

object itself, deselect the "Object" check box and only the pattern will rotate, as discussed in Chapter 8. If none of the selected objects has a pattern fill, these check boxes are dimmed.

You can confirm your rotation specifications by clicking on either the OK or COPY button. Clicking COPY retains any selected object at its original position, while creating a clone rotated the specified number of degrees.

You can also access the ROTATE dialog box by double-clicking on the rotate tool icon in the toolbox. Illustrator automatically rotates the object with respect to its exact center. If multiple objects are selected, Illustrator rotates the objects with respect to the center of the selection. Use this technique when you can't figure out where the center point is.

Slanting objects

Slanting (more accurately called *skewing*) is perhaps the most difficult transformation to conceptualize. To skew an object is to slant its vertical and horizontal proportions independently of each other. For example, a standard kite shape is a skewed version of a perfect square. As shown in Figure 11-30, the vertical lines in the square are slanted backward and the horizontal lines are slanted upward.

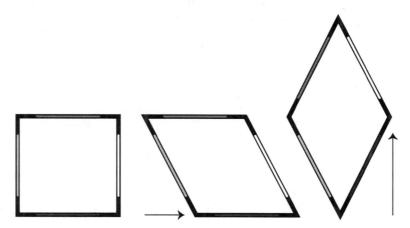

Figure 11-30: Transforming a square into a kite by skewing the shape in two steps.

For some reason, Adobe calls this process *shearing*, like maybe it has something to do with sheep. Who knows? But it follows that the feature used to skew objects in Illustrator is the *shear tool*.

Using the shear tool

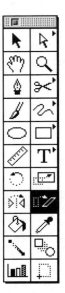

The shear tool, eighth tool on the right side of the toolbox, is used to skew text blocks and graphic objects. It is operated by *both* clicking *and* dragging, each at a separate location. The following steps explain how to use this tool:

1. Select the object you wish to skew. Then select the shear tool. Your cursor will appear as a small cross.

2. Click with the shear tool at some location in your drawing area. This location will act as the *shear origin*, the center of the skewing operation. Elements on opposite sides of the origin will be skewed in opposite directions.

3. After you establish a shear origin, your cursor changes to an arrowhead. Drag from one side of the origin to the other to skew the selected object in that direction.

In general, the shear tool functions like any other transformation tool. However, it may take some experimenting before you're able to accurately predict the results of your actions. In the following exercise, you can experiment by skewing the telephone shape from Figure 11-9:

1. Select the shear tool and click near the middle of the selected shape to establish the shear origin.

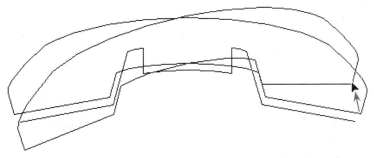

Figure 11-31: Drag with the shear tool to skew the right half of the selected shape up and the left half of the shape down.

The **Illustrator 5** Book

2. Drag upward from the bottom right corner point in the shape, as shown in Figure 11-31. The right half of the phone shrugs upward with your drag. The left half shrugs downward, because it is located on the opposite side of the shear origin.

 Like the rotate tool, the shear tool offers the most control when the distance between the shear origin and the point at which you begin your drag is greater than or equal to the length of the selected object.

If you find that the shear tool consistently behaves erratically for you, try constraining the tool's performance by SHIFT-dragging, as described in the following section. This generally makes the tool more manageable.

Constrained skewing

After establishing the shear origin, press the SHIFT key to slant an object exclusively horizontally (forward and backward) or vertically (up and down). If you SHIFT-drag diagonally from the shear origin, you can also skew a shape equally vertically and horizontally, although the effect of a diagonal drag is much more difficult to predict.

You can alter the effect of SHIFT-dragging with the shear tool by rotating the constraint axes using the "Constrain angle" option in the PREFERENCES dialog box. For more information, see *Transforming rotated objects*, later in this chapter.

Skewing partial paths

Selected elements can be slanted independently of their deselected neighbors in the same path. Simply select the desired points and segments that you wish to skew, and use the shear tool as directed in the previous sections.

For example, suppose you want to skew the selected elements in the skyline path shown back in Figure 11-27:

1. Click with the shear tool on the bottom right selected point, as indicated by the small cross cursor in Figure 11-27.

2. Begin dragging at the point on the left side of the segment along the top of the tallest building.

3. Drag leftward with the shear tool as shown in Figure 11-32. As you drag, press the SHIFT key to constrain the transformation to a horizontal slant. All selected points move with the shear tool based on their proximity to the shear origin; points close to the origin move less than points farther away. All selected vertical segments are slanted backward; all selected horizontal segments are unaffected.

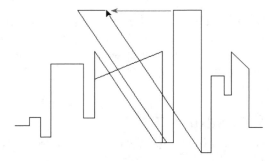

Figure 11-32: Shift-drag to the left with the shear tool to slant the selected elements so they lean backward.

Skewing a clone

You can retain both the original and current positions of a skewed object by OPTION-dragging with the shear tool; that is, press the OPTION key after beginning a drag and hold the key down until after the drag is completed. This creates a *clone* of the selected object that can be manipulated independently of the original. (A more complete discussion of cloning is included in the *Cloning objects* section, later in this chapter.) After you OPTION-drag with the shear tool, the cloned object remains selected, but its original is deselected.

Using the Shear dialog box

If you press the OPTION key before clicking with the shear tool the first time, the cross-shaped cursor gains an ellipsis in the lower right corner and the information bar changes to read "Shear: click to choose origin." This shows that once you click with the mouse, the SHEAR dialog box will display.

Press OPTION and click with the shear tool to simultaneously determine the location of the shear origin and display the SHEAR dialog box, shown in Figure 11-33, which allows you to skew one or more selected objects numerically along a specified *shear axis* (the imaginary straight line along which the selected object will slant).

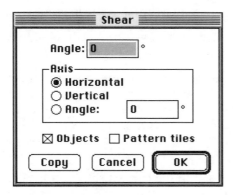

Figure 11-33: The Shear dialog box allows you to specify the angle of the shear axis and determine the angle of the slant.

The "Axis" box contains three radio buttons, any one of which may be selected to determine the angle of the shear axis. These options produce the following results:

- Select "Horizontal" to slant an object forward or backward.

- Select "Vertical" to slant an object up or down.

- Select "Angle" and enter a value between –360 and 360 in the nearby option box to slant an object along an angled axis.

The value in the lower "Angle" option box is measured in degrees from the mean horizontal (0°). Because the axis extends to either side of the shear origin, values over 180° are repetitious. (For an explanation of degrees, see the *Constrained movements* section of Chapter 6.)

Regardless of the selected "Axis" option, you will want to enter a value for the "Angle" option at the top of the dialog box. Here's where things get tricky. In almost every option box that is measured in degrees, Illustrator interprets the value in a counterclockwise direction. This is true for rotations, angled axes, and directional movements.

The single exception is this "Angle" option, where a value is interpreted in a clockwise direction.

- A positive horizontal value slants a selected object forward.

- A negative horizontal value slants a selected object backward.

- A positive vertical value slants anything to the right of the origin down and anything to the left of the origin up.

- A negative vertical value slants anything to the right of the origin up and anything to the left of the origin down.

The reason for this is probably because the shear tool is commonly used with text. Oblique or italicized type is slanted forward; backward-sheared type is considered to be backslanted. Therefore, the clockwise angle measurement makes sense in this context. You may nonetheless find yourself slightly confused when you skew an object by a positive value vertically and see it slant downward.

If some object in the current selection is filled or stroked with a tile pattern, select the "Pattern tiles" option to transform the tiles along with the selection. If you wish to shear the pattern and not the object itself, deselect the "Objects" check box and only the pattern will shear, as discussed in Chapter 8. If none of the selected objects has a pattern fill, these check boxes will be dimmed.

You may confirm your skew specifications by clicking on either the OK or COPY button. Clicking COPY retains any selected object at its original position, while creating a clone slanted along the specified axis by the specified number of degrees.

You can also access the SHEAR dialog box by double-clicking on the shear tool icon in the toolbox. Illustrator automatically skews the object with respect to its exact center. If multiple objects are selected, Illustrator skews the objects with respect to the center of the selection. Use this technique when you can't figure out where the center point is.

Transformation nightcaps

The following are a couple of quick notes about transformations before I close the subject entirely. Although they are not absolutely necessary to your understanding of transformation tools, they can be helpful in sticky situations.

The **Illustrator 5** Book

Recording transformations

Each of the four transformation dialog boxes previously discussed in this chapter acts as a recorder of the most recent scaling, flip, rotation, or skew. After transforming an object by hand, OPTION-click with or double-click on the current transformation tool while the object remains selected. The appropriate dialog box appears, containing the exact percentage, number of degrees, and so on, corresponding to the previous transformation. You can use this information to repeat the transformation, apply a similar transformation to another object, or simply as a reference for tracking purposes.

> If you are sharing a file with one or more colleagues, or filling in for a person in the middle of an illustration, you may want to track your transformations by entering them into the "Note" option in the ATTRIBUTES dialog box (⌘-⌥-A) for each affected object. In this way, your manipulations can be undone well after the fact if they are inadequate or inaccurate.

Transforming with respect to the center point

When you transform a selected object by double-clicking on one of the transformation tools, the object transforms with respect to the object's center. This is great if you know the exact numerical value by which you want to transform the object. If, on the other hand, you want to transform the object by hand with respect to its center, you have to make a best guess while manually positioning the origin. Unless, that is, you tell Illustrator to find the center point for you.

With Illustrator 5.0, you can add a center point automatically to any graphic object. Choose the ATTRIBUTES... command from the OBJECT menu (⌘-⌥-A). The ATTRIBUTES dialog box will display. In addition to tagging a particular object with a note, as discussed in the above tip, you can click on the "Show center point" check box to add a center point to a selected graphic object. Like the center point of an ellipse or rectangle, this new center point displays as an × in the artwork mode and displays only when the object is selected in the preview mode. It becomes an intricate part of the object and can't be removed unless you deselect the "Show center point" check box in the ATTRIBUTES dialog box. Center points are also very useful for aligning multiple objects.

Transforming rotated objects

As we have mentioned, the performance of the scale tool, the reflect tool, and the shear tool are affected by the current orientation of the constraint axes. If you rotate the constraint axes by entering a value between –360 and 360 in the "Constrain angle" option inside the GENERAL PREFERENCES dialog box (⌘-K), you alter the angle at which an object is transformed.

Generally, you will be able to most accurately predict the results of a transformation when the constraint axes are not rotated; that is, when the "Constrain angle" option is set to 0. An exception arises when transforming an object that has been rotated. In this case, you will find that the object is most easily transformed when the constraint axes are likewise rotated.

For example, suppose that you rotate an object. Later on, you decide you want to enlarge the object. The following exercise describes how this might work:

1. Draw a rectangle with the rectangle tool.

2. Select the rotate tool and click on the center point of the rectangle to establish the rotation origin. Drag the shape by one of its corners to rotate the rectangle, as shown in Figure 11-34.

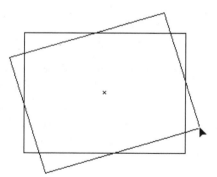

Figure 11-34: Rotate an object a random number of degrees.

3. The rectangle turns out to be too short for your purposes, although its width is correct. Select the scale tool and click on the center point of the shape to establish the scale origin. Drag downward from the lower side of the shape to increase its

height. Whether or not you press SHIFT to constrain the scaling, the enlargement distorts the rectangle so that its corners are no longer perpendicular, as shown in Figure 11-35. The sides slant as if you had skewed the shape with the shear tool. This is because you are scaling the rectangle along an axis that is not aligned with the rectangle itself.

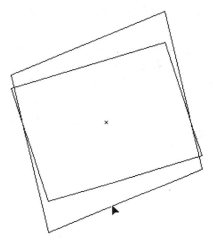

Figure 11-35: Scaling the rotated
rectangle vertically distorts the shape.

4. Choose the UNDO SCALE command (⌘-Z).
5. Select the measure tool and click on each of the two points bordering the bottom segment in the rectangle.

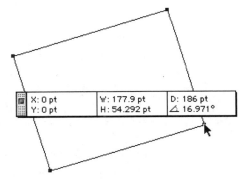

Figure 11-36: The Info palette displays the
angle of the rotated rectangle.

6. The INFO palette will appear, as shown in Figure 11-36 on the previous page. The bottom right value indicates the angle of the measured segment. Since this segment used to be horizontal (0°), the new angle reflects the degree of the previous rotation. Record the angle, which in the case of the figure is 16.971°.

7. Choose the PREFERENCES… command (⌘-K) and enter the recorded value into the "Constrain angle" option box. Press RETURN to implement the change.

8. Select the scale tool again and click on the center point of the rectangle to establish the scale origin. Press SHIFT and drag downward from the lower side of the shape to increase its height. This time, the rectangle does not distort. As shown in Figure 11-37, all corners remain perpendicular as you increase the height of the shape.

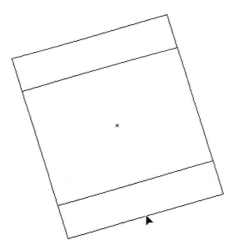

Figure 11-37: By rotating the constraint axes to the same angle as the rotated rectangle, you preserve the form of the object as you scale it vertically.

9. Restore the constraint axes to their original orientation.

The process for flipping and skewing rotated objects is similar. The only transformation tool that is not affected by the orientation of the constraint axes is the rotation tool, since objects are always rotated from their current orientation.

🜨 The **Illustrator 5** Book

Duplicating objects

To *duplicate* an object is to create and control one or more copies of an existing object. Some of these techniques use the Macintosh Clipboard, where one set of objects can be stored for future retrieval. Others work without the Clipboard or in combination with manipulation techniques, including the transformation tools. All repeat the composition of an object, a movement, or a transformation procedure.

Cut, copy, and paste

The CUT, COPY, and PASTE commands under the EDIT menu are available in any Macintosh application. CUT and COPY store one or more selected objects so they can be used later in the current session. The PASTE command retrieves the stored objects and displays them in the drawing area. Each command works with Apple's built-in *Clipboard*, which can hold only one object or one set of objects at a time.

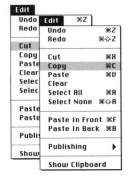

To cut an object is to remove the object from the current illustration and place it inside the Clipboard. This is done by selecting an object and choosing the CUT command from the EDIT menu (⌘-X). The COPY command (⌘-C) works very similarly. But rather than removing the selected object, this command makes a copy of a selected object and puts it in the Clipboard.

Both CUT and COPY put something into the Clipboard. Since the Clipboard can only hold one set of items at a time, each command disposes of the current occupant in the Clipboard and replaces it with the newly cut or copied object. If no object is selected in the drawing area, the CUT and COPY commands are dimmed.

The PASTE command (⌘-V) works exactly opposite the COPY command. To paste an object is to copy the contents of the Clipboard and place them inside the current drawing area. The object still exists in the Clipboard and may be pasted into your illustration over and over again. You must have cut or copied an object into the Clipboard sometime previously during the current session in order to use the PASTE command. Otherwise, the command is dimmed.

The PASTE command pastes the contents of the Clipboard at the exact center of the current window and in front of all other objects in the illustration. (You can also paste an object at the exact location at which it was cut or copied, while additionally altering its layering, by choosing the PASTE IN FRONT (⌘-F) or PASTE IN BACK (⌘-B) command

---

from the Edit menu, as described in the section *Layering objects*, later in this chapter.) Pasted objects appear selected in the illustration window. In this way, you can easily find an object and move it to its proper location.

Duplicating type

You can also duplicate characters, words, and paragraphs of type. Select the type tool and highlight the type that you want to use later. Choose Cut to remove the highlighted type from the text block and store it in the Clipboard. Choose Copy to copy the highlighted type to the Clipboard. Choose Paste to replace the highlighted type with type from the Clipboard or paste the type after the insertion marker.

Pasted type retains all character formatting. However, it will assume the paragraph formatting of the paragraph into which it is pasted (unless an entire paragraph was copied, and it is pasted between paragraphs).

Cut or copied objects (selected with the selection tool) cannot be pasted into a text block. Cut or copied type (selected with the type tool) cannot be pasted outside a text block.

Duplicating partial paths

You can cut or copy individually selected points and segments in an object independently of their deselected neighbors. In the first example of Figure 11-38 on the following page, I have selected a single curved segment, copied it, and then pasted it. The pasted segment is offset slightly from the original path. Notice that although the points that border the curved segment are not selected in the original path, they are copied and pasted. This is because a segment must always be bordered on both sides by a point.

If you select a point, the result of choosing the Copy and Paste commands is slightly different. By selecting an interior point, you also select both the segment that enters the point and the segment that exits the point. Therefore, copying and pasting a point also copies and pastes the two segments associated with the point, as shown in the second example of Figure 11-38 on the next page. Once again, two points that were not selected in the original path are pasted in the offset path, since these are the endpoints belonging to the two copied segments.

The **Illustrator 5** Book

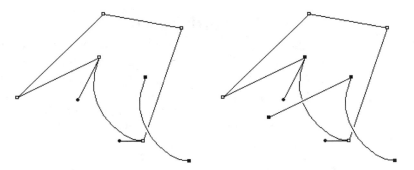

Figure 11-38: Copying and pasting a segment (left) pastes the points bordering the segments as well; copying and pasting a point (right) pastes the two bordering segments and their bordering points.

Cloning objects

Cloning is much like the COPY command with two important exceptions: First, cloning bypasses the Clipboard. It neither displaces the current occupant in the Clipboard nor does it replace that object with the cloned object. Second, cloning acts like combined COPY and PASTE command. The cloned object immediately appears in your illustration, in front of all other objects in the current illustration.

Cloning is accomplished in one of three ways:

- Press OPTION and drag a selected object with the selection tool; that is, press the OPTION key after beginning the drag and hold the key down until after the drag is completed. This moves and clones the object in a single gesture.

- Press OPTION and drag a selected object with one of the transformation tools (scale, reflect, rotate, or shear) to transform and clone the object in a single gesture.

- Click on the COPY button in the MOVE, SCALE, ROTATE, REFLECT, or SHEAR dialog box. This feature allows you to determine the placement of a clone with numerical precision.

After you clone one or more objects, the original objects remain unaffected while their clones appear at the new position or orientation. Only the cloned objects are selected.

Cloning partial paths

Just as you can clone whole objects, you can also clone selected elements within objects independently of their deselected neighbors. The first example of Figure 11-39 shows a selected curved segment being OPTION-dragged with the selection tool. The result is shown in the second example in the figure. The segment and its two bordering points have been cloned and reshaped simultaneously.

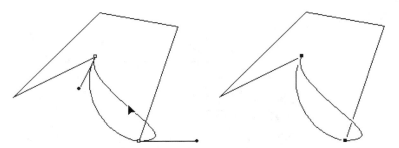

Figure 11-39: Option-drag a segment (left) to simultaneously reshape and clone the segment (right).

If you instead OPTION-drag at a selected interior point in an otherwise deselected path, as shown in the first example of Figure 11-40, you clone the selected point, its two bordering segments, and each segment's bordering points. As shown in the second example of the figure, the form of each cloned segment is again reshaped, since each is bordered by one moving point and one stationary point.

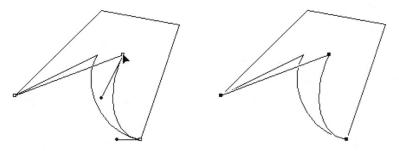

Figure 11-40: Option-drag a point (left) to simultaneously reshape and clone both bordering segments (right).

Duplicating a transformation

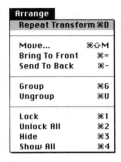

Most drawing programs offer a command that duplicates the effects of a recent transformation. In Illustrator, this is the REPEAT TRANSFORM command under the ARRANGE menu (⌘-D), which repeats any newly completed transformation, including a movement.

The first example of Figure 11-41 shows two rectangles: the deselected rectangle represents the original location of an object, and the selected rectangle demonstrates the location to which it has been dragged. After you move the shape, you can choose the REPEAT TRANSFORM command to duplicate the distance and direction of the movement, as shown in the second example of the figure. The third example shows the results of choosing the REPEAT TRANSFORM command a second time. Each application of REPEAT TRANSFORM repeats the most recent transformation.

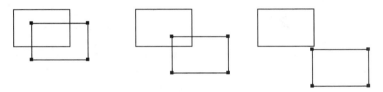

Figure 11-41: After the selected rectangle is dragged from its original deselected position (left), the Repeat Transform command is applied two consecutive times (middle and right) to twice repeat the transformation.

To fine-tune the transformation of an object, you can apply a slight transformation the first time and then repeatedly apply the REPEAT TRANSFORM command. When the eventual transformation exceeds your requirements, choose UNDO TRANSFORM to return it to the exact position or size required.

Suppose you have created a complicated object that is too small to match the size of another object in your illustration. Rather than going back and forth, scaling the object by guess and by golly, you can perform a slight enlargement—about a quarter of what you think is required—and repeat the transformation several times using REPEAT TRANSFORM. With each application of the command, the selected object grows by the incremental percentage. When the size of the object surpasses the desired size, choose UNDO TRANSFORM (⌘-Z) to reduce it to the size that most accurately matches your requirements.

If an object becomes deselected after a transformation or between one application of the REPEAT TRANSFORM command and another, then REPEAT TRANSFORM is dimmed.

Duplicating transformation and object

If the newly completed transformation included a cloning, the REPEAT TRANSFORM command duplicates both transformation and cloning operations. This allows you to create a string of objects, the placement of which follow a constant trend.

In the first example in Figure 11-42, the selected rectangle has been both cloned and moved from the location represented by the deselected shape. The second example shows the result of choosing the REPEAT TRANSFORM command. Notice that, like the second example of Figure 11-41, the movement of the rectangle has been repeated. But this time, the shape is also recloned, resulting in three rectangles instead of two. If REPEAT TRANSFORM is chosen a second time, there will be four rectangles, each offset from the others a consistent distance, as shown in the last example of Figure 11-42.

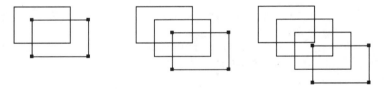

Figure 11-42: After the selected rectangle is option-dragged (left), the Repeat Transform command is applied two consecutive times (middle and right) to twice repeat the transformation and twice duplicate the rectangle.

By duplicating both transformation and object, you can achieve very interesting effects. The following exercise demonstrates how to use the REPEAT TRANSFORM command to create a perspective gridwork of objects. This exercise makes use of the grouped object shown in Figure 11-43 on the following page, which contains three paths. The bottom segment of the outermost path is longer than the top segment, giving it an illusion of depth. The inner ellipses are positioned slightly closer to the top segment of the outer shape, enhancing the illusion.

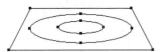

Figure 11-43: The following exercise explains how to transform and duplicate this grouped object to create a perspective effect.

1. Select the shear tool. Click above the group at the location indicated by the small cross cursor at the top of Figure 11-43 to establish the shear origin.

2. Press SHIFT and OPTION and drag leftward from the bottom right corner of the grouped object, skewing it horizontally while also cloning it, as shown in Figure 11-44. Notice that the cloned object appears to lean into the original, extending back into the same visual horizon. This is a result of experimenting with the position of the shear origin.

Figure 11-44: Shift-option-drag the object with the shear tool to simultaneously skew and clone the group.

Figure 11-45: Choose Repeat Transform to repeat the skew and clone operations.

3. Choose REPEAT TRANSFORM (⌘-D) to create another clone and repeat the horizontal skew. Figure 11-45 shows the result, which further enhances the illusion of perspective.

4. Select the two groups farthest to the left. In this step, you will flip a clone of these objects about the center of the original group, creating five symmetrical images. Press OPTION and click with the reflect tool in the center of the deselected group to display the REFLECT dialog. Select the "Vertical" option and click on the COPY button. The result is shown in Figure 11-46: five symmetrical images emerging from the surface of the page.

Figure 11-46: Select the two left groups and flip clones of these objects about the center of the deselected group.

5. You have now managed to impart a sense of perspective through the use of skewing, flipping, and cloning. But the illustration lacks drama. What's needed are additional rows of slanting tiles, which are most easily created by scaling the existing rows over and over. To begin, choose SELECT ALL from the EDIT menu (⌘-A).

6. Select the scale tool and OPTION-click above the group at the location indicated by the small cross cursor at the top of Figure 11-47. Not only does this establish a scale origin at the location previously occupied by the shear origin, but it also displays the SCALE dialog box.

⁖

Figure 11-47: Select the entire row of groups and option-click with the scale tool to display the Scale dialog box.

7. Enter 150% into the "Uniform" option box and click the COPY button. Figure 11-48 on the following page shows how a second, larger row of shapes is created. Again because of the placement of the transformation origin, the second row lines up perfectly with the first. By scaling the cloned shapes to 150% of original size, you enlarge both the size of the shapes and the distance between the shapes and the scale origin.

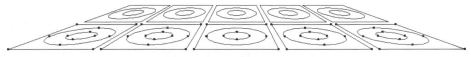

Figure 11-48: Scale clones of the top row of groups to 150% to create two perfectly aligned rows.

8. Choose the REPEAT TRANSFORM command (⌘-D) to create a third row of larger clones directly beneath the second row.

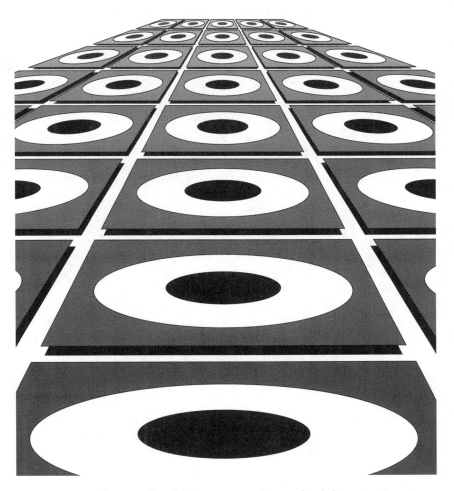

Figure 11-49: The completed illustration is the result of choosing Repeat Transform several times and filling and stroking the resulting paths.

To create the illustration shown in Figure 11-49, press ⌘-D several more times. Each series of shapes increases in size and distance from the group above it, thereby creating an even and continuous sense of perspective. Figure 11-49 is shown as it appears when printed. All shapes are filled and stroked. Foreground images are filled with darker shades of gray than background images, heightening the sense of depth. A layer of shadows has also been added.

Layering objects

When you preview or print an illustration, Illustrator describes it one object at a time, starting with the first object in the drawing area and working up to the last. The order in which the objects are described is called the *layering order*. The first object described is behind all other objects in the drawing area. The last object is in front of all other objects. All other objects exist at some unique layer between the first and the last object.

Left to its own devices, layering would be a function of the order in which you draw. The oldest object would be in back; the most recent object would be in front. But Illustrator provides a number of commands that allow you to adjust the layering order of existing text blocks and graphic objects.

Absolute front and back

Like many Macintosh programs, Illustrator offers two commands for manipulating the layering of objects. These are the BRING TO FRONT (⌘-=, COMMAND-EQUALS) and SEND TO BACK commands (⌘- –, COMMAND-HYPHEN) from the ARRANGE menu. If you select an object and choose BRING TO FRONT, this object is treated exactly as if it were the most recently created path in the current illustration. It will be described last when previewing or printing. By choosing SEND TO BACK, a selected object is treated as if it were the first path in the file and is described first when previewing or printing.

You can apply BRING TO FRONT and SEND TO BACK only to whole objects. If a path is only partially selected when choosing either command, the entire path is moved to the front or back of the current illustration.

If more than one object is selected when choosing BRING TO FRONT or SEND TO BACK, the relative layering of each selected object is retained. For example, if you select two objects and then choose the BRING TO FRONT command, the frontmost of the two selected objects becomes the frontmost object in the file, the backmost of the two selected objects becomes the second-to-frontmost object.

Relative front and back

When creating complicated illustrations, it is not enough to be able to send objects to the absolute front or back of an illustration. Even a simple illustration may contain over a hundred objects. Adjusting the layering of a single object from, say, 14th-to-front to 46th-to-front would take days using BRING TO FRONT and SEND TO BACK.

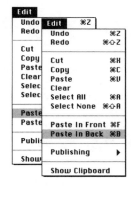

Fortunately, Illustrator provides two commands that make relative layering manipulations possible: They are PASTE IN FRONT (⌘-F) and PASTE IN BACK (⌘-B), available from the EDIT menu. Both commands make use of the Macintosh Clipboard. As described in the *Cut, copy, and paste* section earlier in this chapter, one or more objects are placed inside the Clipboard by choosing the CUT or COPY command. The PASTE IN FRONT and PASTE IN BACK commands retrieve the contents of the Clipboard, placing them at the exact horizontal and vertical location at which they were cut or copied. PASTE IN FRONT pastes the contents of the Clipboard directly in front of a selected object in the drawing area; PASTE IN BACK pastes the contents of the Clipboard directly in back of a selected object. Therefore, both commands affect only the layering of a cut or copied object, and not its positioning.

Figure 11-50 shows two columns of examples demonstrating the PASTE IN FRONT command. The objects in the left-hand column are shown in the artwork mode; the objects in the right-hand column are shown in the preview mode. The following exercise explains the examples in the figure:

1. The first example shows four layered shapes. Select the black shape and choose the CUT command (⌘-X), removing the shape from the illustration and placing it in the Clipboard.

2. Select the backmost remaining shape, as shown in the second example, and choose the PASTE IN FRONT command (⌘-F). The path is pasted at the exact horizontal and vertical position from which it was cut, but it is moved in front of the selected path, as shown in the second previewed example.

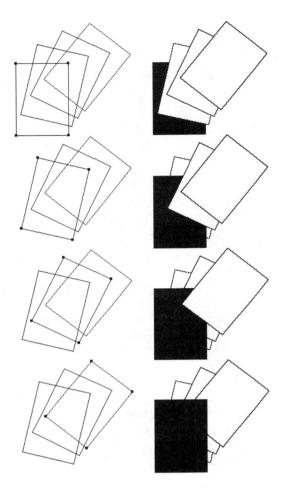

Figure 11-50: The effects of cutting a black path and pasting it in front of selected paths as viewed in the artwork (left) and preview modes (right).

3. The third and fourth examples show the results of selecting other paths and choosing PASTE IN FRONT. Throughout the figure, the layering of the black shape is altered, but the horizontal and vertical positioning of all shapes is constant.

If you select multiple objects when choosing one of the relative pasting commands, the contents of the Clipboard are placed in front

🔬 The **Illustrator 5** Book

of the frontmost selected object, or in back of the backmost selected object. If no object is selected, the Clipboard contents are pasted to the absolute front or back, just as if the BRING TO FRONT or SEND TO BACK commands had been chosen.

The relative layering commands can be used to insert an object into a group, a clipping path, a compound path, or some other combined object. Simply cut the object to the Clipboard (⌘-X), select an object in the combined object using the direct-selection tool, and then choose PASTE IN FRONT or PASTE IN BACK.

Layering in combined objects

Any command that combines selected objects together can also affect the layering of objects in an illustration. These include GROUP (⌘-G), MAKE (COMPOUND) (⌘-8), LINK BLOCKS (⌘-⇧-G), and MAKE TEXT WRAP. All objects in a group, compound path, linked object, or wrapped object must be consecutively layered. To accomplish this, Illustrator uses the frontmost selected object as a marker when you choose one of these commands. All other selected objects are moved to consecutive layers in back of the frontmost object.

Choosing UNGROUP (⌘-U), RELEASE (COMPOUND) (⌘-9), UNLINK BLOCKS (⌘-⇧-U), or RELEASE TEXT WRAP neither restores an object to its original layer nor otherwise affects its layering.

Drawing layers

In addition to the previous layering functions, all of which Illustrator has offered for several years now, version 5.0 introduces self-contained *drawing layers* (or simply *layers*), an almost essential capability for creating complex illustrations. Layers have long been a staple of competing drawing programs like FreeHand and Canvas. But while Illustrator may be late to join the fray, it does so with a vengeance. Its layers are possibly the best around.

Using the LAYERS palette, you can create layers that act like transparent pieces of acetate. You can draw an object on any layer and see it clearly through all layers in front of it. An illustration can contain any number of layers, each layer can contain any number of objects, and you can name layers and alter their order as you see fit.

Assigning layers

The LAYERS palette is an independent palette that appears in front of the foreground illustration. It is displayed by choosing SHOW LAYERS from the WINDOW menu (⌘-⌃-I). All existing drawing layers in the current illustration are displayed in a scrolling list inside the LAYERS palette. You can define and manipulate these layers by choosing commands from the pop-up menu, as shown in Figure 11-51.

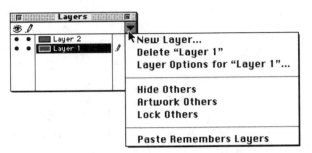

Figure 11-51: Click on the down-pointing arrowhead icon to display the Layers palette pop-up menu.

When you select an object in the illustration window, the corresponding drawing layer becomes highlighted in the scrolling list. If you select multiple objects on different layers or if no object is selected, the highlighted layer name is the active drawing layer, on which future objects will be created. To change the active drawing layer, click on a layer name in the scrolling list.

Creating a new layer

Only named layers can be assigned to graphic objects and text blocks in Illustrator 5.0. To introduce a drawing layer to the list of named layers in the LAYERS palette, choose the NEW LAYER... command from the palette's pop-up menu. The NEW LAYER dialog box displays, as shown in Figure 11-52. Enter a layer name up to 31 characters long into the "Name" option box. (Note that Illustrator does *not* allow you to replace an existing drawing layer by creating a new layer with the same name.)

You can specify the color that Illustrator assigns to selection outlines by selecting an option from the "Selection color" pop-up menu.

⚛ The **Illustrator** 5 Book

If you want to hide all objects on the layer, deselect the "Show" check box. If you want to view the objects on the layer in the artwork mode but not in the preview mode, deselect the "Preview" check box. When the "Print" check box is selected, all objects on the layer will print. Select the "Lock" option to lock the objects so they can't be accidentally altered. Select "Dim placed images" to gray imported EPS images so that you can easily distinguish them from graphic objects and text blocks created in Illustrator. (Remember that to view placed images, the "Show placed objects" option in the DOCUMENT SETUP dialog box must be selected.)

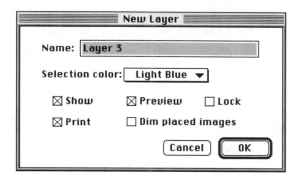

Figure 11-52: The Layers dialog box allows you to name layers, specify the color of selections, and assign attributes to new layers.

Your new layer name will display at the top of the LAYERS palette. By default, the new drawing layer is a foreground layer that is positioned in front of all other layers in the current illustration.

Deleting an existing layer

You can delete any existing drawing layer—even if it's chock-full of text and graphic objects—by clicking on the layer name in the scrolling list in the LAYERS palette and choosing DELETE... from the pop-up menu. If the layer contains any objects, an alert box displays, warning you that you are about to delete a layer that contains artwork. Press RETURN or click on the DELETE button to delete the layer and all of its contents. Click on CANCEL or press COMMAND-PERIOD to cancel the operation and retain the objects on the current layer.

If you delete a layer by mistake, choose the UNDO DELETE LAYER command from the EDIT menu (⌘-Z) to restore the layer and all its objects to the current illustration.

Changing layer attributes

Any drawing layer displayed in the LAYERS palette can be renamed, assigned a different color, or have any of its attributes changed. To do so, either double-click on the layer name in the LAYERS palette or select the layer and choose the LAYER OPTION FOR... command from the pop-up menu. The LAYER OPTIONS dialog box appears, displaying the name, color, and attributes associated with the selected layer. (In fact, with the exception of the title bar, the LAYER OPTIONS dialog box looks exactly like the NEW LAYER dialog box in Figure 11-52.) After making the desired alterations, click on OK or press RETURN to close the dialog box and implement your changes.

Displaying and hiding layers

A solid or hollow circle in front of a layer name under the eyeball icon indicates that all objects on that layer appear on screen. A solid circle means that the layer shows up in both the artwork and preview modes, while a hollow circle means that the layer displays in the artwork mode at all times. Click on the circle to hide it and, by so doing, hide all objects on that layer in the drawing area. This technique enables you to isolate a detail on another layer so you can examine it more closely or make corrections to it.

To display objects on a hidden layer, click in front of the layer name under the eyeball in the LAYERS palette to display the circle.

To hide all layers other than the highlighted one in the current illustration, choose the HIDE OTHERS command from the pop-up menu. Then click in front of specific layer names under the eyeball to indicate the additional layers you want to display. To display all layers choose the SHOW ALL command, which replaces the HIDE OTHERS command when any layer is hidden.

You can also hide or show the contents of a layer by double-clicking on the layer's name and clicking on the "Show" check box in the LAYER OPTIONS dialog box.

Mixing display modes

When working in the preview mode, you can choose the ARTWORK OTHERS command from the LAYERS palette pop-up menu to view all layers but the selected layer in the artwork mode. The selected layer remains previewed. This technique is useful when you want to view one layer independently of others in a complex illustration. Layers confined to the artwork mode display a hollow circle under the eyeball icon next to the layer's name. To display all layers in the preview mode, choose the PREVIEW ALL command from the pop-up menu, which replaces the ARTWORK OTHERS command when any layer appears in the artwork mode.

 You can confine a single layer to the artwork mode by OPTION-clicking on the solid circle under the eyeball icon. To again preview the layer, OPTION-click on the hollow circle.

Protecting layers

Just as you can protect a selected object from being altered by choosing the LOCK command from the ARRANGE menu, you can protect entire layers of objects in Adobe Illustrator. One way to protect a layer is to hide it, as I mentioned a moment ago. Objects on a hidden layer can't be manipulated because they're invisible. But if you want to protect layers without losing sight of their contents, you need to manipulate the circles under the pencil icon.

A solid circle in front of a layer name under the pencil icon indicates that the layer is unlocked and you can manipulate the objects on that layer. Click on the circle to hide it and, by so doing, lock all objects on that layer in the drawing area. This allows you to work in another layer without risking accidentally manipulating or deleting an object in the locked layer.

You can also protect all layers except the highlighted layer by choosing the LOCK OTHERS command from the LAYERS palette pop-up menu. Then click in front of specific layer names under the pencil to indicate the additional layers you want to unlock. To display all layers choose the UNLOCK ALL command, which replaces the LOCK OTHERS command when any layer is locked. You can also lock or unlock a layer by double-clicking on the layer's name and clicking on the "Lock" check box in the LAYER OPTIONS dialog box.

Copying and pasting

One way to move an object from one layer to another layer is to select the object, cut or copy it using the Cut (⌘-X) or Copy (⌘-C) command from the Edit menu, click on the target layer in the Layers palette, and paste the object into its new layer using the Paste command (⌘-V). To disable this function, choose the Paste Remembers Layers command from the pop-up menu. A check mark in front of the command name indicates that all Clipboard functions are confined to the same layer. For example, if you copy an object from Layer #2, Illustrator will paste it back into Layer #2. Use this function when you want to duplicate objects on multiple layers and you want Illustrator to sort the duplicates back onto their original layers.

The "Paste remembers layers" option in the General Preferences dialog box correlates directly to the Paste Remembers Layers command from the Layers palette pop-up menu. Selecting one chooses the other and vice versa.

Reordering a layer

The order in which layer names appear in the Layers palette determines the layering order in the illustration. The first name in the list represents the foremost layer; the last name is the rearmost layer.

To change the order of layers in the current illustration, simply drag a layer name to a different position in the Layers palette scrolling list. Objects assigned to that layer will be repositioned behind or in front of objects in other layers.

Moving objects between layers

To move objects between layers, select one or more objects in a layer that is neither hidden nor locked. A small square in the layer's color appears to the right of the layer's name in the Layers palette. Drag the colored square up or down the scrolling list to a different layer that is also neither hidden nor locked. The cursor becomes a finger to indicate that you are moving objects between layers. Upon releasing the mouse button, Illustrator transfers all selected objects to the new layer. The paths and points in the selected objects appear in the new layer's color to show that the move is complete.

To clone selected objects between layers, OPTION-drag the colored square on the right side of the LAYERS palette. Upon releasing, the selected objects will exist independently in both layers, just as though you had copied them from one layer and pasted them into another.

Although you can select objects from different layers simultaneously by SHIFT-clicking on each object, you can only move or clone objects from one layer to another layer at a time.

Working in layers

Any object in any layer in your illustration is subject to all the commands and options included in Illustrator. For example, in addition to locking or hiding an entire layer, you can lock or hide individual objects within any layer using the commands in the ARRANGE menu.

You can also change the relative layering of objects within a single layer using the SEND TO BACK and BRING TO FRONT commands. For example, if you apply the BRING TO FRONT command to an object on Layer #1, Illustrator brings it to the front of that layer only, not to the front of all layers in the current illustration.

When you save an illustration that contains multiple layers, the layers and their attributes are saved with the illustration. When you go to print a document that contains layers, be sure that all layers intended for printing have the "Print" check box selected in the LAYER OPTIONS dialog box.

Blending objects

The last feature to discuss in this chapter is a combination transformation and duplication feature called *blending*. To blend two selected paths is to create a series of intermediate paths between them. For example, suppose you have created two paths, one that represents a caterpillar and one that represents a butterfly. By blending these two paths, you can create several additional paths that represent metamorphic stages between the two life forms, as shown in Figure 11-53 on the next page. The first intermediate path is formed much like the caterpillar. Each intermediate path after that becomes less like the caterpillar and more like the butterfly.

Figure 11-53: Blending a caterpillar and a butterfly creates a series of transformed duplicates between the two objects.

Using the blend tool

In any blend, two paths must be selected. Of the two, the rear path acts as the *source path* and the forward path acts as the *concluding path.* You create blends using the *blend tool*, the second-to-last tool on the right side of the toolbox. Operate the blend tool by clicking on each of two selected points, one in the source path and one in the concluding path. Any number of points can be selected in each path, and each path can contain any number of points. Only paths can be blended in Illustrator. Placed art cannot be blended.

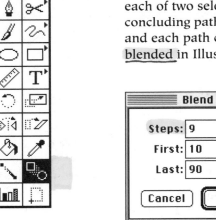

Figure 11-54: The Blend dialog box allows you to specify the number of intermediate paths to create between two selected paths.

After you click on a selected point in each of two paths, the BLEND dialog box displays, as shown in Figure 11-54. This dialog box contains three options that allow you to control the nature of the intermediate paths, called *steps*, in a blend.

- **Steps**. Enter the number of intermediate paths that you want Illustrator to create in this option. Any number between 1 and 1000 is acceptable. The "First" and "Last" values update accordingly.

- **First**. The value in this option determines the location of each point in the first step as a percentage of the total distance between each selected pair of points in the source and concluding paths. This value also affects how the first step is painted as a percentage of the difference between the fills and strokes of the source and concluding paths.

- **Last**. The value in this option determines the location of each point in the last step as a percentage of the total distance between each selected pair of points in the source and concluding paths. This value also affects how the last step is painted as a percentage of the difference between the fills and strokes of the source and concluding paths.

If you can make sense of all of that, you've probably used the tool before. If not, don't keep reading it over and over; you'll just turn your brain to mush. These options are better demonstrated by example: Say that you specify 9 steps between your source and concluding paths. Illustrator determines the positioning of each step as a percentage of the distance between both paths. The source path occupies the 0% position and the concluding path occupies the 100% position. To space the steps evenly, Illustrator automatically assigns the nine steps positions 10% through 90%. Therefore, the "First" option updates to display 10%, and the "Last" option displays 90%.

You can change the "First" and "Last" values to alter the percentage placement of the first and last steps. The second through eighth steps are automatically spaced evenly between them. If you change the "First" value to 30% and the "Last" value to 70%, you squash the steps closer together while leaving some breathing room between the steps and the source and concluding paths.

The "First" and "Last" values also control the fill and stroke of the intermediate paths. Suppose the source path is filled with white and stroked with a 100% black, 11-point line weight; the concluding path is filled with 100% black and stroked with a 50% black, 1-point line weight. The painting attributes of the steps are averaged incrementally as a function of the number of steps. To determine this average, Illustrator divides the difference in the painting attributes by the number of steps. In this case, the differences between source and concluding path are as follows:

- The difference in fill color = 100% black – 0% black (white) = 100%.

- The difference in stroke color = 100% black – 50% black = 50%.

- The difference in line weight = (11-point) – (1-point) = 10-point.

With 9 steps, a "First" value of 10%, and a "Last" value of 90%, your blend will appear as shown in Figure 11-55. Each step is painted as follows:

Step	% change	Fill color	Stroke color	Line weight
1	10%	10% black	95% black	10-point
2	20%	20% black	90% black	9-point
3	30%	30% black	85% black	8-point
4	40%	40% black	80% black	7-point
5	50%	50% black	75% black	6-point
6	60%	60% black	70% black	5-point
7	70%	70% black	65% black	4-point
8	80%	80% black	60% black	3-point
9	90%	90% black	55% black	2-point

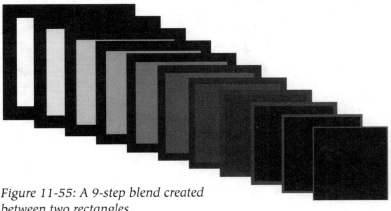

Figure 11-55: A 9-step blend created between two rectangles.

The **Illustrator** 5 Book

Press RETURN to exit the BLEND dialog box and create the specified number of steps, beginning and ending at the prescribed locations. Illustrator creates the steps as a grouped object, layered between the source and concluding paths. Within the group, the steps ascend in layering order as they approach the concluding (frontmost) path.

If either the source path or concluding path lacks a fill or stroke, all steps created with the blend tool will also lack a fill or stroke. The blend tool affects dashed strokes only if both the source and concluding paths are dashed; otherwise, all steps are stroked solid.

Selecting points in a blend

Your mastery of the blend tool depends upon your ability to control the appearance of intermediate paths rather than simply relying on Illustrator's automation. The quantity and location of points in the steps, as well as the form of the segments between points, are based on two criteria:

- The number of points you select in the source and concluding paths before clicking with the blend tool.

- The specific point in each path on which you click with the blend tool.

The blend tool relies on selected points as guidelines. It tries to couple each selected point in the source path with a selected point in the concluding path. The blend tool then determines the form and number of segments required between each consecutive pair of selected points. Therefore, you can acquire the most control over your blend by selecting as many points as possible in each path.

 For the most predictable results, your source and concluding paths should contain an identical number of points, all of which should be selected. If you must blend between paths with different numbers of points, do *not* select every point in each path. Instead, select points with discrimination, making sure that each selected point in the source path clearly corresponds to a selected point with a similar identity (smooth or corner) in the concluding path.

The left example in Figure 11-56 shows a source path (top) and a concluding path (bottom) that contain different numbers of points.

However, for every selected point in the source path, there is a similar selected point in the concluding path. If you look closely, you will see that the selected points occupy pivotal positions in their paths.

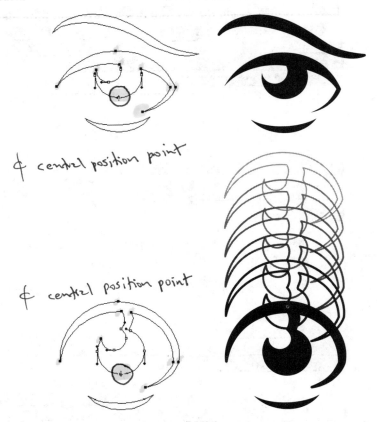

Figure 11-56: When blending two paths with different numbers of points, each selected point in the source path should correspond to a selected point in the concluding path whose identity is similar.

Which points to click?

The points that you click with the blend tool also control the appearance of the steps in a blend. The blend tool uses the click points as origin points for its path creations. It then progresses around the paths in a consistent direction, from one pair of points to the next.

The **Illustrator** 5 Book

Try to click on a similar selected point in each path. If possible, each point should occupy a central position in its path (unless the paths are open, in which case you *must* click on a selected endpoint in each path).

In the case of Figure 11-56, I click with the blend tool on the smooth points along the bottom of each eyeball, indicated by small cross cursors. After the dialog box appears, I specify 5 steps and change the "First" option to 40% to create a large gap between the source path and the first path. The result is shown on the right side of the figure. The fills of the steps in this figure have been made transparent after the fact to make them easier to see. Notice that the distance is greater between the source path and the first step than between the last step and the concluding path because we changed the "First" value. The shade and line weight of the stroke in the first step is also affected by this change.

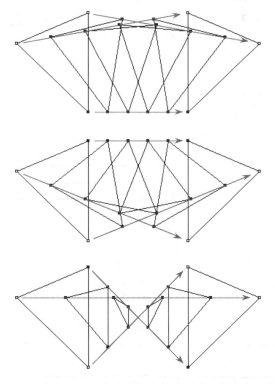

Figure 11-57: Clicking with the blend tool on three different pairs of points (shown as selected in each example) affects the appearance of the steps.

If you click on points that occupy different positions in the source and concluding paths, Illustrator creates distorted steps. Figure 11-57 shows three examples. In each example, I create four blends by clicking on different pairs of points—shown as selected—in the two triangles. Each point in one triangle blends toward a point in the other triangle based on its proximity to the click point, as demonstrated by the arrows.

When blending, the source and concluding paths must both be closed or both be open. If the paths are open, you must click on a selected endpoint in each path. Also, you cannot blend text blocks or paths associated with text blocks.

Blending multiple paths

Although you can blend only two paths at a time, you can blend as many pairs of paths as you desire within a single illustration.

Figure 11-58: Blending five separate open paths to create a late-show metamorphosis.

The first image and the last image in Figure 11-58 each contain five open paths. The images were specifically designed so that for each path in the man's face there is a path performing a similar function in the werewolf. Carefully selecting pairs of points in each like path and entering identical values every time the BLEND dialog displayed produced a series of 30 blends that overlap to form six metamorphic images. With the exception of a slight stroking alteration (that of changing the stroke of the source path to black), the final blend appears exactly as it was created with the blend tool. It is natural when creating such a difficult series of blends that some paths will suffer from a variety of aesthetic imperfections, as do those in the figure. Such paths require reshaping.

Creating custom gradations

Despite the amazing visual metamorphoses that you can produce using this feature, you will probably find the blend tool most helpful in creating custom gradations that are not limited to the linear or radial styles offered by the GRADIENT palette, as discussed in the *Gradient fills* section of Chapter 8. For example, suppose you created two rectangles, both without strokes, in which the rear shape was larger and had a black fill and the front one was smaller and had a white fill. If you then reshaped the forward rectangle using the direct-selection tool, selected both shapes, and applied the blend tool, you would create a gradation something like the one shown in Figure 11-59.

Figure 11-59: A square gradation created by blending two concentric squares of different sizes and colors.

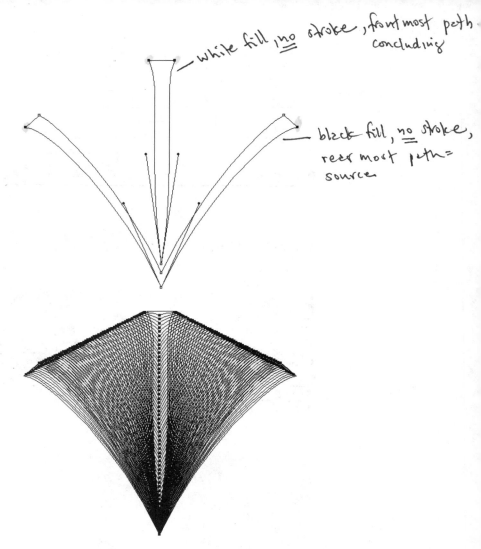

white fill, no stroke, frontmost path concluding

black fill, no stroke, rearmost path = source

*Figure 11-60: After selecting a white path (top, central)
and a black path (top, V-shaped), the paths are blended
to create a gradation containing 49 steps.*

When creating a complex custom gradation with the blend tool,
you will be concerned with the color values of the source and concluding paths as well as with the shapes themselves. The top example
of Figure 11-60 shows two paths: the central path is filled with white,
and the V-shaped path is filled with black. Neither path is stroked,

since a repeating stroke would interrupt a continuous gradation. Also, the central path is in front, making it the concluding path.

After selecting the points shown in the example, I click on the rightmost point in each path with the blend tool. By default, the "Number of steps" option in the BLEND dialog box contains the value 254. PostScript printers can produce a maximum of 256 gray values, including black and white. Subtract 2 for black and white, and you have 254. Thus, 254 steps will produce the most fluid gradation; however, 254 paths also greatly complicate your illustration. A more reasonable value might be 49 steps. This means that each blend will be 2% lighter than the blend behind it. The second example of Figure 11-60 displays the 49 evenly spaced steps created by the blend tool.

After creating a gradation, you can incorporate it into a clipping path. In Figure 11-61, I have grouped the gradation from Figure 11-60 with a masking object to create a glistening charm. To create the outlines around the charm, I added two copies of the mask, each stroked with different line weights and with transparent fills.

Figure 11-61: The result of incorporating the gradation from the previous figure into a clipping path.

If you'll be printing your final illustration to a 300 dot-per-inch laser printer, you won't need more than 24 steps, since a device of this type can produce only 26 gray values. However, if you'll be printing to a higher resolution device, such as a Linotronic or Compugraphic imagesetter, such a small number of steps may result in *banding*—an effect in which each step in a gradation appears clearly distinguishable from its neighbor. To determine the optimal number of steps for a specific imagesetter, use the following formula:

$$[(dpi \div lpi)^2 + 1] \times \% \Delta c - 2$$

in which *dpi* is the resolution of the printer in dots per inch, *lpi* is the screen frequency in lines per inch, and $\% \Delta c$ is the percentage change in color. For example, the percentage change in color between a 40% source path and a 70% concluding path is 30%. If you intend to print this gradation to a Linotronic 100 with a resolution of 1270 dots per inch and a default frequency of 90 lines per inch, the optimal blends contain 58 steps, because $[(1270 \div 90)^2 + 1] \times 0.3 - 2 = 58$.

If math isn't your strong point, just use the default values Illustrator displays in the BLEND dialog box. For small blends, divide the default value by an integer, such as 2, 3, or 4.

CHAPTER

THE HODGE- PODGE WORLD OF FILTERS

Nearly half of Illustrator 5.0's new features are expressed as commands under the FILTER menu. They affect just about every aspect of your drawing, from creating objects to reshaping objects to transforming objects. In other words, while they have very little to do with each other, they are nonetheless crammed into the same menu. The only tie that binds these commands is the fact that none of them are built into Illustrator. Instead, every one of them originates from an external module located in a folder called Plug-Ins inside the same folder that contains the Illustrator application.

Frankly, I struggled to decide whether to integrate my discussions of the FILTER menu commands into the other chapters in this book or to discuss them in one big lump as I do in this chapter. Though I leaned heavily toward the integrated solution, no matter how I worked it out, there were a handful of commands that didn't fit anywhere, commands that actually qualify as *filters*—which, for what it's worth, are functions that enhance or alter the appearance of selected objects, sort of like a cross between the effects of reshaping and the automation of certain transformation operations. That's what filters are supposed to be anyway. This meant I would have to create a filters chapter of some kind for the leftovers and name it *The Filters that are Actually Filters* or maybe something pompous like *The Way the Filters Menu Ought to Be*. I ultimately decided that a single filters chapter would be less confusing and more helpful for the widest variety of users.

The one exception is that I decided a couple of commands, namely EXPORT and FIND under the TEXT submenu, should go with the text discussion in Chapter 7. No matter how I reasoned it out, those two commands just *had* to stay with the rest of the text features.

Can you sense the inner turmoil at work here? I hope so.

So, anyway, just in case you get lost, which seems unlikely, you'll find every command in this chapter under the FILTERS menu. To keep things simple, most commands get their own sections. I know, I know, it's a very rudimentary organizational structure. I thought it up in the bathroom one day. (Not really, it's a joke.) And it'd be just like the manual, if only the manual did anything close to a decent job of describing the filters. So what you have here is a manual-like approach to a random collection of functions. Get off my case already.

Things you should know

If you can't locate one or more of the commands I describe, read through these items to see what's the matter.

- If your FILTER menu is empty, Illustrator is looking at the wrong folder when loading filter modules. Choose PLUG-INS from the PREFERENCES submenu under the FILE menu. Locate the folder that contains the filter modules and press the RETURN key. Then quit Illustrator and restart the application.

- If you're missing just a few filters, someone—perhaps you before that nasty case of amnesia—has relocated some filters to a different folder. Put them all in the Plug-Ins folder, use the PLUG-INS command to make sure that's where Illustrator is looking for them, quit Illustrator, and restart the application.

- Maybe you didn't install all the filters. See Appendix A for instructions on reinstalling your software.

- Is it just the PATHFINDER filters and a couple of the commands in the OBJECTS submenu that you're missing? Aha! Then the problem is your Mac. The Pathfinder filters require that your machine be equipped with a *math coprocessor* (also called a *floating-point unit*, or *FPU*). If you own an LC, IIsi, or Centris 610, your computer lacks a math coprocessor. You can either try to purchase an FPU, which can be a very expensive and complicated upgrade, or accept that you can't use the PATH-FINDER, OFFSET PATH..., and OUTLINE STROKED PATH filters and get on with your life.

The first command

One more thing before I start describing filters: After you apply a filter, Illustrator makes that filter the first command in the FILTERS menu. The idea is that since you applied it once, you'll probably want to apply it once more, whether because you messed up the first time or because you want to apply the filter to different objects.

KE Press COMMAND-SHIFT-E to reapply the last filter you used. Illustrator applies the filter just as you did before, using the same settings. If the filter previously displayed a dialog box and you want to redisplay that dialog box and change the settings, press the OPTION key while choosing the first command from the FILTERS menu.

Messing around with colors

The COLORS submenu in the FILTERS menu contains filters that affect the colors of fills and, in the case of the last five filters, the colors of strokes. All nine filters work best when the fills or strokes of the selected objects are process colors. For more information on fills and strokes, see Chapters 8 and 9, respectively.

Changing process fills

Choose the ADJUST COLORS... filter to display the ADJUST COLORS dialog box, as shown in Figure 12-1. Here you can adjust the percentage composition of cyan, magenta, yellow, and black in the selected objects. The fill of each selected object must be a process color. If none of the selected objects contain a process fill, a warning box will display informing you that you're messing up. If the selected objects contain an assortment of fills with at least one process fill, all objects not containing a process fill become deselected.

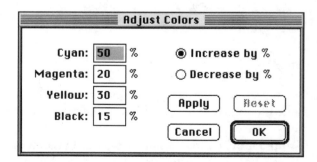

Figure 12-1: The Adjust Colors dialog box allows you to increase or decrease the percent composition of a process fill.

The ADJUST COLORS dialog box allows you to either increase or decrease the selected process fills by the amounts entered in the four percentage option boxes. For example, if you were to assign the values shown in Figure 12-1 to an orange object composed of 20% magenta and 40% yellow, the object would change to 50% cyan, 40% magenta, 70% yellow, and 15% black, better known as really ugly sickly green.

Use this option only when you want to change several differently colored objects by the same degree. Otherwise, it's easier to use the PAINT STYLE palette.

Creating color blends

With at least three objects selected, choosing the BLEND FRONT TO BACK filter assigns the middle selected objects a sequence of intermediate process colors between the fill colors of the frontmost and rearmost objects. For example, suppose you select three objects. The frontmost object's fill consists of C10 M20 Y30 K40 and the rearmost object's breakdown is C70 M80 Y90 K100. After you apply BLEND FRONT TO BACK, the middle objects fill will be C40 M50 Y60 K70. Get it? No? Well, it's just like using the blend tool except that it works after the fact. Rather than creating objects and filling them at the same time, the BLEND FRONT TO BACK filter applies blended fills to objects that already exist between two extremes.

Variations on the BLEND FRONT TO BACK filter include BLEND HORIZONTALLY and BLEND VERTICALLY. With BLEND HORIZONTALLY, Illustrator blends between the colors of the leftmost and rightmost objects in the selection. BLEND VERTICALLY blends between the colors of the top and bottom objects.

Desaturating colors

Applying the DESATURATE filter decreases the percent values of cyan, magenta, yellow, and black in the fill and stroke of all selected objects. The percentages do not decrease uniformly. Instead, they decrease relatively so that, after applying the filter several times in a row, all four colors arrive at zero at the same time. If an object is filled with a spot color, the DESATURATE filter converts the color to its CMYK equivalent and then reduces the CMYK percentages.

The DESATURATE MORE command is just an exaggerated version of the DESATURATE filter. The CMYK values arrive at 0 faster.

If you're familiar with Photoshop, keep in mind that Illustrator's definition of saturation has nothing to do with the *true* definition of saturation. In Photoshop, for example, saturation is the difference between a color picture and a black-and-white picture. The color picture is intensely saturated, the black-and-white picture has no saturation whatsoever. By contrast—no pun intended—Illustrator's strange breed of saturation is the difference between a color picture and a blank white page. Since the levels of cyan, magenta, yellow, and black diminish uniformly, zero saturation results in white.

Inverting colors

When you choose the INVERT COLORS filter, the CMYK values for the fill and stroke of all selected objects change to their opposite values. For example, a fill of C10 M20 Y30 K40 becomes C90 M80 Y70 K60. Black fills and strokes change to white, white ones change to black— it's just like a photographic negative. Only spot colors are unaffected.

Adding saturation

I hope that this isn't too anticlimactic, but as you have probably already guessed, the SATURATE and SATURATE MORE filters work like the DESATURATE and DESATURATE MORE filters except that they *increase* the CMYK percent values for the fill and stroke of all selected objects.

Creating special shapes

The CREATE submenu in the FILTERS menu contains six filters that allow you to create specialized graphic objects. The first and last filters, FILL & STROKE FOR MASK and TRIM MARKS, both create graphic objects based on existing graphic objects in your illustration. The MOSAIC filter requires a PICT file previously created in an image editor such as Photoshop. The other three filters, CREATE POLYGON..., CREATE SPIRAL..., and CREATE STAR..., all produce specialized graphic objects from scratch.

The **Illustrator 5** Book

Adding color to the mask

Back in the *Clipping paths* section of Chapter 8, you may remember, you had to add a stroke to the bomb-pop example because the stroke of the clipping path was lost when you applied the MAKE (MASK) command. To create a stroke then, I told you to copy the rounded trapezoid shape that was the clipping path, paste it in front, and assign a stroke with no fill. Not too difficult, but definitely a pain in the butt.

The FILL & STROKE FOR MASK filter performs this step automatically. Simply select the clipping path (and only the clipping path), assign a new fill and stroke in the PAINT STYLES dialog box, and choose the FILL & STROKE FOR MASK command. An alert box comes up as if you did something wrong, but that's just Illustrator's way of bumping up your blood pressure. Just click on the OK button and everything will be fine. Illustrator creates two clones, both with the same shape as the clipping path. Illustrator assigns the stroke—and only the stroke—to the first clone and places it just in front of the clipping path. The program then assigns the fill to the second clone and places it just behind the masked elements. The end result is a stroked path surrounding your clipping path and an additional fill that shows through the mask from behind the masked elements.

For example, I created the incredibly realistic planet on the right side of Figure 12-2 by applying the MAKE (MASK) command to the objects on the left side of the figure. Next, I selected just the circle that serves as the clipping path, selected a green fill and a black stroke with a 1-point weight from the PAINT STYLE palette, and chose the FILL & STROKE FOR MASK command. The result is shown on the right of Figure 12-3.

In the case of Chapter 8's bomb-pop, the selection of fill would not matter when using this filter since the masked elements (the colored ice chunks) fill the entire clipping path. The easiest thing to do is select a "None" fill and black stroke and Illustrator will then create only one shape with a black stroke in front of the clipping path. In other words, Illustrator will create only one shape when "None" is selected for either the fill or the stroke.

Don't be surprised if you encounter some problems when you first use this filter. During one of my first attempts, I encountered unexpected and wholly undesirable results when I selected both the clipping path and some of the masked elements. An error message displayed and when I pressed RETURN, Illustrator proceeded to wreak havoc on my defenseless graphic. That's why they invented the UNDO command, I guess.

Figure 12-2: After creating the circle and land masses (left), I bring the circle to front and choose the Make (Mask) command, causing both the fill and stroke of the circle to disappear (right).

Figure 12-3: By selecting only the clipping path (left), selecting the appropriate fill and stroke, and choosing the Fill & Stroke for Mask command, I restore the fill and stroke to the circle (right).

⚛ The **Illustrator** 5 Book

Making a mosaic

The CREATE MOSAIC... filter allows you to create a *mosaic* from a file saved in the PICT format. If you have ever dove into a swimming pool that was not deep enough, you probably saw a mosaic right before losing consciousness. It was the group of little square tiles that spelled out "3.6 ft." in black on white. In Figure 12-4 I used a PICT file of a map of the United States—the one in the System 7.1 Scrapbook, in fact—to create the mosaic.

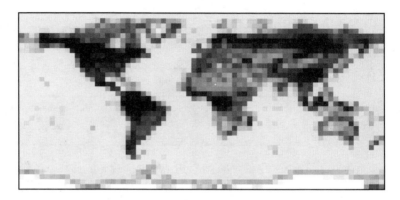

Figure 12-4: The Create Mosaic... filter allows you to create mosaics consisting of rectangles that mimic the image in a PICT file.

Choose the CREATE MOSAIC... filter to display a typical OPEN dialog box that shows only files saved in the PICT format. Double-click on one of the files. The OPEN dialog box disappears and the MOSAIC dialog box appears, as shown in Figure 12-5, showing the dimensions of the image in the PICT file in points. Here you enter the dimensions of the mosaic picture in the "New Size" option boxes. You can elect to have the rectangles that make up the mosaic fit snugly together, or you can enter the amount of space you want between the rectangles in the "Tile Spacing" option boxes. Enter the number of rectangles you want to make up the mosaic horizontally and vertically in the "Number of Tiles" option boxes.

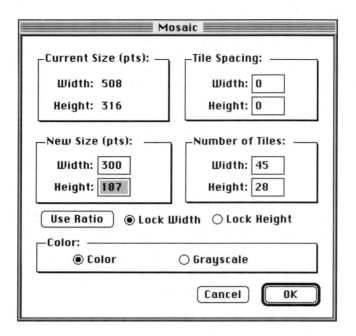

Figure 12-5: The Mosaic dialog box allows you to control the size of the mosaic, the number of and the space between rectangles in the mosaic, and the color of the mosaic.

If you want the "New Size" and the "Number of Tiles" values to conform to the ratio of the original image (represented by the "Current Size" numbers), then first enter the desired values into either the two "Width" or the two "Height" option boxes. For example, maybe you know that you want the mosaic to be 300 points wide with 30 tiles. Next, click on either the "Lock Width" or the "Lock Height" radio button, whichever conforms to the values you just changed. And finally, click on the USE RATIO button and the option boxes that you did *not* assign values to change in accordance to the ratio of the original image. For example in Figure 12-5, I entered 300 into the "New Size Width" option box and 45 into the "Number of Tiles Width" option box. I then selected the "Lock Width" radio button and clicked on the USE RATIO button. The values in the two "Height" option boxes changed automatically in accordance with the ratio of the PICT image.

Equilateral polygons

Choose the CREATE POLYGON... filter to display the POLYGON dialog box, as shown in Figure 12-6. Here you can enter the number of sides that you want to assign to your equilateral regular polygon and the radius of the polygon. An *equilateral polygon*, incidentally, is a multisided shape in which all the sides are the same length and all the internal angles are equal. The polygon must have at least three sides and no more than 4,000 sides. (A polygon with that many sides would look for all the world like a circle so what's the point?) You can assign a "Radius" value as large as 4,000 points. The radius is the distance from the center point to any one of the anchor points along the outline of the shape. Click on the OK button or press RETURN and Illustrator creates the polygon you specified, using the fill and stroke attributes from the PAINT STYLES palette.

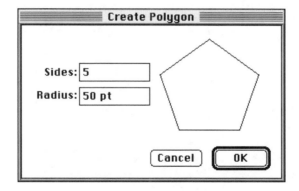

Figure 12-6: You can assign the number of sides and the radius of your equilateral polygon in the Create Polygon dialog box.

Spiraling lines

Choose the CREATE SPIRAL... filter to display the CREATE SPIRAL dialog box, which appears in Figure 12-7. The "Winds" value represents the number of times that the line loops around the center of the spiral. The "Radius" value is the distance from the center to the end of the line. In Figure 12-8, I've represented the center as an ×. Both values

---

can be as high as 4,000. After you click on the OK button or press RETURN, Illustrator creates a spiral as you have specified, using the fill and stroke attributes in the PAINT STYLES dialog box.

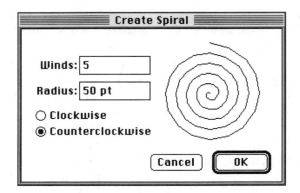

Figure 12-7: You assign the number of winds and the radius of your spiral in the Create Spiral dialog box.

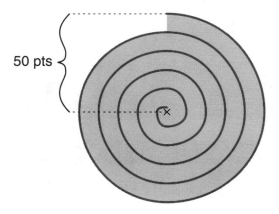

Figure 12-8: This is the result of clicking on the OK button in the Create Spiral dialog box shown above. The radius of the spiral is the distance from the center point, marked by the ×, to the last point on the outside of the spiral.

The **Illustrator** 5 Book

One final note about this filter: If you enter 1 for the number of loops, you can get a good start on Groucho's nose from Chapter 4. You would need to create a second 1-loop spiral positioned just to the right of the first spiral and reshape this spiral with the direct-selection tool. Finally, join the endpoints of the two paths to create a calligraphic line. It may not be exactly what you want, but it's a heck of a lot easier than drawing one from scratch.

Star shapes

Choose the CREATE STAR... filter to display the CREATE STAR dialog box shown in Figure 12-9. Here you can enter the number of points you want on your star and the distances for the "1st Radius" and "2nd Radius" values. Your star must have at least 3 points and no more than 4,000. Each of the "Radius" values can be up to 4,000 points. The first radius is the distance from the center of the star to any one of the outer points. The second radius is the distance from the center of the star to any one of the inner points. This, of course, assumes that the first radius is larger than the second. If the second radius is larger, it goes to the outer points instead. In Figure 12-11, I created a star with the CREATE STAR dialog box shown below. The small × marks the center point. Each radius is labeled.

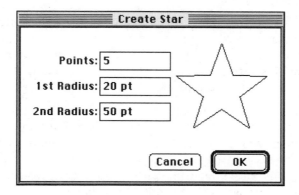

Figure 12-9: You assign the number of points and the first and second "Radius" values of your star in the Create Star dialog box.

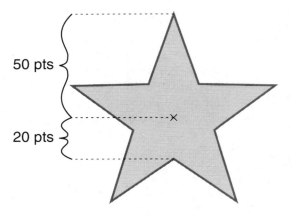

50 pts

20 pts

Figure 12-10: This is the result of applying the settings shown in Figure 12-9. Both the first and second "Radius" values are measured from the center point.

Adding trim marks

When you choose the TRIM MARKS filter, eight lines appear that just encompass the selected objects, as shown in Figure 12-11. Both examples in the figure show the rectangles that the trim marks are based on. These rectangles don't print; I added them to the figure merely to demonstrate the origin of the trim marks.

Trim marks, incidentally, are not the same as crop marks. Where only one set of crop marks can exist in an illustration at a time, multiple sets of trim marks can appear in an illustration. Crop marks cannot be selected or manipulated. You can manipulate trim marks just like any other graphic elements.

When you print multiple pieces of artwork that you want to ultimately cut apart into the individual graphics, the trim marks serve as guides for the cutting. For example, if you want to design your own business cards, you would probably create eight to ten cards per page. By assigning trim marks around each, you create convenient guides for cutting, especially if you have access to one of those big paper cutters that seem to be required equipment in any elementary school front office. You know, it used to sit right next to the mimeograph machine, that antiquated copier that printed those wonderfully aromatic blue pages. I swear, that's why kids don't do as well on tests these days. They can't sniff the paper for inspiration.

The **Illustrator 5** Book

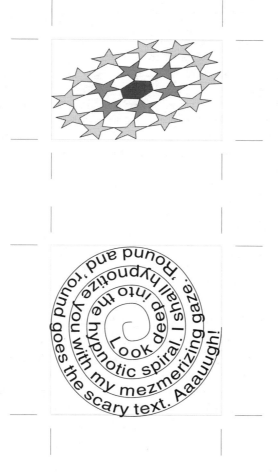

Figure 12-11: I want to cut these two images out after I print them. Adding the trim marks gives me convenient guides to cut along.

Uh, sorry, sort of got off the subject there. (Ahem.) Trim marks are created as eight grouped lines. If you don't need all eight lines, or if lines from multiple trim marks overlap, you can manipulate the trim marks with the direct-selection tool or ungroup the trim marks and delete a few. If you are planning to move artwork that has trim marks, you'll probably want to group the artwork and trim marks to keep them together.

The way filters ought to be

To paraphrase a certain well-fed talk-show host—if one can call a show where a guy sits around and talks about *himself* for an hour a talk show (not that he *likes* to talk about himself, noooo, it's just sort of a compulsion)—where was I? Oh, yeah, to paraphrase etc. etc., the DISTORT submenu offers the first glimpse of the way the FILTERS menu ought to be. With the exception of the FREE DISTORT... command, which really transforms a selected object, the other commands in this submenu take an object and mess it up in the finest of filtering traditions. Imagine, for example, the Great Limboid himself subject to the ROUGHEN filter. Truly a sight to behold.

(To those who are offended by the previous paragraph, I apologize. But I figure a guy who refuses to call the President of the United States anything besides Slick Willy—regardless of the President's party affiliation—deserves to be ribbed. Assuming you can reach his ribs, of course.)

Distortion in a dialog box

To use the FREE DISTORT... filter, select one or more objects in your illustration and choose the filter from the DISTORT submenu. The FREE DISTORT dialog box will display, as shown in the first example of Figure 12-12, which allows you to distort the selected objects, similarly to how you can distort objects with the direct-selection tool. The difference is that in the FREE DISTORT dialog box, you distort the selected objects as though they were printed on a rectangular sheet of impossibly flexible material.

In the FREE DISTORT dialog box, the selected objects will display by default inside the rectangle. The objects appear without either fill or stroke—as in the artwork mode—so overlapping objects may look a bit different in the FREE DISTORT dialog box than they do in the preview mode. To distort the objects in the dialog box, click and drag on one of the four corner handles. You can drag the handles in any direction. You can even drag outside the boundaries of the dialog box, as shown in the second example of Figure 12-12. However, if you do so, you won't be able to retrieve the handle except by clicking on the RESET button to restore the rectangle.

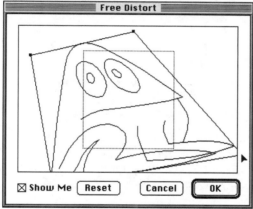

Figure 12-12: The Free Distort dialog box allows you to drag on any of the four corners of the rectangular boundary to distort the selected objects.

If you use the FREE DISTORT... filter to distort an object and then apply the filter later to second object, the rectangular boundary shows the result of the first distortion, thus allowing you to repeat the same distortion several times. If you do *not* want to work from the previous distortion, simply click on the RESET button to return the boundary to a rectangle.

If you want to see the rectangular boundary without the selected object, deselect the "Show Me" check box. You'll only want to do this when distorting very complex objects that take a long time to display.

Roughing it

The ROUGHEN... filter adds points to the selected objects and then moves each point in a random direction, granting your artwork a serrated, spiky look. When you choose the ROUGHEN... command, the ROUGHEN dialog box appears, as shown in Figure 12-13.

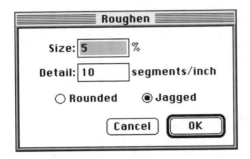

Figure 12-13: In the Roughen dialog box enter the number of points that you want for every inch of segment and the amount that you want every point moved.

The value you enter into the "Detail" option box determines the number of points that Illustrator adds to each inch of segment. For example, if you have a 3-by-2-inch rectangle and you enter 5 into the "Detail" option box, then the rectangle will have a total of 50 points — 5 points times a total of 10 inches of segments. The value you enter into the "Size" option box is the distance—expressed as a percentage of the longest segment in each selected object—that each point will move. Selecting the "Rounded" radio button converts the points of all selected objects into smooth points (except endpoints of open paths), while selecting the "Jagged" option makes them all corner points.

After the points are added to the selected objects, the ROUGHEN... filter moves each point. Each point is moved in a random direction and a distance less than or equal to the "Size" value. In Figure 12-14,

I applied the ROUGHEN... filter to a single 1-by-2-inch rectangle in all nine examples. In the top row, with the "Jagged" radio button selected, I used a "Detail" value of 10 for each and a "Size" value of 5, 10, and 20, respectively. So in the first example, each point was moved in a random direction, up to 0.1 inch—5% of 2 inches. In the second example, each point moved up to 0.2 inch in a random direction; in the third, 0.4 inch is the maximum. In the second row of examples, I varied the "Detail" values while keeping the "Size" value fixed. It gives them that cool treasure map look, don't you think? The third row of examples is the same as the first row except that the "Rounded" radio button is selected.

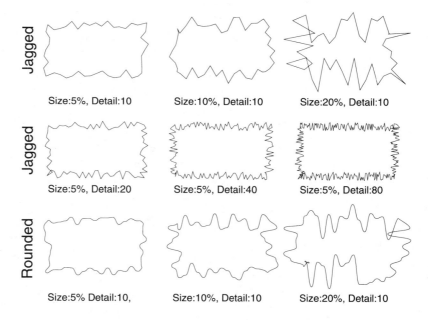

Figure 12-14: Nine rectangles subject to the whims of the Roughen filter.

That English dish, scribble and tweak

Actually, the dish is called *bubble and squeak*, but the SCRIBBLE... and TWEAK... filters offer access to the next best thing. Unlike the ROUGHEN... filter, neither the SCRIBBLE... nor the TWEAK... filter adds points to selected objects. Rather, they both move existing points as well as Bézier control handles in random directions and distances. Choose either SCRIBBLE... or TWEAK... from the DISTORT submenu to display the corresponding dialog box, as shown in Figure 12-15. The two dialog boxes offer the same function. The only difference is that the move executed by the SCRIBBLE... filter is measured as a percentage of the longest segment (as with the ROUGHEN... filter), while the TWEAK... filter measures movement in points, inches, or centimeters.

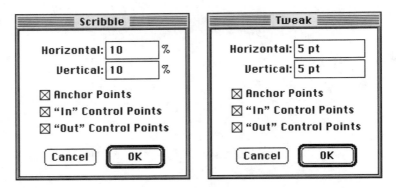

Figure 12-15: The Scribble and Tweak dialog boxes offer the same options. They just measure their moves differently.

Now, before I discuss how the specific options work, I need to mention an additional point about Bézier control handles. Each handle can be categorized as *in* or *out*, or better yet, *innies* and *outties*, like belly buttons, depending on whether it's associated with the segment going into the point or out from the point. This idea is illustrated in Figure 12-16, which shows an open path consisting of three points. The path was drawn from left to right. The middle point is a smooth point with two Bézier control handles. The left one is an innie control handle, so named because it's on the side of the point where the segment goes into the point. The right one is an outtie control handle, because it's on the outgoing side of the point. These are the same "In" and "Out" referred to in the SCRIBBLE and TWEAK dialog boxes.

Select the "Anchor Points" check box to move the points of the selected objects. Select the "'In' Control Points" to move all innie control handles and select the "'Out' Control Points" to move all outtie handles. If you want to move all Bézier control handles regardless of

The **Illustrator 5** Book

where they lie, select both options. If a corner handle doesn't have any control handles, Illustrator obligingly adds control handles and then moves them independently of one another. In Figure 12-17, for example, after I applied the CREATE OUTLINE command to some type, I applied the SCRIBBLE... filter with both the "'In' Control Points" and the "'Out' Control Points" options selected. As a result, Illustrator gave all corner points—like the ones along the once-straight sides of the *i*, *l*, and *T*—Bézier control handles so that each of them could be moved.

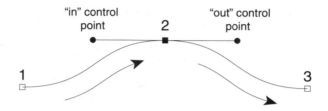

Figure 12-16: A Bézier control handle can be thought of as either an innie or an outtie, depending on whether it is on the in-going or outgoing side of a point.

Figure 12-17: "Wow," says your friend, "I didn't know that you could use your computer while driving a 4 × 4 over rocky terrain!"

The Scribble... and Tweak... filters work best on objects that contain many points. In the figure above, I prepared the letters by applying the Add Anchor Points filter three times to ensure that I got a realistically scribbly appearance.

Hanging ten the easy way

With the Twirl... filter, you can give a selected object a wavy appearance. Choose the Twirl... filter to display a dialog box containing a single "Angle" option. If you get a dialog box with a warning, Illustrator doesn't think you have enough points to work with. To optimize the filter's performance, click on the Cancel button, choose the Add Anchor Points filter a couple of times, and again apply the Twirl... filter.

The Twirl... filter transforms the selected objects by rotating all the points around the center. The nearer the point is to the center, the more the point moves. It's sort of like twirling spaghetti around a fork. Say you have a straight strand of thin spaghetti stuck in the fork's prongs. As you twirl the fork, the part of the spaghetti strand that is closest to the fork rotates more than the parts that are further away. Now imagine the you can twirl your fork anywhere from –4,000° to 4,000°, and you have the Twirl... filter.

A positive value in the "Angle" option box produces a clockwise twirl; a negative value produces a counterclockwise twirl. If multiple objects are selected, they are all rotated around the same center. Figure 12-18 shows a sample application of the Twirl filter. I selected the objects on the right, chose Add Anchor Points three times in a row, and then applied the Twirl filter with an "Angle" value to 300°.

Figure 12-18: The Twirl filter can produce automatic yin yang.

A random collection of filters

The commands under the OBJECTS submenu don't have an awful lot to do with one another. The first filter simply adds points to selected objects. The next three filters move the selected objects to align or distribute them. The MOVE EACH..., ROTATE EACH..., and SCALE EACH... filters allow you to transform several selected objects individually. And the two filters nestled between MOVE EACH... and ROTATE EACH... do special things to the outline of a path. If these commands do not appear in your OBJECTS submenu, it's because you don't have an FPU chip, as I described at the beginning of this chapter.

Doubling the points in a path

Choose ADD ANCHOR POINTS to double the number of points in a selected path. One point is added midway between each pair of points in the path. Illustrator makes the new points smooth points or corner points depending on the identity of the existing points in the path.

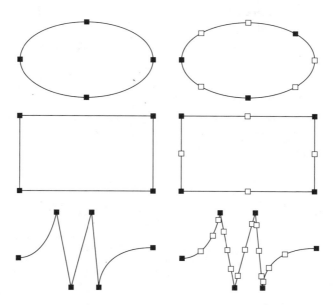

Figure 12-19: The results of applying the Add Anchor Points filter to three paths. The original paths appear on the left, the new paths appear on the right. The new points appear as hollow.

In Figure 12-19 on the previous page, for example, the ellipse gains four smooth points and the rectangle gains four corner points. I applied the ADD ANCHOR POINTS filter twice to the open path at the bottom of the figure. This resulted in three new smooth points along each curved segment and three new corner points along each straight segment.

Note that ADD ANCHOR POINTS has no immediate effect on the appearance of a path. Its primary purpose is to prepare a path for the application of other filters, especially those in the DISTORT submenu.

Aligning and distributing objects

Choose the ALIGN OBJECTS... command to display the ALIGN OBJECTS dialog box, as shown in Figure 12-20. Here you can align or distribute two or more selected objects horizontally, vertically, or both.

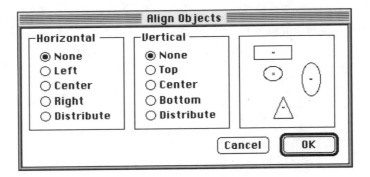

Figure 12-20: The Align Objects dialog box lets you to align selected objects horizontally, vertically, or both. Here you can also opt to distribute the aligned objects.

The "Horizontal" radio buttons let you align selected objects along their left or right sides or down the middle. You can also distribute them evenly from left to right.

- Selecting the "Left" radio button moves all the selected objects so that the left sides of the objects align in perfect formation.

- When you select the "Center" option, Illustrator averages the centers of all selected objects and then aligns them in formation.

- Selecting the "Right" radio button aligns the right sides of the selected objects.

The **Illustrator** 5 Book

- Select the "Distribute" radio button to arrange the selected objects at regular intervals between the far left and far right objects in the selection.

The "Vertical" radio buttons work similarly, except from top to bottom. It's worth noting that if you select alignment options—excluding the "Distribute" radio buttons—from both the "Horizontal" and "Vertical" lists, the selected objects will overlap to some extent or other. Generally, you just want to select an option from a single list and leave the other list set to "None." The only exception is the "Distribute" options. If you select both of these, Illustrator evenly distributes the selected objects both horizontally and vertically.

The DISTRIBUTE HORIZONTALLY filter works exactly as if you had chosen the ALIGN OBJECTS... filter and selected the "Distribute" radio button from the "Horizontal" list and the "None" radio button from the "Vertical" list. The top row of Figure 12-21 shows a series of five objects prior to distribution. The bottom row shows the same objects after applying the DISTRIBUTE HORIZONTALLY filter. The dotted lines show how the three objects in the middle move so they are equal distances apart while the left and right objects remain stationary.

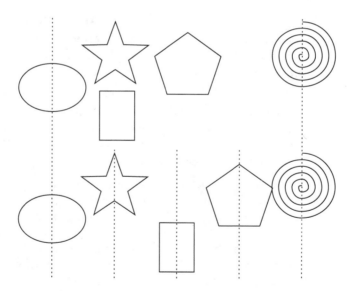

Figure 12-21: With at least three objects selected, the Distribute Horizontally filter repositions the middle objects at regular intervals between the far left and far right objects.

The DISTRIBUTE VERTICALLY filter works exactly as if you had chosen the ALIGN OBJECTS... filter and selected the "Distribute" radio button from the "Vertical" list and the "None" radio button from the "Horizontal" list. Big surprise.

Moving objects randomly

The MOVE EACH... filter works a lot like the MOVE dialog box. But unlike the MOVE dialog box, which affects only selected points, the MOVE EACH... filter affects all points of the selected objects regardless of how many points are selected. Also, the MOVE EACH dialog box provides a "Random" check box, which is missing from the standard MOVE dialog box. When the "Random" check box is selected, Illustrator moves the selected objects random distances within the confines of the values set in the "Horizontal" and "Vertical" option boxes. For example, say the values in the "Horizontal" and "Vertical" option boxes are 20 and 35 points, respectively. With "Random" selected, the objects move anywhere between 20 points left or right and 35 points up or down.

Offsetting paths and outlining strokes

Both of the filters I'm about to describe require that your computer be equipped with an FPU, as I explained at the beginning of this chapter. If you use an LC, IIsi, or Centris 610, you'll probably want to skip to the next section.

The OFFSET PATH... command traces a new path around the selected path according to your specifications. The filter generally works best if you select only one closed path. The filter can really misbehave when applied to open paths.

When you choose OFFSET PATH..., Illustrator displays the dialog box shown in Figure 12-22. Enter the distance between the new path and the original in the "Offset" option box. A positive value creates a path around the outside of the selected object; a negative value traces the inside of the object. Select an option from the "Line Join" pop-up menu to determine the appearance of the corners of the traced path. And enter a value into the "Miter limit" option box to specify the point at which Illustrator bevels off overly sharp corners. Figure 12-23 shows the result of applying the settings from Figure 12-22 three times in succession.

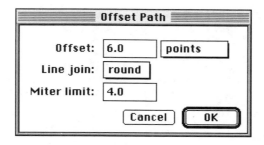

Figure 12-22: The Offset Path dialog box enables you to trace a selected object with a new path.

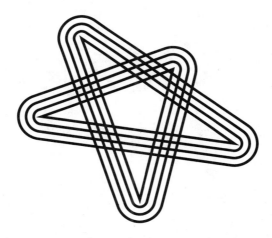

Figure 12-23: The result of tracing a hand-drawn star three times using the settings in the previous figure.

The OUTLINE STROKED PATH filter automatically traces around the stroke of a selected object using a compound path. Figure 12-24 on the next page shows a path with a 9-point stroke, followed by the same path after applying the OUTLINE STROKED PATH command. I've taken the liberty of applying a transparent fill and thin black stroke to the traced object so you can see the structure of the new compound path. If I hadn't changed the fill and stroke, the two objects would appear identical.

Figure 12-24: Objects with 9-point strokes (left) and the same objects traced with the Outline Stroked Path command.

You might think that one of the uses for this filter would be to create calligraphic outlines. Unfortunately, editing the outline paths can be more than a little difficult thanks to Illustrator's unusual approach to tracing the joins. So I recommend you use the Outline Stroked Path filter under two conditions. First, if you want to stroke a path with a gradation, you can apply the command and then select a gradient fill from the Paint Styles dialog box. Second, you can create variable line weight effects by scaling an outline path. The bottom examples of Figure 12-24, for example, show the results of scaling both a stroked path and an outline path 200% vertically. While the outline of the stroked path remains uniform, the outline path becomes distorted.

🔬 The **Illustrator** 5 Book

Rotating and scaling objects independently

The ROTATE EACH... filter works just like the MOVE EACH... filter, except that it actually has a purpose. Unlike the rotate tool, which rotates all selected objects about a single rotation origin, the ROTATE EACH dialog box rotates each selected object independently around its center. Figure 12-25 shows three rectangle with drop shadows, followed by the same rectangles rotated first with the rotate tool and next with the ROTATE EACH filter. Notice that the independently rotated rectangles remain in their original positions.

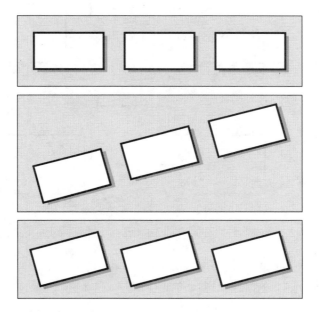

Figure 12-25: Three rectangles (top) rotated with the rotate tool (middle) and the Rotate Each command (bottom).

Likewise, the SCALE EACH filter scales each selected object independently around its center. Figure 12-26 on the following page shows how this works. Notice that when you use the scale tool, you scale the gaps between selected objects as well as the objects themselves. When using the SCALE EACH filter, gaps are ignored.

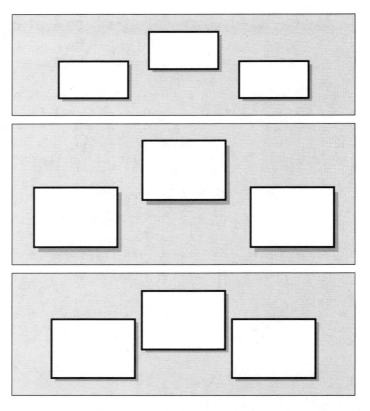

Figure 12-26: Three rectangles (top) scaled with the scale tool (middle) and the Scale Each command (bottom). I scaled the shapes 120% horizontally and 160% vertically.

The SCALE EACH filter is quite honestly something I've been hoping Illustrator would add since I was a toddler. It's really a lifesaver. For example, consider this: When I first created Figure 12-19, I represented the points in the figure using 3-by-3-point squares. After placing the graphic into PageMaker and scaling it down to size, the points were too small. I now wanted them to be 6-by-6-point squares. In the old days, I would have had to scale each square separately. Generally in these cases, I would have just redrawn a single square and cloned it several billion times. With Illustrator 5.0, I just selected all the squares and applied the SCALE EACH filter at 200%. Not only does it save time, it saves considerable frustration.

Both the ROTATE EACH and SCALE EACH dialog boxes provide "Random" check boxes for transforming objects randomly within the confines specified by the option box values. Also, these commands affect entire objects, even if you have selected specific points and segments with the direct-selection tool.

Combining objects

The PATHFINDER submenu is available only if your computer is equipped with an FPU. If you own an LC, IIsi, or Centris 610, you're out of luck. See the beginning of this chapter for complete information.

All right, the commands under the PATHFINDER submenu enable you to combine objects with each other to create variations on those objects. The objects must overlap to take advantage of these commands. For example, let's say you want to draw a chunk of Swiss cheese with a hole cut into the side of it. Draw a rectangle, draw a circle that partially overlaps the rectangle, then select both shapes and choose the BACK MINUS FRONT filter.

Here are the filters in the PATHFINDER submenu and how they work:

- **Unite** fuses the selected objects into a single object in which overlapping strokes are removed. The final object takes on the paint attributes of the original foreground object. Figure 12-27 on the next page shows an example of this filter, as well as of the four that follow.

- **Intersect** forms an object out of each overlapping region of the selected objects. If more than one shape is formed, the shapes are automatically grouped. Each of the final objects takes on the paint attributes of the original foreground object.

- **Exclude** forms an object out of each non-overlapping region of the selected objects. This is just the opposite effect of the INTERSECT filter. Once again, all shapes are grouped automatically and each of the final objects takes on the paint attributes of the original foreground object.

- **Back Minus Front** removes everything but the non-overlapping regions of the rearmost object. The remaining paths are automatically converted to shapes and grouped. The final objects take on the paint attributes of the original background object.

- **Front To Back** removes everything but the non-overlapping regions of the frontmost object. The remaining paths are automatically converted to shapes and grouped. The final objects take on the paint attributes of the original foreground object.

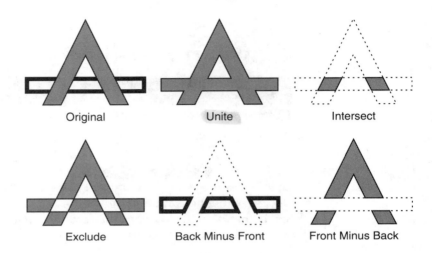

| Original | Unite | Intersect |

| Exclude | Back Minus Front | Front Minus Back |

Figure 12-27: Examples of the five filters in the Combine section of the Pathfinder submenu.

- **Divide Fill** breaks up all overlapping and non-overlapping regions of the selected objects into individual shapes. All the new shapes get no stroke and are filled so that they look as they did before. For example, in Figure 12-28, the second example in the top row shows the result of the DIVIDE FILL filter. The fill of each shape matches the fill of the original object from which it was divided. All the final shapes are automatically grouped.

- **Divide Stroke** breaks up all overlapping regions of the selected objects into individual open paths. All the new paths get no fill and are stroked with the fill of the closest original object. In Figure 12-28, for example, the mess of lines on the right side of the top row is the result of the DIVIDE STROKE filter. The strokes of the open paths each receive the color of the fill of the circle that was closest in the layering order of the three circles. Strangely enough, each path is assigned a 1-point line weight despite the line weights of the original objects. All the open paths are automatically grouped.

🜚 The **Illustrator** 5 Book

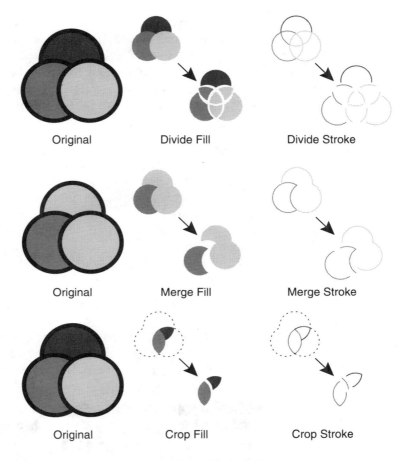

Original	Divide Fill	Divide Stroke
Original	Merge Fill	Merge Stroke
Original	Crop Fill	Crop Stroke

Figure 12-28: Examples of the six filters in the Divide/Merge and Crop sections of the Pathfinder submenu. The arrows point to the separated versions of the divided, merged, and cropped shapes.

- **Merge Fill** fuses all the selected overlapping objects that have the same fill as the frontmost object into a single shape. Any of the selected objects that have a different fill are clipped into their own shapes. The center example in Figure 12-28 shows that the front and back circles fuse into one shape and the other circle becomes an independent shape. All new shapes get no stroke and are automatically grouped.

- **Merge Stroke** fuses all selected overlapping objects that have the same fill as the frontmost object into a single open path. Differently filled objects are separated into distinct open paths. The strokes of the open paths each receive their colors from the fills of the original objects. Each path is automatically assigned a 1-point line weight. All the open paths are automatically grouped.

- **Crop Fill** forms a shape out of each region in which the frontmost (and only frontmost) object in the selection overlaps one or more other selected objects. Each new shape gets no stroke, but retains the fill of the original background object. The middle shapes in the bottom row of Figure 12-28 were clipped from the two original circles that were behind the front circle. It's as if the front circle were a cookie cutter and the two rear circles were the dough. And no chocolate chips. All new shapes are automatically grouped.

- **Crop Stroke** forms open paths out of each region in which the frontmost object in the selection overlaps one or more other selected objects. The strokes of the open paths each receive their colors from the fills of the original objects. Each path is automatically assigned a 1-point line weight. All the open paths are automatically grouped.

- **Mix Hard** simulates how the colors of selected objects will look when printed if you have the "Overprint" option selected in the PAINT STYLES dialog box. If two objects overlap, the overlapping region's fill is a mix of the darkest CMYK values. For example, if you have two overlapping objects, one filled with C10 M20 Y80 K90 and the other filled with C90 M80 Y70 K60, choosing MIX HARD creates an intersecting object filled with C90 M80 Y80 K90. It takes the darkest values for each of the primary colors, just like an overprint.

- **Mix Soft** allows you to change the transparency of the overlapping regions of the selected objects. In the MIX SOFT dialog box, enter a percent in the poorly named "Rate" option box. The option should really be named "Transparency." A value of 0% means that the frontmost object is not transparent at all and thus entirely opaque; a value of 100% makes the frontmost object entirely transparent. Values in between mix the colors in the frontmost object with those of other objects in the selection, as demonstrated in Figure 12-29. Strokes are deleted and the selected objects are grouped.

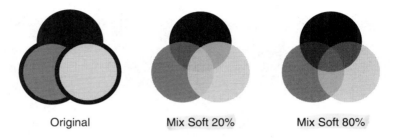

| Original | Mix Soft 20% | Mix Soft 80% |

Figure 12-29: Two examples of the Mix Soft… filter applied at different percentages.

Selecting elements automatically

The SELECT submenu offers seven filters that provide unique and helpful methods for selecting elements in your illustration. The first four filters select graphic objects based on similar paint style attributes. The fifth filter switches the selected status of all objects in your illustration. And the last two filters select specialized objects.

Selecting objects with the same fill

The SAME FILL COLOR filter selects all graphic objects that are filled with the color or gradation that is currently active in the PAINT STYLE palette. For some reason, the filter does not select text objects (nor do any of the other filters in this submenu except SELECT INVERSE) nor is it sensitive to tile patterns.

To use the filter, start by getting the desired color or gradient into the "Fill" box in the PAINT STYLE palette. The easiest way to do this is to click with a selection tool or the eyedropper tool on an object that contains the desired fill. Next, choose the SAME FILL COLOR filter. Illustrator then selects all graphic objects in your illustration that have this fill. Any stroke is ignored. Once the objects are selected, you can manipulate them as desired.

The SAME FILL COLOR filter is very useful for changing the colors used in your illustration. For example, in Figure 12-30, I decided that the two darker grays in the image on the left were too dark to suit my peculiar needs. I selected one of the objects filled with the darkest gray, chose SAME FILL COLOR to select the others, and used the options in the PAINT STYLE palette to specify a more appropriate gray. After repeating this process for the objects filled with the next darkest shade of gray, I arrived at the far more aesthetically pleasing image on the right.

Figure 12-30: Using the Same Fill Color filter, I easily changed all the occurrences of the two darkest gray fills in the left-hand illustration.

Selecting objects with the same fill and stroke

The SAME PAINT STYLE filter selects all graphic objects that share the same fill, stroke, and line weight attributes that are displayed in the PAINT STYLE palette. This filter combines the functions of the SAME FILL COLOR, SAME STROKE COLOR, and SAME STROKE WEIGHT filters, the last two of which I discuss below.

Selecting objects with the same stroke

The SAME STROKE COLOR filter selects all graphic objects that are stroked with the stroke color that is currently active in the PAINT STYLE palette. This filter ignores line weight, caps, joins, and all other stroke attributes except color.

If you want to select all objects that are stroked with a certain line weight, click on an object with that line weight with a selection tool or the eyedropper tool and choose the SAME STROKE WEIGHT filter. This filter ignores color, caps, joins, and everything else except line weight.

Selecting what's not selected and deselecting what is

The SELECT INVERSE filter is a handy command that allows you to quickly select many unrelated objects in your illustration. Choose the filter to select all objects that are *not* selected—both graphic objects and text—and deselect all objects that *are* selected.

This is especially useful if you want to select most of the objects in a complicated drawing. Oh sure, you could select everything with the SELECT ALL command and then SHIFT-click on each of the objects that you don't want to select. The problem is that it can be rather difficult to SHIFT-click on the right objects when so many of them overlap. You might find yourself clicking and reclicking on the same objects because you can't get to the object that you want to deselect. So instead, SHIFT-click on all the objects that you ultimately don't want to select and then choose the SELECT INVERSE filter. Believe me, it can't be much easier.

Selecting other stuff

Choose the SELECT MASKS filter to select all the clipping paths in your illustration. The masked elements (the objects inside the clipping path) will not become selected. This command is useful for selecting the masks prior to applying the FILL & STROKE FOR MASK filter. Other than that, it's just there in case you need it.

The SELECT STRAY POINTS filter is primarily designed to help you clean up your illustration. Inadvertently clicking with either the pen tool or the freehand tool can sometimes leave a single point in the file. To delete such points, choose the SELECT STRAY POINTS filter and press DELETE. The command is especially useful for getting rid of gunk created by illustrators who are less careful than you.

Some more real filters

The last group of filters I'll be discussing are those in the STYLIZE submenu. Like the filters in the DISTORT submenu, many of these qualify as real filters, commands that thoroughly abuse selected objects in some automated fashion or other. The first, third, and fourth filters—ADD ARROWHEADS, CALLIGRAPHY, and DROP SHADOWS—are the enhancement options. You can tack on arrowheads, make the object look like it was drawn with a calligraphic pen, and add dopey little drop shadows. The other three filters change the appearance of the selected objects by moving points and changing the curvature of segments, much like the filters from the DISTORT submenu.

Fashioning arrowheads without flint

The ADD ARROWHEADS... filter allows you to add predefined arrowheads to open paths in your illustration. (Don't bother assigning arrowheads to closed paths; it just won't work.) To use this filter, select an open path and choose the ADD ARROWHEADS... command. The ADD ARROWHEADS dialog box displays, as shown in Figure 12-31. Scroll through the different arrowhead choices by clicking on the two hand icons. When you have found an acceptable arrowhead, select whether the arrowhead will appear at the beginning, at the end, or at both ends of the open path by clicking on the corresponding radio button. If you want to change the size of the arrowhead, enter the desired percentage value into the "Scale" option box. Click on the OK button or press RETURN to add the arrowheads to the selected paths.

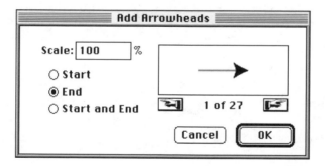

Figure 12-31: The Add Arrowheads dialog box allows you to select from 27 different arrowheads that you can add to either end of an open path.

The ADD ARROWHEADS... filter provides 27 arrowheads. Illustrator automatically groups the arrowheads with the open path to which they are added. The arrowheads also take on the color of the path's stroke.

The left portion of Figure 12-32 shows a few examples of some possible arrowheads, all scaled to 100%. The figure demonstrates that, in addition to the scaling value you enter, the sizes of arrowheads depend on the line weights. For example, the right-hand path in Figure 12-32 features a 5-point gray line with two arrowheads. The arrowheads on the right are larger that those on the left because the path on the right is thicker than any of the paths on the left.

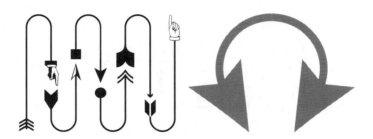

Figure 12-32: The arrowheads on the left are smaller than the ones on the right because the paths on the left are stroked with a thinner line weight.

What happens when you eat too much salt

The BLOAT... filter distorts the selected object by moving the points inward and rounding the segments outward. Choosing the BLOAT... filter displays a dialog box that contains a single "Amount" option box. Here you enter the percentage by which you want the selected object to bloat. This percentage represents the distance that the points move toward the center of the object as well as the distance that the Bézier control handles move away from the center. In Figure 12-33 on the following page, for example, the BLOAT... filter was applied to the shapes along the top of the figure. For the rectangle, I bloated it by 10%. This means that each of the four corner points moved inward by a distance of 10% of its original distance from the center point. Conversely, the control handles go outward by 10%, creating a sort of blobular effect. Negative values move the points in the object outward from the center point and the Bézier control handles inward (like the PUNK... filter, described on page 536).

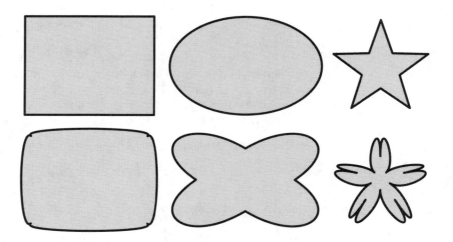

Figure 12-33: I created the bottom shapes by bloating the top ones by 10%, 35%, and 50%, respectively.

Giving it that calligraphic touch

The CALLIGRAPHY... filter lets you transform any path into a calligraphic stroke. Choose the CALLIGRAPHY... filter to display a dialog box with two option boxes, "Pen Width" and "Pen Angle." Enter the thickness of the stroke into the "Pen Width" option box and the angle of the stroke into the "Pen Angle" option box. These options function just like the "Width" and "Calligraphic angle" options in the BRUSH dialog box. To see how these work, read *The brush tool* section in Chapter 5.

The CALLIGRAPHY... filter generally works best on paths that don't have sharp corners. Since the CALLIGRAPHY... filter creates its illusion by duplicating the selected object and forming a compound path out of the two paths, it leaves gaps around sharp corners. Also, applying the CALLIGRAPHY... filter to compound paths (such as type that has been converted to graphic objects with the CREATE OUTLINE command in the TYPE menu) will not give them a calligraphic appearance. Nevertheless, it does add an interesting effect to the text, as shown in Figure 12-34.

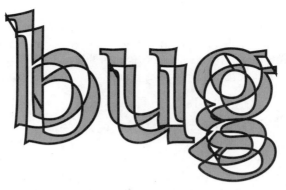

Figure 12-34: After converting this text to paths, I applied the Calligraphy... filter. The effect isn't exactly calligraphic, but it's pretty darn cool.

Taking the work out of drop shadows

The DROP SHADOW... filter lets you add drop shadows to selected objects. A drop shadow gives the appearance that the selected object is floating above the page. Choose DROP SHADOW... to display the DROP SHADOW dialog box, as shown in Figure 12-35. Here you enter the distance between the drop shadow and the object. Enter the horizontal distance in the "X Offset" option box and the vertical distance in the "Y Offset" option box. Illustrator colors the shadow with a darkened shade of the color that fills the object. You can specify how much darker the shadow is by entering a value into the "Darker" option box. A value of 100% guarantees that the shadow will be solid black.

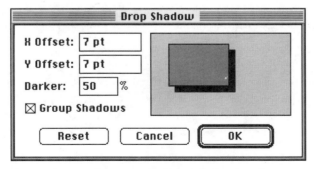

Figure 12-35: The options in this dialog box let you specify the distance between a selected object and its shadow as well as the color of the shadow.

Click on the "Group Shadows" check box to ensure that each shadow is automatically grouped with its object. Click on the RESET button to return the options in the DROP SHADOW dialog box to their default settings, which appear in Figure 12-35.

Not quite what the Sex Pistols had in mind

The PUNK... filter distorts the selected object by moving its points outward and rounding its segments inward. They sort of end up looking like they've all sucked on too many lemons. Choosing the PUNK... filter displays a dialog box that contains a single "Amount" option box. Here you enter the percentage by which you want the selected object to punk. This percentage represents the distance that the points move away from the center of the object as well as the distance that the Bézier control handles move toward the center. In Figure 12-42, for example, I applied the PUNK... filter to the shapes along the top of the figure. I punked the rectangle 10%, the ellipse 35%, and the star 50%. And in case you haven't guessed this already, the PUNK... filter is the exact opposite of the BLOAT... filter. In fact, any negative value bloats the objects instead of punking them.

Figure 12-36: I created the bottom shapes by punking the top ones by 10%, 35%, and 50%, respectively.

The **Illustrator** 5 Book

Rounding off corners

The ROUND CORNERS... filter rounds off the corners in a selected object. It's great for rounding off corners in a rectangle after the fact, but you can also apply it to stars, polygons, and other shapes that have a lot of corners. It's really supereasy. Give it a try.

CHAPTER

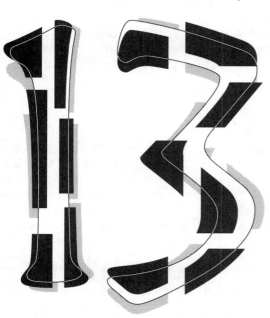

CREATING
AND
EDITING
GRAPHS

Graphing applications abound on all varieties of computers. Microsoft Excel satisfies the needs of users who are interested primarily in number-crunching but sometimes require basic graphs. If you need a dedicated or scientific graphing program, then the only application worth the price of admission is DeltaGraph Professional. A range of presentation applications—including Microsoft PowerPoint and Aldus Persuasion—also offer charting features. And if you want a program that walks you through the process, you'll want to switch computers and try out Harvard Graphics or Lotus FreeLance on the PC. Yes, this is one of those areas in which the PC is easier to use than the Mac.

So why would you ever use Illustrator's graphing tools? The answer is freedom of manipulation. Other software is capable of producing a wider variety of charts with more bells and whistles, but few allow you to so much as reposition the legend in an existing chart. In Illustrator, you can reshape, transform, and duplicate any element in a graph to your heart's content. Only a drawing program can turn graphs into artwork.

Creating a graph

Style...
Data...

Design...
Column...
Marker...

Illustrator provides six *graphing tools*. Instead of providing the different graphing tools as alternates for the graph tool (eleventh tool on the left in the toolbox), you select the different tools from the GRAPH STYLE dialog box. Either choose STYLE... from the GRAPHS submenu under the OBJECT menu or double-click on the graph tool slot to display the GRAPH STYLE dialog box. Each tool allows you to create a different kind of chart. All these tools are operated in the following manner:

1. Choose the desired graphing tool from the GRAPH STYLE dialog box.

2. Use the tool to define the chart's boundaries in your illustration.

3. Enter the desired data into the resulting GRAPH DATA dialog box.

4. Press ENTER to instruct Illustrator to process the data and generate the chart corresponding to the selected tool.

The main purpose of any graphing tool is to determine the rectangular dimensions of a chart. You draw with a graphing tool just as if you were drawing with the rectangle tool or oval tool. This means you can use any of the following techniques:

- Drag to draw the chart boundary from corner to corner.

- Press OPTION and drag to draw the boundary from center to corner.

- SHIFT-drag or SHIFT-OPTION-drag to draw a square boundary.

- Click to display the GRAPH dialog box shown in Figure 13-1. Enter the horizontal and vertical dimensions of the desired chart into the "Width" and "Height" option boxes and press RETURN. The click point becomes the upper left corner of the chart boundary.

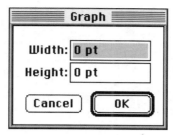

Figure 13-1: Click with any graphing tool to display the Graph dialog box, which allows you to enter the dimensions of the chart boundary.

- Press OPTION and click to display the GRAPH dialog box. Enter the horizontal and vertical dimensions of the desired chart into the "Width" and "Height" option boxes, and press RETURN. The click point becomes the center of the chart boundary.

After you define the width and height of your chart, the GRAPH DATA dialog box automatically displays, as shown in Figure 13-2 on the next page. This dialog box is actually a mini-spreadsheet window, containing its own size box and scroll bars. Unlike with other dialog boxes, you can click outside the GRAPH DATA window to bring the illustration window to the front of the desktop. Although it disappears from view, the GRAPH DATA window remains open behind the illustration window, so that you don't lose any changes you have made while inside the dialog box. To bring the GRAPH DATA window to the front of the desktop, choose the GRAPH DATA... command from the GRAPH menu.

Using the Graph Data dialog box

The *worksheet matrix* in the lower portion of the GRAPH DATA dialog box is similar to the worksheet provided in a standard spreadsheet program such as Microsoft Excel or MacCalc. The worksheet contains rows and columns of individual containers, called *cells*. Numbers entered into the cells can represent dollar amounts, times and dates, or percentages. You can even enter words for labels and legends. Unlike with a true spreadsheet, however, you cannot enter formulas, since Illustrator provides no calculation capability.

Data entered from the keyboard appears in the *value entry line* at the top of the worksheet (below the buttons). Press RETURN or TAB to transfer the data from the value entry line into the current cell and advance to another cell.

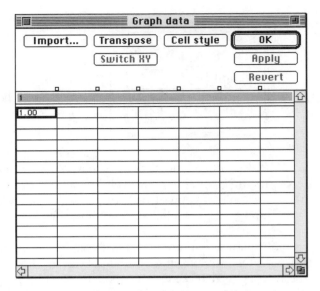

Figure 13-2: The Graph Data dialog box contains a worksheet matrix made up of rows and columns of cells. Enter the data you want to graph, as well as label text, into these cells.

As you type, most keys insert the standard character that appears on the key. Some characters, however, perform special functions:

- **Quotation marks** ("). Enter quotes around numeric data to use a number as a label, such as a product number or year. If a cell consists of only numbers without quote marks, Illustrator interprets the data as a value and graphs it or merely does not display it at all.

 To display quotes around a numeric label, use the opening and closing quotation marks, " and " (⌥-[and ⇧-⌥-[), rather than the straight quote " (⇧-').

- **Vertical line character** (|). If you want a label to contain multiple lines of text, enter the vertical line (⇧-\) to represent a carriage return character.

- **Tab** or **right arrow** (→). Accepts the data in the value entry line and moves one cell to the right (to the next cell in the row).

- **Left arrow** (←). Accepts the data in the value entry line and moves one cell to the left (to the previous cell in the row).

- **Return** or **down arrow** (↓). Accepts the data in the value entry line and moves one cell down (to the next cell in the column).

- **Up arrow** (↑). Accepts the data in the value entry line and moves one cell up (to the previous cell in the column).

- ⌘-**Z** (UNDO CELL TYPE-IN command). Restores the original data in the value entry line.

- **Enter**. Accepts the data in the value entry line and selects the OK button, exiting the GRAPH DATA dialog box.

For most kinds of charts, both the first row and the first column of cells can be reserved for labels. To use cells as labels, delete the data from the very first cell (at the intersection of the first row and column) and leave it empty. Every other cell in the first row and the first column should contain at least one non-numeric character or quote marks around the numbers to instruct Illustrator to display the data as is.

Because different kinds of charts require different kinds of information, the specific manner in which you organize data varies from one kind of chart to the next. The following sections describe the functions of the basic chart types and explain how you should enter data for each.

Bar chart data

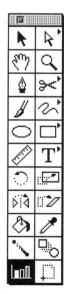

If you use the *bar-graph tool* (what Illustrator calls the *grouped-column-graph tool*) to create the chart boundary in the drawing area, Illustrator expects you to organize your data in *standard bar chart* form. Bar charts are most commonly used to demonstrate a change in data over a period of time. The horizontal axis (*X-axis*) may be divided into time units, measured in days, months, or years. The vertical axis (*Y-axis*) tracks values, which may be measured in units sold, dollars or other currency, or any number of other possibilities. As shown in Figure 13-3 on the following page, bars (sometimes called *columns*) rise up from the X-axis to a height equivalent to a value on the Y-axis. The taller the bar, the greater the value it represents. If more than one *series* of data is included in the chart, like bars from each series are *clustered* together. Hence, this type of chart is known in some circles as a *cluster bar chart*, or a *grouped column chart*. In Illustrator, bars from different series are filled with different gray values. The colors representing the series are itemized in a *legend*.

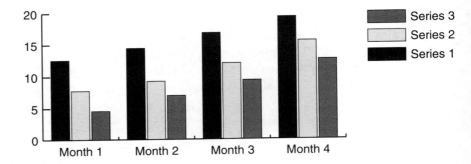

Figure 13-3: An example of a standard bar chart, also known as a cluster bar chart or a grouped column chart. Series of bars are clustered together. Each series is identified in the legend (right).

When the GRAPH DATA dialog box displays for a standard bar chart, arrange your data as demonstrated in Figure 13-4.

- Delete the contents of the first cell, and leave it empty.

- Enter series labels in the first row of cells. The label text will appear in the legend.

- Enter X-axis labels in the first column.

- Organize series of data into columns under the series labels. If you enter a dollar sign ($), the symbol will be ignored. If you enter other currency symbols (such as £ or ¥), Illustrator will not graph the value.

- Y-axis labels correspond automatically to the data.

	Series 1	Series 2	Series 3	
Month 1	12.57	77.60	45.70	
Month 2	14.44	92.50	69.90	
Month 3	16.84	12.04	93.60	
Month 4	19.34	15.55	12.63	

Figure 13-4: Organize bar chart data into columns under series labels. This data corresponds to the bar chart shown in Figure 13-3.

The **Illustrator 5** Book

Stacked bar chart data

Graph type
○ Grouped column
◉ Stacked column
○ Line
○ Pie
○ Area
○ Scatter

If you use the *stacked-bar-graph tool* (what Illustrator calls the stacked-column-graph tool) to create the chart boundary in the drawing area, Illustrator expects you to organize your data in *stacked bar chart* form. Stacked charts are much like standard bar charts, except that like bars from different series are stacked on top of each other, rather than clustered side by side. A stacked bar chart is most useful for showing the sums of all series. You can create a *percentage chart* by organizing your data so that all values for each series add up to 100, as shown in Figure 13-5. Percentage charts are useful for demonstrating the relative performance of various series over time.

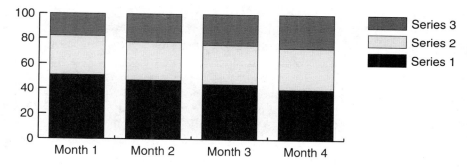

Figure 13-5: An example of a specific variety of stacked bar chart, called a percentage chart. Series of bars are stacked on top of one another. As in the standard bar chart, each series is identified in the legend (right).

When the GRAPH DATA dialog box displays for a stacked bar chart, arrange your data as demonstrated in Figure 13-6.

- Delete the contents of the first cell, and leave it empty.

- Enter series labels in the first row of cells. The label text will appear in the legend.

- Enter X-axis labels in the first column.

- Organize series of data into columns under the series labels. If you enter a percentage symbol (%) with a value, the symbol will be ignored.

- Y-axis labels correspond automatically to the data.

	Series 1	Series 2	Series 3	
Month 1	51.00	31.00	18.00	
Month 2	47.00	30.00	23.00	
Month 3	44.00	31.00	25.00	
Month 4	40.00	33.00	27.00	

Figure 13-6: Organize stacked bar chart data into columns under series labels. This data corresponds to the percentage chart shown in Figure 13-5. Notice that the values in each row add up to 100.

Line graph data

If you use the *line-graph tool* to create the chart boundary in the drawing area, Illustrator expects you to organize your data in *line chart* form. Like bar charts, line charts are generally used to show changes in items over a period of time. Straight segments connect points representing values, as shown in Figure 13-7. Several straight segments combine to form a line, which represents a complete series. The inclination of a segment clearly demonstrates the performance of a series from one point in time to the next. Because large changes result in steep inclinations, line charts are best used to graph data that includes dramatic fluctuations.

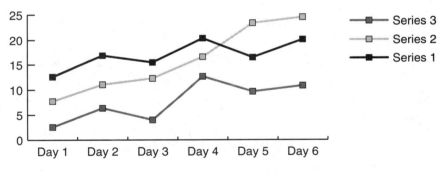

Figure 13-7: An example of a line chart. Lines are composed of straight segments that connect value points and represent complete series. Each series is identified in the legend (right).

The **Illustrator 5** Book

When the GRAPH DATA dialog box displays for a line chart, arrange your data as demonstrated in Figure 13-8:

- Delete the contents of the first cell, and leave it empty.

- Enter series labels in the first row of cells. The label text will appear in the legend.

- Enter X-axis labels in the first column.

- Organize series of data into columns under the series labels.

- Y-axis labels correspond automatically to the data.

	Series 1	Series 2	Series 3	
Day 1	12.57	7.76	2.57	
Day 2	16.84	11.04	6.36	
Day 3	15.44	12.25	3.99	
Day 4	20.34	16.55	12.63	
Day 5	16.42	23.35	9.65	
Day 6	20.08	24.49	10.82	

Figure 13-8: Organize line chart data into columns under series labels. This data corresponds to the line chart shown in Figure 13-7.

Although line chart data may fluctuate dramatically, you don't want series to cross each other more than one or twice in the entire chart. If series cross too often, the result is a *spaghetti chart*, which is difficult to read and typically ineffective.

Pie chart data

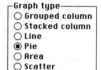

If you use the *pie-graph tool* to create the chart boundary in the drawing area, Illustrator expects you to organize your data in *pie chart* form. A pie chart is the easiest kind of chart to create. However, pie charts are not nearly as versatile as the other charts discussed so far. Only one series may be expressed per pie. If you want to show more than one series for comparative purposes, each series must be given a pie of its own, as shown in Figure 13-9 on the next page. The advantage of a pie chart is that it always displays values in a series in relation to the whole. A series inhabits a 360° circle and each value within the series occupies a percentage of that circle.

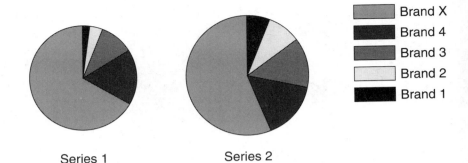

	Brand X
	Brand 4
	Brand 3
	Brand 2
	Brand 1

Series 1   Series 2

Figure 13-9: An example of two pie charts, each representing a single series. Values are labeled in the pie or in a legend (right). Series 1 is smaller than Series 2 because the latter includes larger values.

When the GRAPH DATA dialog box displays for a pie chart, arrange your data as demonstrated in Figure 13-10.

- Delete the contents of the first cell, and leave it empty.

- Enter value labels in the first row of cells. The label text will appear in the legend.

- Enter series labels in the first column. If more than two series of data are required, use a different kind of graph.

- Organize series of data into rows to the right of the series labels. The labels will appear as titles below the pie, as demonstrated in Figure 13-9.

	Brand 1	Brand 2	Brand 3	Brand 4	Brand X	
Series 1	0.98	1.56	4.07	6.76	26.57	
Series 2	3.24	4.67	6.99	8.25	29.34	

Figure 13-10: Organize pie chart data into rows to the right of series labels. This data corresponds to the pie charts shown in Figure 13-9.

Area graph data

Graph type
- ○ Grouped column
- ○ Stacked column
- ○ Line
- ○ Pie
- ● Area
- ○ Scatter

If you use the *area-graph tool* to create the chart boundary in the drawing area, Illustrator expects you to organize your data in *area chart* form. In its simplest form, an area chart is little more than a filled-in line chart. However, the series of an area chart are stacked one upon another as in a stacked bar chart to display the sum of all series, as shown in Figure 13-11.

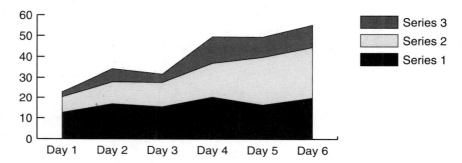

Figure 13-11: An example of an area chart. The area between one line and the next is filled in. Different fills represent different series. Each series is identified in the legend (right).

If you encounter a spaghetti effect when creating a line chart —that is, segments frequently overlap each other—you may quickly and easily remedy the problem by converting the line chart into an area chart.

When the GRAPH DATA dialog box displays for an area chart, arrange your data as demonstrated in Figure 13-12.

- Delete the contents of the first cell, and leave it empty.

- Enter series labels in the first row of cells. The label text will appear in the legend.

- Enter X-axis labels in the first column.

- Organize series of data into columns under the series labels.

- Y-axis labels correspond automatically to the data.

	Series 1	Series 2	Series 3	
Day 1	12.57	7.76	2.57	
Day 2	16.84	11.04	6.36	
Day 3	15.44	12.25	3.99	
Day 4	20.34	16.55	12.63	
Day 5	16.42	23.35	9.65	
Day 6	20.08	24.49	10.82	

Figure 13-12: Organize area chart data into columns under series labels. This data corresponds to the area chart shown in Figure 13-11. (This is the same data that was used to create the line chart shown in Figure 13-7.)

Scatter graph data

If you use the *scatter-graph tool* to create the chart boundary in the drawing area, Illustrator expects you to organize your data in *scatter chart* form. Like a line chart, a scatter chart plots points and connects these points with straight segments. However, rather than merely aligning series of values along a set of X-axis labels, the scatter graph pairs up columns of values. The first column of data represents Y-axis (series) coordinates; the second column represents X-axis coordinates. Scatter charts are most accurately used to map scientific data or to graph multiple series that use slightly different time increments.

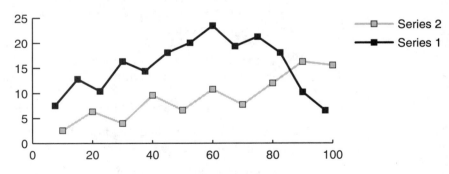

Figure 13-13: An example of a scatter chart. Points plotted at specified X,Y-coordinates are connected with straight segments. Each series is identified in the legend (right).

The **Illustrator 5** Book

When the GRAPH DATA dialog box displays for a scatter chart, arrange your data as demonstrated in Figure 13-14.

- Enter series labels in the first row of cells, at the top of odd columns (first, third, fifth, and so on). In the first row, leave even-numbered cells empty. The label text will appear in the legend.

- Enter Y-axis (series) data in odd columns.

- Enter X-axis data in even-numbered columns. Side-by-side columns of data are plotted as paired points. In other words, each row of values in the first and second columns is plotted as a point in the first series, each row in the third and fourth columns will be plotted as a point in the second series, and so on.

- Y-axis and X-axis labels correspond automatically to the data.

Series 1		Series 2		
7.57	7.50	2.57	10.00	
12.84	15.00	6.36	20.00	
10.44	22.50	3.99	30.00	
16.34	30.00	9.63	40.00	
14.42	37.50	6.65	50.00	
18.08	45.00	10.82	60.00	
20.06	52.50	7.76	70.00	
23.49	60.00	12.04	80.00	
19.35	67.50	16.25	90.00	
21.26	75.00	15.55	100.00	
18.05	82.50			
10.24	90.00			
6.56	97.50			

Figure 13-14: Organize scatter chart data by series
in pairs of columns under series labels. This data
corresponds to the scatter chart shown in Figure 13-13.

Importing data

Because Illustrator provides no calculation capability, and its cell-editing functions are limited (cells cannot be inserted, deleted, exchanged, sorted, and so on), you may prefer to import values into the GRAPH DATA worksheet, rather than enter them from the keyboard. You can create your data in any spreadsheet program capable of saving as a *tab-delineated*, text-only file. Such programs include Microsoft Excel, Claris Resolve, MacCalc, and Lotus 1-2-3 just to name a few. In a tab-delineated file, individual cells are separated by tab characters; rows of cells are separated by carriage returns.

Because Illustrator accepts any tab-delineated, text-only file, you can also create your data in a word processor such as Microsoft Word or WriteNow. When entering the data, insert tabs between values and insert carriage returns between rows of values. Then save the finished file as a text-only, or *ASCII*, document.

To import a data file, display the GRAPH DATA dialog box and click on the cell that you want to act as the upper left cell in the imported data. Click the IMPORT... button, or choose the IMPORT GRAPH DATA... command from the FILE menu, to display the PLEASE OPEN TEXT FILE dialog box, as shown in Figure 13-15. (The IMPORT GRAPH DATA... command appears in place of the PLACE ART... command in the FILE menu only when the GRAPH DATA dialog box is displayed.)

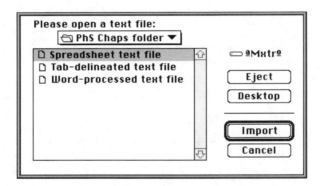

Figure 13-15: The Please Open Text File dialog box allows you to select a tab-delineated text file to import into the Graph Data worksheet.

To import a data file, double-click on its name in the scrolling file list, or select the file and click the IMPORT button or press RETURN. The DESKTOP and EJECT buttons, the folder bar, and keyboard equivalents operate as described in the section *Creating a new illustration* in Chapter 3.

The imported data appears in the worksheet in rows and columns starting in the selected cell. If any of these cells already contain data, their contents are replaced.

Adjusting data

Unlike more sophisticated spreadsheets, the GRAPH DATA dialog box does not allow you to insert cells, delete cells, or in any way move cells inside the worksheet. However, you can move data within cells using one of the following techniques:

- Cut data from one location and paste it into another. You can also copy data and clear multiple cells using keyboard equivalents or by choosing commands from the EDIT menu.

- Click on the TRANSPOSE button to swap rows and columns of data.

- Click on the SWITCH XY button to swap columns of data in a scatter chart. This button is dimmed when you're creating or editing any kind of chart except a scatter chart.

You select multiple cells in the worksheet by dragging across them, or by pressing the SHIFT key while pressing one of the arrow keys ($\uparrow$, $\rightarrow$, $\downarrow$, or $\leftarrow$). All selected cells except the current cell become highlighted, as shown in Figure 13-16.

	Series 1	Series 2	Series 3		
Month 1	12.57	7.76	4.57		
Month 2	14.44	9.25	6.99		
Month 3	16.84	12.04	9.36		
Month 4	19.34	15.55	12.63		

Figure 13-16: When you select multiple cells, all cells except the current cell become highlighted.

You can remove the contents of selected cells and transfer the data to the Clipboard by choosing the CUT command (⌘-X). Choose the COPY command (⌘-C) to copy the contents of highlighted cells.

To paste the contents of the Clipboard into the worksheet, click on the cell that you want to act as the upper left cell in the pasted data and choose the Paste command (⌘-V). The Paste command is dimmed if the Clipboard does not contain data. Cells are pasted into the same number of cells from which they were cut or copied. Cells are always pasted in the rows and columns including and following the current cell, even if multiple cells are highlighted and the selected cell is in the lower right corner of the selection. If any affected cells already contain data, their contents are replaced.

 Illustrator allows you to paste any type into the Graph Data worksheet. Therefore, you can copy words or paragraphs from a block of text in the drawing area and paste them into a graph. You may also copy data from the worksheet window and paste it into a text block.

You can delete the contents of multiple selected cells by choosing Clear from the Edit menu or by pressing the clear key. (Pressing delete or backspace deletes only the contents of the current cell.)

Transposing data

The Graph Data dialog box also allows you to *transpose* data; that is, swap the way in which the data is plotted on the X and Y axes. Click the Transpose button to swap rows and columns in a matrix. The data in the first row will appear in the first column, the data in the first column will appear in the first row, and so on. For example, if we click the Transpose button for the data shown back in Figure 13-4, the data is transposed as shown in Figure 13-17. The series data is mapped along the X axis, and the time labels appear in the legend, as shown in Figure 13-18.

	Month 1	Month 2	Month 3	Month 4	
Series 1	12.57	14.44	16.84	19.34	
Series 2	7.76	9.25	12.04	15.55	
Series 3	4.57	6.99	9.36	12.63	

Figure 13-17: The data from Figure 13-4 as it appears after clicking the Transpose button.

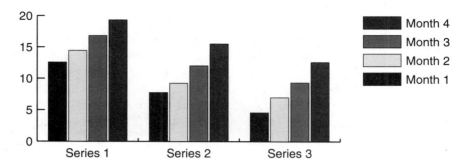

Figure 13-18: The bar chart from Figure 13-3 as it appears after transposing rows and columns of data.

Because data is organized differently in a scatter chart, a special SWITCH XY button is provided. Click on this button to swap even and odd columns of data in the worksheet. The data in the first column moves to the second, the data in the second column moves to the first, the data in the third column moves to the fourth, and so on. For example, if we click the SWITCH XY button for the data shown back in Figure 13-14, the data is transposed as shown in Figure 13-19. Y-axis coordinates are transposed to the X-axis and X-axis coordinates are transposed to the Y-axis, as shown in Figure 13-20, on the following page.

	Series 1		Series 2	
7.50	7.57	10.00	2.57	
15.00	12.84	20.00	6.36	
22.50	10.44	30.00	3.99	
30.00	16.34	40.00	9.63	
37.50	14.42	50.00	6.65	
45.00	18.08	60.00	10.82	
52.50	20.06	70.00	7.76	
60.00	23.49	80.00	12.04	
67.50	19.35	90.00	16.25	
75.00	21.26	100.00	15.55	
82.50	18.05			
90.00	10.24			
97.50	6.56			

Figure 13-19: The data from Figure 13-14 as it appears after clicking the Switch XY button.

Notice in Figure 13-20 that the "Series 2" and "Series 1" labels no longer appear in the legend, due to the fact that the locations of these labels were altered in the GRAPH DATA dialog box.

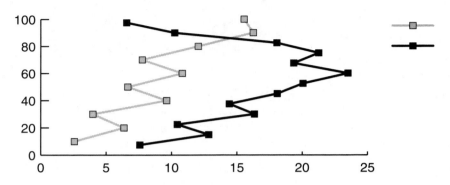

Figure 13-20: The bar chart from Figure 13-13 as it appears after transposing odd and even columns of data.

The changes effected by both the TRANSPOSE and SWITCH XY buttons apply to all data in the worksheet, regardless of the cells selected when the buttons are clicked.

Adjusting cell style

The final cell adjustment that you can make in the GRAPH DATA dialog box is cosmetic. The CELL STYLE button allows you to adjust both the width of the columns in the worksheet and the number of digits that can follow a decimal point. These controls affect only the appearance of data in the worksheet; they do not affect the appearance of the current chart.

Click the CELL STYLE button to display the CELL STYLE dialog box shown in Figure 13-21. Enter any value between 0 and 10 into the "Number of decimals" option box. This option determines the number of *significant digits*; that is, the number of characters that can appear after a decimal point in a cell. Enter any value between 3 and 20 into the "Column width" option box. This option controls the default width of each cell in the GRAPH DATA dialog box, measured in digits (characters).

The **Illustrator 5** Book

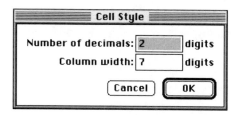

Figure 13-21: These options let you specify the numerical format and width of cells.

	Month 1	Month 2	Month 3	Month 4	
Series 1	12.57	14.44	16.84	19.34	
Series 2	7.76	9.25	12.04	15.55	
Series 3	4.57	6.99	9.36	12.63	

	Month 1	Month 2	Month 3	Month 4	
Series 1	12.57	14.44	16.84	19.34	
Series 2	7.76	9.25	12.04	15.55	
Series 3	4.57	6.99	9.36	12.63	

Figure 13-22: Drag the column handle above the value entry line (top) to change the width of a column of cells (bottom).

 To adjust the width of a single column of cells, drag the corresponding *column handle* above the value entry line, as shown in Figure 13-22. The column is widened or narrowed by the nearest number of whole digits.

Implementing your data

Click on the APPLY button to display the results of your data in the drawing area without leaving the GRAPH DATA dialog box. If you cannot see the drawing area because the dialog box is in the way, drag its title bar to move the box partially off screen. This allows you to make changes if the current data is not satisfactory.

Click on REVERT to restore the settings from when you entered the GRAPH DATA dialog box, or since the last time your clicked on the APPLY button.

Click OK to exit the dialog box and implement your changes. If you want to exit the GRAPH DATA dialog box without implementing your changes, click the close box, then click the DON'T SAVE button in the resulting alert box (or press COMMAND-D), shown in Figure 13-23.

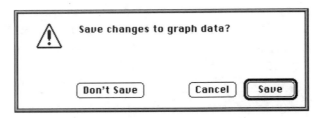

Figure 13-23: This alert box appears if you click the close box in the title bar of the Graph Data dialog box after making changes to the data.

You can undo the creation or alteration of a chart after clicking on the OK or APPLY button by choosing the UNDO GRAPH DATA OK command from the EDIT menu (⌘-Z).

Editing a graph

There are four basic ways to edit a graph created in Adobe Illustrator: 1) edit the data; 2) convert the graph into a different kind of graph; 3) reposition axes, legends, and other elements using options; and 4) customize elements using tools discussed in previous chapters. Each of these methods is discussed in the following section.

Editing data

To edit the data in an existing graph, select the entire graph with the selection tool and choose the DATA... command in the GRAPHS sub-menu from the OBJECT menu. The GRAPH DATA dialog box displays, containing all data pertinent to the current chart. Edit the data as desired, and press the ENTER key to implement your changes.

Converting a graph

Style...
Data...

Design...
Column...
Marker...

To convert a selected chart, choose the STYLE... command in the GRAPH submenu from the OBJECT menu or double-click on the graph tool slot in the tool box. The GRAPH STYLE dialog box shown in Figure 13-24 displays. This dialog box provides access to a heap of options that allow you to edit various facets of a graph.

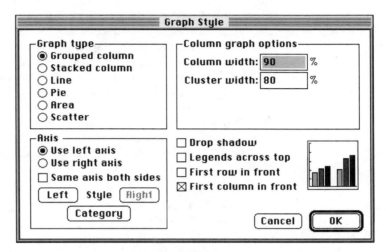

Figure 13-24: The Graph Style dialog box allows you to convert a graph to a different kind of graph as well as edit various facets of a selected chart.

The options in the "Graph type" box control the identity of the current chart. The options to the right of this box change depending on which radio button is selected in the "Graph type" box. These radio buttons include the following:

- **Grouped column.** Select this option to change the selected graph to a standard bar chart. Two options will appear in the "Column graph options" box on the right. The "Column width" option box controls the width of each bar in the chart, measured as a percentage of its *flush width*. A value of 100% causes bars to be flush with each other; the default value of 90% allows slight gutters between bars; and values greater than 100% cause bars to overlap. The "Cluster width" option controls the width of each cluster of bars between different series, again measured as a percentage of the flush width of the clusters. The default value of 80% allows a gutter between clusters.

- **Stacked column**. Select this option to change the selected graph to a stacked bar chart. The "Column graph options" box includes the same options described in the previous item.

- **Line**. Select this option to change the selected graph to a line chart. Four options appear in the "Line graph options" box on the right, as shown in Figure 13-25. When selected, the "Mark data points" check box creates square markers at the data points in each line. The "Connect data points" check box creates straight segments between points in a line graph. If this option is deselected, stray points will appear without lines. When "Connect data points" is selected, the "Fill lines" check box becomes available, allowing you to create lines thicker than the default line weight. Enter the desired line weight in the "Fill line width" option box. The units are those selected in the "Ruler units" option in the GENERAL PREFERENCES dialog box. Select "Edge-to-edge lines" to draw lines that extend the entire width of the chart, extending to both edges of the X-axis.

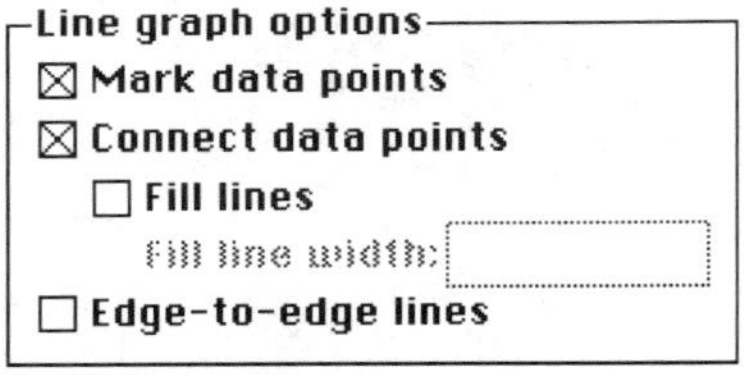

```
┌Line graph options────────────┐
│ ⊠ Mark data points           │
│ ⊠ Connect data points        │
│    □ Fill lines              │
│      Fill line width: [     ]│
│ □ Edge-to-edge lines         │
└──────────────────────────────┘
```

Figure 13-25: The "Line graph options" box in the Graph Style dialog box allows you to change aspects of a selected line chart.

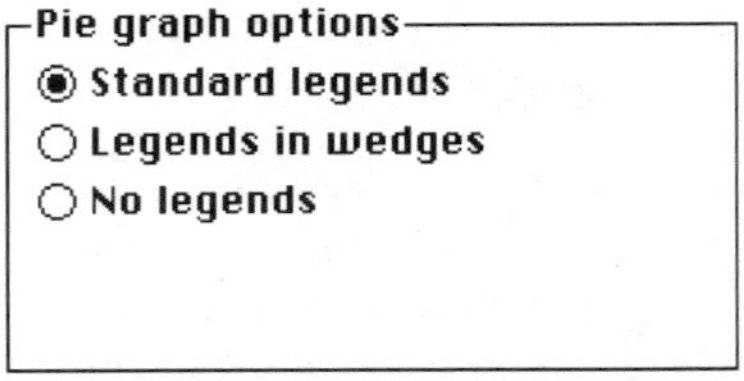

```
┌Pie graph options─────────────┐
│ ⦿ Standard legends           │
│ ○ Legends in wedges          │
│ ○ No legends                 │
│                              │
│                              │
└──────────────────────────────┘
```

Figure 13-26: The "Pie graph options" box in the Graph Style dialog box allows you to change aspects of a selected pie chart.

- **Pie**. Select this option to change the selected graph to a pie chart. Three options will appear in the "Pie graph options" box on right, as shown in Figure 13-26. By default, the "Standard legends" radio button is selected, which results in a legend that identifies the values in the graph. If you instead select "Legends in wedges," the wedges themselves are labeled. Select "No legends" to include no labels for the values in the pie chart.

- **Area**. Select this option to change the selected graph to an area chart. No additional option appears to the right of the "Graph type" box.

- **Scatter**. Select this option to change the selected graph to a scatter chart. Four options will appear in the "Scatter graph options" box on right. These are the same options that appear in the "Line graph options" box as shown in Figure 13-25, except without the "Edge-to-edge lines" option.

Changing the identity of the selected chart may require that you reorganize the data in the GRAPH DATA dialog box.

Adjusting miscellaneous attributes

In the lower right corner of the GRAPH STYLE dialog box are four check boxes. These options include the following:

- **Drop shadow**. Select this option to create drop shadows behind the bars, lines, pie slices, or areas in a chart, as demonstrated in Figure 13-27.

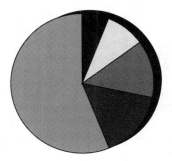

Series 1

Figure 13-27: Select the "Drop shadow" option to create a drop shadow behind the series elements in a chart.

- **Legends across top**. Select this option to move the legend from the right side of the chart to the top of the chart, as shown in Figure 13-28. Labels are listed horizontally instead of vertically.

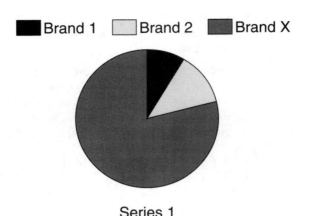

Series 1

Figure 13-28: Select the "Legend across top" option to move the legend to the top of the chart in horizontal formation.

- **First row in front**. Select this option to layer elements representing rows of data in the selected chart in descending order, with the first row in front and the last row in back. If this is a little difficult to visualize, consider the example of a bar chart with overlapping bars and clusters. (Both the "Column width" and "Cluster width" values are set to 110%.) The rows of data in a bar chart represent clusters of values. In Figure 13-29, the "First row in front" option is deselected, so the clusters are layered in ascending order, with the first cluster in back and the last cluster in front. In Figure 13-30, the option has been selected, so the clusters are layered in descending order with the first cluster in front and the last cluster in back.

- **First column in front**. Select this option to layer elements representing columns of data (series) in the selected chart in descending order, with the first series in front and the last series in back. In Figure 13-29, the "First column in front" option has been selected, so the bars are layered in descending order with the first bar in each cluster in front and the last bar in each cluster in back. In Figure 13-30, the option is deselected, so the bars are layered in ascending order with the first bar in back and the last bar in front.

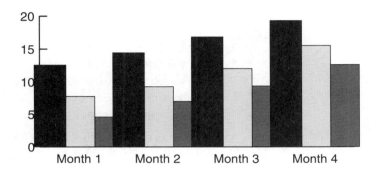

Figure 13-29: Overlapping bars and clusters with the first row (cluster) in back and the first column (series bar) in front.

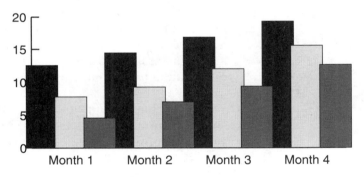

Figure 13-30: Overlapping bars and clusters with the first row (cluster) in front and the first column (series bar) in back.

The "First row in front" and "First column in front" options are most useful when applied to bar charts in which bars or clusters overlap. The "First column in front" option can also be applied to line and scatter charts, to determine the layering order of series lines. Though never dimmed, the options are not applicable to area charts or pie charts.

Adjusting legends and axes

The "Axis" box in the lower left corner of the GRAPH STYLE dialog box allows you to control the appearance and positions of the vertical and horizontal axes in a selected chart. The first three options control the placements of the Y-axis (vertical axis):

- **Use left axis**. Select this radio button to make the Y-axis appear on the left-hand side of the chart, as it does by default. This axis uses the attribute settings determined by clicking on the LEFT button at the bottom of the "Axis" box. (The RIGHT button will appear dimmed.)

- **Use right axis**. Select this radio button to make the Y-axis appear on the right-hand side of the chart. This axis uses the attribute settings determined by clicking on the RIGHT button at the bottom of the "Axis" box. (The LEFT button will appear dimmed.)

- **Same axis both sides**. Select this check box to make the Y-axis appear on both sides of the chart. This axis uses the attribute settings determined by clicking the LEFT or RIGHT button at the bottom of the "Axis" box, whichever is currently available. If you have specified different attributes for the left and right axes, select the "Use left axis" or "Use right axis" radio button to determine which set of attributes are used.

Three "Style" buttons appear at the bottom of the "Axis" box; only two of the buttons are available at any time. The LEFT and RIGHT buttons control the attributes of the Y-axis, and the CATEGORY button (called the BOTTOM button when the current selection is a scatter chart) controls the appearance of the X-axis (horizontal axis).

Clicking on any of these buttons displays the GRAPH AXIS STYLE dialog box shown in Figure 13-31. Here you specify the location of tick marks and labels on the current axis. The options in the "Axis label and tick line values" box control the way in which an axis is labeled; those in the "Axis tick lines and marks" box control the size of tick marks.

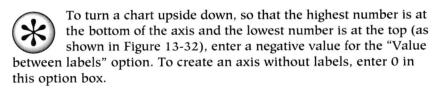

Figure 13-31: The Graph Axis Style dialog box allows you to control various attributes affecting the appearance of the X-axis or Y-axis.

The "Axis label and tick line values" options are available when you are setting attributes for the Y-axis of any chart or the X-axis for a scatter chart only. Therefore, they are dimmed if you have accessed the GRAPH AXIS STYLE dialog box by clicking on the CATEGORY button. These options include the following:

- **Calculate axis values from data**. By default, this radio button is selected. Illustrator automatically determines the number of tick marks and labels that appear on the axis.

- **Use manual axis values**. If you want to specify a range of labels in an axis to enhance the appearance of a chart, select this radio button and enter values in the three option boxes that follow. The "Minimum label value" determines the lowest number on the axis; the "Maximum label value" determines the highest number. The "Value between labels" determines the increment between labels.

To turn a chart upside down, so that the highest number is at the bottom of the axis and the lowest number is at the top (as shown in Figure 13-32), enter a negative value for the "Value between labels" option. To create an axis without labels, enter 0 in this option box.

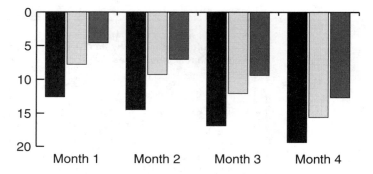

Figure 13-32: Flip a chart by entering a negative value in the "Value between labels" option when editing the attributes of the Y-axis.

- **Labels before/after**. These option boxes allow you to enter symbols or words up to nine characters long to precede or follow each label in a chart. For example, enter $ into the "Before" option box to precede every label with a dollar sign, as shown in Figure 13-33. Enter g in the "After" option box to indicate that each value is to be interpreted in thousands of dollars.

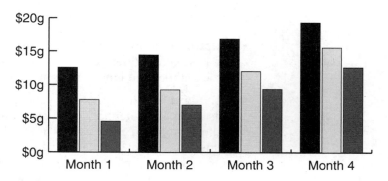

Figure 13-33: Enter characters to precede and follow the labels, such as the $ and g in the Y-axis, using the "Labels before/after" option.

Most of the "Axis tick lines and marks" options are available when setting attributes for the X- or Y-axis. These options include:

- **None**. Select this radio button to display no tick mark on the current axis. This option does not affect the placement or appearance of labels.

- **Short**. Select this radio button to display short tick marks that extend from the axis toward the chart, as by default.

- **Full width**. Select this radio button to create tick lines that extend the full width or height of the chart, as in Figure 13-34.

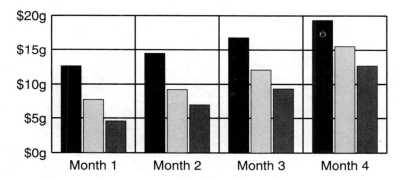

Figure 13-34: Select the "Full width" option to extend the tick marks across the entire chart. Here, the option has been selected for both the X- and Y-axes.

- **Draw tick lines between labels**. This check box is available only if you displayed the GRAPH AXIS STYLE dialog box by clicking on the CATEGORY button. When selected, as by default, tick marks appear centered between labels, as demonstrated by the vertical lines in Figure 13-34. When deselected, each tick mark is centered above a single label, as shown in Figure 13-35.

- **Draw __ tick marks per tick line**. This option should read *Tick marks per label*, because it allows you to control the number of tick marks per labeled increment. In Figure 13-36, we have entered 5 for this option, creating a total of four tick marks per every label along the Y-axis. (The value for this option includes the tick mark for the next label, hence a value of 5 creates four tick marks per label.)

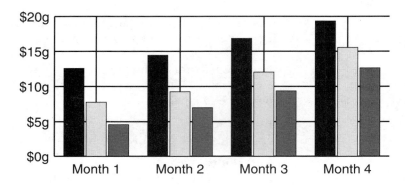

Figure 13-35: For the X-axis of a bar, line, or area chart, deselect the "Draw tick lines between labels" option to create tick marks at the label rather than between labels.

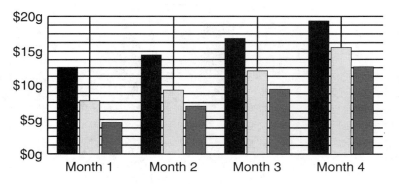

Figure 13-36: The same chart after entering 5 for the "Draw __ tick marks per tick line" option.

All options in the "Axis" box of the GRAPH STYLE dialog box are dimmed when the "Pie" option is selected in the "Graph type" box. If "Scatter" is selected, the "Use left axis" and "Use right axis" radio buttons are dimmed.

Customizing a graph

Illustrator provides several options for editing the appearance of a selected chart. However, if you want to truly customize a chart, you'll have to apply the reshaping and transformation principles covered in Chapters 6 and 11. After all, the elements in a chart are no more than standard graphic objects that you can manipulate like any other object in Adobe Illustrator.

The elements in a chart are organized into a small network of grouped objects. If you ever want to edit the data associated with a chart or adjust attribute options, do *not* ungroup any of these groups. Instead, use the direct-selection tool to select and manipulate specific elements.

Charts are composed of groups within groups within groups. The following list demonstrates how you can select each of the groups using the direct-selection tool:

- Click to select a specific point or segment in a series object.

- Press OPTION and click to select a whole object in the chart, such as an axis or column.

- Press OPTION and click a second time to select an entire axis, including tick marks and labels, or an entire series.

- Press OPTION and click a third time to select an entire series as well as its representation in the legend.

- Press OPTION and click a fourth time to select all series and legend representation in the chart.

- Press OPTION and click a fifth time to select the entire chart.

After selecting the appropriate elements, you can manipulate them as desired. The only manipulation that you have to be careful with is layering. Only layer entire series, entire axes, and so on. Do *not* alter the layering of a single element, such as a bar, an axis label, or a tick mark.

 To use multiple chart types within a single chart, as shown in Figure 13-37, select the entire series that you want to change by clicking on it with the selection tool. Then choose STYLE... (GRAPHS) and select a new option in the "Graph type" box. The options to the right of the "Graph type" box are not available when only a single series is selected.

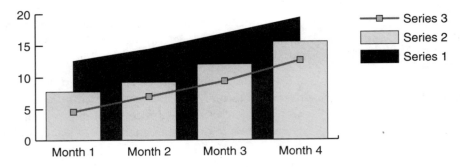

Figure 13-37: A graph containing series represented as an area chart (series 1), a bar chart (2), and a line chart (3).

Graph designs

Illustrator 5.0 allows you to create *pictographs*, graphs in which series are represented by graphic objects. The graphics can be stretched to form columns in a bar chart, or they can appear as markers in a line or scatter chart. The following sections describe how this works.

Creating a graph design

You create pictographs by establishing and using *graph designs*, special graphic objects that can be applied to a chart. Like tile patterns, graph designs are rectangular. Therefore, your graph design must include a rectangle, sent to back and generally painted with a transparent fill and stroke. Use the pen tool to draw a horizontal line the width of the graph design. In the case of a *sliding design*, position this line at the spot at which you want to see the object elongated. For example, if you are creating a graph design that looks like a hammer, you should position the horizontal line some place on the handle, as shown in Figure 13-38. The hammer will then be stretched at this location to represent a large value when a sliding design is specified.

After you have filled and stroked all graph design elements in front of the rectangle, select design elements, rectangle, and horizontal line and choose GROUP (⌘-G). Select the horizontal line with the direct-selection tool and choose MAKE (GUIDE) from the OBJECT menu (⌘-5). Then choose the LOCK (GUIDE) command (⌘-7) to unlock all guides. Select the whole design with the selection tool and choose DE-SIGN… from the GRAPH submenu under the OBJECT menu. The DESIGN dialog box will display, as shown in Figure 13-39.

Style...
Data...

Design...
Column...
Marker...

The **Illustrator 5** Book

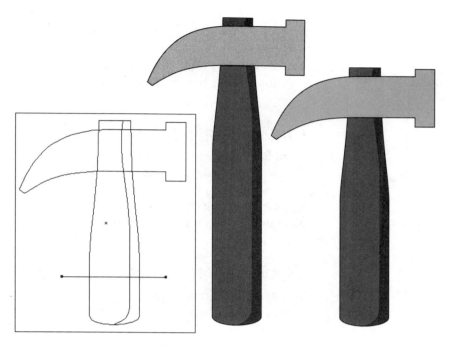

Figure 13-38: Add a horizontal line to a graph design (left) to indicate the location at which the graph design should be elongated in a sliding design (middle and right).

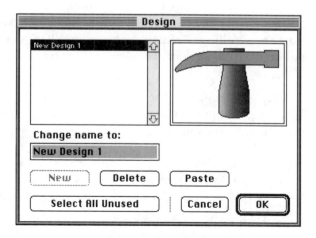

Figure 13-39: The Design dialog box allows you to create new graph designs and organize existing ones.

Enter a name for your graph design in the "Change name to" option box. The name takes the place of *New Design 1* in the scrolling pattern list. Click on the OK button or press RETURN to confirm the creation of your new graph design.

Organizing graph designs

In addition to allowing you to create new graph designs, the DESIGN dialog box provides options for organizing and editing existing graph designs. These options operate identically to those in the PATTERN dialog box. Read the *Organizing tile patterns* section of Chapter 9 for complete information on the use of these options.

Applying graph designs to a bar chart

You can apply graph designs to bar charts, stacked bar charts, line charts, and scatter charts. They are not applicable to area charts or pie charts.

To apply a design to an existing bar chart or stacked bar chart, select the specific series to which you want to apply the graph design by clicking on it with the selection tool. Then choose the COLUMN... command in the GRAPH submenu from the OBJECT menu. The GRAPH COLUMN DESIGN dialog box shown in Figure 13-40 displays. Select the desired "Column design type" option, select an existing graph design from the scrolling "Column design name" list, and click on the OK button or press RETURN. The design appears in the selected series.

The manner in which a design is applied to represent the values in a series depends on the radio button you select in the "Column design type" box in the GRAPH COLUMN DESIGN dialog box. These options include the following:

- **None**. Select this option only when you want to remove a graph design from the selected series. The "Column design name" box and the scrolling list inside it become dimmed.

- **Vertically scaled**. Select this option to enlarge or reduce the vertical proportion of the graph design in order to represent various values, as demonstrated in Figure 13-41.

```
Style...
Data...

Design...
Column...
Marker...
```

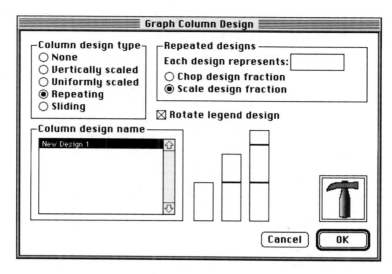

Figure 13-40: The Graph Column Design dialog box allows you to apply a graph design to the current bar chart or stacked bar chart.

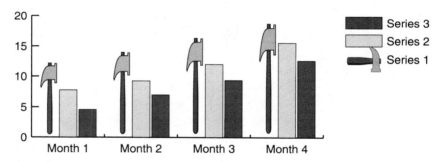

Figure 13-41: A series with a vertically scaled graph design.

- **Uniformly scaled**. Select this option to enlarge or reduce the graph design proportionally in order to represent various values, as demonstrated in Figure 13-42 on the following page.

- **Repeated**. Select this option to repeat the graph design over and over to represent various values. When the "Repeated" radio button is selected, the otherwise-dimmed "Repeated designs" options become available. Enter a value in the "Each design represents" option box to determine the value represented by each graph design. For example, if a value in the selected series is 500, and you enter 200 for "Each design represents," the design will be repeated two and a half times. Select the "Chop design fraction" to slice off the extraneous portions of the top repeated graph design, as shown in Figure 13-43; select "Scale design fraction" to scale the top graph design to the size of the fractional space, as shown in Figure 13-44.

- **Sliding**. Select this option to elongate the graph design at the spot indicated by the horizontal guide line when defining the design, as shown in Figure 13-45.

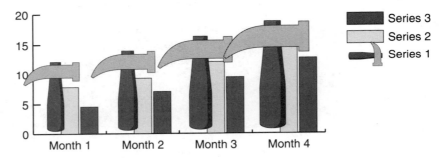

Figure 13-42: A series with uniformly scaled graph designs.

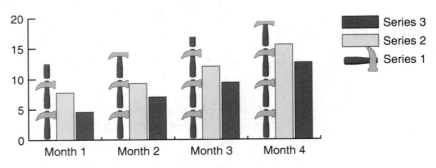

Figure 13-43: A series with repeated graph designs. Fractional designs at the top of each bar are chopped off.

The **Illustrator 5** Book

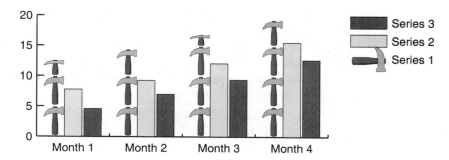

Figure 13-44: A series with repeated graph designs.
Fractional designs at the top of each bar are scaled.

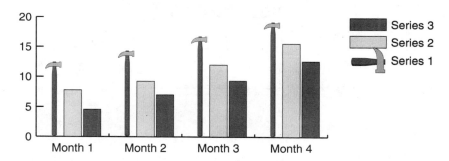

Figure 13-45: A series with sliding graph designs, which
have been elongated at the spot specified with the
horizontal guide line back in Figure 13-38.

Select the "Rotate legend design" check box in the GRAPH COLUMN
DESIGN dialog to display the graph design on its side in the legend, as
in the previous five figures. If you deselect this option, the design appears standing upright in the legend.

Applying graph designs to a line chart

To apply a design to an existing line chart or scatter chart, select the
specific series to which you want to apply the graph design by clicking on *a marker* in the series with the selection tool. (Do not select
the line segments.) Then choose the MARKER... command in the

GRAPH submenu from the OBJECT menu. The GRAPH MARKER DESIGN dialog box shown in Figure 13-46 displays. Select "On data point" from the "Marker design type" options, select an existing graph design from the scrolling "Marker design name" list, and click on the OK button or press RETURN. The design appears in the selected series, as shown in Figure 13-47.

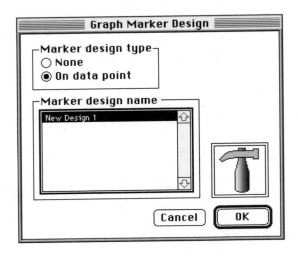

Figure 13-46: The Graph Marker Design dialog box allows you to select a graph design to apply to the current line chart or scatter chart.

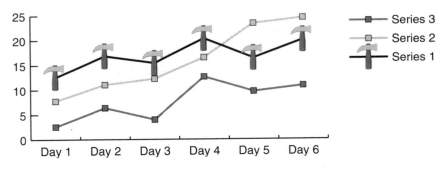

Figure 13-47: Graph designs applied to the markers of a series in a line chart.

The **Illustrator** 5 Book

The size at which a graph design appears in a line or scatter chart is determined by the size of the rectangle you draw when defining the graph design. When applied to a chart, the rectangle is reduced to match the size of the square marker that normally appears at a point in a series. Therefore, to create a design that scales to a reasonable size when applied to a line chart or scatter chart, draw a small rectangle when defining the graph design.

Select the "None" radio button in the "Marker design type" box to remove the graph design from the selected line or scatter chart.

PART 5
FINAL STEPS

CHAPTER

14

IMPORTING AND EXPORTING ARTWORK

579

Illustrator allows you to use documents from other applications in the creation of artwork. In Chapter 3, you saw how you can introduce MacPaint and PICT files for use as tracing templates. In Chapter 7, you learned how to add type from a word processor to a text block. And Chapter 13 explained how to import spreadsheet data for use in a graph.

In this chapter, I will demonstrate how you can place Encapsulated PostScript documents that have been created in other drawing programs into an Illustrator file. You can also save an Illustrator file as an EPS document and import it to page-composition applications that run on the Macintosh or on the IBM PC and compatibles.

Importing graphics

Illustrator allows you to import graphics saved in the *Encapsulated PostScript* (EPS) format. An EPS document is a pure PostScript file that is accompanied by a screen representation, in the PICT format on the Mac or the Metafile format on the PC. The EPS format was designed by Altsys Corporation (the developers of FreeHand) in co-operation with Aldus and Adobe for swapping high-resolution images from one PostScript-compatible application to another. The screen representation is accompanied by a PostScript-language definition that is downloaded directly to the output device during the printing process.

An EPS file can be imported into an illustration as an actual portion of the artwork. It can be transformed, duplicated, layered, and printed. However, it can not be reshaped or blended. In other words, even though an EPS file may have been constructed as a series of points and segments, just like an Illustrator drawing, those points and segments can not be altered.

The EPS format is notoriously inefficient for storing bitmapped artwork. A color EPS bitmap is typically twice as large as the same bitmap saved in the TIFF format. However, Illustrator does not support TIFF or any other graphic format. If you want to manipulate and transform scanned images or other bitmaps in a drawing program, we recommend that you use Aldus FreeHand.

Placing EPS graphics

You can introduce an EPS document into the current illustration by choosing the PLACE ART... command from the FILE menu. This displays the PLEASE OPEN ENCAPSULATED POSTSCRIPT FILE dialog box, shown in Figure 14-1. Notice that four files are displayed. This dialog box displays both EPS files and plain-text files. A standard Illustrator file is saved as an ASCII PostScript document. You can import such a graphic, but since there is no screen preview associated with the file, you cannot view it accurately on screen. Instead, it will appear as a gray box representing the physical proportions of the image. The file will print correctly, but it may be difficult to position the image relative to other elements in an illustration.

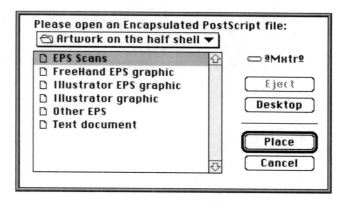

Figure 14-1: The Please Open Encapsulated PostScript File dialog box allows you to import an EPS graphic.

Other plain-text files display as well, such as those created in word processors. But unless they describe a graphic in the PostScript printer language, they cannot be imported using the PLACE ART... command. (You can, of course, import any plain-text file using the IMPORT TEXT... command as described in Chapter 7, *Creating and Editing Type*.)

The PLEASE OPEN ENCAPSULATED POSTSCRIPT FILE dialog box also displays any documents saved in the EPS format. These may originate from the Macintosh or PC; however, only Macintosh-format EPS files with PICT screen previews will display correctly on screen.

Viewing a placed graphic

After you select the desired file from the scrolling list and press RETURN, the selected graphic appears in the middle of the current window as a large box inset with two diagonal lines that cross the box from corner

to corner, as shown in the first example of Figure 14-2. Choose the PRE-
VIEW command (⌘-Y) to display the placed image as it appeared when
created and previewed in its original software.

If you select the "Show placed images" check box in the DOCU-
MENT SETUP dialog box (introduced in the *Document setup* section of
Chapter 3), you can view the graphic in the artwork mode, as shown
in the second example of Figure 14-2. Although the screen-redraw
speed is slower when the "Show placed images" option is selected,
you can manipulate the graphic more accurately in this mode. Placed
images always display accurately in the preview mode, regardless of
the setting of the "Show Placed Images" option.

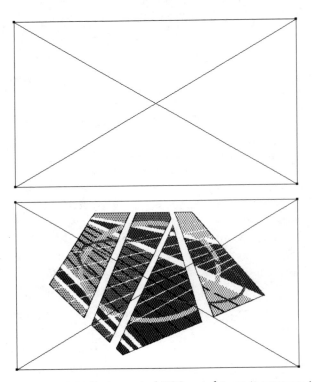

*Figure 14-2: An imported EPS graphic as it appears in
the artwork mode when the "Show placed images" option
is deselected (top) and selected (bottom).*

The **Illustrator 5** Book

Masking imported graphics

Figure 14-3 shows how an EPS image might be integrated into an illustration. Here I have scanned an enhanced image of a floppy disk, saved it in the EPS format, and imported it into Illustrator using the PLACE ART... command. I then created a path shaped like an apple using the pen tool. After selecting the path with the selection tool, I SHIFT-clicked to select the imported EPS image and chose the MAKE command from the MASK submenu under the OBJECT menu. The result is a scanned image set inside an apple, an effect possible only in an advanced drawing application like Adobe Illustrator.

Figure 14-3: A gray-scale bitmapped image saved in the EPS format, imported into Illustrator, and masked by a clipping path.

Opening illustrations that contain EPS graphics

An illustration that contains an EPS image must always be able to reference its original EPS file in order to preview or to print the placed image successfully. Therefore, when you save an illustration, Illustrator remembers the location of the original imported EPS file on disk. If you try to open an existing illustration after having moved its imported EPS file to a different disk or folder, Illustrator will produce the PLEASE LOCATE dialog box, as shown in Figure 14-4. This dialog box asks you to locate your EPS file on disk. If you click on the CANCEL button, the illustration previews with a white box covering all objects in back of the EPS image; such an EPS image will not print at all.

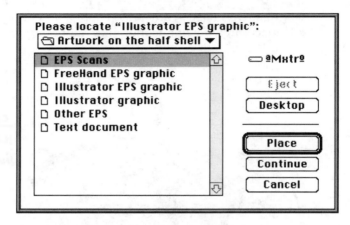

Figure 14-4: The Please Locate dialog box asks you to specify the current location of an imported EPS file on disk.

Exporting an illustration

You can use illustrations created in Illustrator 5.0 in any Macintosh or PC application that supports the EPS format. In this way, an illustration can become part of a full-fledged document, such as a newsletter, flyer, or catalog, or part of a video or on-screen presentation.

Saving an illustration in the EPS format

You can store an illustration as an EPS document by choosing the SAVE AS... command from the FILE menu. Figure 14-5 shows the SAVE ILLUSTRATION dialog box that will display. (This dialog box is the same one I introduced in the *Saving an illustration* section of Chapter 3.) At the bottom of the dialog box are three options that allow you to save an illustration for use in other applications. These include the "Preview" and "Compatibility" pop-up menus and the "Include Placed images" check box.

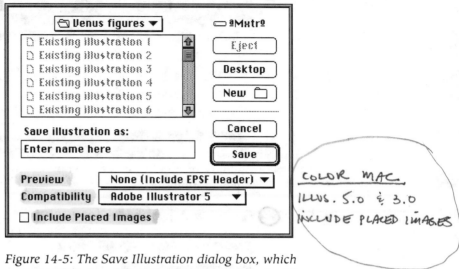

Figure 14-5: The Save Illustration dialog box, which appears when you choose the Save As… command from the File menu, allows you to export an EPS document for use in another Macintosh or PC application.

The "Preview" pop-up menu allows you determine whether the current illustration is saved as an EPS file. It includes the following options:

- **None (Omit EPSF Header)**. Select this option to save the illustration as a standard PostScript file that cannot be imported into most other applications. The "Include Placed Images" check box will be dimmed.

- **None (Include EPSF Header)**. Select this option to save the illustration with an EPS header in order to import it into any application that supports the EPS format. No preview, however, will be included with the illustration. Instead, the illustration will appear as a gray box on screen in another application, but it will print correctly.

- **Black&White Macintosh**. Select this option to save the illustration as an EPS file with a black-and-white screen preview for use in any Macintosh program that supports the EPS format.

8 Bit Macintosh

- **Color Macintosh**. Select this option to save the illustration as an EPS file with a color screen preview for use in any Mac program that supports the EPS format and runs in color. Color EPS files take up more room on disk than black-and-white EPS files.

- **IBM PC**. Select this option to save the illustration as an EPS file with a black-and-white screen preview for use in any PC program that supports the EPS format.

The "Compatibility" pop-up menu allows you specify whether the current illustration is compatible with earlier versions of Illustrator as well as with other applications that support early formats. It includes the following options:

- **Adobe Illustrator 5**. Select this option to save the illustration as a standard Illustrator 5.0 file. Such a file cannot be opened in previous versions of Illustrator.

- **Adobe Illustrator 4**. Select this option to save the illustration as a standard Illustrator 4.0 file. Such a file can be opened in Illustrator 4.0 or 5.0 but not in Illustrator 1.1, 88, or 3.0.

- **Adobe Illustrator 3**. Select this option to save the illustration as a standard Illustrator 3.0 file. Such a file can be opened in Illustrator 3.0, 4.0, or 5.0 but not in Illustrator 1.1, or 88.

- **Adobe Illustrator 88**. Select this option to save the illustration as an Illustrator 88 file. Such a file can be opened in Illustrator 88, 3.0, 4.0, and 5.0 but not in Illustrator 1.1.

- **Adobe Illustrator 1.1**. Select this option to save the illustration as an Illustrator 1.1 file. Such a file can be opened in any version of Adobe Illustrator as well as in several other drawing applications such as Aldus FreeHand on the Mac and Corel-Draw on the PC.

 Depending on the complexity of the current illustration, any format but "Adobe Illustrator 5" may result in some loss of information. Techniques such as tile patterns, masking, and placing EPS graphics are incompatible with the Illustrator 1.1 format; compound paths and

The **Illustrator 5** Book

area or path text blocks are not supported by Illustrator 88. In the Illustrator 1.1 format, objects painted with patterns will become filled or stroked with 100% black. Though the form of a clipping path or a compound path will remain intact, its purpose will be ignored; objects will not be masked, nor will they create holes. If an illustration contains a placed EPS image, that image will not appear when the file is opened in Illustrator 1.1. If an illustration contains text objects, they will be converted to point text blocks with fewer than 256 characters when saved in the Illustrator 88 format.

Saving to the Illustrator 3 or 4 format results in minor losses only. Namely, these versions of Illustrator do not support gradations. Any gradient fills are therefore converted to blends.

 When saving an illustration in any of the old formats, be sure that you have previously saved it in the Illustrator 5 format to avoid the permanent loss of information. For example, you might want to save to the Illustrator 3 format to ensure a gradation will print when imported into PageMaker or QuarkXPress. But unless you also save the illustration in the Illustrator 5 format, you won't be able to edit the gradation later on.

Saving illustrations with placed EPS graphics

If the current illustration that you are saving as an EPS file contains one or more EPS images that have been imported with the PLACE ART... command, be sure to select the "Include Placed Images" check box in the SAVE ILLUSTRATION dialog box. This option directs Illustrator to include a PostScript description of all imported EPS graphics as part of the saved illustration file.

If you do not check the "Include Placed Images" option when you save an illustration that contains a placed image, upon clicking the SAVE button or pressing RETURN, the dialog box shown in Figure 14-6 displays giving you another chance to include the placed image with the illustration. Click on the SAVE WITH PLACED IMAGES button or press RETURN if you decide to include the placed images in your document. Click on the SAVE WITHOUT PLACED IMAGES or press COMMAND-PERIOD if you decide to stick with your original decision. You can also cancel the entire saving process by clicking on the CANCEL button or pressing COMMAND -C.

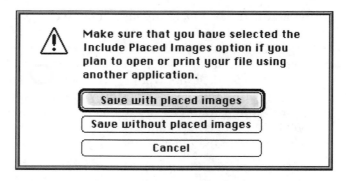

Figure 14-6: If you do not take advantage of it in the Save Illustration dialog box, you get a second chance to include placed images with your illustration.

Note that selecting the "Include Placed Images" option does not free Illustrator from requiring access to the original EPS file when you open the illustration at some later point in time. This is very important; folks always get mixed up on this point, so I recommend that you read that sentence again and assign it to memory. However, selecting the option does ensure that an EPS illustration that contains EPS graphics will preview and print correctly from within another application, such as a page-composition or presentation program. If this option is not selected when saving an EPS illustration, any placed EPS graphics will appear on-screen but will not print successfully.

CHAPTER

15

PRINTING
YOUR
ILLUSTRATIONS

Illustrator describes every text block and graphic object in an illustration as a combination of mathematically defined points and segments. This pure-math model allows Illustrator to translate the illustration to various hardware devices, regardless of device resolution. On a day-to-day basis, the primary display device is your monitor. However, finished illustrations are best displayed on a page printed from a high-resolution output device. In this chapter, I discuss how to print Illustrator 5.0 files, including black-and-white standard prints, color composite prints, and color separations.

Printing from Illustrator

You can print black-and-white, grayscale, and color composites (using a color laser printer) directly from inside the Illustrator application. To create color separations for four-color process printing, you must use the Adobe Separator utility, as discussed in the *Printing from Separator* section later in this chapter.

Printing from Adobe Illustrator is a four-step process.

1. Use the Chooser desk accessory to select the LaserWriter driver.
2. Choose the PAGE SETUP... command from the FILE menu to determine the size of the printed page.
3. Position the page-size boundary in the drawing area.
4. Choose the PRINT... command from the FILE menu (⌘-P) to print the current illustration to the selected output device.

Each of these steps is described in detail in the following sections.

Choosing the PostScript printer

Illustrator prints high-resolution artwork only to PostScript-compatible output devices. Although you can print an illustration to a non-PostScript printer, such as an ImageWriter or LaserWriter SC, it will print as a low-resolution bitmap, exactly as it appears on screen. For any but the most rudimentary proofing purposes, such a print is useless.

To select a PostScript-compatible printer, choose the CHOOSER from the list of desk accessories under the APPLE menu. The Chooser desk accessory appears, as shown in Figure 15-1. One or more *printer drivers* display on the left side of the window. Printer drivers help the current application translate the contents of a printed file to a specific variety of output device. Click on the icon labeled "LaserWriter," which is the driver for all PostScript-compatible printers. This allows you to prepare your illustration to be printed to a PostScript printer even if no such printer is currently hooked up to your Mac. If your computer is networked to one or more PostScript devices, select the desired printer from the "Select a LaserWriter" list on the right-hand side of the Chooser window. Then click in the close box to return to the Illustrator desktop.

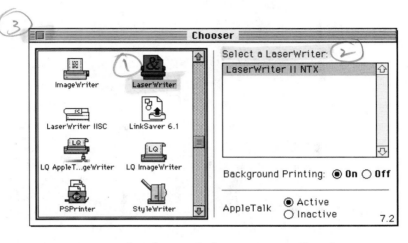

Figure 15-1: Use the Chooser desk accessory to select the LaserWriter printer driver.

Setting up the page

The next step is to define the size of the page on which your illustration will be printed. Choose the PAGE SETUP... command from the FILE menu to display the LASERWRITER PAGE SETUP dialog box shown in Figure 15-2 on the next page. I first introduced this dialog box in the *Adjusting the page size* section of Chapter 3, where I explained how to set the page size for a new document. Remember, if you want to see the page boundaries in your illustration, you must toggle the SHOW PAGE TILING command in the VIEW menu so that the page boundaries display. Let's now take a more complete look at this dialog box.

The most important options presented in this dialog box are the "Paper" radio buttons, which control the size of the printed page. Apple's LASERWRITER PAGE SETUP dialog box offers five page sizes: "US Letter," "US Legal," "A4 Letter," "B5 Letter," and "Tabloid." "Tabloid" is a pop-up menu that offers five specialized sizes or styles, including two envelope choices.

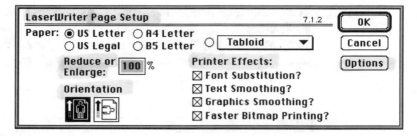

Figure 15-2: Use the LaserWriter Page Setup dialog box to determine page size and orientation. The LaserWriter driver version number is displayed to the left of the OK button.

As discussed in Chapter 3, the selected page size also determines the current *margin size,* displayed within the page-size boundary in the drawing area. The margin size specifies the *imageable area* of a page; that is, the amount of the page on which objects can be printed. For example, a "US Letter" page measures 8½ inches by 11 inches, but only 7.68 inches by 10.16 inches is imageable. Objects that fall in the remaining margin will not print on Apple LaserWriters or most other PostScript-compatible laser printers. (High-resolution printers, such as the Linotronic family of imagesetters, print the entire page size, regardless of the margin size.) You can enlarge the margin size by selecting the "Larger Print Area" option in the LASERWRITER OP-TIONS dialog box, as described later in this section.

The LASERWRITER PAGE SETUP dialog box also allows you to set a reduction or enlargement to alter the size of your document. On the Apple LaserWriter, reductions may be as small as 25% and enlargements as large as 400%. If you enter a value in the "Reduce or Enlarge" option box that is beyond the capability of your printer, an alert box warns you as soon as you click on the OK button or press the RETURN key.

The "Orientation" icons are the next options. As in other Macintosh software, you can specify whether your page is upright (the portrait setting) or on its side (the landscape setting). Changing the orientation setting in this dialog box also changes the orientation of the page size in the drawing area. Text blocks and graphic objects will *not* be repositioned or rotated to match the new orientation.

Four "Printer Effects" options are available, all of which are ignored when printing from Adobe Illustrator.

The OPTIONS button brings up the LASERWRITER OPTIONS dialog box shown in Figure 15-3. The check boxes in this dialog can be very useful in adjusting the appearance of a printed illustration. The sample page on the left-hand side of the dialog box demonstrates the effect of the selected options. The dog represents the illustration on the page, and the dotted line represents the margin size.

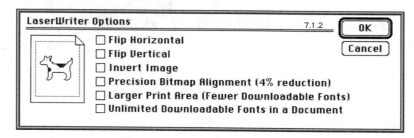

Figure 15-3: The LaserWriter Options dialog box allows you to adjust the appearance of an illustration on the printed page.

The options in the LASERWRITER OPTIONS dialog box work like so:

- **Flip Horizontal**. Select this option to flip the objects in an illustration horizontally on the printed page. When printing film negatives, deselect "Flip Horizontal" to specify *emulsion up*; select the option to specify *emulsion down*. The creation of film negatives is discussed more thoroughly later in this chapter.

- **Flip Vertical**. Select this option to flip the objects in an illustration vertically on the printed page. You can also use this option to determine the emulsion side of a film negative. However, if you select *both* "Flip Horizontal" and "Flip Vertical," you will nullify the effect (emulsion up).

- **Invert Image**. Select this option to change all blacks to white and all whites to black. For example, black becomes white, 40% black becomes 60% black, and 20% black becomes 80% black. This option prints a *negative* of the current illustration and is used primarily when printing to film on high-resolution Linotronic or Compugraphic imagesetters.

- **Precision Bitmap Alignment** (**4% reduction**). This option reduces 72-dot-per-inch MacPaint images to 96% of their current size, making them compatible with the resolution of a 300-dot-per-inch laser printer. Since bitmapped MacPaint images can be used only as nonprinting tracing templates in Illustrator, this option is useless when printing an illustration.

- **Larger Print Area** (**Fewer Downloadable Fonts**). This option allows you to enlarge the imageable area of an illustration when printing to a laser printer. The margin size displayed in the drawing area becomes larger when this option is selected. The standard and enlarged imageable areas for each page size are listed below. (All above imageable area measurements are notated in picas and points. For example, *60p9* means 60 picas and 9 points.)

Page size			Imageable area		Larger image area	
NAME	WIDTH	HEIGHT	WIDTH	HEIGHT	WIDTH	HEIGHT
US Letter	8.5″	11″	46p0	60p9	48p0	64p8
US Legal	8.5″	14″	40p4	75p0	48p0	81p6
Tabloid	11″	17″	63p6	99p0	63p6	99p0
A4 Letter	210mm	297mm	44p9	66p0	46p6	66p5
B5 Letter	176mm	250mm	38p9	58p6	38p9	58p6

- **Unlimited Downloadable Fonts in a Document**. When selected, this option forces a change in the PostScript commands that define your illustration. Normally, documents can contain only as many fonts as will fit into printer memory at once, but this option allows downloadable fonts to swap in and out of printer memory. Although you can select this option to avoid printer out-of-memory errors, Adobe warns against using it, since it may cause printing complications of its own.

Adjusting the page size

The appearance of the page boundaries in the drawing area is determined by the selected radio button in the "View" area of the DOCUMENT SETUP dialog box (first introduced in the *Document setup* section of Chapter 3).

The **Illustrator** 5 Book

These radio buttons include the following:

- **Single full page**. Select this radio button to display a single page size and margin size.

- **Tile full pages**. Select this radio button to display as many whole pages as will fit inside the artboard.

- **Tile imageable areas**. Select this radio button to subdivide the artboard into multiple partial margin sizes, called *tiles*.

After selecting one of these options, use the page tool to position the page size in relation to the objects in your illustration. Be sure to choose the SHOW PAGE TILING command from the VIEW menu if the dotted page boundaries are not visible. If you select the "Tile imageable areas" option, the page number of each tile is listed in the lower left corner of the tile. This way, you can specify the particular pages that you want to print from inside the LASERWRITER PRINT dialog box.

For more information about using "View" options and the page tool, refer to the sections *Moving the page size in the drawing area* and *Creating a two-page layout* which begin on page 99 of Chapter 3.

Printing pages

To initiate the printing process, choose the PRINT... command from the FILE menu (⌘-P). The standard LASERWRITER PRINT dialog box displays, as shown in Figure 15-4 on the next page. Enter the number of copies you want to print in the "Copies" option box. Then select a range of pages using the "Pages" options. By default, the "All" radio button is selected. If the drawing area displays a single page size, only that page will be printed. If the drawing area displays multiple pages or tiles, Illustrator will print all pages that contain type or graphic objects. To define a specific range of pages or tiles to be printed, enter the page numbers in the "From" and "To" option boxes. These numbers should correspond to the page numbers displayed in the lower left corners of pages in the drawing area.

The "Cover Page" options allow you to print an extra page that lists the user name, application, document name, date, time, and printer for the current job. This page can precede or follow the illustration pages.

```
┌─────────────────────────────────────────────────────────────┐
│ LaserWriter  "LaserWriter II NTH"              7.1.2  ┌─────────┐│
│                                                       │  Print  ││
│ Copies: 1         Pages: ◉ All  ○ From:    To:       └─────────┘│
│                                                       ┌─────────┐│
│ Cover Page:    ◉ No ○ First Page  ○ Last Page        │ Cancel  ││
│                                                       └─────────┘│
│ Paper Source: ◉ Paper Cassette  ○ Manual Feed                   │
│ Print:         ◉ Black & White   ○ Color/Grayscale              │
│ Destination:   ◉ Printer         ○ PostScript® File             │
└─────────────────────────────────────────────────────────────┘
```

*Figure 15-4: The LaserWriter Print dialog box allows you
to print a composite of an illustration to a PostScript-
compatible output device.*

If you want to print your illustration on a letterhead or another
special piece of paper, select "Manual Feed" from the "Paper Source"
options. Your laser printer will display a manual feed light directing
you to insert the special paper. The "Paper Source" options are ignored when printing to a color laser printer or to an imagesetter or
other film-based output device.

Two "Print" radio buttons appear near the bottom of the LASER-
WRITER PRINT dialog box: "Black & White" and "Color/Grayscale."
These options affect the printing of PICT images only and are ignored
when printing PostScript or Encapsulated PostScript illustrations.

The last two radio buttons, "Printer" and "PostScript File," allow
you to either send the document directly to your printer or to a Post-
Script text file on disk. Selecting the "PostScript File" option changes
the PRINT button into a SAVE button. Clicking on the SAVE button displays a standard SAVE dialog box that lets you name and determine
the destination folder of the PostScript file. I don't recommend that
you use this option with Illustrator since the program automatically
generates PostScript files when you save an illustration.

Click on the PRINT button or press RETURN to initiate the printing
process. If the current illustration contains color and your output device is not capable of printing colors, your printer will use gray values
to represent the colors, much like a black-and-white television shows
Gone with the Wind in grayscale. Color documents output on color
printers produce *color composites*, which are prints that contain all
colors used in the current illustration. To create color separations of
illustrations that include color, use the Adobe Separator utility as described in the *Printing from Separator* section later in this chapter.

The new PostScript printer driver

PSPrinter

If you own the Adobe Illustrator 5.0 Deluxe CD-ROM, you have access to Adobe's newest printer driver, PSPrinter 8.0. It's contained in the PSPrinter 8.0.1 folder on the CD and must be installed separately from Illustrator. Once you install PSPrinter, an additional printer icon appears in the Chooser. Select the icon labeled "PSPrinter" as you would select the "LaserWriter" icon. Then click in the close box.

With "PSPrinter" selected, choose the PAGE SETUP command from the FILE menu in Illustrator. The PSPRINTER PAGE SETUP dialog box appears, as shown in Figure 15-5. Click on the OPTIONS button to display the PSPRINTER OPTIONS dialog box, as shown in Figure 15-6.

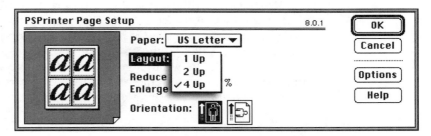

Figure 15-5: The PSPrinter Page Setup dialog box provides access to basically the same features as does the LaserWriter dialog box.

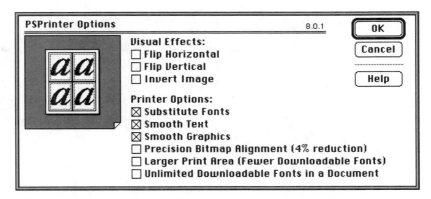

Figure 15-6: The PSPrinter Options dialog box lets you adjust the orientation, size, and appearance of an illustration on the printed page.

Chapter 15: **Printing Your Illustrations** 597

For the most part, the options in the PSPRINTER PAGE SETUP and OPTIONS dialog boxes are identical to those discussed on pages 568 through 570. Certainly, the options are distributed differently—for example, some that appear in the LASERWRITER PAGE SETUP dialog box are now found in the PSPRINTER OPTIONS dialog box—but the only real dissimilarities when using the PSPrinter driver are the lack of a "Faster Bitmap Printing" option and the addition of the "Layout" pop-up menu, which lets you output 1, 2, or 4 tiles on a single printed page. This allows you to reduce tabloid illustrations to fit on a letter-size page. For example, with PSPrinter you can print the illustration shown in Figure 15-9 in one pass by selecting the "4" option from the "Layout" pop-up menu. Illustrator will automatically resize the illustration to fit within the confines of a single printed page.

When you print with the PSPrinter driver, Illustrator displays the dialog box shown in Figure 15-7. The "Paper Source" options let you print the first page on special paper. The other options work as discussed earlier. Click on the OPTIONS button to display the PRINT OPTIONS dialog box shown in Figure 15-8. Using the "PostScript Errors" pop-up menu, you can request that printing errors remain on screen for your inspection or print along with your illustration.

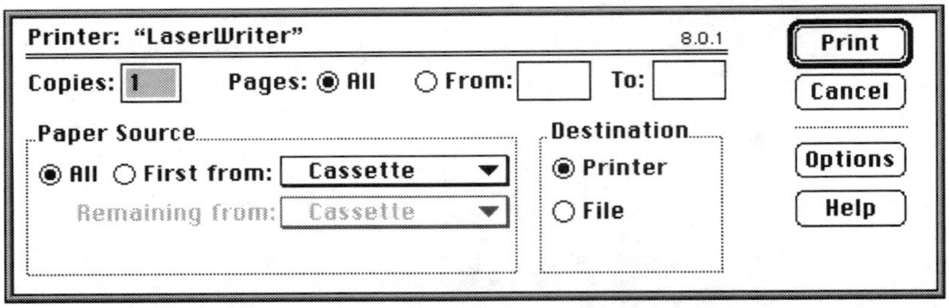

Figure 15-7: This dialog box allows you to choose a different paper source for the first page.

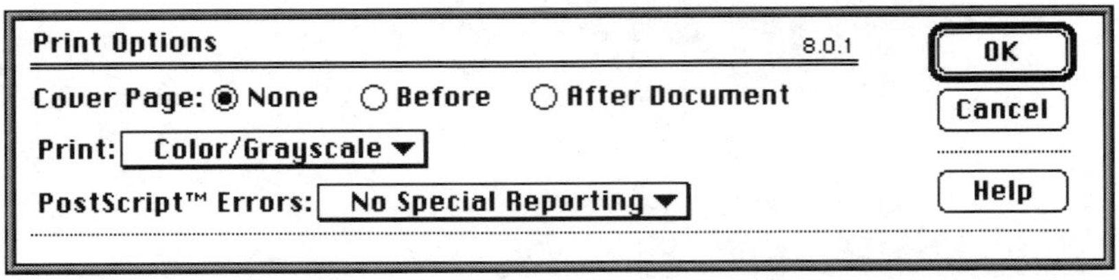

Figure 15-8: The Print Options dialog box allows you to decide how and where Illustrator reports printing errors.

Special printing considerations

No two print jobs are the same. Although the process itself is straight-forward, your illustration may require special treatment not addressed by the PRINT... command. Alternatively, your illustration may seem fine, but complications occur that prevent the printing process from completing successfully. In either of these cases, the following sections may be of some assistance. They explain how to: 1) print oversized art-work, 2) create crop marks, 3) avoid "limitcheck" errors, and 4) solve "out of memory" errors.

Printing oversized documents

By virtue of the LASERWRITER PAGE SETUP dialog box, Illustrator pro-vides access to various common page sizes. But many artists require custom page sizes that Illustrator cannot accommodate. And even if it could, most laser printers are set up to print letter-size pages only. So how do you proof oversized artwork using a typical laser printer, and how do you print the final artwork from an imagesetter?

To proof your artwork, select the "US Letter" option in the LASER-WRITER PAGE SETUP dialog box, then select "Tile imageable areas" from the "Artwork board" options in the PREFERENCES dialog box. Your illus-tration will be sectioned onto separate tiles as indicated by the dotted lines in the drawing area. If these breaks are not at the most opportune locations in terms of easily reassembling your artwork, use the page tool to manually reposition the dotted lines. Then print your document one page at a time, manually repositioning the tile for each page before each print, as demonstrated in Figure 15-9 on the next page.

To print the finished illustration, use the Adobe Separator utility, which can take full advantage of the larger printable areas found on certain PostScript output devices, including Linotronic and Compu-graphic imagesetters. Separator ignores tile locations, instead allow-ing you to specify a *bounding box* to define the custom size of your imageable area. (See the *Printing from Separator* section later in this chapter for complete information.)

Figure 15-9: Using the page tool to reposition the tiles with respect to an oversized illustration.

Creating crop marks

Illustrator 5.0 provides new commands for creating *crop marks*, which are used to indicate the boundaries of an illustration. When printed to an Linotronic 100 imagesetter, for example, all illustrations are printed on pages 12 inches wide, regardless of their actual size. When you go to have the illustration commercially reproduced, the printer will want to know the dimensions of the final page size and how the illustration should be positioned on the page. Crop marks specify the boundaries of the reproduced page. Properly positioned crop marks prevent miscommunication with your commercial printer, as well as help avoid additional commercial printing expenses.

To create crop marks, draw a box with the rectangle tool that represents the size of the paper onto which the final illustration will be reproduced. While the rectangle remains selected, choose the MAKE command from the CROPMARKS submenu under the OBJECT menu. The rectangle will be converted into crop marks, as shown in Figure 15-10. Notice that the marks are positioned outside the boundary, preventing them from appearing on the final, reproduced page.

🔬 The **Illustrator 5** Book

If no object is selected and a single page is displayed in the drawing area (as per the "Single full page" option in the DOCUMENT SETUP dialog box), choose MAKE (CROPMARKS) to create crop marks to match the current page size.

Only one set of crop marks can exist inside any illustration. When you choose MAKE (CROPMARKS), you delete any previous crop marks while creating new ones.

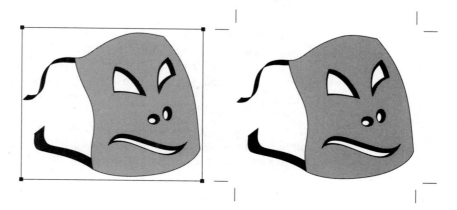

Figure 15-10: After drawing a rectangle to specify the size of the trimmed illustration (left), choose the Set Cropmarks command to convert the rectangle to crop marks (right).

Crop marks can also be useful for defining the boundaries of an EPS illustration that you intend to import into a page-layout or presentation program. In Aldus PageMaker, for example, you might import an illustration with crop marks, and then use the crop tool to trim the illustration to the proper size.

You can also export EPS illustrations with crop marks in order to combine multiple illustrations with multiple sets of crop marks on a single page. This saves imagesetting costs and provides any number of required crop marks for paste-up purposes.

To delete the crop marks from an illustration, choose the RELEASE command from the CROPMARKS submenu under the OBJECT menu. The crop marks will be converted back to a rectangle.

Splitting long paths

You might encounter several errors when printing an illustration. One of the most common is the "limitcheck" error, which results from a limitation in your printer's PostScript interpreter. If the number of points in the mathematical representation of a path exceeds this limitation, the illustration will not print successfully.

Unfortunately, the "points" used in this mathematical representation are not the points you used to define the object. Instead, they are calculated by the PostScript interpreter during the printing process. When presented with a curve, the PostScript interpreter has to plot hundreds of tiny straight lines to create the most accurate possible rendering. So rather than drawing a perfect curve, your printer creates a many-sided polygon whose exact number of sides in determined by a device-dependent variable known as *flatness*. The default flatness value for the Apple LaserWriter is 1.0 device pixel, or $\frac{1}{300}$ inch. This means the center of any tiny side of the polygon rendering may be at most $\frac{1}{300}$ inch from the farthest X,Y-coordinate of the actual mathematical curve, as demonstrated by Figure 15-11.

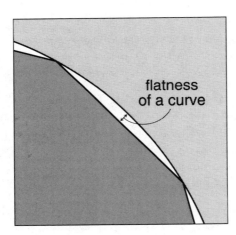

Figure 15-11: The flatness of a curve determines the greatest distance between any one of the tiny straight lines used to represent the curve and its true mathematical description.

The **Illustrator 5** Book

Each tiny line in the polygon rendering is joined at a "point." If the number of "points" exceeds your printer's built-in "path" limit, an alert box displays, warning you that the printer has encountered a limitcheck error, and the print job is canceled. The "path" limit for the original LaserWriter was 1500, seemingly enough straight lines to imitate any curve. But every once in a while, you may create a curve that proves too much for the printer. For example, a standard signature contains several complex loops that might tax the limitations of the most advanced output device.

There are two ways to avoid limitcheck errors. The first and most preferred method is to select the "Split long paths" check box in the DOCUMENT SETUP dialog box. Then enter the resolution for the *final* output device in the "Output resolution" option box at the bottom of the dialog. The next time you save or print the current illustration, Illustrator will automatically break up every path that it considers to be at risk into several smaller paths. The integrity of your illustration will not be affected.

Unfortunately, there is no way to automatically reassemble paths that have been split. They must be joined back together manually if and when you decide to make alterations the illustration. And finally, Illustrator's automated path-splitting feature only accounts for the complexity of a path. It does not account for whether a path is filled or stroked with a complex tile pattern, which is the most likely cause of a "limitcheck" error.

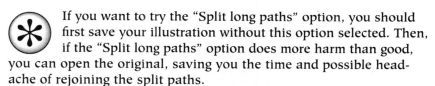 If you want to try the "Split long paths" option, you should first save your illustration without this option selected. Then, if the "Split long paths" option does more harm than good, you can open the original, saving you the time and possible headache of rejoining the split paths.

If the automatic splitting technique does not solve your problem, you can change the flatness of individual paths. Select the path that seems responsible—keeping in mind that long paths painted with tile patterns are the most likely culprits—and choose ATTRIBUTES... from the OBJECT menu (⌘-⌥-A) to display the ATTRIBUTES dialog box. The "Output resolution" option box lets you control the printed appearance of a selected path without affecting the rest of the illustration. The flatness equals the resolution of your printer divided by the "Output resolution" value. For example, if you are printing to a 2400-dpi imagesetter, entering a value of 600 into the "Output resolution" option box changes the flatness of the selected path to 4.

Printing pattern tiles

As described in the previous section, tile patterns may cause limit-check errors. But more often they cause "out of memory" errors, especially if several patterns are used in a single illustration. To accelerate the printing process, Illustrator downloads tiles to your printer's memory, much as if they were nonresident fonts. In this way, the printer accesses tile definitions repeatedly throughout the creation of an illustration. However, if the current illustration contains too many tile patterns, or if a single tile is too complex, the printer's memory may become full, in which case the print operation is cancelled and an alert box warns you that an out-of-memory error has occurred.

Out-of-memory errors are less common in high-resolution output devices, such as imagesetters, because these machines tend to include updated PostScript interpreters and have increased memory capacity. Therefore, you will most often encounter an out-of-memory error when proofing an illustration to an old-model LaserWriter or other low-memory device. Try any one of these techniques to remedy the problem:

- Change all typefaces in the current illustration to Times, Helvetica, or some other printer-resident font. In this way, Illustrator will not have to download both patterns and printer fonts.

- Print objects painted with dissimilar tile patterns in separate illustrations. Then use traditional paste-up techniques to combine the pages into a composite proof.

- Deselect the "Preview and print patterns" option in the GENERAL PREFERENCES dialog box. All patterned fills and strokes will print as gray. This technique allows you to proof all portions of your illustration except the patterns themselves.

When you print the illustration to an imagesetter, it will probably print successfully because of the imagesetter's increased memory capacity. If the illustration still encounters an out-of-memory error, you will have to delete some patterns or resort to traditional paste-up techniques, as suggested in the second item of the list above.

Most service bureaus charge extra for printing complex documents that tie up their imagesetters for long periods of time. Tile patterns almost always complicate an illustration and slow down printing time. Therefore, use masks and compound paths instead of patterns whenever possible.

Printing from Separator

Adobe Separator is a utility application that creates and outputs *color separations* from files created with Illustrator 5.0. The process of creating color separations results in a separate printed page, either on paper or film, for each of the four process colors and for each custom color used in the document. Each page displays only those objects, or portions of objects, that contain the specified color.

Before discussing Adobe Separator any further, it must be made clear that this software's relative ease of use belies the complexity of the process that it facilitates. Creating color separations for four-color printing is an exacting and demanding undertaking. It requires specific knowledge of the four-color printing process, the press on which documents will be reproduced, and the imagesetter on which the separation positives or negatives will be output. This does not mean that you cannot successfully create and use separations from Adobe Illustrator and Adobe Separator, but I strongly advise that you work very closely with your commercial printer, and be sure that the service bureau or print department that will be outputting your separations understands your requirements exactly.

Starting Separator

Prior to using Adobe Separator, you must install the Separator application and the PPD folder on your hard disk as described in Appendix A. Once you've installed them, double-click on the Separator icon at the Finder level to launch the application.

The PLEASE OPEN ADOBE ILLUSTRATOR OR (EPSF) FILE dialog box appears, requesting that you select a PostScript-language file, as shown in Figure 15-12 on the next page. Locate the file you wish to separate in the scrolling list, and either double-click on the file name or select the file and click on the OPEN button. Separator allows you to open not only Illustrator files, but also compatible Encapsulated PostScript files created in other applications. If the file name that you select is not compatible with the Separator application, a dialog box notifies you, and the file is not opened. If the file you select is compatible, but not capable of being printed with the Separator application, the file opens but you are alerted that you will not be able to print separations. This may occur when opening PostScript files that have been improperly modified in a word processor.

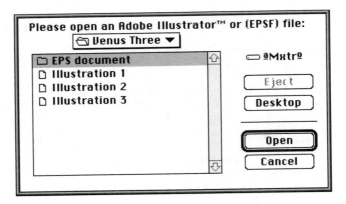

Figure 15-12: This dialog box allows you to select the illustration or Encapsulated PostScript document that you want to print.

Following this, the SETUP window appears, as shown in Figure 15-13. In the SETUP window, the current printer is listed below the OPEN PPD... button.

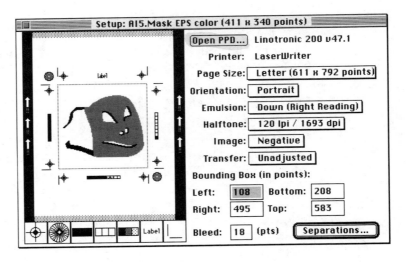

Figure 15-13: The Setup window displays after you successfully launch Adobe Separator and open an Illustrator file.

Setting Separator options

The SETUP window is divided into two parts: the *separation preview* on the left side of the window and a series of separation options along the right-hand side. The separation preview allows you to determine the *margin notes* that print with each separation, as described in the *Margin notes* section on page 613. The title bar lists the name of the open Illustrator or EPS file. To open a different file, click in the close box (or choose CLOSE from the FILE menu, ⌘-W) to first close the current window. Then choose the OPEN... command from the FILE menu (⌘-O) to display the PLEASE OPEN ADOBE ILLUSTRATOR OR (EPSF) FILE dialog box displayed in Figure 15-12, and select a different illustration. Adobe Separator allows only one open window at a time.

The upper right corner of the SETUP window contains an OPEN PPD... button, which allows you to change the selected PPD file. The current selection is listed to the right of the button. Click the button to display the OPEN POSTSCRIPT PRINTER DESCRIPTION (PPD) FILE dialog box, shown in Figure 15-14, and select a different PPD file.

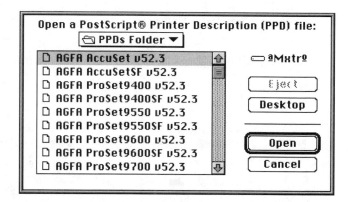

Figure 15-14: The Open PostScript Printer Description (PPD) File dialog box allows you to select the PPD file corresponding to the intended output device.

The OPEN POSTSCRIPT PRINTER DESCRIPTION (PPD) FILE dialog box asks you to select the *PostScript printer description* (PPD) file that corresponds to the intended output device. You will find the PPD files included with Adobe Illustrator 5.0 inside a PPD folder, which reside in the folder containing the Separator application. Each PPD file is named for the printer model it describes. Some PPD files have numbers following the printer name, indicating the specific version of the PostScript ROM chips that the printer may contain. It is important to use the correct PPD file for your output device in order for the Adobe Separator to work properly. If you do not have a PPD file corresponding to your printer ROM, contact Adobe Systems or the printer manufacturer for information on obtaining the correct PPD file.

To avoid searching through the long list of PPD files over and over every time you use Separator, copy the PPD files you use regularly to a new folder. At the Finder level, choose the NEW FOLDER command from the FILE menu (⌘-N), name the folder something like *My PPDs*, and OPTION-drag the specific PPD files that you wish to copy from the original PPD folder to the new PPD folder. (Pressing OPTION copies the files rather than simply relocating them.)

Locate the desired PPD file in the scrolling list, and either double-click on the file name or select the file and click the OPEN button. You can select a different printer using the Chooser, as described in the *Choosing the PostScript printer* section earlier in this chapter.

Beneath the current printer are a series of pop-up menu options, all of which are described in the following sections.

Page size

Based on information contained in the selected PPD file, the "Page Size" pop-up menu lists the page sizes available for your output device. Next to the common name of each page size is the imageable area of the page, measured in points. The area required for the margin notes, which Separator prints on each page, has been subtracted, so the area you see is the area you get. Select a page size that is large enough to contain both illustration and margin notes, the latter of which consume about four picas all around.

If the selected printer allows you can define custom page sizes, you can select the "Other..." option to display the PAGE SIZE dialog box, shown in Figure 15-15. The default values for the "Width" and "Height" options are the dimensions of the smallest page that will contain the current illustration. The "Offset" option allows you to add space between your illustration and the right edge of the paper.

If the "Offset" value is left at 0, the custom page will be centered in the width of the paper or film used by the current output device.

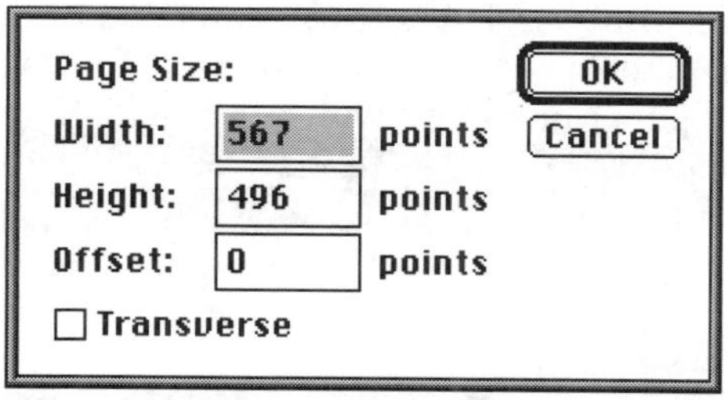

Figure 15-15: *The Page Size dialog box allows you to specify a custom page size.*

The "Transverse" option controls the position of your custom page relative to the paper or film on which it will be printed. This is most commonly used when printing on imagesetters that use long rolls of paper or film. The default positioning for any page on a Post-Script printer places the long edge of the page parallel to the long edge of the paper. In most cases this is correct, but when printing to an imagesetter you can usually reduce paper or film waste by setting pages *transverse*; that is, with their short edges parallel to the long edge of the paper.

Orientation

Unlike the "Transverse" option, which controls the position of the page on the printer's paper, the "Orientation" option controls the position of an illustration on the page, just like the "Orientation" option in the LASERWRITER PAGE SETUP dialog box. By default, all Separator documents are output with the "Portrait" option selected, even if the "Landscape" option was selected in the LASERWRITER PAGE SETUP dialog box when the document was created and saved in Illustrator 5.0.

Selecting the "Landscape" option in the "Orientation" pop-up menu rotates the illustration 90°. Separator performs this rotation regardless of whether the rotated image correctly fits on the paper, so be careful when altering this option.

Emulsion

The "Emulsion" option, like the "Flip Vertical" option in the LASER-WRITER OPTIONS dialog box (shown in Figure 15-3), controls how the document is printed relative to the emulsion on photosensitive paper or film. The names given to the options, "Up" and "Down," refer to the sides of the paper or film on which the emulsion is laid. When printing film negatives, you will probably want to select "Down" from the pop-up menu; when printing on paper, "Up" is usually the correct setting.

Halftone

The "Halftone" option controls the *resolution* (the number of pixels printed in a linear inch) and *screen frequency* (the number of *halftone cells* in a linear inch) of the output device. Halftone cells are the dots used to represent gray values and tints. Resolution is measured in *dots per inch*, or dpi, with "dots" being device pixels. Frequency is measured in *lines per inch*, or lpi. For example, the default resolution for an Apple LaserWriter is 300 dpi; the default screen frequency is 60 lpi.

Since a setting of 60 lpi assigns 60 halftone cells to every linear inch, every halftone cell printed on a 300-dpi laser printer measures five pixels wide by five pixels tall ($300 \div 60 = 5$), for a total of 25 pixels per cell. If all pixels in a cell are turned off, the cell appears white; all pixels turned on produces black; any number between 0 and 25 produces a shade of gray. You can create a unique tint by turning on each of 0 through 25 pixels, for a total of 26 gray values.

Therefore, when choosing a "Halftone" option, consider how your change affects the number of gray values printable by the current output device. Raising the resolution increases the number of gray values by providing more pixels. However, raising the frequency value decreases the number of gray values because it decreases the size of each halftone cell, and therefore the number of pixels per cell.

Image

Like the "Invert" option in the LASERWRITER OPTIONS dialog box, the "Image" option controls whether the document is printed as a positive or a negative image. If printing to paper, the default "Positive" is usually the correct setting. However, when printing to film, "Negative" is probably the preferred setting. Be sure to confirm your selection with your commercial printer.

Transfer

The "Transfer" pop-up menu allows you to temporarily adjust the *transfer function* for the current output device and is specifically applicable to film output. The transfer function determines the *density* of various tints; that is, their lightness or darkness. If tints tend toward high density, your output will appear too dark when printing film positives and too light when printing film negatives. If tints tend toward low density, just the opposite is true.

By default, the "Unadjusted" option is selected. This option instructs Separator to rely on its default density settings. Unless you are specifically instructed to do so by a commercial printer, or you are skilled in the use of an *optical densitometer* (a typically hand-held device that measures reflected light), do *not* change the "Transfer" option. However, if you know what you're doing, you can select the "Adjust tints..." option, which displays the UNADJUSTED TINT DENSITIES dialog box, as shown in Figure 15-16. This dialog box allows you to adjust the density settings for 10% incremental tints of the four process colors (cyan, magenta, yellow, and black) as well as a sample custom color. The values inside each cell can vary between 0.000 and 3.000. Each value represents the densitometer reading for that tint. You can take readings from the *gray bar* included on each separation produced by Separator (see *Margin notes* on page 613).

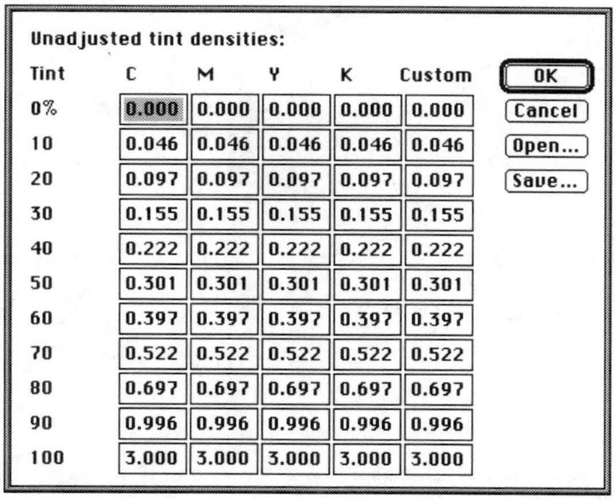

Tint	C	M	Y	K	Custom	
0%	0.000	0.000	0.000	0.000	0.000	OK
10	0.046	0.046	0.046	0.046	0.046	Cancel
20	0.097	0.097	0.097	0.097	0.097	Open...
30	0.155	0.155	0.155	0.155	0.155	Save...
40	0.222	0.222	0.222	0.222	0.222	
50	0.301	0.301	0.301	0.301	0.301	
60	0.397	0.397	0.397	0.397	0.397	
70	0.522	0.522	0.522	0.522	0.522	
80	0.697	0.697	0.697	0.697	0.697	
90	0.996	0.996	0.996	0.996	0.996	
100	3.000	3.000	3.000	3.000	3.000	

Unadjusted tint densities:

Figure 15-16: The Unadjusted tint densities dialog box allows you to adjust the density settings for the current output device. The large difference between 90% and 100% is typical.

Restoring pop-up menu settings

Choose USE DEFAULT SETTINGS from the SETTINGS menu (⌘-T) to re-store all pop-up menus in the SETUP window to their original settings.

Bounding box

The "Bounding Box" options allow you to adjust the size of the area Separator allots to the current illustration. The default values represent the smallest *bounding box* that can be drawn around the illustration. Margin notes appear in the margins around the bounding box.

The values in the "Left," "Right," "Bottom," and "Top" option boxes represent the distance from the edge of the page size and the corresponding edge of the bounding box. Therefore, entering smaller values for any of these options increases the size of the bounding box; entering larger values shrinks the bounding box.

You can also adjust the size of the bounding box by dragging directly on the dotted rectangle that represents the bounding box in the separation preview. Your cursor changes to a four-headed cursor if you are on a corner or a two-headed arrow if you are on a side, as shown in Figure 15-17. All margin notes move with the bounding box. Or, if you prefer, you can drag the illustration to reposition it within the bounding box. In this case, your cursor appears as a hand.

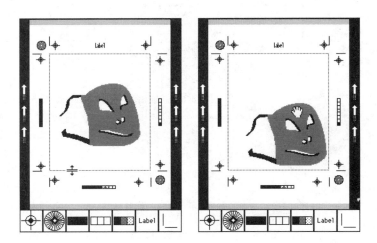

Figure 15-17: Dragging an edge of the bounding box in the separation preview (left) and moving the illustration (right).

🌀 The **Illustrator 5** Book

Enter a value between 0 and 72 points for the "Bleed" option, which determines the distance between the bounding box and any margin note.

Choose USE DEFAULT BOUNDING BOX from the SETTINGS menu (⌘-B) to restore the original bounding box and bleed values, as well as the positioning of the illustration in the separation preview.

Margin notes

As mentioned earlier, each page output from Separator includes a variety of *margin notes*:

- A *page label*, which lists the document name, separation color, line frequency, screen angle, and page number of the separation. This page label is printed both backward and forward, so it can be read either emulsion up or emulsion down.

- The right edge of each page includes a *progressive color bar*, and the left edge includes an *overprint bar*, which is a progressive color bar with process black overprinting all colors.

- Centered on the bottom of the page is a *gray bar* with 10% gradations. You can measure this bar with a densitometer to gauge density readings.

- A *star target* is placed in the upper left and lower right corners of the separation.

- In each corner of the page are both *crop marks*, used to determine the trim size, and *registration crosshairs*, used to help align separations.

Most, if not all, of these margin notes are used by the commercial printer reproducing your illustration, so be sure they are not removed when trimming excess paper or film from your printed separation.

Figure 15-18 on the following page shows how the margin notes appear in the separation preview. If you wish to adjust the placement of margin notes, you can do so by dragging them. The new coordinates of the margin note will be listed at the top of the preview. You can add a margin note by dragging from one of the icons at the bottom of the preview. The margin note associated with each icon displays when you click on it at the top of the preview. To delete a margin note, drag the item out of the window.

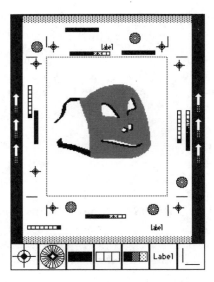

Figure 15-18: You can move, add, and delete margin notes in the separation preview.

Choose the USE DEFAULT MARKS command from the SETTINGS menu (⌘-M) to restore the original margin notes to their original positions in the separation preview.

 If you move, add, or delete a margin note inadvertently or incorrectly, Separator provides an UNDO command under its EDIT menu (⌘-Z) that allows you to undo the alteration.

Separation techniques

Once you have set the basic parameters of the separations using the options described above, it is time to actually select and print the separations. The number and type of separations that should be created for any document is dependent upon the color printing process you will use to reproduce the document. There are two ways in which a specific color can be printed on a sheet of paper. Using the first method, *spot-color printing*, inks are premixed to the desired color and then applied to the paper. Spot-color printing is usually used when only one or two colors (in addition to black) are used in an illustration. This printing method is neither exceedingly expensive nor very technically demanding. Spot-color printing allows for selecting and applying precise colors with perfect color consistency.

In order for an illustration to be reproduced using the spot-color printing process, it must be separated by printing a page for each custom color of ink used in the illustration. Process colors should *not* be used in illustrations that will be printed using the spot-color process, because spot-color separations cannot be created from process colors.

In the alternative printing method, *four-color process printing*, cyan, magenta, yellow, and black ink are blended in specific percentages to create a visual effect that approximates thousands of other colors. Four-color process printing is technically demanding and tends to be more expensive than spot-color printing, which is why many commercial print shops do not offer this service. But when available, it delivers more colors than any other printing method.

Documents that are to be reproduced using the four-color process printing method require four separations, one for each of the component inks. Every color object in an illustration is broken down into its component color separations, which conform to the original definition of the process color in Illustrator 5.0. For example, Figure 15-19 contains four color separations followed by a monochrome composite print of the image. The square field behind the star in the image is filled with a process color that is defined as 100% cyan, 60% magenta, 0% yellow, and 10% black. It therefore outputs as solid on the cyan separation, a 60% tint on the magenta separation, transparent on the yellow separation, and a 10% tint on the black separation. When these colors are printed in these percentages, the placement of the halftoned dots will visually simulate a deep blue.

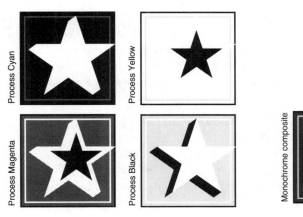

Figure 15-19: Four process-color separations (left) and a monochrome composite (right) of the same image.

It is possible in some cases to combine four-color process printing with spot-color printing. Although this process is more expensive, and is subject to the capabilities of your commercial printer, it provides the advantages of both four-color process (many colors with few inks) and spot colors (precise colors) in one printed piece. Many magazines, for example, are printed using four-color process colors for photos and spot color for advertisements.

In Chapter 10, *Filling and Strokng in Color*, I discussed the two types of colors used in Illustrator 5.0 — process colors and custom colors — and mentioned that, traditionally, process colors are applied to illustrations that will be reproduced using four-color process printing, and custom colors are applied to illustrations that will be reproduced using spot-color printing.

When an illustration is opened in Adobe Separator, colors that were specified as process colors are automatically prepared for output as four-color separations, and custom colors are prepared for output as additional spot-color separations. It is possible, however, to *decompose* one or more custom colors back into their primary color components (as specified in the CUSTOM COLOR dialog box in Illustrator 5.0) so that they can be output as process-color separations. The following section describes how to decompose custom colors while creating separations.

Defining separations

To define the separations that you wish to print from Separator, click on the SEPARATIONS... button in the lower right corner of the SETUP window or choose the SEPARATIONS... command from the FILE menu. The SEPARATION window shown in Figure 15-20 displays. This dialog box allows you to change the label, select the process colors that you want to print, and select custom colors that you want to decompose, as well as change the frequency and angle of the spot colors.

Enter a new illustration name in the "Label" option box. This label will print on each separation name with the separation color and other margin notes. By default, the label is the file name under which the illustration is saved. Since file names tend to be rather cryptic, you may want to change the name to something more familiar that will help your commercial printer keep track of your job.

File	
Open...	⌘O
Close	⌘W
Get Info...	⌘I
Separations...	
Save Selected Separations...	
Save All Separations...	⌘S
Print Selected Separations	
Print All Separations	⌘P
Print Composite	
Quit	⌘Q

The **Illustrator 5** Book

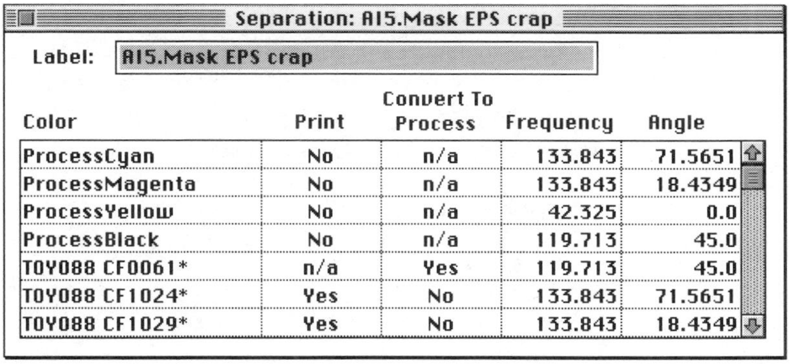

Separation: AI5.Mask EPS crap				
Label: AI5.Mask EPS crap				
Color	Print	Convert To Process	Frequency	Angle
ProcessCyan	No	n/a	133.843	71.5651
ProcessMagenta	No	n/a	133.843	18.4349
ProcessYellow	No	n/a	42.325	0.0
ProcessBlack	No	n/a	119.713	45.0
TOYO88 CF0061*	n/a	Yes	119.713	45.0
TOYO88 CF1024*	Yes	No	133.843	71.5651
TOYO88 CF1029*	Yes	No	133.843	18.4349

Figure 15-20: The Separation window allows you to specify the separations that you wish to print.

To decompose a custom color into its process color components, click on the "No" to the right of the custom color name in the "Convert To Process" column. A "Yes" will appear in its place. To prevent a custom color from being decomposed, click on the "Yes" to change it to a "No."

To print a custom color to its own separation, click on the "No" to the right of the custom color name in the "Print" column to change it to a "Yes." You cannot select a decomposed custom color, because it will print to process separations automatically. In Figure 15-20, for example, the first process color (TOYO88 CF0061) will decompose to CMYK separations. The other two (TOYO88 CF1024 and TOYO88 CF1029) will print to their own separations.

The last two options in the SEPARATOR dialog box allow you to set the frequency and angle of the color halftone cells. Most of the time, you will never have to concern yourself with these numbers. Illustrator automatically assigns each of the four process colors a different angle so that each contribution to a composite color shows through distinctly and not as a glommy mess. Figure 15-21 on the next page shows four halftone cells with different angles and four that have the same angle. The right examples in each row show how the four colors look when printed on top of one another.

One case in which you might need to adjust the angle of a color is when two spot colors are mixed together in a gradation or blend. For example, suppose you have two spot colors, PMS 2587 purple and PMS 2995 blue, as the first and last colors in a gradation. If both colors were assigned the same angle in the SEPARATION dialog box, then the areas where the two colors converge won't print correctly. One set of halftone cells will print directly on top of the other, resulting in a murky mess. To correct the problem, change the angle of one of the colors to an angle used by a process color—0°, 18.5°, 45°, or 72.5°.

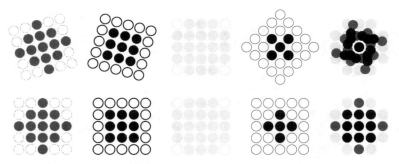

Figure 15-21: Four halftone cells with different angles (top) and four with the same angle (bottom).

Click in the close box to confirm your settings and return to the SETUP window.

Printing separations

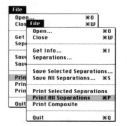

To print only those separations specified in the SEPARATION window, choose the PRINT SELECTED SEPARATIONS command from the FILE menu. A separation will be printed for every process color and every custom color whose check box is selected in the SEPARATION window.

To print all separations, regardless of whether they are selected in the SEPARATION window, choose the PRINT ALL SEPARATIONS command from the FILE menu (⌘-P). Only dimmed colors (process colors that do not exist in the current illustration and decomposed custom colors) will not receive their own separations.

Choose PRINT COMPOSITE from the FILE menu to print the entire document at once—including all process colors and custom colors. This creates a full-color composite on a color printer or a black-and-white composite on a monochrome printer. In either case the result is identical to that obtained by selecting the PRINT... command while inside the Illustrator 5.0 application.

Saving separations

It is also possible to print separations to disk as PostScript files, allowing for easy transport, storage, or modification. To save only those separations specified in the SEPARATION window, choose the SAVE SELECTED SEPARATIONS... command from the FILE menu. A separation will be saved to disk for every process color and every custom color whose check box is selected in the SEPARATION window.

To save all separations, regardless of whether they are selected in the SEPARATION window, choose the SAVE ALL SEPARATIONS command from the FILE menu (⌘-S). Only dimmed colors (process colors that do not exist in the current illustration and decomposed custom colors) will not receive their own separation file.

Getting information

Choose the GET INFO... command from the FILE menu (⌘-I) to display the GET INFO window shown in Figure 15-22. This window contains information about the current illustration. As well as a general information field, the window displays a list of all fonts, tile patterns, and placed EPS documents included in the illustration. Click on the PRINT button or press RETURN to print the contents of the GET INFO window. Click in the close box in the title bar to close the window.

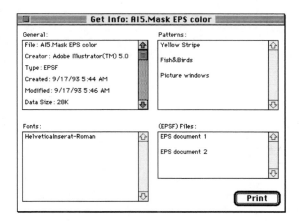

Figure 15-22: The Get Info window contains general information about the current illustrations, as well as lists of fonts, tile patterns, and placed EPS images that the illustration contains.

Quitting Separator

When you have finished working in the Separator utility, choose the QUIT command from the FILE menu (⌘-Q). Control of your computer is returned to the Macintosh Finder. Changes to the settings, margin notes, and bounding box are automatically saved with any illustration opened inside Adobe Separator.

APPENDIX
&
INDEX

APPENDIX

INSTALLING
ADOBE
ILLUSTRATOR 5.0

621

To use Adobe Illustrator, Adobe Separator, and Adobe Type Manager, you must *install* these applications onto your Macintosh computer's hard drive. The process is simple, and you have to install each application only once, not every time you want to operate the program. If Illustrator and its related utilities are already installed, you can begin using the program as described in Chapter 3, *A Brief Tour of Adobe Illustrator 5.0.*

Taking stock

The Adobe Illustrator 5.0 package includes seven 800K disks, which contain the Illustrator application and all accessory files. Each disk and its contents are listed below.

- **Disk 1**. The Adobe Illustrator 5.0 Installer program, the Installer Script, a ReadMe file, and TeachText.

- **Disk 2**. The first portion of the Adobe Illustrator 5.0 application.

- **Disk 3**. The second portion of the Illustrator 5.0 application, the plug-in modules, and the PostScript printer descriptions.

- **Disk 4**. The first portion of the Adobe fonts folder that contains a total of 40 Type 1 fonts. *Postscript*

- **Disk 5**. The second portion of the Adobe fonts folder.

- **Disk 6**. The third portion of the Adobe fonts folder, Adobe Type Manager 3.6, the related ATM document, the color systems, the plug-in modules that require an FPU, and the utilities, including the Adobe Separator application.

- **Disk 7**. Several predefined gradients and patterns, and the translators for importing and exporting documents into or out of Illustrator.

Hardware requirements

Before beginning any installation procedure, it is important that your Macintosh hardware configuration is complete and compatible with Adobe Illustrator 5.0. You must have a Macintosh equipped with:

- A 30 megabyte hard drive.

- 3.1 megabytes of RAM (5M are recommended).

- Macintosh System version 6.0.7 or later. (System 7.0 or 7.1 is recommended.)

- A PostScript-compatible printer is optional, but highly recommended.

Keep in mind that this is the minimal configuration. A larger hard drive and more RAM will certainly work as well or better. If your computer lacks a hard drive or sufficient RAM, you will need to upgrade your computer. Call your local computer dealer or discount house for more information. If your system software is too old, you can obtain the newest system software for a nominal fee from your Authorized Apple Dealer. If you do not own a PostScript printer, you can probably locate a service bureau in your area that will allow you to output your Illustrator files on their PostScript printers for a per-page charge.

The installation process

To use the Adobe Illustrator 5.0 Installer utility to install Illustrator onto your hard drive, power up your Macintosh as normal. If you use any antivirus programs, such as the Symantec Utilities' Shield Init or Symantec AntiVirus Macintosh (SAM) program, you may want to temporarily deactivate these because the installation process will set them off. It is not required that you deactivate them, but it is a good idea. You cannot have any other programs running when you run the Installer.

Installing Illustrator

Insert Disk 1, and double-click on the Installer utility. The Install startup screen displays after a few seconds. Click the OK button or press RETURN. The EASY INSTALL dialog box then displays, as shown in Figure A-1 on the next page. You can either select the INSTALL button or the CUSTOMIZE button. Clicking on the INSTALL button (or pressing RETURN) installs all the Illustrator files that your computer can use. For example, if your Mac doesn't have a math coprocessor, the plug-in modules that require an FPU will not install.

Clicking on the CUSTOMIZE button displays the CUSTOMIZE dialog box. Here you can select exactly which Illustrator files you want installed on your Mac. For example, you might decide that you don't need the tutorial that Adobe provides. (After all, you already have me, your personal Illustrator trainer). In this case, click and drag over all files in the scrolling list to select them all, then SHIFT-click on the files you don't want. Once the desired files are selected, click on the INSTALL button. If you change your mind and decide you want all compatible files, click on the EASY INSTALL button. If any other programs are running, the Installer offers to quit these applications before continuing the installation.

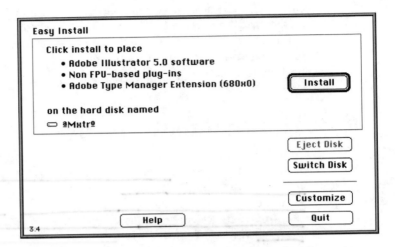

Figure A-1: The Easy Install dialog box allows you to either install all pertinent Illustrator files or to select only the files you want.

Throughout the installation process, you may be requested to exchange disks. Do so as prompted. After Illustrator 5.0 has been installed successfully, the installation program quits and you are returned to the Finder. A new folder called *Adobe Illustrator 5.0* now exists on your hard drive. This folder contains the Illustrator application and all the other related folders and files.

Installing Adobe Type Manager

To save space on your hard drive you might decide that you can do without some of the Illustrator 5.0 files. If you don't need the zillions of custom colors, don't install the Color System folder. If you decide that you don't want all the utilities that install with the Separator &

Utilities folder, simply throw the undesirables away. But one Adobe file that you definitely want to install is Adobe Type Manager (ATM) 3.6, a utility that accurately displays PostScript fonts on your computer screen. The program reads the definition of the typeface provided by the printer font and generates high-resolution characters at any type size inside virtually every Macintosh program.

When you choose the easy install route, the following Adobe Type Manager related files are installed:

- One ATM control panel, called simply *~ATM™*.

- One of two ATM driver files, either *~ATM 68000* or *~ATM 68020/030/040*.

- Screen and printer fonts for the Courier, Helvetica, Times, Symbol, and several other font families included in the Adobe Type folder (all of which are optional).

Adobe Type Manager requires both screen and printer versions of each font that you want to use. The screen font must be loaded into the System file or attached to the System using a font utility such as Suitcase II or MasterJuggler.

Very likely, you have already installed all the screen fonts that you need. If you haven't installed the Courier, Times, Helvetica, and Symbol screen fonts, open the Adobe Base 13 folder in the Adobe Type folder, which is automatically installed in the Adobe Illustrator 5.0 folder when you do the easy install, and drag all the needed fonts onto the System folder. A dialog box displays asking whether it's okay to place the fonts in their proper folder. Simply click on the OK button. Do the same with all the other fonts that you want to use throughout your Macintosh applications.

Choose the CONTROL PANELS folder from the APPLE menu. Double-click on the ~ATM control panel icon. A personalizing dialog box appears, requesting that you enter your name and organization. Type this information and click on the OK button. The ATM window then appears, as shown in Figure A-2 on the next page.

Figure A-2: The Adobe Type Manager control panel device allows you to allot memory for ATM.

The ATM window contains four options. Set them as follows:

- **ATM**. Select "On" to activate ATM; select "Off" to turn it off.

- **Font Cache**. Set the amount of memory that can be used by ATM on a regular basis. A large *font cache* (512K) improves ATM's performance, but takes away memory that could otherwise be used for applications. For best results, set this option to 256K if your computer has 4 megabytes of RAM; set it to 512K or higher if you have more than 8 megabytes of RAM.

- **Preserve**. Select the "Line Spacing" radio button to retain the line breaks and page breaks in documents that were previously opened without ATM. However, the tips of ascenders and descenders of some characters may appear chopped off when using this option. To avoid chopped characters, select the "Character shapes" option. You may have to reformat a few documents, but your printed type will look better.

- **Substitute for missing fonts**. You may try to open a document that you did not create, just to find that it contains fonts that you do not have on your Mac. With this option selected, a dialog box displays informing you which fonts you lack and which font will serve as a substitute in the document.

After you set the ATM options as desired, you will be informed that the changes will not take effect until you restart you Mac. Click in the Control Panel close box. Choose the RESTART command from the SPECIAL menu to restart your computer and load Adobe Type Manager.

You are now ready to begin using Adobe Illustrator 5.0 and its related utilities. Return to the beginning of the book to get started.

INDEX
(O-RAMA)

---

command key (⌘) 16
control key (ʌ) 16
option key (⌥) 16
shift key (⇧) 16
shift-tab 17
spacebar 22
tab key 17
keyboard equivalents and
  shortcuts 58–68
knocked out color 418

L

Label option 616
Labels before/after option 566
Larger Print Area option 592, 594
LaserWriter 590
LaserWriter driver 8 97
LaserWriter Options dialog
  box 592
LaserWriter Page Setup
  dialog box 591
  introduced 38
LaserWriter Print dialog box 595
  introduced 38
Last Filter command 498
  introduced 55
Last option 485
Latin computer term 258
launch 69–71
  double-click an Illustrator 5.0
    document 70
  Illustrator for first time 71
Layer Option for... option 480
layering
  combined objects 477
  order 474
layers 477
  creating 478
  moving objects between 482
Layers palette 478
  introduced 56
Layout pop-up menu 598
leading 302
Leading before ¶ option
  in Paragraph dialog box 271,
    317
Leading command 302, 312
  introduced 52

Leading option 302
Left (Alignment) command 303
  introduced 52
left and right side bearings 304
Left indent option 316
Left option 518
legend 543
letter spacing 306
Letter spacing option 318
limitcheck errors 599, 602
line breaks 263
line caps 389
  and dash pattern 398
  specifying 389
Line Join option 520
line joins 391
  and dash pattern 401
  specifying 391
Line option 560
line weight 384
  hairline 389
  specifying 389
line-graph tool 546
  introduced 34, 35
linear gradations 357
lines 118, 119
  properties 121
Link Block command
  introduced 53
Link Blocks command 281, 283
linked object 279
linking a story 273
linking order 282
Linotype 54
Lock (Guides) command 430
  introduced 48
Lock command 433
  introduced 43
Lock Height option 504
Lock option 479
Lock Width option 504
Locking objects 432

M

MacCalc 541, 552
MacConnection 205
MacDraft 78
MacDraw 78, 148, 156, 243

Twirl... filter   516
two-page layout   99
type
    converting into paths   326
    cool dazed observer effect   534,
        535
    filled with tile patterns   357
    gradient fills   363
Type 3 fonts   54
Type menu
    introduced   51
type size   302
type tool   262
    introduced   29
typefaces   270, 301

U

Unadjusted tint densities dialog
        box   611
undo   258
Undo command   258
    introduced   40
Undo Levels option   259
Ungroup command   424
    introduced   43
Uniform scale option   443
Uniformly scaled option   573
Unite filter   525
Unlimited Downloadable Fonts in a
        Document option   594
Unlink Block command   285
    introduced   53
Unlock All command   433
    introduced   43
upside down graphs   565
Use Default Bounding Box
        command   613
Use Default Marks command   614
Use Default option   109
Use Default Settings
        command   612
Use left axis option   564
Use Page Setup option   98
Use page setup option   102
Use precise cursors option   106
Use printer's default option   103

Use Ratio button   504
Use right axis option   564
using artwork mode   139
using preview mode   140
using tile patterns   350

V

Variable option   175
Vertical only option   252
Vertical option
    in Align Objects dialog box   519
    in Move dialog box   222
    in Move Each dialog box   520
    in Reflect dialog box   448
    in Rotate dialog box   459
    in Scale dialog box   444
vertical shift   293
Vertically scaled option   572
View menu   44
view size   23
view sizes   87
    maximum and minimum   89

W

Wacom drawing tablet   175
weight   121
White fill type box   340
White stroke type box   387
Whole Word option   330
Width option
    in Oval dialog box   157
    in Rectangle dialog box   150
Wind option   505
window close box   79
Window menu   56
window size box   79
window title bar   79
window zoom box   79
Wingz   552
word spacing   306
Word spacing option   318
worksheet matrix   541
wrap   263
Wrap Around option   330

X, Y, Z